D0890046

CHIRONOMIDAE

Ecology, Systematics
Cytology and Physiology

CHIRONOMIDAE

Ecology, Systematics Cytology and Physiology

Proceedings of the 7th International Symposium on Chironomidae, Dublin, August 1979

Editor

D. A. MURRAY

Department of Zoology, University College Dublin

PERGAMON PRESS

OXFORD · NEW YORK · TORONTO · SYDNEY · PARIS · FRANKFURT

U.K.	Pergamon Press Ltd., Headington Hill Hall, Oxford OX3 0BW, England
U.S.A.	Pergamon Press Inc., Maxwell House, Fairview Park, Elmsford, New York 10523, U.S.A.
CANADA	Pergamon of Canada, Suite 104, 150 Consumers Road, Willowdale, Ontario M2J 1P9, Canada
AUSTRALIA	Pergamon Press (Aust.) Pty. Ltd., P.O. Box 544, Potts Point, N.S.W. 2011, Australia
FRANCE	Pergamon Press SARL, 24 rue des Ecoles, 75240 Paris, Cedex 05, France
FEDERAL REPUBLIC OF GERMANY	Pergamon Press GmbH, 6242 Kronberg-Taunus, Pferdstrasse 1, Federal Republic of Germany

First edition 1980

British Library Cataloguing in Publication Data

International Symposium on Chironomidae, *7th, Dublin, 1979*
Chironomidae - ecology, systematics, cytology and physiology.
1. Chironomidae - Congresses
I. Title II. Murray, D A
595.7'71 QL537.C456 79-41622

ISBN 0-08-025889-1

In order to make this volume available as economically and as rapidly as possible the authors' typescripts have been reproduced in their original forms. This method has its typographical limitations but it is hoped that they in no way distract the reader.

Printed in Great Britain by A. Wheaton & Co., Ltd., Exeter

Contents - Inhalt

Introduction

At the termination of the Sixth International Symposium on Chironomidae, in Prague, 1976, the assembled delegates voted Ireland as the host country for the next symposium. Accordingly the Seventh International Symposium was organised in Dublin and held on the campus of University College, Dublin on August 27-29, 1979.

Eighty three registered delegates from twenty one countries convened in Dublin on Monday August 27 for the opening of the symposium by Professor C.F. Humphries. The first August Thienemann Lecture on the topic "Methods and principles of phylogenetic biogeography" was delivered by Professor Lars Brundin. Following this lecture participants presented, during the succeeding two and a half days, a total of forty five papers in ten scientific sessions.

Fig. 1. Professor Lars Brundin delivering the first August Thienemann Lecture.

Lectures were delivered on the following themes:- Cytology and physiology; Systematics and geographic distribution; Ecology, including aspects of lotic, lentic and pollution biology.

The proceedings of the symposium are published by the camera ready method in an attempt to reduce costs and produce the volume as rapidly as possible. The editor is grateful to the contributors for their co-operation in this undertaking.

The Eight International Symposium is to be held in the United States of America in 1982 at a venue yet to be decided.

Twenty six delegates participated in the three day post symposium excursion. On the first day the tour went south west, via the Japanese Gardens at Tully and the Rock of Cashel, to Killarney. Here on the banks of the River Flesk, to the satisfaction of many colleagues, isolated swarms of Buchonomyia thienemanni Fitt. were observed and individual specimens collected eagerly. On the second day the group travelled northwards across the River Shannon estuary to visit the Cliffs of Moher on the Atlantic coast and the limestone Burren region of County Clare before enjoying a medieval banquet at Dunguaire Castle. On the last day of the excursion participants travelled eastwards across the central plain to see the megalithic passage graves at Newgrange, County Meath.

Financial assistance for the symposium is gratefully acknowledged from: Tara Mines Ltd., whose generous support assisted the publication of the scientific proceedings of the symposium; The Electricity Supply Board for assistance towards the administrative costs and the National Board for Science and Technology for providing grants to help defray the accommodation and living expenses of several delegates from east European Socialist Countries.

Thanks are also extended to the Lord Mayor of Dublin, Clr. William Cumiskey, for hosting the delegates to a civic reception at the Mansion House; to Bord Failte Eireann and Aer Lingus for advice and assistance and to the post graduate students of the Limnology Unit, Department of Zoology, University College, Dublin for many hours of enthusiastic help.

D.A. Murray, Editor.
Department of Zoology,
University College, Dublin.
September 1979.

List and Addresses of Participants

AAGAARD, K., Tromso Museum, N. 9000 Tromso, Norway.

ASHE, P., Department of Zoology, University College, Dublin, Belfield, Dublin 4, Ireland.

BADCOCK, R, MRS., Department of Biology, The University, Keel, Staffs. ST 5 5BG, U.K.

BECK, W.M., Florida A & M, University, P.O. Box 111, Tallahasse, Florida 32307, U.S.A.

BROWN, A.E., School of Life, Sciences, Leicester Polytechnic, P.O. Box 143, Leicester, U.K.

BRUNDIN, L., Department of Entomology, Swedish Museum of Natural History, S10405 Stockholm, Sweden.

BUTLER, M.G., Division of Biological Sciences, University of Michigan, Ann Arbor, MI 48109 U.S.A.

BUTLER, J. MRS. Same Address.

BYRNE, R., Department of Zoology, Trinity College, Dublin 2, Ireland.

CARTER, C., Limnology Laboratory, New University of Ulster, Magherafelt, Co. Derry, N. Ireland.

CRANSTON, P., British Museum, Natural History, Cromwell Rd., London.

CREDLAND, P., Department of Zoology, Bedford College, University of London, Regents Park, London NW1 4NS.

DEGELMANN, A., Max Planck Institut für Biologie, Abt. Beerman, Spemannstrasse 34, D74 Tübingen, West Germany.

DEVAI, G., Department of Zoology and Anthropology, L. Kossuth University, H4010 Debrecen, Hungary.

DOUGLAS, D., Department of Science, Regional Technical College, Dundalk, Co. Louth, Ireland.

DOWLING, C. Department of Zoology, University College Dublin, Belfield, Dublin 4, Ireland.

DUKE, E.J., Department of Zoology, University College, Dublin, Belfield, Dublin 4, Ireland.

ERIKSSON, L., Entomology Department, Institute of Zoology, University of Uppsala, Box 561, S 751 22 Uppsala, Sweden.

EVALDSSON, I., Institute of Zoology, Helgonavägen, 3, S-223-62 LUND, Sweden.

FERRARESE, U., Institute Biologia Animale, Universita di Padova, Via Loredan 10, I 35100 Padova, Italy.

FISCHER, J., Universitat Bern Zoologisches Institut Sahlistrasse 8, CH 3012 Bern, Switzerland.

FITTKAU, E.J., Zoologisches Staatssammlung, Maria Ward Str. 1b, D 8 München 19 West Germany.

FRANK, C., Institut für Tierphysiologie, Frei Universität Berlin, Haderllebenerstr 9, D 1000 Berlin 41, West Germany.

GEIGER, H., Universitat Bern Zoologisches Institut Sahlistrasse 8, CH 3012 Bern, Switzerland.

GODDEERIS, B., Koninklijk Belgisch Institut voor Naturwetenschappen, Vautierstraat 31, 1040 Brussels, Belgium,

GRODHAUS, G., California Department of Health Services, 2151 Berkley Way, CA 97404 U.S.A.

HALVORSEN, G., Zoologisk Museum, Museplass 3, N 5014 Bergen - Univ., Norway.

HARDY, P., Max Planck Institut für Biologie, Abt. Beerman, Spemannstrasse 34, D74 Tübingen, West Germany.

HOFFRICHTER, O., Institut f. Biologie der Universität Albertstr 21a, D.78 Freiburg, West Germany.

HOWARD, S., Department of Zoology, Cambridge University, Downing St., Cambridge, U.K.

JANKOVIC, M., Institute for Biological Research, University of Belgrade, 29 November 142, Beograd, Yugoslavia.

KAJAK, Z., Polish Academy of Sciences, Institute of Ecology, 05-150 Lomianki, Dziekanow Lesny, Warsaw, Poland.

KÖHN, T., Institut für Tierphysiologie, Frei Universität Berlin, Haderllebenerstr 9, D 1000 Berlin 41, West Germany.

KOSKENNIEMI, E., Department of Biology, University of Jyväskylä, Yliopistonkatu 9, SF 40100 Jyväskylä, Finland.

KOVACS, A., Department of Zoology and Anthropology, L. Kossuth University, H 4010 Debrecen, Hungary.

KOWNACKA-MARGEREITER, M, Institut für Zoologie Universität Innsbruck, A6020 Innsbruck, Austria.

KREBS, B., Planketnet 3, s'Heer Arendskerke, Holland.

KURECK, A., Zoologische Instituet, Universität Köln, Wyertal 119, D. 5000 Köln 41, West Germany.

KUGLER, J., Department of Zoology, Tel-Aviv University, Tel-Aviv, Israel.

LANGTON, P., 1 Brooks Road, March, Cambs. PE 15 8AR, England.

LELLAK, J., Hydrobiological Department, Faculty of Science, Charles University, Vinicna 7, 128 44 Prague 2, Czechoslovakia.

LICHTENBERG, R., Naturhistorisches Museum Wien, 2. Zoologische Abt. Burgring 7, Postfach 417 A 1014 Wien, Austria.

LINDEBERG, B., Zoological Museum, Helsinki University P. Rautatiek 13, Helsinki 10, Finland.

LINDEGAARD, C., Freshwater Biological Laboratory, University of Copenhagen, 51 Helsingorsgade, DK 3400 Hillerød, Denmark.

MACKEY, A.P., Freshwater Biological Association, River Laboratory, East Stoke, Wareham, Dorest, BH 20 6BB, England.

MAIRTIN, F., Department of Zoology, University College Dublin, Belfield Dublin 4, Ireland.

McGARRIGLE, Department of Zoology, University College Dublin, Belfield Dublin 4, Ireland.

MICHAILOVA, P., Institute of Zoology, Ruski 1, Sofia, Bulgaria.

MOLLER-PILLOT, H., Leyparkweg 37, 5022 AA Tilburg, Holland.

MORRIS, D., UWIST, Department of Applied Biology Newbridge on Wye, Llandrindood Wells, Powys, Wales.

MOUNTAIN, T., Department of Biology, The University, Keele, Staffs. ST 5 5BG, England.

MURRAY, D., Department of Zoology, University College Dublin, Belfield, Dublin 4, Ireland.

MURRAY, F. Mrs, (same address)

NEUBERT, I., Institut für Tierphysiologie, Frei Universität Berlin, Haderllebenerstr 9, D 1000 Berlin 41, West Germany.

O'CONNOR, J., National Museum of Ireland, Natural History Division, Kildare St., Dublin 2.

PALOMAKI, L., Department of Biology, University of Jyväskylä, Yliopistonkatu 9, SF 40100 Jyväskylä, Finland.

PINDER, L.C.V. Freshwater Biological Association, River Laboratory, East Stoke, Wareham, Dorset, BH 20 6BB England.

PRAT, N., Dept. Ecologia, Universidad Barcelona Gran Via 585, Barcelona 7, Spain.

REISS, F., Zoologisches Staatssammlung, Maria Ward Str. 1b D8 München 19, W. Germany.

RIPLEY, M., Limnology Laboratory, New University of Ulster, Magherafelt, Co.Derry, N. Ireland.

ROBACK, S.S., Academy of Natural Sciences of Philadelphia.

ROBACK, H. Mrs, (same address)

ROSENBERG, D., Freshwater Institute, 501 University Crescent, Winnipeg, Manitoba, R 3T 2N6 Canada.

ROSSARO, B., Institute of Zoology, Univ. degli Studi di Milano, Via Celoria 10, I 20133, Milan, Italy.

RYSER, H., Universitat Bern, Zoologisches Institut, Sahlistrasse 8, CH 3012 Bern, Switzerland.

SAETHER, O.A., Department of Systomatic Zoology, Museum of Zoology, Museplass 3, n-5014 Bergen/Univ. Norway.

SÄWEDAL, L., Zoological Institute, Department of Systematics, Helgonavägen 3, S 223 62 Lund, Sweden.

SWEENEY, P., Department of Zoology, University College, Dublin, Belfield, Dublin 4, Ireland.

SCHOLL, A., Universitat Bern, Zoologisches Institut, Sahlistrasse 8, CH 3012 Bern, Switzerland.

TAIT-BOWMAN, C., Department of Biology, University of Salford, Salford M5 4WT, England.

TALLANDINI, L. Instituto di Biologia Animale, Universita di Padova, Via Loredan 10, I 35100 Padova, Italy.

TICHY, H., Max Planck Institut f. Biologie, abt. Beerman, Spemanstrasse 34, D74 Tübingen, West Germany.

TITMUS, G., Department of Biology, The University Keele, Staffs. ST5 5BG, England.

TOSCANO, J., Department of Zoology, The University, Newcastle-upon-Tyne, NE1 7RU, England.

TURCHETTO, M., Instituto di Biologia Animale, Universita di Padova, Via Loredan 10, I 35100 Padova, Italy.

WALENTOWICZ, T., Department of Zoology, The University, Newcastle-upon-Tyne, NE1, 7RU, England.

WEBB, C., Department of Zoology, University of Bristol, Woodland Rd., Bristol BS8, 1UG, England.

WEBB, MRS. C. (Same Address).

WHELAN, K. Inland Fisheries Trust Inc., Mobhi Boreen, Glasnevin, Dublin 9, Ireland.

WILLASSEN, E., Zoologisk Museum, Museplass 3, N 5014 Bergen/Univ., Norway.

WILLIAMS, K. Freshwater Biological Association, River Laboratory, East Stoke, Wareham, Dorset BH 20 6BB, England.

WILSON, R., Department of Zoology, University of Bristol, Woodland Rd., Bristol BS8 1UG, England.

WÜLKER, W. Biological Institute, 1 (Zoology), Albert Str. 21a, D 78 Freiburg, West Germany.

1. D. L. Morris
2. M. McGarrigle
3. P. Cranston
4. A. E. Brown
5. L. Brundin
6. D. A. Murray
7. P. Ashe
8. R. S. Wilson
9. W. Wulker
10. M. G. Butler
11. W. Beck
12. L. Eriksson
13. F. Murray
14. C. Dowling
15. B. Goddeeris
16. S. Howard
17. L.C.V. Pinder
18. P. Credland
19. T. Mountain
20. C. Webb
21. M. Kownacka-Margreiter
22. M. Ripley
23. C. Carter
24. G. Titmus
25. C. Tait-Bowman
26. N. Prat
27. B. Krebs
28. P. Langton
29. R. Badcock
30. R. Lichtenberg
31. E. Koskenniemi
32. I. Evaldsson

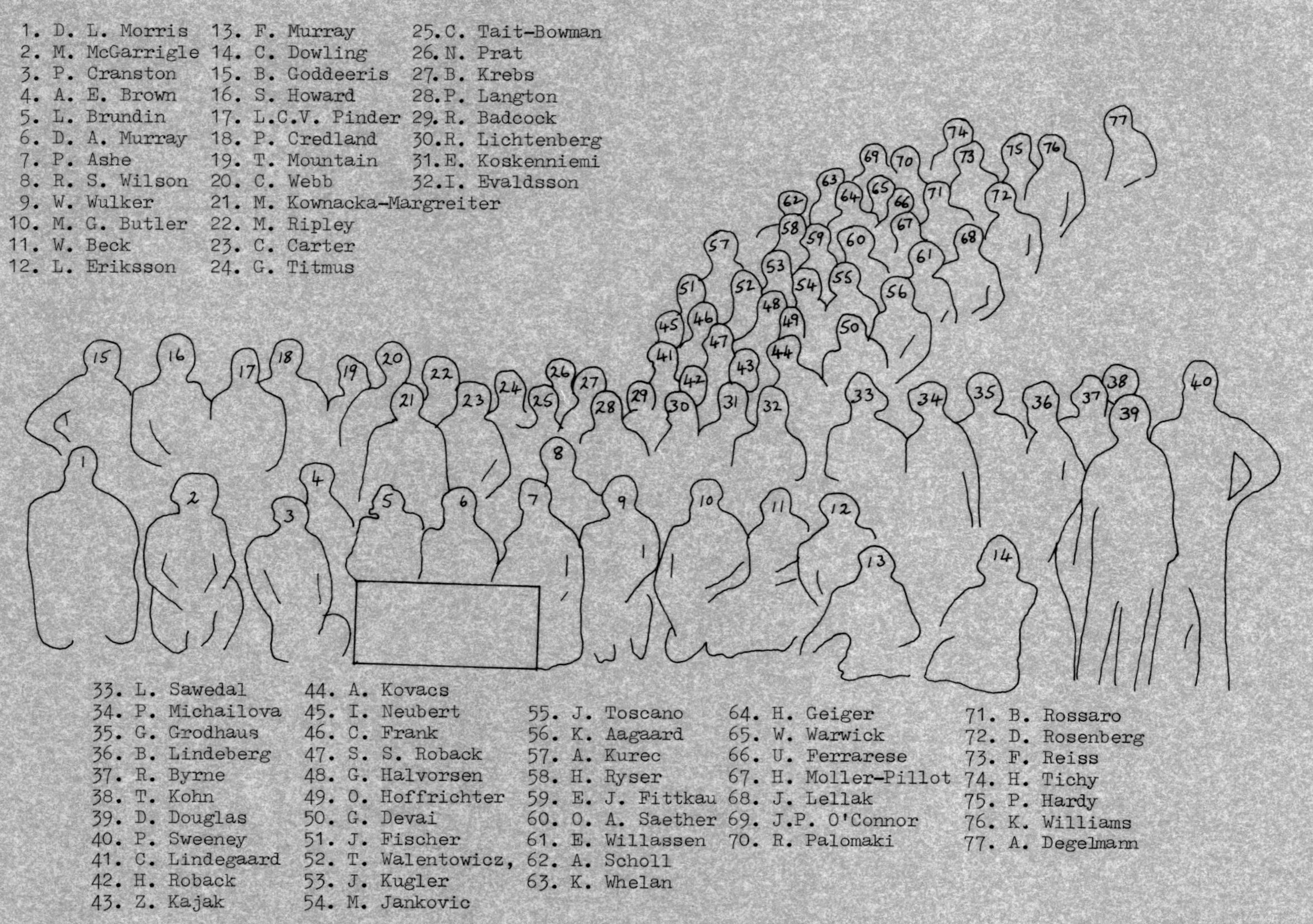

33. L. Sawedal
34. P. Michailova
35. G. Grodhaus
36. B. Lindeberg
37. R. Byrne
38. T. Kohn
39. D. Douglas
40. P. Sweeney
41. C. Lindegaard
42. H. Roback
43. Z. Kajak
44. A. Kovacs
45. I. Neubert
46. C. Frank
47. S. S. Roback
48. G. Halvorsen
49. O. Hoffrichter
50. G. Devai
51. J. Fischer
52. T. Walentowicz,
53. J. Kugler
54. M. Jankovic
55. J. Toscano
56. K. Aagaard
57. A. Kurec
58. H. Ryser
59. E. J. Fittkau
60. O. A. Saether
61. E. Willassen
62. A. Scholl
63. K. Whelan
64. H. Geiger
65. W. Warwick
66. U. Ferrarese
67. H. Moller-Pillot
68. J. Lellak
69. J.P. O'Connor
70. R. Palomaki
71. B. Rossaro
72. D. Rosenberg
73. F. Reiss
74. H. Tichy
75. P. Hardy
76. K. Williams
77. A. Degelmann

1. D. W. Morris 13. F. Murray 25. C. Tait-Bowman
2. M. McGarrigle 14. C. Dowling 26. N. Fret
3. P. Cranston 15. B. Goddeeris 27. B. Krebs
4. A. E. Brown 16. S. Howard 28. P. Langton
5. L. Brundin 17. J. C. V. Pinder 29. K. Badcock
6. D. A. Murray 18. P. Credland 30. H. Lichtenberg
7. P. Ashe 19. I. Mountain 31. H. Kockenkemi
8. R. S. Wilson 20. C. Webb 32. L. Evaldsson
9. W. Walker 21. M. Kownacka-Margreiter
10. M. G. Lottier 22. M. Sipley
11. W. Beck 23. C. Carles
12. L. Eriksson 24. G. Pittman

33. L. Sæwedal 44. A. Kovacs 55. J. Toscano 64. R. Geiger 71. B. Rossaro
34. P. Michailova 45. I. Neubert 56. K. Aagaard 65. W. Warwick 72. D. Rosenberg
35. G. Grodhaus 46. O. Frank 57. A. Kuree 66. V. Ferrarese 73. P. Zeiss
36. P. Lindeberg 47. S. S. Roback 58. H. Ryser 67. E. Moller-Pillot 74. H. Tichy
37. R. Byrne 48. G. Halvorsen 59. W. J. Fittkau 68. J. Dellak 75. P. Hardy
38. T. Kohn 49. O. Hoffrichter 60. O. A. Sæther 69. J. P. O'Connor 76. K. Williams
39. D. Douglas 50. H. Deval 61. E. Willassen 70. B. Palomaki 77. J. Dagelmann
40. E. Sweeney 51. J. Fischer 62. A. Schoell
41. S. Lindegaard 52. T. Walentowicz
42. H. Roback 53. S. Kugler 63. K. Whelan
43. Z. Kajak 54. M. Jankovic

VII INTERNATIONAL
CHIRONOMID
SYMPOSIUM
DUBLIN - AUG '79

List of Papers

SECTION II - SYSTEMATICS AND DISTRIBUTION Page

SECTION III - ECOLOGY

Lotic Environment

SECTION I

CYTOLOGY AND PHYSIOLOGY

In Vitro Translation of Balbiani Ring RNA from *Chironomus tentans*

P. A. Hardy and C. Pelling

Max-Planck Institut für Biologie, Abteilung Beermann, Spemannstrasse 34, 7400 Tübingen 1, Federal Republic of Germany

ABSTRACT

Balbiani rings are sites of particularly active RNA synthesis on the polytene chromosomes of Chironomids. Three such sites occur on the fourth chromosome in the salivary glands of Chironomus tentans. The RNA products of two of them (BR1 and BR2) have molecular weights of over 10×10^6 Daltons and are thought to code salivary proteins, which include fractions of more than 5×10^5 Daltons. In order to obtain insight into the nature of their primary translation products, RNA was isolated from salivary glands and translated in a cell-free system from rabbit reticulocytes. Salivary gland RNA induces the synthesis of a set of polypeptides, having molecular weights of up to 5×10^5. Immunoprecipitation studies, using an antiserum directed against total saliva, indicate that the very large species synthesized in vitro are immunologically related to constituents of saliva. These data provide evidence to support the contention that the unusually large proteins present in saliva are primary products of translation and are most probably coded by Balbiani ring RNA.

KEYWORDS

Balbiani ring RNA; in vitro translation; reticulocyte lysate; immunoprecipitation; salivary proteins.

INTRODUCTION

The fourth polytene chromosome in the salivary glands of Chironomus tentans is characterized by the presence of three Balbiani rings. These chromosomal sites synthesize large amounts of RNA (Pelling, 1964). The RNA products of two of these giant puffs, BR1 and BR2, have been isolated and characterized biochemically and by in situ hybridization. The kinetics of in situ hybridization indicate that both Balbiani rings contain repeated sequences. The RNA is polyadenylated and has a sedimentation constant of 75S (For review, see Case and Daneholt, 1977). Its size has been determined by electron microscopy to be about 12×10^6 Daltons (Case and Daneholt, 1978). 75S RNA emerges from the nucleus without detectable size change and is incorporated into polysomes. It thus functions as messenger RNA. The main protein products of the salivary gland are constituents of the saliva, which is secreted into the lumen of the gland and eventually the medium. They have been investigated by Grossbach (1969, 1977) and include species whose molecular weights

exceed 500,000 Daltons. The observed correspondence between the high rate of RNA synthesis at BR1 and BR2 and the production of salivary proteins has been taken to indicate that Balbiani ring RNA codes for fractions of saliva. It has been suggested that BR RNA is translated into small units of 40 - 60K. which are later polymerized into the larger forms found in saliva in the lumen (Rydlander and Edström, 1975), but Grossbach (1977) could find no evidence to support this hypothesis.
In order to gain some insight into the nature of the primary translation products of Balbiani ring RNA, we have isolated RNA from salivary glands and translated it in vitro in the reticulocyte lysate system.

MATERIALS AND METHODS

Isolation of Salivary Gland RNA

Total salivary gland RNA was isolated by a modification of the method of Strohmann et al. (1977). Glands were homogenized in 50mM Tris pH8.0, 5mM EDTA; 2mM aurin tricarboxylic acid; 70mM mercaptoethanol; 8M guanidinium chloride. The homogenate was extracted three times with an equal volume of chloroform: isobutanol (4:1). RNA was precipitated by the addition of a half-volume of ethanol at $-20^{o}C$ and extracted twice more with 8M guanidinium chloride. The final pellet was washed with 3M acetate pH5.2 and with 80% ethanol and used for translation.

Preparation of Antiserum to Salivary Proteins

Salivary proteins were isolated by brief fixation of the glands with 35% ethanol and subsequent mechanical removal of gland cells. This material was injected into rabbits using the double emulsion technique (Weir, 1978). Antiserum was characterized using a protein A binding test (Kronvall and coworkers, 1970)and by rocket immunoelectrophoresis (Axelsen, Kroll, and Weeke, 1973).

In Vitro Translation of Salivary Gland RNA

Aliquots of RNA were translated in the reticulocyte lysate kit from New England Nuclear (Dreieich, FRG) using the following salt conditions: 160mM K^{+}, 1mM Mg^{++}, and including 5uM S-adenosylmethionine. 35S methionine was the labelled amino acid. Incubation was for 2 hrs. at $30^{o}C$.
Immunoprecipitates were isolated with fixed Staphylococcus aureus cells after the method of Kessler (1975).
The products of translation were examined by electrophoresis on SDS polyacrylamide gradient gels (3 - 20%) with the buffer system of Laemmli (1970). Labelled bands were detected by fluorography (Bonner and Laskey, 1974).

RESULTS AND DISCUSSION

Figure 1 shows the pattern obtained on electrophoresis of cellular and salivary proteins in SDS polyacrylamide gradient gels (3 - 20%). The saliva contains two prominent proteins (referred to as A and B) with mol.wts. of 55oK and 18oK respectively (these are probably equivalent to fractions 1 - 3 of Grossbach (1964)) as well as fractions of 15 - 20K. In addition, several minor bands are present.

Figure 2 shows the results of a pulse-chase experiment in which larvae were injected with 1uCi of ^{35}S-methionine (Pelling, 1964). Cellular and salivary proteins were isolated after the times indicated and separated on gels. Labelled bands were detected by fluorography. It can be seen that 55oK material becomes labelled within 5 mins. Several discrete bands can be distinguished in this region of the gel. After some time, smaller polypeptides appear, including two bands of about 18oK, one of which is actually a doublet. The first protein to emerge into the lumen is

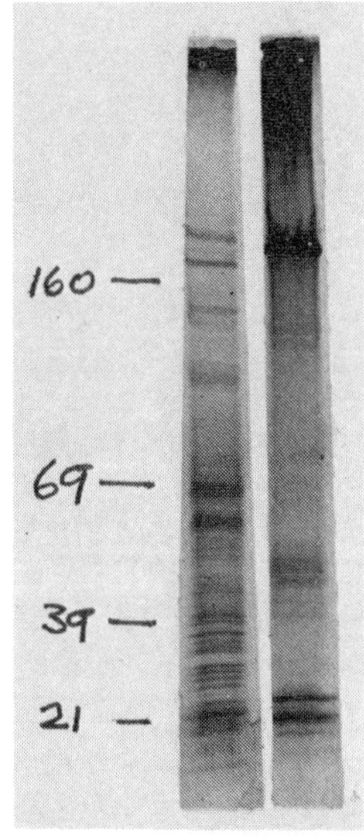

Fig. 1

Figure 1 shows gel separations of cellular (left) and salivary proteins (right). Positions of markers are also shown.

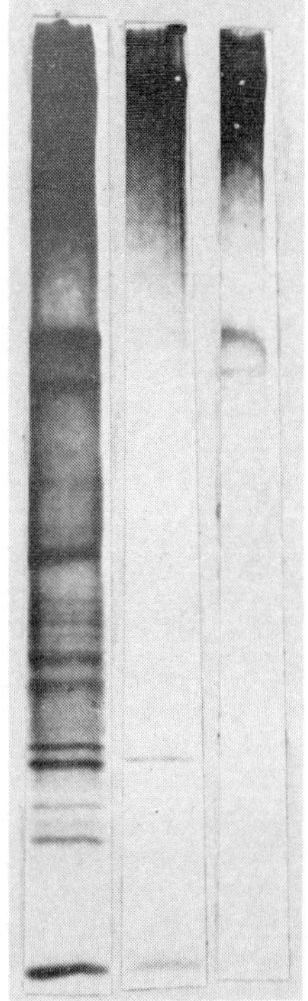

Fig. 2.

Figure 2 shows a fluorograph of cellular and salivary proteins separated after injection of larvae with 1µCi of ^{35}S-methionine.
Left: Cell proteins 5 mins. after injection.
Centre: Cell proteins 30 mins. after injection.
Right: Salivary proteins 30 mins. after injection.

TABLE 1 Protein A Binding Test

Experiment	% Input Bound
Antiserum + Protein A	0.2
Antigen (Salivary Protein) + Protein A	0.6
Antigen + Antiserum + Protein A	58

Table 1: A constant amount of ^{125}I-labelled Protein A was incubated with aliquots of antiserum and/or isolated saliva in phosphate-buffered saline containing 1% BSA at 37°C for 2 hrs. Bound Protein A was recovered by centrifugation and counted in a gamma-ray counter. Results are expressed as a percentage of the input counts. Binding is observed only in the presence of both antiserum and antigen, indicating that Protein A is specifically recognizing immune complexes.

a single species of 550K. A group of bands of 20 - 25K are also detectable after 30 min. Of the two heavily labelled proteins of 180K and 150K, which are present in cells, only one (B) appears in saliva.

The observation that several species are found in the region of fraction A in cellular material but only the largest is apparently secreted into the lumen, possibly indicates that some post-translatory modifications occur. Indeed it is known that the salivary proteins are glycosylated (Grossbach, 1969) and the extra bands may represent intermediates in this process.

Antiserum was prepared against total saliva as described in Materials and Methods. The serum was tested for the presence of anti-salivary antibodies using a protein A binding test. The results shown in Table 1 confirm that antibodies are present. Rocket immunoelectrophoresis revealed that at least four distinct antigenic species are present in saliva (data not shown). In order to reveal possible cross-reactions between individual components of saliva, immunological studies with monospecific antisera will be necessary.

Isolation of Salivary Gland RNA

Total RNA was isolated from salivary glands by a modification of the guanidinium chloride method of Strohmann and others (1977). The original method was found to be inapplicable to salivary glands because salivary protein coprecipitates with nucleic acid from 8M guanidinium on addition of ethanol. Thus, it was necessary to insert an extraction step with organic solvents before precipitation. Aurin tricarboxylic acid was added to all buffers as a further nuclease inhibitor. After washing the pellet with acetate and ethanol, the RNA can be translated with high efficiency in the reticulocyte lysate system.

Isolated RNA was analyzed for the presence of intact 75S Balbiani ring RNA by electrophoresis on 1% agarose gels. The 75S peak was recovered from the gel and further characterized by in situ hybridization to squash preparations of salivary gland chromosomes. The material was shown to contain BR1 and BR2 sequences (data not shown).

Translation of Total Salivary Gland RNA

Benoff and Nadal-Ginard (1979a) have described conditions under which the reticulocyte lysate system can efficiently translate tissue RNA to yield high molecular weight products. We have used a modification of these conditions to translate total salivary gland RNA (see Material and Methods).

Figure 3a shows a fluorograph of a gel profile of the products of such a translation experiment. The lower region of the gel has been overexposed to reveal the presence of two very high molecular weight bands. Immunoprecipitation (Fig. 3b) confirms that both are antigenically related to saliva. The smaller of the two bands has a mol.wt. of over 200K and does not seem to correspond to any of the fractions labelled in vivo. It may be a form of Fraction B which is very prominent in vivo but is not otherwise detected among the in vitro products. The larger of the two has a mol.wt. of about 500K. This appears to be somewhat smaller than Fraction A, but the result does demonstrate that it is possible to translate salivary gland RNA into Fraction A-like proteins.

Figure 4 shows a similar separation of immunoprecipitates on which the low molecular weight products can be distinguished. Several discrete bands are specifically precipitated. At least one of these can be unequivocally identified with a species labelled in vivo. A number of other bands in this area of the gel can be identified with salivary constituents on the basis of electrophoretic mobility. Thus, with the possible exception of Fraction B, the major components of saliva can be synthesized in this cell-free system.

The repetitive nature of the RNA products of BR1 and BR2, together with the unusual size of the putative protein products, has led to the proposal that the RNA might be polycistronic and that the primary products of translation might be small polypeptides which are polymerized into the mature form found in saliva, after completion of translation (Rydlander and Edström, 1975). The results presented here demonstrate that salivary gland RNA can be translated in a heterologous system into products which include proteins of over 500K. These very large species most probably represent primary translation products, since it is unlikely that the reticulocyte lysate contains the enzymes responsible for the hypothetical post-translational polymerization of smaller units. It cannot be excluded, however, that such an activity might itself be a product of in vitro translation.

The fact that the amount of Fraction A-like protein synthesized in vitro is extremely small does not necessarily support the polycistronic model, as it is known that the translation of large RNA in cell-free systems is relatively inefficient. Poly A-containing RNA, translated under the conditions described above, does not induce synthesis of products larger than about 60K (Hardy, unpublished results). This may be due to poor retention of giant RNA on oligo dT-cellulose or possibly implies that 75S RNA possesses a short poly A tail. In this case, 75S RNA would be underrepresented in poly A-containing RNA. Taken together with a low translational efficiency, this would account for the lack of synthesis of Fraction-A-like protein. Similar observations have been reported by Benoff and Nadal-Ginard (1979b) for myosin.

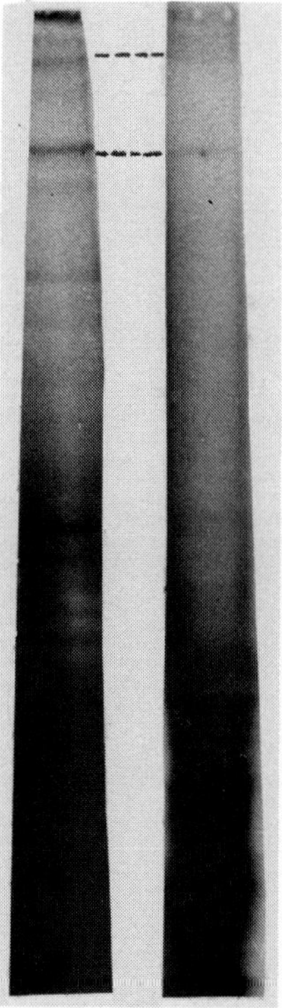
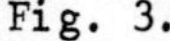

Fig. 3.

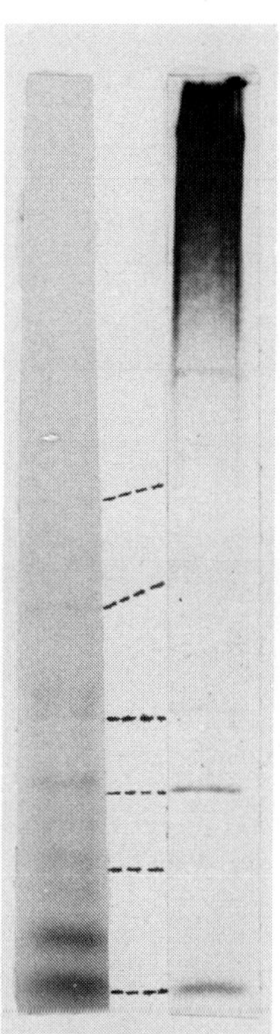

Fig. 4.

Figure 3 shows products of in vitro translation (left) and corresponding immunoprecipitates. Gel was overexposed to reveal large proteins.
Figure 4 shows a similar immunoprecipitate pattern (left) and, for comparison, saliva labelled in vivo for 30 mins. (right).

In summary, the evidence presented here suggests that the largest fraction(s) of *Chironomus tentans* salivary protein is the product of translation of single cistron(s), whose length must exceed 15,000 bases. The products of BR1 and BR2 are the only known candidates for such giant messenger RNAs. The question remains, which RNA codes for which polypeptide. This problem can only be solved by in vitro translation of purified RNA from individual Balbiani rings.

Abbreviation: K = kilodaltons

ACKNOWLEDGEMENTS

The authors are very grateful to Prof. Wolfgang Beermann for his continuous interest and support. We thank Mr. J. Perkovic and Miss S. Stangl for excellent technical assistance. We are indebted to P. Symmons (Max-Planck-Institut für Virusforschung, Tübingen) for a gift of labelled Protein A. Special thanks are due to Mrs. I. Darenberg for her painstaking preparation of the typescript. During part of this work, P. A. H. was supported by a postgraduate stipendium from the Max Planck Society.

REFERENCES

Axelsen, N. H., J. Kroll and B. Weeke. (1973). In *A Manual of Quantitative Immunoelectrophoresis*, Universitetsforlaget, Oslo.
Benoff, S. and B. Nadal-Ginard (1979a). *Biochemistry*, *18*, 494.
Benoff, S. and B. Nadal-Ginard (1979b). *Proc.Natl.Acad.Sci. USA*, *76*, 1853.
Bonner, W. T., and R. Laskey (1974). *Eur.J.Biochem.*, *46*, 83.
Case, S. T., and B. Daneholt. (1977). In J. Paul (Ed.), *Internatl.Rev.Biochem.*, Vol. 15. University Park Press, Baltimore.
Case, S.T. and B. Daneholt (1978). *J.Mol.Biol.*, *124*, 223.
Grossbach, U. (1969). *Chromosoma (Berl.)*, *28*, 136.
Grossbach, U. (1976). In W. Beermann (Ed.), *Results and Problems in Cell Differentiation*, Vol. 8. Springer-Verlag, Berlin, Heidelberg, New York.
Kronvall, G., U. S. Seal, J. Finstad, and R. C. Williams (1970). *J.Immunol.*, *104*, 140.
Laemmli, U. (1970). *Nature*, *227*, 680.
Pelling, C. (1964). *Chromosoma (Berl.)*, *15*, 71.
Rydlander, L., and J.-E. Edström. (1975). In *Proc. Tenth FEBS Meeting*, Paris.
Strohmann, R. C., P.S. Moss, J. Micou-Eastward, D. Spector, A. Przybyla, and B. Paterson (1977). *Cell*, *10*, 265.
Weir, D. M., (1978). *Handbook of Exp.Immunol.*, Blackwell Scientific Publications, London.

Comparative External Morphological and Karyological Characteristics of European Species of Genus Clunio Haliday, 1855 (Diptera, Chironomidae)

P. Michailova

Institute of Zoology, Bulgarian Academy of Sciences, 1 Boul. Rousski, Sofia, Bulgaria

ABSTRACT

The present work gives the external morphological particularities of taxonomic value in adults of the species Cl. marinus Haliday, Cl. balticus Heimbach, Cl. ponticus Michailova established with a scanning electronic microscope. The karyological features of the separate species allowing species differentiation as early as in the larva stage are noted. The role of the chromosome aberrations in the karyotype evolution of the genus are treated. Discussed is the matter concerning existence of genetic isolation between the three species.

KEYWORDS

Cl. marinus, Cl. balticus, Cl. ponticus, facets, hypopygium, chromosome diploid set, salivary gland chromosomes, aberrations, karyotype evolution, homologues, pairing.

INTRODUCTION

In the process of evolution of the representatives of genus Clunio the species differentiation is not accompanied by accumulation of severe external morphological differences. For a long period of time Strenzke (1960), Koskinen (1968), Pankratova (1970) have treated populations of the European Atlantic coast, the Baltic sea coast, the Mediterranean sea coast, the Caspian sea coast and the Black sea coast as belonging to the species Cl. marinus. But later Neumann (1971) and Heimbach (1978) have, on the basis of a detailed etologic and ecological analysis, examined the Mediterranean population as "Cl. mediteraneus" without a species description, and the populations of the Baltic sea like Cl. balticus Heimbach, 1978. The external morphological etologic-ecological and karyological particular features allowed the specimens of the Black sea population to be referred to the species Cl. ponticus Michailova, 1979. Because of the interesting ecology of the representatives of the genus (marked lunar periodicity in the specimens of the Atlantic coast and lack of such periodicity in those of the Baltic sea, the Mediterranean sea and the Black sea, difference in the day-night cycle of imago emergence) the studies are directed primarily to the etological and ecological analysis of the species; detailed data on the external morphology and karyology of the species are missing. In the present report an account is given of the results from the comparative external morphological and karyological analysis of representatives of the genus from different geographical regions.

MATERIAL AND METHODS

The material used is of Cl. marinus from the Helgoland coast, of Cl. balticus from Normandy and Cl. ponticus from the whole Bulgarian Black sea coast. IVth age larvae, pupae and imago of the three species have been analysed. A scanning electronic microscope Jeol type is used as to establish the external morphological differences in imago of the three species. Due to a number of methodological difficulties the karyological analysis has been carried out on fixed as well as live material.

RESULTS AND DISCUSSIONS

The detailed analysis on the external morphology of imago in the three species rendered possible determination of signs having a taxonomic value which help in differentiation of the three species. By means of the conventional light microscope differences are found mainly in morphology of the antenna segments. Use of the scanning electronic microscope gives the possibility still greater details in the external morphology of the three species to be discovered. Eye facets in Cl. marinus are heptagonal, in Cl. balticus are almost rounded and in Cl. ponticus concave with a complex undulated surface (Fig. 1, a, b, c). Evolution in this species has probably gone further and brought in result reduction in eye function. This raises an interesting question concerning eye functioning and whether it is connected with the particularities in etology of the specimens from the Black sea coast. We have noticed also differences as regards the thickened hairs on the tenth segment of the antenna in the separate species. In Cl. ponticus they are getting thinner towards the apex, while in Cl. marinus and Cl. balticus they are elongated, bow-shaped and in Cl. marinus are curved in the middle (Fig. 2, a, b, c). The separate species are differentiated also by the morphological particularities in one of the hairs on the second segment of the antenna as well as by the "formation" on the dorsal-medial plate of the hypopygium. The comparative morphological analysis made shows a greater similarity in the two sympatric species Cl. marinus and Cl. balticus than with Cl. ponticus.

The specific features in the morphology of the salivary gland chromosomes gives the possibility the species to be differentiated in the larva stage. The chromosome diploid set in the three species is 2n = 6. In Cl. balticus the salivary gland chromosomes have granular structure and in this they differ sharply from the salivary gland chromosomes of the remaining species (Fig. 3).

When comparing the salivary gland chromosomes of Cl. marinus with those of Cl. ponticus it is seen that the Ist chromosome of Cl. marinus has the nucleolus and the Balbian ring (Fig. 4), while in Cl. ponticus the Ist chromosome has the nucleolus and the Balbian

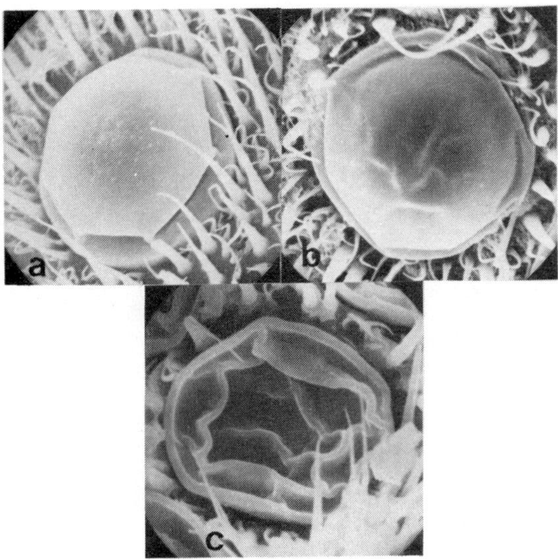

Fig. 1. Facets, SEM - 6000X; a. Cl. marinus, b. Cl. balticus, c. Cl. ponticus.

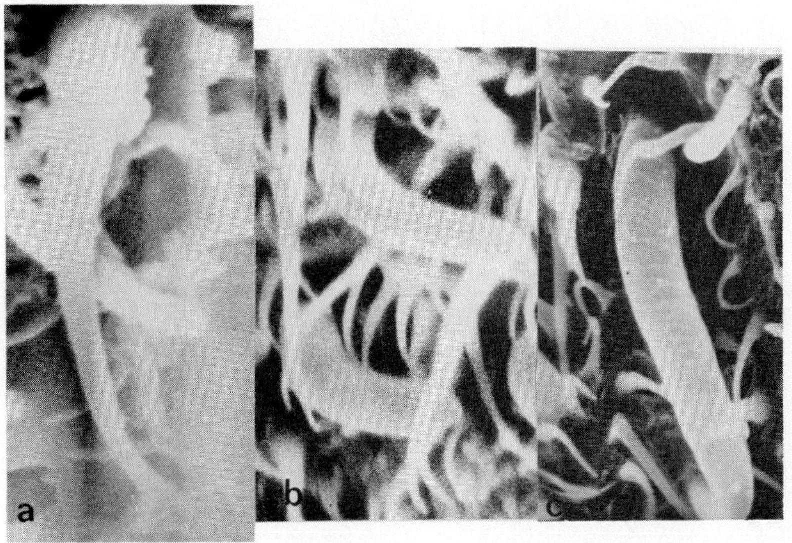

Fig.2.Hairs on the 10th antennal segment, SEM - 6000X; a. Cl. ponticus, b. Cl. marinus, c.Cl. balticus.

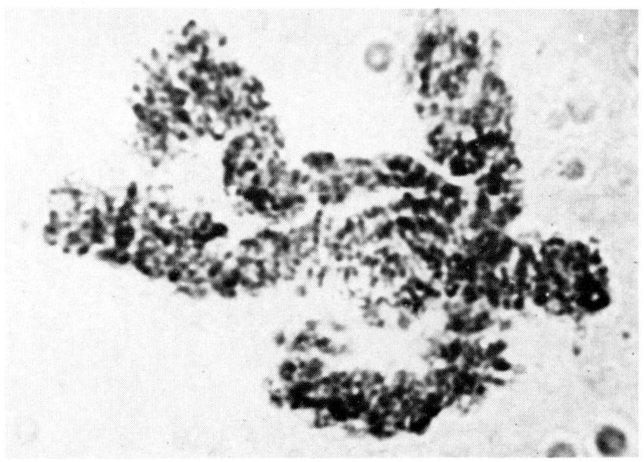

Fig. 3. Ist, IInd and IIIrd chromosome of the species Cl. balticus 40X.

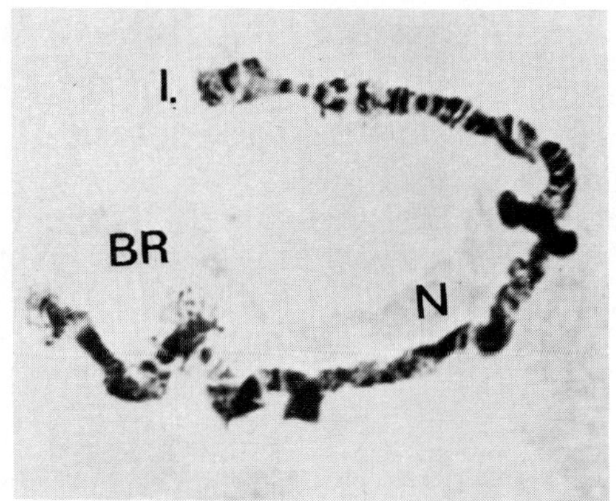

Fig. 4. Ist chromosome of the species Cl. marinus - 40X.

ring is translocated to the second chromosome (Fig. 5, 6). The

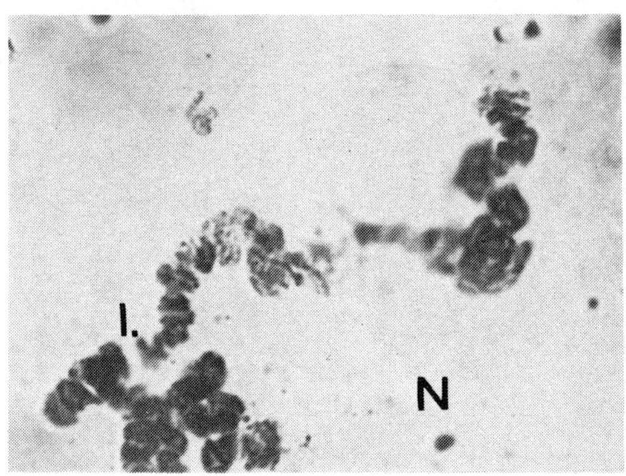

Fig. 5. Ist chromosome of the species Cl. ponticus - 40X.

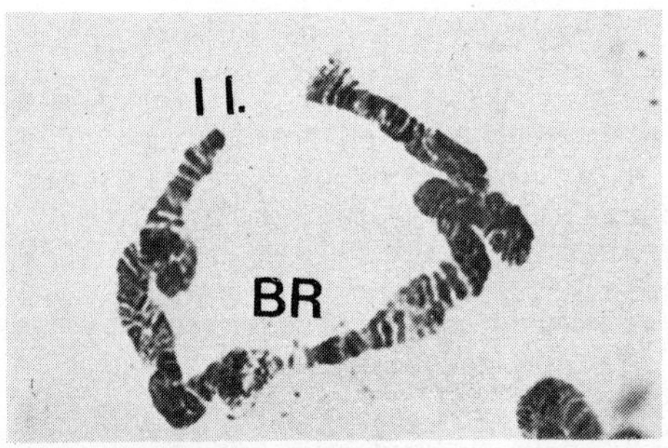

Fig. 6. IInd chromosome of the species Cl. ponticus - 40X.

homozygous inversions play an important role in the karyotype divergence of the two species. Separate sections of the Ist and the IInd chromosome of Cl. ponticus have been inverted in comparison with definite sections in the Ist chromosome of Cl. marinus. The IInd and the IIIrd chromosome of Cl. marinus show a complex heterozygous inversion (Fig. 7). Interesting is also the observed frequent pairing between the separate sections of one and the same chromosome in Cl. marinus. The paired sections have a similar structure. It makes us think that in the karyotype evolution of Cl. marinus an important role has been played by the duplications expressed in repetition of certain sections by the length of the chromosomes. The karyological differences could lead in result to building-up of genetic isolation between the species. Differences in the chromosome structure would

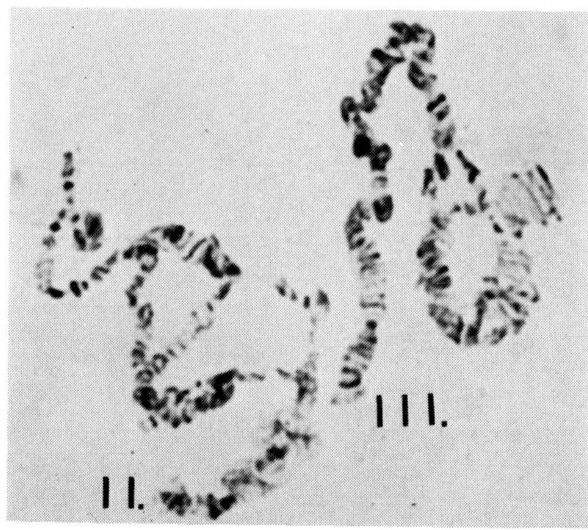

Fig. 7. IInd qnd IIIrd chromosome of the species Cl. marinus - 40X.

not give the possibility of correct meiosis process as only in a small number of sections homology can be observed. These results are a good basis to be assumed that between the investigated species not only etological-ecological isolation but also genetic isolation is existing.

On the other hand, the heterozygous inversions in the IInd and the IIIrd chromosomes of all the studied specimens of Cl. marinus and the rather unstable karyotype expressed in existence of different types of chromosome aberrations prove that in this species the speciation process has not been completed yet. In support of it comes also the frequent occurrence of incomplete pairing between the homologues of the chromosomes accompanied by disparity in the bands. These results lead us to the thought that the Helgoland population is not completely isolated from the neighbouring populations. Very likely the specimens of the Helgoland population are crossing with specimens from some of the neighbouring populations, discussed by Neumann (1976) as geographical races. And namely the specimens with disparity in the band structure - a fact observed by us - are the result of such crossing.

ACKNOWLEDGEMENT

I am deeply indebted to Prof. Dr. D. Neumann and to Dr. Heimbach for their kindness in sending me the material of Cl. marinus and Cl. balticus.

REFERENCES

Heimbach, F. (1978). Oecologia, 32, 195-202.
Koskinen, R. (1968). Ann. Zool. Fenn., 5, 71-75.
Michailova, P. (1979). Genetica, in print.
Neumann, D. (1971). Oecologia, 8, 1-20.
Neumann, D. (1976). Annual Review of Entomology, 21, 387-414.
Pankratova, V. (1970). Larven und Puppen der Unterfamilie Orthocladiinae (Diptera, Chironomidae).
(Leningrad), 117-120.
Strenzke, K. (1960). Ann. Zool. Soc., "Vanano", 22, 4, 1-30.

Untersuchungen ueber die Verbreitung der Zuckmuecken Gattung Chironomus in der Schweiz, mit Besonderer Beruecksichtigung von Drei Cytologisch nicht Beschreibenen Arten

H. M. Ryser*, H. J. Geiger*, A. Scholl* und W. Wülker**

*Zoologisches Institut, Sahlistr. 8, CH-3012 Bern, Switzerland
**Biologisches Institut I, Albertstr. 21a, D-7800 Freiburg, Federal Republic of Germany

ABSTRACT

The distribution of the genus Chironomus has been investigated in the area of Bern (lakes, ponds, pools), Grindelwald (ponds and pools in the alpine region) and the Swiss Jura (ponds in a swamp). Species diagnosis was based on cytological examination of larval salivary gland chromosomes. Twenty-two species have been found, including three species with unknown karyotypes; two of these are very closely related to Ch. plumosus and coexist with it in the Murtensee.

KEYWORDS

Genus Chironomus; distribution; area of Bern; alpine species; plumosus group; new karyotypes; cytotaxonomy.

EINLEITUNG

Zuckmücken der Gattung Chironomus sind eine taxonomisch schwierige Gruppe. In der von Strenzke (1959) begonnenen und bisher noch nicht abgeschlossenen Revision der Gattung hatten cytologische Untersuchungsergebnisse an Speicheldrüsen-Chromosomen der Larven entscheidenden Anteil an der Neufassung der Arten (Keyl, 1959-1962). Es zeigte sich, dass mehrere Arten bisher nur anhand der cytotaxonomischen Unterscheidungsmerkmale determiniert werden können (Keyl, 1960; Wülker, 1973; Klötzli, 1974). Schon daraus folgt, dass ältere Veröffentlichungen über Vorkommen und Biologie der Arten in vielen Fällen mit Unsicherheit bezüglich der Artdiagnose behaftet sein dürften.

Die von Strenzke und Keyl (lit. zit.) revidierten Arten entstammten vorwiegend Untersuchungsmaterial aus Norddeutschland. Ergänzungen folgten aus andern Untersuchungsgebieten Mitteleuropas (Wülker, 1973; Wülker und Klötzli, 1973). Dennoch dürften damit noch nicht alle in Mitteleuropa vorkommenden Arten erfasst sein, besonders auch deshalb, weil weite Gebiete bisher noch nicht bearbeitet worden sind. Formal kann darauf hingewiesen werden, dass für 12 gültige mitteleuropäische Arten (Fittkau und Reiss, 1978) Karyotypbeschreibungen fehlen.

Aus diesen Gründen schien es uns von Interesse, das Artenvorkommen in der Schweiz unter Anwendung cytologischer Unterscheidungsmerkmale zu untersuchen. Ueber das Artenvorkommen in der Umgebung von Bern wurde bereits an anderer Stelle berichtet (Ryser et al., 1978). Diese Befunde werden in der vorliegenden Arbeit ergänzt durch Ergebnisse aus Untersuchungsgebieten in den Alpen und einem Hochmoor im Jura. Für drei im Untersuchungsgebiet vorkommende, cytologisch bisher nicht bekannte Arten, bei welchen es sich vermutlich um neue Arten handelt, werden vorgängig einer Artbeschreibung die cytologischen Erkennungsmerkmale genannt.

METHODISCHES

Die Untersuchungen konzentrierten sich auf drei Regionen.

1. Bern und Umgebung (400-900 m NN). Es wurden Kleingewässer (mehrheitlich Löschteiche, aber auch Weiher, Tümpel und Wegpfützen) sowie Seen und seeartige Gewässer (ein Stausee und Bootshäfen) untersucht. Bei Seen erfolgte die Probenentnahme im Uferbereich und im Profundal bis zu 30 m Wassertiefe. Insgesamt wurden mehr als 5'000 Larven von etwa 50 Fundorten untersucht.

2. Umgebung der Grossen Scheidegg bei Grindelwald im Berner Oberland (1500-2000 m NN). Die Proben stammen ausschliesslich aus Alpentümpeln. Von über 10 Fundstellen wurden mehr als 1'000 Larven diagnostiziert.

3. Ein Hochmoor im Neuenburger Jura bei Le Cachot (1000 m NN). Aus drei Moortümpeln und Moorgräben wurden etwa 500 Larven untersucht.

Die Ergebnisse über das Artenvorkommen stützen sich ausschliesslich auf Larvenfunde. Bezüglich Einzelheiten der Probengewinnung und -verarbeitung verweisen wir auf Ryser et al. (1978).

Die Artdiagnose basiert auf cytologischen Unterscheidungsmerkmalen an Speicheldrüsen-Chromosomen von Larven des vierten Stadiums nach Keyl (1960, 1961, 1962), Keyl und Keyl (1959), Wülker (1973) und Wülker und Klötzli (1973). Die Präparation der Drüsen erfolgte nach Rosin und Fischer (1965).

Zur näheren Kennzeichnung der drei cytologisch nicht bekannten Arten (Ch. sp.2, Ch. sp.3 und Ch. sp.7) haben wir während der Sommer 1978 und 1979 am Murtensee Laichmücken eingesammelt, deren Laiche bei Zimmertemperatur aufgezogen wurden. Die Geschwisterschaften wurden jeweils z.T. als Larven cytologisch und morphologisch untersucht, z.T. als Imagines abgesammelt und nach Schlee (1966) präpariert. Von jeder der drei Arten haben wir mehr als 20 Geschwisterschaften erhalten.

Speicheldrüsen-Präparate und Präparate der Imagines stehen auf Anfrage für Vergleichszwecke zur Verfügung.

ERGEBNISSE UND DISKUSSION

Das Artenvorkommen

Die Tabelle 1 gibt Auskunft über die Artenfunde in den drei Untersuchungsgebieten. Für das Untersuchungsgebiet Bern sind die Artenfunde in Seen und seeartigen Gewässern einerseits, sowie in Kleingewässern andererseits getrennt ausgewiesen. Von den 26 aus Mitteleuropa cytologisch beschriebenen Chironomus-Arten sind 19 Arten gefunden worden. Weiterhin sind drei cytologisch nicht beschriebene Arten aufgetreten, von diesen sind Ch. sp.2 und Ch. sp.3 bereits früher erwähnt (Rosin und Fischer, 1972; Ryser et al., 1978) während Ch. sp.7 in dieser Arbeit erstmals behandelt wird.

In Tabelle 1 haben wir durch Punkte summarisch die Häufigkeit der Arten angegeben. Zur Ergänzung sei erwähnt, dass wir in Seen unterhalb einer Wassertiefe von ca. 5 m fast ausnahmslos Ch. plumosus gefunden haben. Am Murtensee konnten wir auffallende Unterschiede in der Häufigkeit chromosomaler Strukturvarianten bei Ch. plumosus-Larven aus dem Literal und dem Profundal feststellen (Bürki et al., 1978) Ch. sp.3 trat bisher nur in Larvenproben aus dem Litoral des Murtensees auf und wurde regelmässig und meist häufig gefunden. Ch. sp.7 wurde im Murtensee weniger häufig als Ch. sp.3 gefunden, konnte aber vereinzelt auch im Wohlensee nachgewiesen werden. Ch. sp.2 ist in Seen und seeartigen Gewässern häufiger und regelmässiger gefunden worden und konnte auch ausserhalb des hier behandelten Untersuchungsgebietes (z.B. Vierwaldstättersee) nachgewiesen werden.

Die Tabelle 1 lässt bezüglich des Artenvorkommens auffallende Unterschiede zwischen den drei Untersuchungsgebieten erkennen, welche als Ausdruck der ökologischen Differenzierung der Gattung gedeutet werden können. Die Unterschiede im Artenvorkommen in Seen und Kleingewässern in der Region Bern entsprechen der Erwartung, soweit zu den ökologischen Ansprüchen der Arten aus der Literatur Angaben verfügbar sind (Strenzke, 1960; Keyl, 1962; Fittkau und Reiss, 1978). Die andersartige Chironomusfauna des Untersuchungsgebietes im Jura kann damit erklärt werden, dass es sich dabei um ein Hochmoor handelt und dass moorartige Gewässer unter den Fundorten der beiden andern Untersuchungsgebiete nicht vertreten sind. Für Ch. holomelas unc Ch. uliginosus, welche neben Ch. melanescens in dem Moor gefunden wurden, nennen auch andere Autoren (Lit. zit.) Moore als Fundorte. Zur Fauna der Alpentümpel scheint uns bemerkenswert, dass keine der im Mittelland häufigen Kleingewässerarten dort gefunden wurde. Diesbezüglich muss angeführt werden, dass die Mehrzahl der untersuchten Larvenproben aus der oberen Stufe des angegebenen Höhenbereiches (1900-2000 m) entstammt. Ch. lacunarius ist aus Almtümpeln bei Garmisch-Patenkirchen beschrieben worden (Wülker und Klötzli, 1973). Die Art ist im Alpengebiet weit verbreitet. Wir haben sie u.a. in der Zentralschweiz gefunden. Da die Larve früher unter dem Namen Ch. "alpestris" geführt wurde (Wülker und Klötzli, 1973), dürfte auch ein Teil des Lunzer Materials von Thienemann (1950) zu Ch. lacunarius gehören. Sehr überraschend ist das häufige Auftreten von Ch. striatus in Alpentümpeln, bei gleichzeitigem Fehlen der Art in Kleingewässern des Mittellandes. Auch Krieger-Wolff und Wülker (1971) haben bei Untersuchungen über die Chironomus-Fauna der Umgebung von Freiburg i.Br. diese Art nur in Tümpeln in höheren Lagen des Schwarzwaldes gefunden. Zu diesen Angaben kontrastieren die von Keyl (1962) genannten Fundorte in Norddeutschland (Schwefelsaurer Tonteich bei Reinbek, Eckertalsperre).

Art	Bern und Umgebung		Berner Alpen	Jura
	Seen	Kleingewässer	Tümpel	Tümpel
Ch. bernensis	● ● ●			
commutatus	● ● ●			
nuditarsis	● ● ●	● ●		
plumosus	● ● ●	●		
sp. 2	● ● ●			
sp. 3	● ● ●			
sp. 7	● ●			
cingulatus	● ●			
obtusidens	●			
dorsalis		● ● ●		
luridus		● ● ●		
thummi		● ● ●		
annularius	●	● ●		
melanotus		● ●		
sororius		●		
lacunarius			● ● ●	
striatus			● ● ●	
aberratus			● ●	
pseudothummi			●	
holomelas				● ● ●
melanescens				● ● ●
uliginosus				● ● ●

TABELLE 1 Die Artenfunde in den drei Untersuchungsgebieten

Durch Punkte werden Angaben zur Häufigkeit gemacht. Ein Punkt bedeutet, dass von der betreffenden Art nur einzelne Individuen gefunden worden sind. Zwei Punkte kennzeichnen Arten, welche an einzelnen Standorten zwar regelmässig, aber nie häufig auftraten. Drei Punkte kennzeichnen Arten, welche in der Mehrzahl der Proben und meist in höherer relativer Abundanz nachgewiesen werden konnten.

Die drei cytologisch nicht bekannten Arten

1. Erkennungsmerkmale. Aus nachfolgend mitgeteilten cytologischen Untersuchungsbefunden an Freiland-Larvenmaterial sowie Larven aus Gelegeaufzuchten geht eindeutig hervor, dass es sich bei diesem Material um drei Arten handelt, welche in die Gattung Chironomus zu stellen sind. Hingegen ist noch nicht abschliessend geklärt, ob es sich um neue Arten handelt. Ch. sp.2 ist bereits von Rosin und Mitarbeitern gefunden und bearbeitet worden, Untersuchungsergebnisse an Imagines führten Klötzli zu der Auffassung, dass es sich hier mit Vorbehalten allenfalls um Ch. winthemi handeln könne (zitiert nach Rosin und Fischer, 1972). Für Ch. sp.3 und Ch. sp.7 führt der Schlüssel von Strenzke (1959) zu Ch. plumosus, wobei es weiteren Untersuchungen vorbehalten bleiben muss, Unterschiede statistisch abzugrenzen.

Ch. sp.2 hat drei grosse mediozentrische und ein kleines telozentrisches Chromosom. Die Chromosomenarme sind mit den Armen anderer Chironomusarten homologisierbar und liegen in der Kombination AB, CD, EF, G (thummi-Komplex) vor. Strukturmodifikationen im A- und F-Arm erschweren die Analyse ihrer Beziehungen zu den betreffenden Chromosomenarmen anderer Chironomusarten. Zur Erkennung der Art kann der E-Arm benutzt werden, dessen Querscheibenfolge nur bei dieser Art auftritt. Diese artspezifische Strukturvariante des E-Armes lässt sich durch eine lange Inversion von der Querscheibenfolge des E-Armes bei Ch. plumosus ableiten. Inversionspolymorphismus wurde bisher in den Armen D und F festgestellt.

Ein bemerkenswertes larval-morphologisches Merkmal ist die Form der Ventraltubuli, welche bei Ch. sp.2 lang und spitz ausgezogen sind. Appendices laterales sind nicht vorhanden. Die Larve entspricht somit dem von Lenz (1954) erwähnten fluviatilis-Typ, dem bisher kein Karyotyp und auch keine Imaginalart zugeordnet ist.

Ch. sp.7 hat nur drei Chromosomen. Sie liegen in der Armkombination AB, CD, FEG vor. Die gleiche Armkombination, welche vom thummi-Komplex abgeleitet ist, haben auch die nordamerikanischen Ch. staegeri und Ch. crassicaudatus (Wülker et al., 1971). Zwischen diesen beiden Arten und Ch. sp.7 dürften jedoch keine näheren Verwandtschaftsbeziehungen bestehen. Es sind weitere Chironomusarten mit nur drei Chromosomen bekannt, bei welchen jeweils das G-Chromosom an den E-Arm transloziert ist: Aus Mitteleuropa Ch. commutatus mit der Armkombination AD, BC, FEG (Keyl, 1962), welche vom lacunarius-Komplex abgeleitet ist, und aus Australien Ch. duplex mit der Armkombination AEG, BF, CD, welche vom pseudothummi-Komplex abgeleitet ist (Martin, 1971). Die von Wülker et al. (1968) vertretene Ansicht, in der Chromosomenevolution von Chironomus seien bestimmte Translokationen bevorzugt und mehrfach realisiert worden, findet mit dem Fund von Ch. sp.7 eine weitere Stütze.

Auch Ch. sp.7 ist von anderen mitteleuropäischen Chironomus-Arten larval-morphologisch klar unterscheidbar. Die Art besitzt keine Ventraltubuli, ein Merkmal, welches sie mit Ch. salinarius teilt. Während bei Ch. salinarius auch die Appendices laterales fehlen, sind diese bei Ch. sp.7 vorhanden. Ch. sp.7 entspricht somit als einzige bisher bekannte Chironomusart dem von Lenz (1954) erwähnten reductus-

Typ. Die larvalen Abdominalanhänge haben jedoch als morphologisches Merkmal jenseits der Artgrenzen wohl nur geringen taxonomischen Wert. Es wurde bisher die Auffassung vertreten, dass die Larven der Gattung Chironomus, und nur diese, im allgemeinen zwei Paar Ventraltubuli besitzen. Wir haben aber in unserem Untersuchungsmaterial zwei neue Einfeldia-Arten gefunden, welche ebenfalls zwei Paar Ventraltubuli besitzen[1].

Ch. sp.3 hat drei grosse mediozentrische und ein kleines telozentrisches Chromosom. Die Chromosomenarme sind auch bei dieser Art mit den Armen anderer Chironomusarten homologisierbar und liegen in der für den thummi-Komplex charakteristischen Kombination AB, CD, EF, G vor. Inversionspolymorphismus wurde vereinzelt in den Chromosomenarmen A und D festgestellt. Zur Erkennung von Ch. sp.3 kann der Arm A herangezogen werden, dessen Querscheibenfolge bisher bei keiner anderen Art getroffen wurde. Diese artspezifische Strukturvariante lässt sich durch eine Inversion von der Strukturvariante AII des Ch. plumosus (Keyl, 1962) ableiten.

2. Vergleich von Ch. sp.3, Ch. sp.7 und Ch. plumosus. Eine detaillierte Analyse der Querscheibenfolgen der einzelnen Chromosomenarme von Ch. sp.3 und Ch. sp.7 weist auf enge Verwandtschaftsbeziehungen der beiden Arten zueinander und zu Ch. plumosus. In Abb. 1 sind diese Beziehungen schematisch illustriert. Es sollen die Arme A, E und F näher besprochen werden, welche von Keyl (1962) bei andern Arten eingehend analysiert worden sind. Besonders klar ist die nahe Verwandtschaft am F-Arm zu erkennen, der bei allen drei Arten identisch ist und eine Querscheibenfolge aufweist, welche bisher nur von Ch. plumosus bekannt war. Im E-Arm sind Ch. plumosus und Ch. sp.7 identisch. Der E-Arm von Ch. sp.3 leitet sich von dieser Struktur durch zwei Inversionen ab, welche die benachbarten Bereiche 5 - 4 und 3f - 11 umfassen. Die Strukturfolge des A-Armes von Ch. sp.3 leitet sich, wie bereits erwähnt, durch eine Inversion von der Strukturvariante AII von Ch. plumosus ab. Von Ch. plumosus AII kann auch die Querscheibenfolge des A-Armes von Ch. sp.7 abgeleitet werden, und zwar durch zwei Inversionen, welche die Querscheiben 4a - 13f und 7 - 8f umfassen.

Ausser diesen cytologischen Untersuchungsergebnissen deuten auch enzymologische Befunde (Scholl et al., in diesem Band) an, dass Ch. sp.3, Ch. sp.7 und Ch. plumosus nächst verwandte Arten sind. Da artunterscheidende imaginale Merkmale zu fehlen scheinen, dürfte es berechtigt sein, die drei Arten einer plumosus Artengruppe zuzuordnen, welche schon von anderen Autoren vermutet worden ist (Strenzke, 1959; Palmen und Aho, 1966). In diesem Zusammenhang wird wiederum die Notwendigkeit unterstrichen, die Artdiagnose bei Chironomus durch cytologische Untersuchungen an Riesenchromosomen abzusichern.

Es ist bemerkenswert, dass diese drei Arten, welche innerhalb der europäischen Arten der Gattung wohl die engsten Verwandtschaftsbeziehungen aufweisen, in einem See koexistieren. Es ist jedoch nicht daran

---

[1]Wir danken Herrn Dr. F. Reiss (München) für die Bestätigung dieses Befundes.

zu zweifeln, dass sie verschiedene Nischen besetzen. Dafür sprechen u. a. Beobachtungen, welche beim Einsammeln von Laichen gemacht wurden. Wir stellten fest, dass die drei Arten im Jahresverlauf in unterschiedlicher relativer Abundanz unter den Laichmücken auftraten.

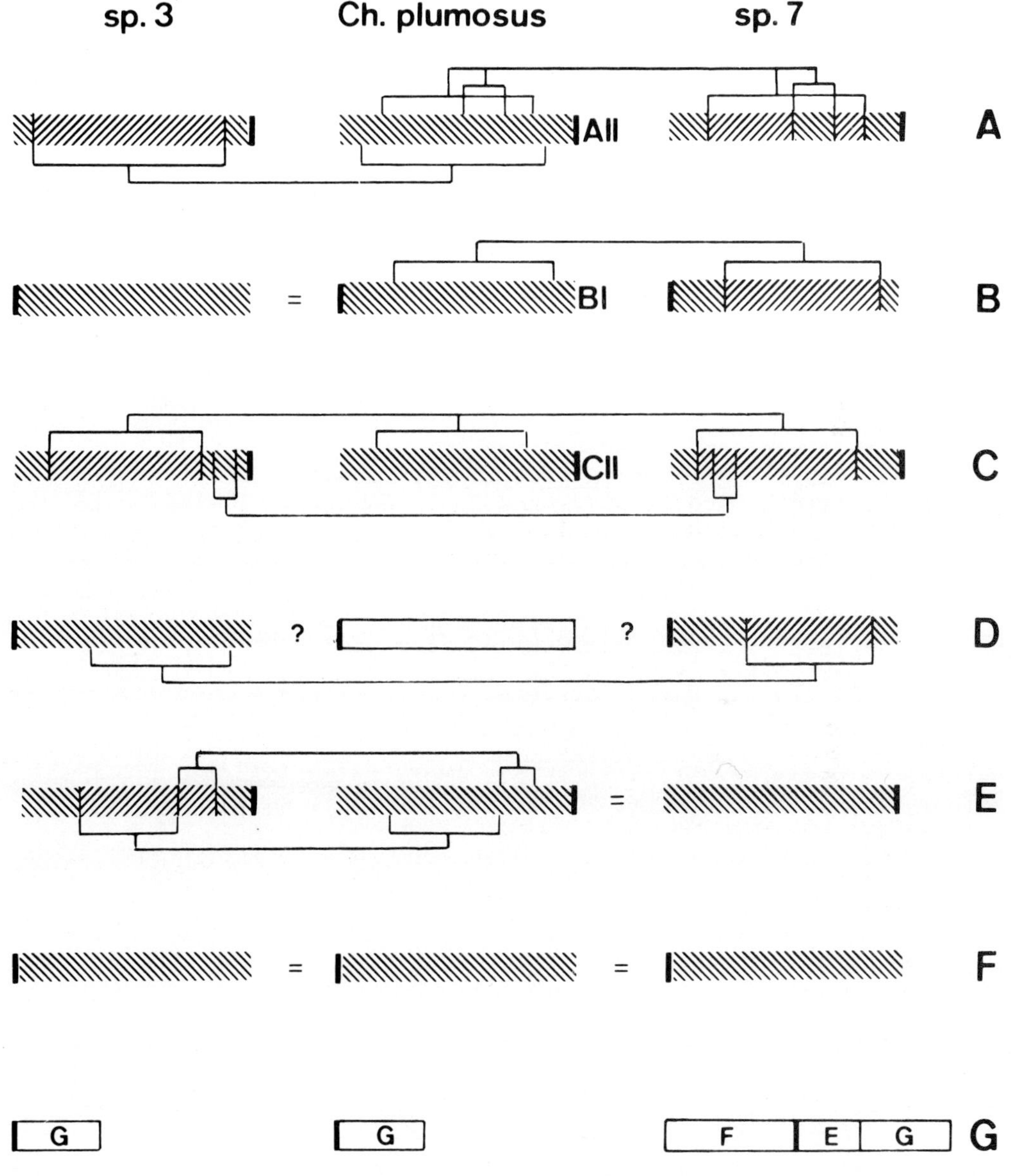

Abb. 1. Vergleich der Chromosomen von Ch. sp.3, Ch. sp.7 und Ch. plumosus.

DANKSAGUNG

Die Arbeit wurde mit finanzieller Unterstützung des Schweizerischen Nationalfonds durchgeführt (Gesuch 3.027.76). Wir danken Herrn R. Fasnacht (Muntelier) sehr herzlich, der uns für die Arbeiten am Murtensee sein Boot zur Verfügung stellte.

LITERATUR

Bürki, E., R. Rothen und A. Scholl (1978). Rev. suisse Zool., 85, 625-634.

Fittkau, D. F. und F. Reiss (1978). In J. Illies (Herausg.), Limnofauna Europaea, Gustav Fischer Verlag Stuttgart. pp. 429-430.

Keyl, H. G. (1960). Arch. Hydrobiol. 57, 187-195.

Keyl, H. G. (1961). Arch. Hydrobiol. 58, 1-6.

Keyl, H. G. (1962). Chromosoma (Berl.) 13, 464-514.

Keyl, H. G. und I. Keyl (1959). Arch. Hydrobiol. 56, 43-57.

Klötzli, A. M. (1974). Arch. Hydrobiol. 74, 68-81.

Krieger-Wolff, E. und W. Wülker (1971). Beitr. naturk. Forsch. SüdwDtl. 30, 133-145.

Lenz, F. (1954-1962). In E. Lindner (Herausg.), Die Fliegen der palaearktischen Region, Bd. III/2 E. Schweizerbart'sche Verlagsbuchhandlung, Stuttgart. pp. 139-260.

Martin, J. (1971). Chromosoma (Berl.) 35, 418-430.

Palmen, E., and L. Aho (1966). Ann. Zool. Fenn. 3, 217-244.

Rosin, S. und J. Fischer (1965). Arch. Julius Klaus-Stift. 41, 37-44.

Rosin, S. und J. Fischer (1972). Rev. suisse Zool. 79, 119-141.

Ryser, H. M., H. J. Geiger und A. Scholl (1978). Mitt. Natf. Ges. Bern NF 35, 69-87.

Schlee, D. (1966). Gewässer und Abwässer 41/42, 169-193.

Strenzke, K. (1959). Arch. Hydrobiol. 56, 1-42.

Strenzke, K. (1960). Ann. Ent. Fenn. 26, 111-138.

Thienemann, A. (1950). Arch. Hydrobiol. Suppl. 18, 1-202.

Wülker, W. (1973). Arch. Hydrobiol. 72, 356-374.

Wülker, W. und A. M. Klötzli (1973). Arch. Hydrobiol. 72, 474-489.

Wülker, W., J. E. Sublette und J. Martin (1968). Ann. Zool. Fenn. 5, 155-158.

Wülker, W., J. E. Sublette, M. F. Sublette, and J. Martin (1971). Stud. Nat. Sci. (Portales, N.M.) 1, 1-89.

Die Evolution der Gattung Chironomus aus Biochemisch-Genetischer Sicht

A. Scholl, H. J. Geiger und H. M. Ryser

Zoologisches Institut der Universität Bern, Sahlistrasse 8, CH-3012 Bern, Switzerland

ABSTRACT

The phylogenetic relationships of eighteen Chironomus species have been investigated by enzyme electrophoresis. A dendrogram is presented. Four lines are recognized which exhibit no or very little similarity with each other. These lines comprise the species as follows: 1. Ch. salinarius, 2. Ch. striatus, 3. five species of the pseudothummi-complex and Ch. thummi, 4. seven species of the thummi-complex (except Ch. thummi) and three species of the lacunarius-complex.

The data suggest that the lacunarius-complex is relatively young and must have originated from the thummi-complex. Furthermore, the lacunarius- and thummi-complex comprise several species of young age, as opposed to the pseudothummi-complex species (including Ch. thummi), which have been separated earlier. The data are in good agreement with conclusions derived from cytotaxonomical investigations.

KEYWORDS

Genus Chironomus; evolution; dendrogram; enzyme electrophoresis; genetic similarity-coefficient; cytotaxonomy; sibling species.

EINLEITUNG

Bei Untersuchungen über die Verwandtschaftsbeziehungen der Organismen finden heute häufig biochemische Methoden Verwendung. Im intragenerischen Bereich wird vor allem die Enzymelektrophorese (Avise, 1974) benutzt.

Mit dieser Methode wird der Grad genetischer Divergenz der zu vergleichenden Arten an einer Stichprobe von Enzymgenen ermittelt, wobei nicht die Gene selbst, sondern die von ihnen determinierten Enzyme untersucht werden. Als Kriterium genetischer Differenzen am betreffenden Locus gilt die elektrophoretische Unterscheidbarkeit homologer Enzyme. Der

Grad genetischer Divergenz der Arten wird aus dem Anteil elektrophoretisch unterscheidbarer Enzyme ermittelt. Aussagen über die Verwandtschaftsbeziehungen basieren auf der Annahme, dass diese dem jeweiligen Grad genetischer Divergenz entsprechen, dass also die jeweils nächst verwandten Arten im Untersuchungsmaterial den geringsten Grad genetischer Divergenz aufweisen.

Die enzymologischen Aussagen differieren gelegentlich beträchtlich von den Vorstellungen, welche aus Untersuchungen mittels klassischer Methoden abgeleitet wurden. Es bleibt in einzelnen Fällen problematisch, welcher Untersuchungsmethode man den Primat für eine Verwandtschaftsaussage zuerkennt, wobei nicht selten die Ueberzeugung des betreffenden Bearbeiters den Ausschlag geben mag (Scholl et al., 1978).

Die vorliegende Untersuchung entstand deshalb primär in der Absicht, die enzymologischen Befunde mit den Aussagen einer anderen genetischen Methode zu vergleichen. Ueber die Verwandtschaftsbeziehungen der Zuckmückenarten der Gattung Chironomus sind von Keyl (1962) konkrete Vorstellungen aus Untersuchungsbefunden an Speicheldrüsenchromosomen formuliert worden. Deshalb bot sich diese Gattung als Untersuchungsobjekt an.

Elektrophoretische Untersuchungen an Zuckmücken schienen uns aber auch aus anderen Gründen von Interesse. Bekanntlich sind die Chironomiden eine taxonomisch weitgehend noch ungenügend erforschte Insektengruppe (Reiss, 1968), welche mit morphologischen Methoden schwer fassbar ist. Es ergab sich somit auch die Gelegenheit, die Anwendbarkeit biochemisch-genetischer Untersuchungsmethoden für taxonomische Fragestellungen bei Chironomiden zu überprüfen.

MATERIAL UND METHODEN

Artdiagnose und untersuchte Arten

Zur Untersuchung gelanten ausschliesslich Larven des vierten Stadiums. Die Artdiagnose erfolgte auf Grund cytologischer Unterscheidungsmerkmale nach Keyl, wie bei Ryser et al. (in diesem Band) zitiert. Pro Enzym wurden von jeder Art mindestens 15 Larven analysiert, welche in der Regel einer Lokalpopulation aus unseren Untersuchungsgebieten (Ryser et al., in diesem Band) entstammten. Folgende Arten wurden untersucht (in Klammern die in Tabelle 1 verwendeten Abkürzungen): lacunarius-Komplex: Ch. lacunarius (lac), Ch. commutatus (com) und Ch. bernensis (ber). thummi-Komplex: Ch. melanotus (mno), Ch. plumosus (pl.1 und pl.2. Hierbei handelt es sich um zwei cytologisch unterscheidbare Formen aus dem Murtensee, welche sich auch ökologisch unterscheiden (Bürki et al., 1978), pl.1 stammt aus dem Profundal, pl.2 aus dem Litoral). Ch. nuditarsis (nud), Ch. aberratus (abe) und Ch. thummi (thu), sowie drei cytologisch nicht bekannte Arten (sp.3), (sp.7), (sp.2), welche bei Ryser et al. (in diesem Band) näher besprochen worden sind. pseudothummi-Komplex: Ch. melanescens (mne), Ch. holomelas (hol), Ch. dorsalis (dor), Ch. luridus (lur) und Ch. uliginosus (uli). Komplex unbekannt: Ch. striatus (str) und Ch. salinarius (sal). Bei Ch. salinarius wurde Freiland-Material aus einer holländischen Lokalpopulation untersucht.

Wir haben ferner zum Vergleich Camptochironomus tentans (ten) in die Untersuchungen einbezogen (Laborstamm, aufgebaut aus Larvenmaterial vom Grossen Plöner See/Deutschland).

Elektrophoresemethoden und Darstellung der Enzyme

Wir präparierten zunächst die Speicheldrüsen der Larven zwecks cytologischer Artdiagnose und verwendeten den restlichen Larvenkörper zur Herstellung eines Gewebehomogenates (mit 80 - 200 µl TRIS-Puffer, 0,1 M, pH 8,0). Durch Zentrifugation wurde eine partikelfreie Homogenat-Ueberstandsfraktion gewonnen, mit welcher die Gele (Stärke-Gele in vertikalen Elektrophorese-Apparaturen von Buchler/USA, mit Schlitzformern für 15 Schlitze) beschickt wurden. Der Extrakt einzelner Larven reichte aus für die Beschickung mehrerer Gele, auf welchen wir nach beendeter Elektrophorese (15 Std. bei 4°C) jeweils verschiedene Enzyme darstellten. In der vorliegenden Untersuchung wurden die Ergebnisse an den folgenden Enzymen ausgewertet (in Klammern die in Tabelle 1 verwendeten Abkürzungen): Isocitrat Dehydrogenase (IDH), Malat Dehydrogenase (zwei genetisch unabhängige Isoenzymsysteme, MDH-1 und MDH-2), Adenylat Kinase (AK), Arginin Kinase (APK), Indophenol Oxydase (IPO), Phosphoglucomutase (PGM), Phosphoglucose Isomerase (PGI), Alkohol Dehydrogenase (ADH), Pyruvat Kinase (PK) und Glutamat-Oxalacetat-Transaminase (GOT).

Die Enzymstichprobe ist relativ klein. Andere Enzyme, welche ebenfalls untersucht worden sind, konnten aus verschiedenen Gründen nicht ausgewertet werden. Bei Esterase- und Amidoschwarz-Färbungen, welche im Gegensatz zu den spezifischen Färbemedien für die obigen Enzyme eine grössere Zahl von Enzym- resp. Proteinbanden auf den Zymogrammen darstellen, war es uns infolge hoher intragenerischer Variabilität der Muster nicht möglich, mit ausreichender Sicherheit Produkte homologer Loci anzusprechen. In anderen Fällen gelang die Darstellung von bestimmten Enzymen nicht bei allen Arten. Es schien uns aus methodischen Erwägungen notwendig, die genetischen Abstände aus einer für alle Arten gleichen Enzymstichprobe zu ermitteln.

Bezüglich der spezifischen Färbemedien für die obigen Enzyme sowie weiterer methodischer Einzelheiten müssen wir aus Platzgründen auf eine frühere ausführliche Veröffentlichung verweisen (Scholl et al., 1978). Es sei jedoch erwähnt, dass für die Darstellung der Enzyme bei Chironomus in einzelnen Fällen Modifikationen dieser bei anderen Organismen verwendeten Färbemedien notwendig waren, welche wir auf Anfrage mitteilen.

Genetische Interpretation der Enzymphänotypen und Allelbezeichnungen

Die genetische Interpretation der aus den Zymogrammen erkennbaren Enzymphänotypen basiert auf Untersuchungsergebnissen an Geschwisterschaften aus Gelegeaufzuchten (Rothen, 1978, eigene unveröffentlichte Befunde).

Die Allelbezeichnungen basieren auf den elektrophoretischen Mobilitäten der Enzyme. Als Referenz wurde Ch. plumosus gewählt. An jedem Enzymlocus trägt das Hauptallel von Ch. plumosus die Bezeichnung loo. Diese Allelbezeichnung tritt auch bei anderen Arten auf, sofern das betreffende Enzym mit der Referenz elektrophoretisch identisch ist. Andere Allelbezeichnungen bei Ch. plumosus ebenso wie bei anderen Chironomusarten geben durch ihre Differenz zu loo die Mobilitätsdifferenz der von diesen Genen determinierten Proteine gegenüber der Referenz zu erkennen (unter unseren Versuchsbedingungen und gemessen in Millimetern). Der Entscheid darüber, ob ein Enzym bei zwei Arten elektrophoretisch identisch ist oder nicht, erfolgte stets auf Grund direkter Vergleiche, wobei Extrakte mehrerer Individuen der betreffenden Arten jeweils in benachbarten Positionen auf einem Gel aufgetrennt wurden.

Berechnung der Aehnlichkeitskoeffizienten

Für die untersuchten Arten haben wir in paarweisem Artvergleich Aehnlichkeitskoeffizienten nach Nei (1972) berechnet. Die Berechnung basiert auf den Frequenzen aller festgestellten Allele (d.h. einschliesslich der aus Platzgründen im Ergebnisteil nicht erwähnten Nebenallele). Die Aehnlichkeitskoeffizienten können zwischen 0,0 und 1,0 variieren. Der Koeffizient 1,0 würde sich beim Vergleich von zwei Populationen ergeben, welche an allen Enzymloci in Haupt- und Nebenallelen und deren Frequenzen übereinstimmen. Da die Berechnung auf einer Stichprobe von elf Enzymen basiert, sinkt der Koeffizient für jeden Enzymlocus, an welchem keine Uebereinstimmung gefunden wird, um den Betrag 0,09, resp. weniger, falls die Differenz sich nur in unterschiedlichen Allelfrequenzen manifestiert. Der Koeffizient 0,0 ergibt sich für Artenpaare, welche an keinem Enzymlocus weder in Haupt- noch Nebenallelen Uebereinstimmungen zeigen.

ERGEBNISSE UND DISKUSSION

Die aus den Elektrophoresebefunden ableitbare Auffassung über die Verwandtschaftsbeziehung der Chironomusarten ist in Abb. 2 in Form eines Dendrogrammes präsentiert. Die Konstruktion des Dendrogrammes stützt sich auf die Aehnlichkeitskoeffizienten (Abb. 1.1 - 1.3), welche aus den bei der Enzymelektrophorese gefundenen Allelen und ihren Frequenzen bei den untersuchten Arten berechnet wurden. Diese Primärbefunde können aus Platzgründen nicht in der gewünschten Ausführlichkeit mitgeteilt werden. Um jedoch einen gewissen Bezug der Aehnlichkeitskoeffizienten zu den Elektrophoreseergebnissen erkennbar zu machen, haben wir in Tabelle 1 für alle Arten die Hauptallele an den untersuchten Enzymloci genannt und Nebenallele, welche in einer Frequenz über 0,1 auftraten, in Klammern erwähnt. Bezüglich der Abkürzungen für die Arten (linke Kolonne) und die Enzyme (obere Kolonne) verweisen wir auf den Methodenteil.

Bei vielen Enzymloci tritt in Tabelle 1 bei Arten des lacunarius- und des thummi-Komplexes die gleiche Allelbezeichnung auf. Dies bedeutet elektrophoretische Identität der betreffenden Enzyme bei diesen Arten. Ebenso sind bei den Arten des pseudothummi-Komplexes häufig Uebereinstimmungen festzustellen. Zwischen den Arten des pseudothummi-Komplexes

	IDH	MDH-1	MDH-2	AK	APK	IPO	PGM	PGI	ADH	PK	GOT
lac	99	100	100	100	106	100	100	100	106	98 (93)	108
com	99	100	100	100	106	100	100	100	100	98 (93)	108 (100)
ber	104	100	100	100	106	100	100	88	106	82	108
mno	99	100 (91)	100	100	100	100	100 (107)	92	109 (105)	91	108
pl 1	100	100 (105)	100	100	100	100	100 (93)	100	100	100	100 (110)
pl 2	100	100 (105)	100	100	100	100	100	100	100	100	100
sp 3	100	100	100	100	100	100	100 (115)	100	100	100	107 (100)
sp 7	100	100	100	100	100	100	100 (93)	100 (92)	100	100	107
sp 2	102	100	111	100	100	100	107	80	106	97	107
nud	102	91	100	102 (97)	90 (100)	100	100 (107)	92	106	93	112
abe	99	83	100	100	90	100	93 (100)	85	92	93 (88)	106
thu	102	100	115	88	100	86	115 (119)	90	99	95	110
mne	106	109	102	95	110	86	115 (107)	90 (100)	107	95	109
hol	96	96	115	97	110 (103)	86	115 (98)	90 (100)	97	95	105
dor	102	103	114 (104)	95	100	86	115	90	105	95	99
lur	108	103	102	88	103	86	115	78	98	95	102
uli	108	109	113	95	103	86	115	90	95	99	99
str	98	81	113	94	108	98	102 (115)	78	96	90	91
sal	89	76	104	95	95	90	102	76	96	90 (86)	98
ten	96	85	100	95	100	95	93	106	108	101	108

TABELLE 1 Die Hauptallele der Chironomusarten an den untersuchten Enzymloci (Erläuterungen siehe Text)

und Arten des thummi- oder lacunarius-Komplexes ergeben sich dagegen fast nie Uebereinstimmungen. Eine bemerkenswerte Ausnahme betrifft Ch. thummi. Die Art zeigt bei vielen Enzymen Mobilitätsidentität mit Arten des pseudothummi-Komplexes, während Uebereinstimmungen mit Arten des thummi-Komplexes nur selten festzustellen sind. Eine sehr isolierte

	commutatus	bernensis	melanotus	plumosus 1	plumosus 2	spec. 3	spec. 7	spec. 2	nuditarsis	aberratus	thummi
lacunarius	0.92	0.73	0.61	0.52	0.50	0.55	0.50	0.37	0.38	0.41	0.09
commutatus		0.63	0.58	0.64	0.62	0.65	0.60	0.29	0.31	0.42	0.10
bernensis			0.49	0.40	0.39	0.44	0.43	0.37	0.35	0.31	0.08
melanotus				0.49	0.48	0.50	0.55	0.34	0.44	0.43	0.15
plumosus 1					0.99	0.89	0.84	0.33	0.31	0.33	0.13
plumosus 2						0.87	0.81	0.31	0.31	0.32	0.13
spec. 3							0.97	0.46	0.29	0.31	0.19
spec. 7								0.48	0.34	0.30	0.19
spec. 2									0.33	0.19	0.30
nuditarsis										0.31	0.13
aberratus											0

Abb. 1.1. Nei Koeffizienten genetischer Aehnlichkeit bei paarweisem Vergleich von Arten des lacunarius- und thummi-Komplexes (Erläuterungen siehe Text).

	melanescens	holomelas	dorsalis	luridus	uliginosus	striatus	salinarius	C. tentans
thummi	0.34	0.42	0.55	0.37	0.26	0.04	0	0.09
melanescens		0.37	0.43	0.36	0.35	0.03	0.09	0.10
holomelas			0.32	0.32	0.26	0.04	0	0.10
dorsalis				0.37	0.47	0.04	0.12	0.19
luridus					0.37	0.14	0	0
uliginosus						0.14	0.09	0.09
striatus							0.23	0
salinarius								0.09

Abb. 1.2. Nei-Koeffizienten genetischer Aehnlichkeit (Fortsetzung).

Stellung nehmen im Untersuchungsmaterial Ch. striatus und Ch. salinarius ein, beide Arten sind bei vielen Enzymen durch artspezifische Varianten gekennzeichnet. Hingegen zeigt Ch. tentans mehrfach Uebereinstimmungen, besonders mit Arten des thummi-Komplexes.

	lacunarius	commutatus	bernensis	melanotus	plumosus 1	plumosus 2	spec. 3	spec. 7	spec. 2	nuditarsis	aberratus	thummi
melanescens	0.03	0.03	0	0	0.03	0.03	0.03	0.02	0.02	0	0	0.34
holomelas	0.03	0.03	0	0	0.03	0.03	0.03	0.02	0.01	0.05	0	0.42
dorsalis	0	0	0.01	0.13	0.10	0.10	0.10	0.10	0.20	0.13	0	0.55
luridus	0	0	0.01	0	0	0	0	0	0.01	0	0	0.37
uliginosus	0	0	0	0	0	0	0	0	0.01	0	0	0.26
striatus	0	0	0	0	0	0	0	0	0.01	0	0	0.04
salinarius	0	0	0	0	0	0	0	0	0	0	0	0
C. tentans	0.19	0.17	0.19	0.30	0.21	0.19	0.20	0.24	0.09	0.14	0.17	0.09

Abb. 1.3. Nei Koeffizienten genetischer Aehnlichkeit (Fortsetzung).

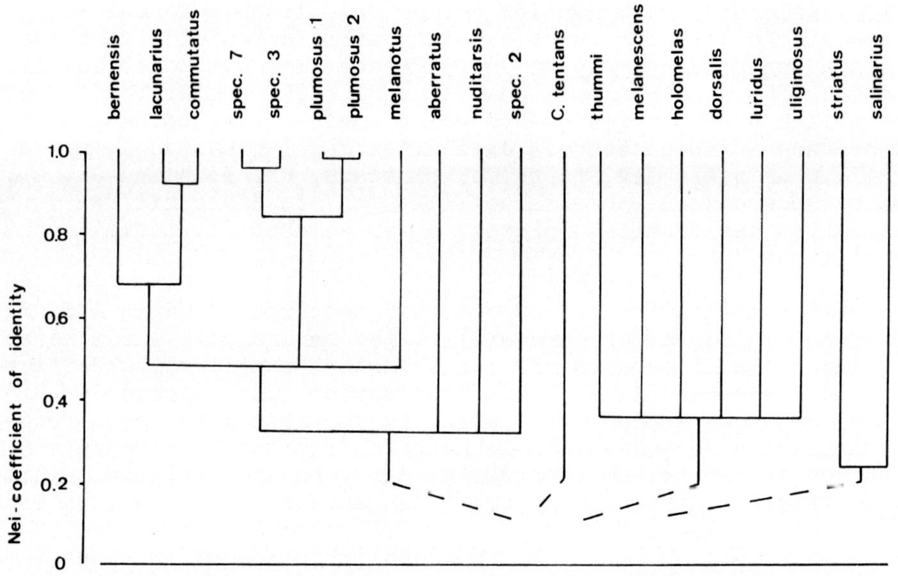

Abb. 2. Dendrogramm der Chironomusarten, basierend auf der enzymologischen Aehnlichkeit (Erläuterungen siehe Text).

In unserem Untersuchungsmaterial sind also Gruppen von Arten nachweisbar, welche mit einander durch ein ihnen gemeinsames Enzymmuster verbunden und von anderen Artengruppen, welche ein anderes Enzymmuster aufweisen, abgesetzt sind. Eine bestimmte Enzymvariante wird vielfach nur innerhalb einer solchen Artengruppe gefunden. Einzelne Arten, welche die gruppentypische Variante des betreffenden Enzyms nicht aufweisen, geben aber ihre Zugehörigkeit zu dieser Gruppe bei anderen Enzymen zu erkennen. Tabelle 1 erlaubt, diesen Befund zu dokumentieren, da die Allelbezeichnungen auf der elektrophoretischen Mobilität der Enzyme basieren. Diese Art von Gruppierung kann nur darauf beruhen, dass die Arten einer Gruppe auf einen gemeinsamen Vorfahren zurückgehen, welcher sich in seinem Enzymmuster von dem nächsten gemeinsamen Vorfahren der Arten einer anderen Gruppe unterschied.

Dem Grad der Uebereinstimmungen in Tabelle 1 entsprechen die berechneten Koeffizienten genetischer Aehnlichkeit in Abb. 1.1 - 1.3. Beim paarweisen Vergleich von Arten innerhalb des lacunarius- und thummi-Komplexes (Abb. 1.1) und auch innerhalb des pseudothummi-Komplexes (Abb. 1.2) sind die Koeffizienten hoch. In allen anderen Fällen (Abb. 1.3) werden dagegen meist sehr niedrige Koeffizienten festgestellt. Als wichtiges Detail sei auf die Sonderstellung von Ch. thummi im thummi-Komplex hingewiesen (Abb. 1.1). Ch. thummi zeigt deutlich höhere Affinitäten mit den Arten des pseudothummi-Komplexes (Abb. 1.2).

Innerhalb des lacunarius und thummi-Komplexes sind Arten zu erkennen, welche mit einander deutlich höhere Aehnlichkeitskoeffizienten ergeben als mit anderen Arten in diesen beiden Komplexen. Diese werden als jeweils nächst verwandte Arten aufgefasst und sind in Abb. 1.1 durch Umrandung sowie durch die gewählte Reihenfolge hervorgehoben. Die beiden Arten Ch. sp.3 und Ch. sp.7 ergeben den höchsten Aehnlichkeitskoeffizienten, welcher nahezu dem der beiden Ch. plumosus-Formen entspricht. Der numerische Wert der Aehnlichkeitskoeffizienten weist auf enge Beziehungen der beiden Arten zu Ch. plumosus hin. Ein hoher Koeffizient wurde auch für das Artenpaar Ch. lacunarius/Ch. commutatus berechnet. Diese beiden Arten lassen nähere Beziehungen zu Ch. bernensis erkennen. Insbesondere ergeben aber die drei Arten des lacunarius-Komplexes mit Ch. melanotus sowie der Gruppe Ch. plumosus, Ch. sp.3 und Ch. sp.7 deutlich höhere Aehnlichkeitskoeffizienten als diese mit den verbleibenden Arten des thummi-Komplexes, unter welchen Ch. thummi nochmals abgesetzt ist.

Diese Beziehungen zwischen den untersuchten Arten sind in Abb. 2 in Form eines Dendrogrammes dargestellt. Das Dendrogramm wurde konstruiert, indem die Artenpaare mit dem höchsten Aehnlichkeitskoeffizienten als nächst verwandte Arten betrachtet wurden. In absteigender Linie des Dendrogrammes wurden mit diesen die weiteren Arten entsprechend dem numerischen Wert des Aehnlichkeitskoeffizienten verbunden. Als Verzweigungspunkt ist im Dendrogramm der durchschnittliche Aehnlichkeitskoeffizient der abzweigenden Arten angenommen worden. Unterhalb eines Aehnlichkeitskoeffizienten von 0,2 wurde auf einen Anschluss der Arten verzichtet, da die niedrigen Aehnlichkeitskoeffizienten infolge der geringen Enzymstichprobe relativ stark von Zufallsübereinstimmungen beeinflusst sein könnten.

In bezug auf die Evolution der Gattung erlauben die Elektrophorese-befunde die Aussage, dass die hier betrachteten Arten auf drei oder vier Linien zurückgehen, welche phylogenetisch bereits sehr lange getrennt sein dürften und zwischen welchen Verwandtschaftsbeziehungen elektrophoretisch nicht mehr oder nur unscharf nachweisbar sind. Eine der beiden Linien, sie umfasst den lacunarius- und thummi-Komplex, hat sich in neuerer Zeit in mehrere Arten aufgespalten. Eine weitere Linie bilden die phylogenetisch älteren Arten des pseudothummi-Komplexes einschliesslich Ch. thummi.

Die vorliegenden Befunde decken sich gut mit den cytotaxonomischen Ergebnissen (Keyl, 1962). Bekanntlich sind die Chironomuskomplexe cytologisch definiert, sie umfassen jeweils Arten mit einer bestimmten Kombination der Chromosomenarme und sind von einander durch reziproke Translokationen getrennt. Ch. salinarius und Ch. striatus konnten keinem Komplex zugeordnet werden, weil mehrere Chromosomenarme nicht identifizierbar sind. Dies lässt vermuten, dass diese beiden mit den anderen Arten entfernter verwandt sind. Der lacunarius-Komplex muss auch nach cytologischen Befunden vom thummi-Komplex abgeleitet sein. Ein phylogenetisch geringeres Alter des thummi-Komplexes wurde vermutet, weil hier im Gegensatz zum pseudothummi-Komplex interspezifische Strukturunterschiede häufig heterozygot erhalten sind. Für Ch. thummi selbst hatte Keyl eine Beziehung über eine von den anderen Arten des Komplexes unabhängige Translokation zum pseudothummi-Komplex erwogen.

Beim Vergleich der beiden Untersuchungsmethoden scheinen die karyologischen Aussagemöglichkeiten an der Gattungsgrenze überlegen zu sein. Der Elektrophorese-Methode stellte sich im vorliegenden Material die Schwierigkeit, dass nur eine kleine Enzymstichprobe auswertbar war und dass sich im Gesamtmaterial unerwartet selten Mobilitätsidentitäten ergeben haben. Dies könnte darauf hindeuten, dass die Gattung Chironomus wesentlich distantere Spezies vereinigt als andere Genera, in welchen die Elektrophorese angewendet wurde. Diese Vermutung lässt sich durch andere Hinweise stützen. Aus zoogeographischer Sicht könnte beispielsweise die weltweite Verbreitung der Gattung erwähnt werden.

DANKSAGUNG

Die Arbeit wurde durchgeführt mit Unterstützung des Schweizerischen Nationalfonds (Gesuch 3.027.76). Wir danken Herrn Prof. W. Wülker (Freiburg i.Br.) für Beratung in cytotaxonomischen Fragen, Herrn Prof. D. Neumann (Köln) für Ch. salinarius Larven und Herrn PD. M. Lezzi (Zürich) für C. tentans Larven.

LITERATUR

Avise, J. C. (1974). Syst. Zool., 23, 465-481.
Bürki, E., R. Rothen und A. Scholl (1978). Rev. suisse Zool., 85, 625-634.
Keyl, H. G. (1962). Chromosoma (Berl.), 13, 464-514.
Nei, M. (1972). Amer. Natur., 106, 283-292.
Reiss, F. (1968). Arch. Hydrobiol., 64, 176-323.
Rothen, R. (1978). Inaugural-Diss. Univ. Bern.
Scholl, A., B. Corzillius und W. Villwock (1978). Z. zool. Syst. Evolut.-forsch., 13, 110-124.

Esterase Evidentiation and Characterization in the Course of Onthogenesis in *Chironomus Thummi* Kieff.

L. Tallandini*, M. Turchetto* and U. Ferrarese**

*Istituto di Biologia Animale, Padova Univ., via Loredan 10, I-35100 Padova, Italy
**Museo Civico di Storia Naturale, Lungadige Porta, Vittoria 9, I-37100 Verona, Italy

ABSTRACT

Esterases from larvae, pupae and adults of *Chironomus thummi* have been studied, as function of time, using α and β naphthyl acetate as substrates. Variation of esterasic activity in relation with pH, temperature, and specific inhibitors has been observed.

KEYWORDS

Esterases; esterasic specific activity; α naphthyl acetate; β naphthyl acetate; eserine; DFP; pCMB.

INTRODUCTION

The study of enzymatic systems can be utilized either for physiological and biochemical, or for taxonomical purposes. For the latter possibility it is necessary to study many enzymes looking for enzymatic systems constant in the course of the onthogenesis. Homogeneous intraspecific and different interspecific patterns, have to be found and carefully controlled on a high number of populations, coming from different places. As a matter of fact our approaches to a biochemical taxonomy have evidentiated significant differences in the electrophoretic pattern of some enzymes in individuals of the same species, collected in the same place, in late spring and autumn. As a part of this large work we are carring out, we are presenting now results on the esterases activity and properties in *Chironomus thummi* during the onthogenesis and in different environmental conditions. These enzymes are largely distributed in living organisms and have been studied by means of electrophoresis and other biochemical assays. Though it is difficult to determine the actual physiological substrates for the various esterases, as many of them probably have broad specificity, however the study of these enzymes is relevant for they have a large range of activity, promoting the utilization of a great variety of substrates.

MATERIALS AND METHODS

Larvae of *Chironomus thummi* have been collected at the Botanical Garden, Padova, University. The fourth instar larvae, were immediately frozen at -30°C. The other ha

ve been kept in the Laboratory;when the pupal and adult stages were reached, individuals were collected and immediately frozen at -30°C. Species determination was performed using the key of Strenzke (1959).
Enzymatic assays were mainly carried out as already stated by Danford and Beardmore (1979). The substrates were α and β naphthyl acetate. The determination of hydrolized substrates as α and β naphthol was performed with Fast Red TR, after the reaction was stopped by adding absolute ethanol. The developed dye, extracted in ethyl acetate, was aestimated spectrophotometrically at 490 nm. Protein determination was performed by the Bradford micromethod (1976). Fig. 1 show the calibration curve.

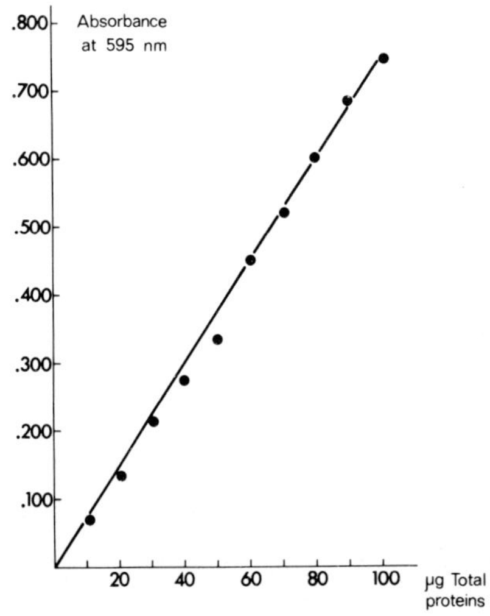

Fig. 1. Calibration of protein content

RESULTS

In Figs. 2 and 3 are shown the calibration for α and β naphthol.

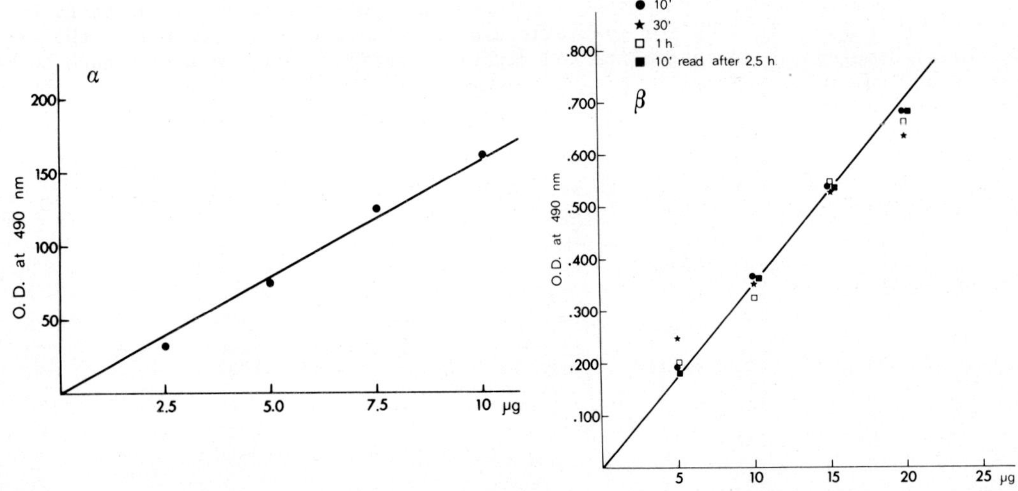

Fig. 2. and Fig. 3. Calibration of α and β naphthol + Fast Red.

As we can see the coloured complex for β naphthol was stable at least till 2.5 h. after the reaction. A similar situation was found also for α naphthol.
In Fig. 4 and Fig. 5 we can follow the break-down of the substrates as a function of time for α and β naphthyl acetate respectively.

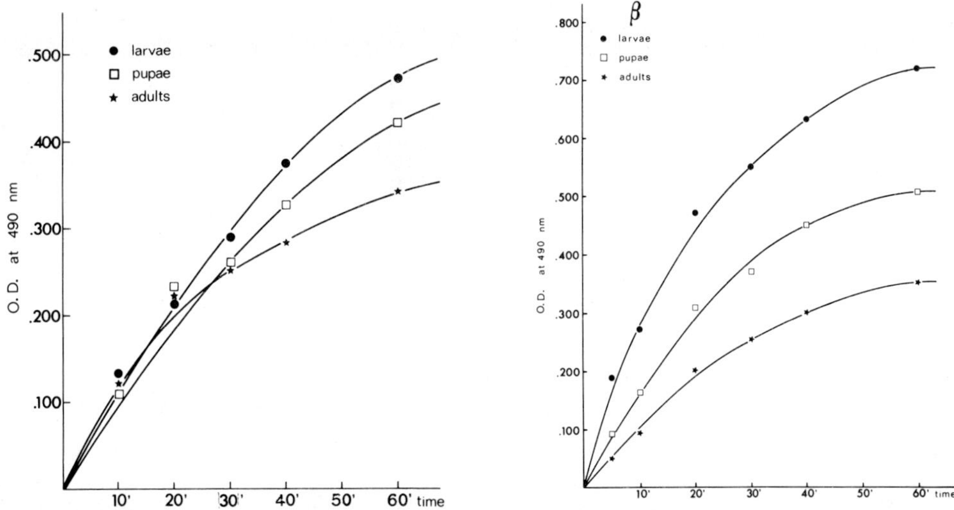

Fig. 4 and Fig. 5. Breakdown of α and β naphthyl acetate as function of time.

The specific enzymatic activity was evaluated in terms of m mol of substrates utilized · mg^{-1} of total proteins · min^{-1}.
The results were :

	naphthyl acetate	naphthyl acetate	mg prot/ml
larvae	$.097 \cdot 10^{-3}$	$.086 \cdot 10^{-3}$	2.63
pupae	$.086 \cdot 10^{-3}$	$.070 \cdot 10^{-3}$	1.73
adults	$.215 \cdot 10^{-3}$	$.113 \cdot 10^{-3}$	0.62

In both cases, but in a more evident way when we follow the substrate, we observe an increase in the esterasic activity in the adults.
In Fig. 6 and Fig. 7 we report the esterasic activity as a function of the temperature. The maximum activity is always reached at 25°C; no significant differences between α and β esterases is observed. Larvae are less sensitive than pupae and adults to the decrease of the temperature (15-5°C); at 60°C esterases from the 3 stages are not completely denatured.
In Fig. 8 and Fig. 9 are shown the calibrations for α and β naphthol at various pH values.
In Fig. 10 we can follow the esterase activity as a function of pH. In the larvae the maximum activity is reached at pH 7 for α and at pH 8 for β esterases. Pupae and adults show similar behaviour. Both adults and pupae in fact have a peak of activity between pH 6.5 and 7.0 and a fall at pH 7.5.
The increase observed at more basic pHs can perhaps be attributed to alkaline phosphatases. We are now controlling this possibility.

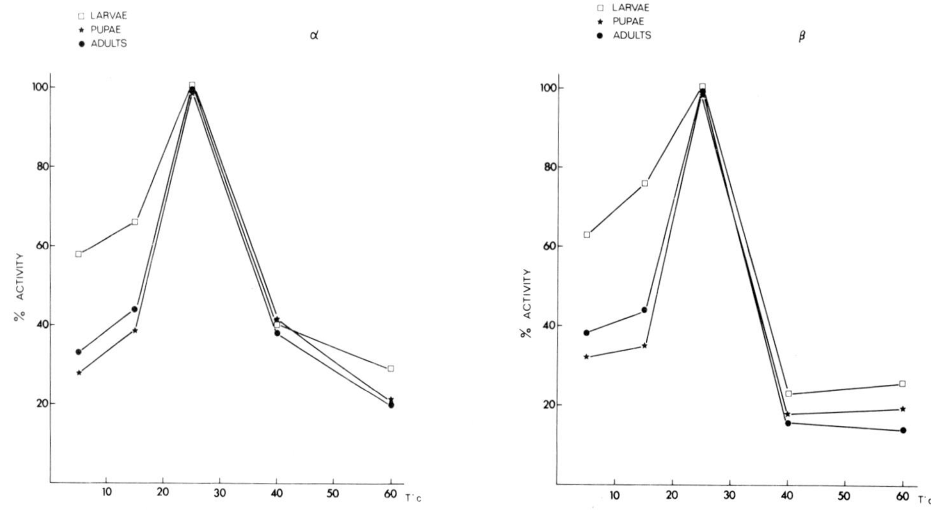

Fig. 6. and Fig. 7. Breakdown of α and β naphthyl acetate as function of temperature.

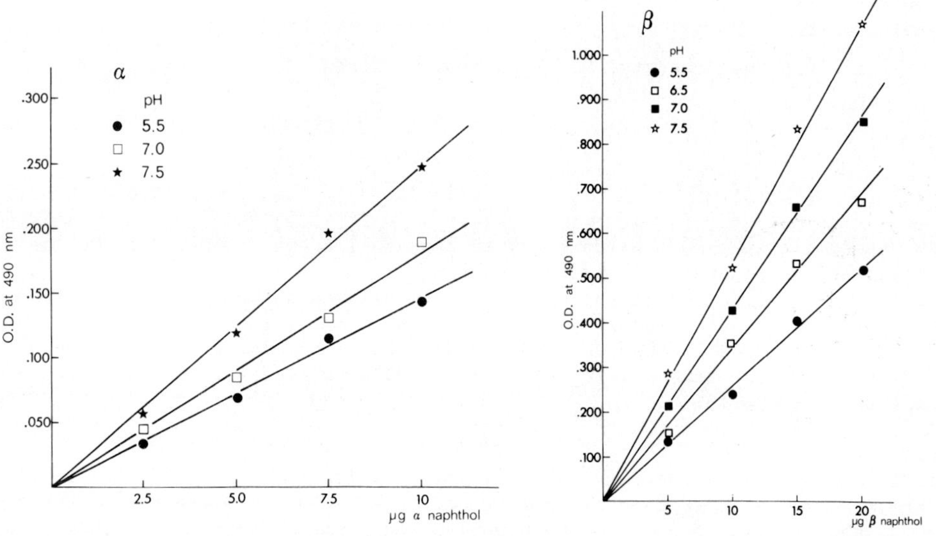

Fig. 8. and Fig. 9. Calibration of α and β naphthol + Fast Red at various pH values.

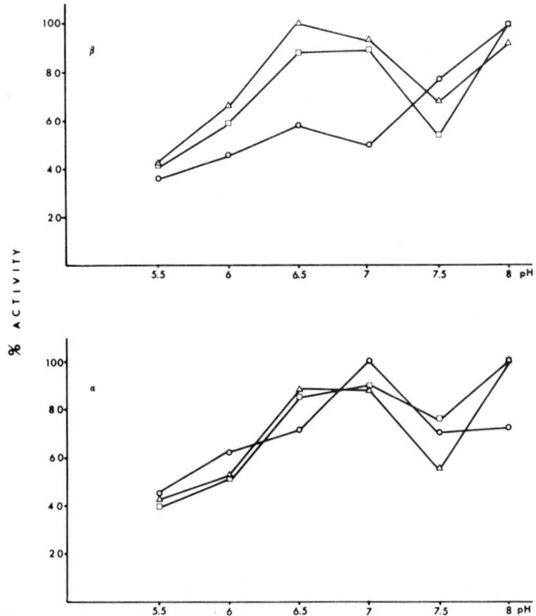

Fig. 10. Percentage activity relative to pH for esterases. Substrates α and β naphthylacetate
O larvae ; △ pupae ; □ adults .

In Fig. 11 we report the esterases activity in the presence of inhibitors. Eserine is a specific inhibitor for cholinesterases and acethyl cholinesterases. At larval stage a smaller quantity of these enzymes is present among α esterases then among β esterases.
The experiments carried out in the presence of DFP (Diisopropyl fluorophosphate), inhibitor of carboxyl esterases, acethyl cholinesterases and cholinesterases, show a high presence of carboxyl esterases among the β esterases. Further inhibition follow the increase of DFP concentration, both in α and β esterases.
We have also tested pCMB (Parachloromercuribenzoate), an inhibitor of aryl esterases, as well as of acetyl cholinesterases and cholinesterases. Using this inhibitor we have not found significant differences between α and β esterases at the three stages (see Table 1).

TABLE 1 Percentage activity of esterases in the presence of inhibitors in larvae (L), pupae (P), and adults (A).

Compound	Conc. (M)	% activity					
		α naphthyl acetate			β naphthyl acetate		
		L	P	A	L	P	A
Eserine	10^{-4}	86	61.4	53.3	73.4	66.5	59
	10^{-3}	80	52.9	56.1	64.2	55.7	51.3
	10^{-2}	76.3	45	39.2	57	46.8	31.3
D F P	10^{-4}	62.5	41.4	41.1	40.6	26.6	29.6
	10^{-3}	30.3	25.7	27.1	26.1	25.3	26
	10^{-2}	3.3	2.1	1.3	6.8	8	7
P C M B	10^{-4}	42.8	35.7	29	35.7	31.6	36.5

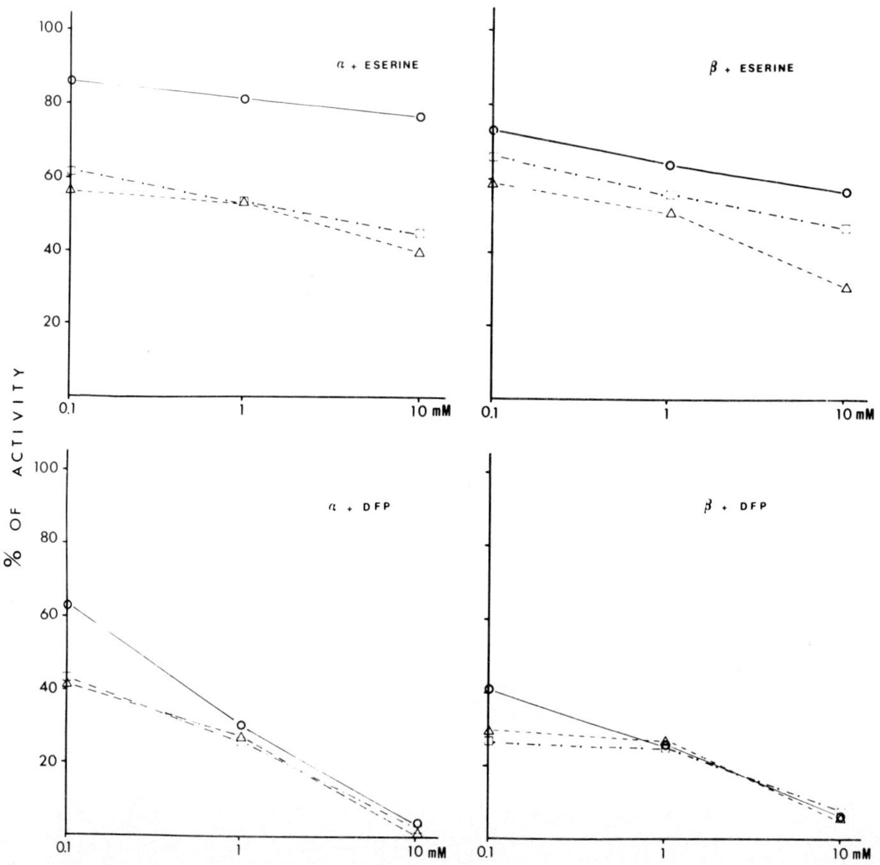

Fig. 11. Breakdown of α and β naphthyl acetate at various concentrations of inhibitors.
—○—larvae ;-·-·□·-·- pupae ;---△---adults.

In summary, we note the increase of esterases in the adults in relation to the total protein content (partly imputable to the loss of the haemoglobins) as well as a differentiation of these enzymes during development showed by the different behaviour with specific inhibitors. From this point of view pupae and adults are very similar.

The same behaviour can be found studing the esterase activity in function of the temperature, which seems to be an interesting limiting factor. It is in fact relevant that at low temperature larval esterase activity decreases less than adult and pupal esterases do. At temperatures higher than 35-40°C we have a strong reduction at all stages, without, however, complete denaturation.

The valuation of the activity in relation to pH shows that pH is not a severe limiting factor for these enzymes. In fact esterases are active in a wide range of pH at every stage of the life of these organisms.

REFERENCES

Bradford, M.M. (1976). A rapid and sensitive method for the quantitation of microgram quantities of protein utilizing the principle of protein-dye binding. *Anal. Biochem.*, 72, 248-254.

Danford, N.D., and J.A. Beardmore (1979). Biochemical properties of Esterase-6 in *Drosophila melanogaster*. *Biochem. Genetics*, 17, 1-22.

Strenzche, K. (1959). Revision der Gattung *Chironomus* Meig. I. Die Imagines von 15 norddentschen Arten und Unterarten. *Arch. Hidrobiol.*, 56, 1-42.

The Haemoglobin Synthesising Tissue of Chironomus

H. Tichy

Max-Planck-Institut für Biologie, Abteilung Beermann, Spemannstrasse 34, D-7400 Tübingen 1, Federal Republic of Germany

ABSTRACT

The haemoglobin of Chironomus is dissolved in the haemolymph of the larva. It was determined that only a negligible haemoglobin turnover takes place and the amount of haemoglobin synthesis during the fourth larval instar could be calculated. By means of cytophotometrical methods, haemoglobin specific absorption could be found only in the oenocytes. Specific immunological methods have also been used to identify the haemoglobin-synthesising tissue and again only the oenocytes gave positive results. The oenocytes are arranged as 4 large cells on each side of the abdominal segments. The measured haemoglobin content of single oenocytes is in good agreement with the calculations of their haemoglobin content and indicates that synthesis in only 60 cells could account for the total haemoglobin production.

KEYWORDS

Chironomus haemoglobin synthesis, haemoglobin turnover, oenocytes, fat body.

INTRODUCTION

One of the most striking features of Chironomids is that the larvae of many groups possess haemoglobin. This haemoglobin is dissolved in the haemolymph and not confined in special cells as in vertebrates and other haemoglobin-synthesising organisms. The haemoglobin of Chironomus has been of great interest and has therefore been investigated from physical, chemical and biological standpoints. The structure of the haemoglobin molecule has been elucidated by X-ray analysis (Huber, Epp, Formanek, 1970). The aminoacide-sequence of many of the different haemoglobins has been determined (Braunitzer, Buse, Gersonde, 1974; Kleinschmidt, Braunitzer, 1978). The physiology of the haemoglobin has been investigated and discussed as an adaptation to the special requirements of oxygen transport and respiration at low oxygen tension (Neumann, 1961; Weber, 1963). Furthermore the different haemoglobins within one species provide a good system for the study of their genetics and evolution (Thompson, English, 1966; Tichy, 1970, 1975, 1976).

One might expect that the tissue or cells, which secrete the haemoglobin into the haemolymph, are also investigated and well known. Indeed, already 1886 described Wielowiejski some celltypes which may be considered as producers of haemolymph

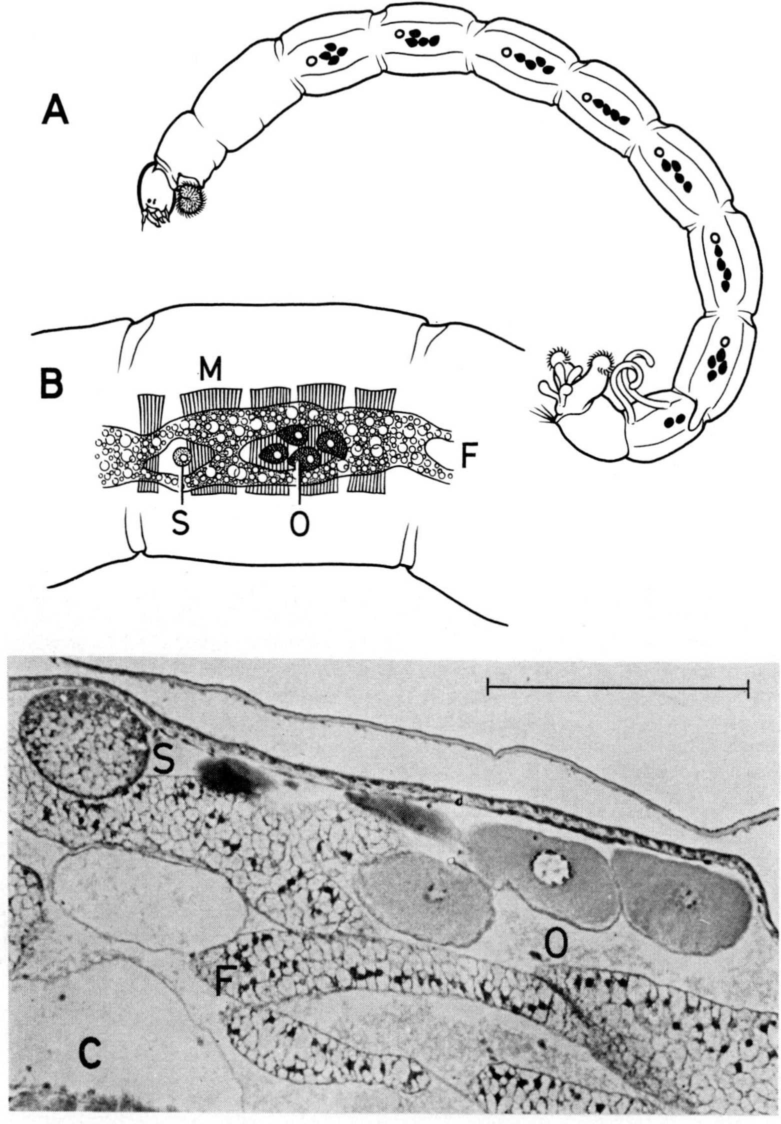

Fig. 1. The morphology of the tissues investigated.
A) The larva with the oenocytes. The four dark spots in each abdominal segment indicate the major oenocytes; the circle in front of them shows the position of the spherical granulous cell.

B) One segment with the oenocytes (O) and the spherical cell (S), with fat body (F) and transverse muscles (M).

C) Histological section of a segment with oenocytes (O), spherical cell (S) and fat body (F). The bar represents 0,1 mm.

proteins including haemoglobin. He describes two types of fat body and another celltype, to which he gave the name oenocytes because of their winelike yellow to red colour.

With the aid of cytochemical methods and cell culture, Laufer and his group investigated the haemoglobin synthesis in Chironomus thummi and published their findings that the so-called lateral fat body is a site of the haemoglobin synthesis (Bergström, Laufer, Rogers, 1976; Schin, Laufer, Carr, 1977). Their results were however based on the use of a rather unspecific haemoglobin reagent and tissue culture of whole body walls, which contains many different types of cells. Hence a reexamination of these results would seem to be in order.

THE TISSUES INVESTIGATED

The tissues investigated are the fat body and the oenocytes. The fat body can be divided into two morphologically different types, following the description of Miall and Hammond (1900). The outer fatty layer which has a green colour lies between the muscles of the body wall more or less segmentally arranged. It consists of a network of lobes with open spaces in which single cells or groups of cells are disposed (Fig. 1B). The inner or lateral fat body of pale white colour surrounds the gut and shows no segmental divisions, it extends through the whole abdomen.

The oenocytes occur only in the abdominal segments, situated between the cuticle and the transverse muscles, surrounded by fat body (Fig. 1B). The oenocytes form paired and segmentally arranged groups of four large cells, which are often, but not uniformly, arranged in a lozenge close together. These yellowish cells, in total 60 cells, are oval with a diameter of up to 0,1mm in the late fourth instar. A dense cytoplasm surrounds the nucleus which includes chromosomes with a low degree of polyteny. In front of the four cells, there is also a fifth cell of spherical shape with two nuclei and a granular cytoplasm (Fig. 1B/C). Even this cell is in direct contact to the oenocytes with the dense cytoplasm by thin plasma-connections, for all the following calculations only the four dense oenocytes have been used.

HAEMOGLOBIN SYNTHESIS AND TURNOVER

The haemoglobin of Chironomus is the major protein constituent of the haemolymph, comprising as much as 75 - 80% of the total blood protein (Manwell, 1966; Wülker, Maier, Bertau, 1969; Firling, 1977). The concentration of the haemoglobin increases during the most interesting fourth instar, excluding the appending prepupal stage, from approximately 2% to an average of 3,7% at the late fourth instar larvae. The maximum increase in some cases to 4,7% (Firling, 1976) and even to 5,6% in the larvae of Chironomus tentans (Tichy, 1970). The fourth instar of this species starts at a larval length of 11 - 12mm and grows up to a maximum length of 23 - 24mm during 30 - 50 days. The increase in haemolymph volume is from 1 µl to 11 - 12 µl/larvae (Fig. 2). The dry weight of haemoglobin rises up under the conditions mentioned from 2 µg/larvae to up to 400 µg/larvae. This drastic magnification in haemoglobin weight provokes the question, whether a turnover of haemoglobin exists.

The investigation of the haemoglobinpolymorphism in a variety of Chironomus species has always shown that the number of haemoglobin bands increases during the fourth larval instar (Thompson, English, 1966; Manwell, 1966; English, 1969; Shrivastava, English, 1970; Tichy, 1970; Schaller, English, 1976). This finding does not exclude that some haemoglobin bands show a decrease in concentration, especially from the middle of the fourth instar. This decrease in concentration, calculated to the dry weight of haemoglobin, shows that the total amount of the haemoglobin band stays nearly constant (Tichy, 1970). It may be argued that different haemoglobin genes become active at different stages and have an up and down of activity or that each haemoglobin has always the same, but one from another different, activity; only the inactivation takes place at different stages. But it seems very unlikely to argue that through a turnover, different for each haemoglobin, the different concentrations have arised.

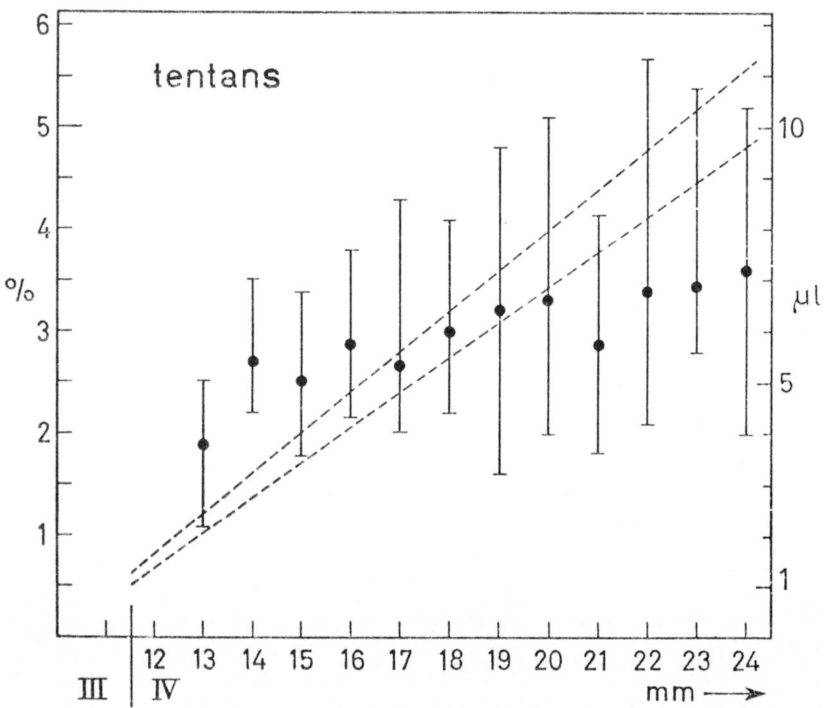

Fig. 2. Haemoglobin concentration and volume increase during the fourth instar of Chironomus tentans larvae. Abscissa: length of the larva in mm, roman numerals indicate the larval instars. Ordinate, left: haemoglobin concentration in %; ordinate, right: volume of the haemolymph in μl. The space between the dotted lines indicates the linear increase of the haemolymph volume, the vertical bars represent the range of haemoglobin concentrations. The average of at least 20 measurements is denoted by a closed circle.

To find out how much haemoglobin turnover, if any, takes place, experiments with radioactively labelled aminoacids and -amino-levulinic-acid, the precursor of the haem group, have been undertaken. The radioactiv material was injected into the larvae of Chironomus tentans, according to the method of Pelling (1964), and then the larvae were kept for 3 - 12 days under normal culture conditions. The haemolymph was investigated electrophoretically and the amount of labelled haemoglobin was measured (Tichy, 1966). The results show that up to three days after the injection, an increase of radioactive labelling in the haemoglobins could be observed, but after that time the radioactivity stays constant for at least nine days. In another experiment, the haemolymph of a larva, prepared as mentioned above, was used for electrophoresis after six days, and also 1 ul of the labelled haemolymph was injected into another larva. This larva was sacrificed after six days, and the haemolymph was electrophorised. The comparison of the radioactive labelling of the haemoglobin before and after the transfusion showed the same amount of labelled haemoglobin in both larvae, when one compensates the dilution of labelled haemoglobin on transfusion. From these findings the conclusion can be drawn that, if any turnover of the haemoglobin exists, it can be only on a very low level.

When one takes this negligible turnover into consideration, the synthetic rate of haemoglobin can be calculated. If an average of 400 µg are synthesised within 40 days, 10 µg haemoglobin will be synthesised per day from one larva and subsequently secreted into the haemolymph. This represents a high synthesis rate even in the absence of a turnover rate.

The lateral fat body, which has been identified as a haemoglobin producing tissue by Laufer and coworkers (1976, 1977), would certainly be capable of achieving this synthetic rate. At first sight, it is a lot to ask that 60 oenocytes should be able to produce 10 µg protein for secretion per day. However, one can calculate that, if haemoglobin synthesis takes place exclusively in the oenocytes, each cell must synthesise 0,15 - 0,2 µg per day. By comparison the rate of salivary secretion has been published with 0,2 - 0,3 µg/cell and day (Grossbach, 1977).

Calculating the volume of an oenocyte from a diameter of 0,1 mm, the volume is approximately 0,0005 mm^3 and the weight of an oenocyte is then 0,5 µg. Under the assumption that an oenocyte synthesise haemoglobin, the calculated rate requires that a cell synthesises half its own weight of haemoglobin/day. If secretion takes place continuously, a steady state concentration of haemoglobin in an oenocyte should be in the region of 1 - 2%. This concentration would be high enough to account for the yellow colour of the cells, as observed at first by Wielowiejski in 1886. Only more concentrated haemoglobin solutions and thick layers show the typical red haemoglobin colour. The fat body, if it is a site of haemoglobin synthesis, would naturally only show a white colour, because the haemoglobin concentration per cell would be much less than 0,1%.

CYTOPHOTOMETRICAL INVESTIGATIONS

The different colours and the expected different amounts of haemoglobin in oenocytes and fat body provide the opportunity to test with spectrophotometric methods whether the absorption of the oenocytes shows similarities with the haemoglobin spectrum. Outer and lateral fat body and single oenocytes were prepared in an insect Ringer solution and were examined with a Zeiss-Ultramicrospectrophotometer (Zeiss UMSP II). For comparison a single human erythrocyte was also investigated. The results are shown in Fig. 3.

It is evident that the oenocyte is the only Chironomus cell type investigated, which shows the prominent haemoglobin peak at 410 - 420 nm. Due to the at least ten times greater thickness of the investigated oenocyte to the erythrocyte, the absorption peak has essentially the same intensity as that of the erythrocyte, which has a haemoglobin concentration of 13%. Hence the concentration of haemoglobin in the oenocytes can be calculated as at least 1%, an amount which is in good agreement with the calculations in the previous section.

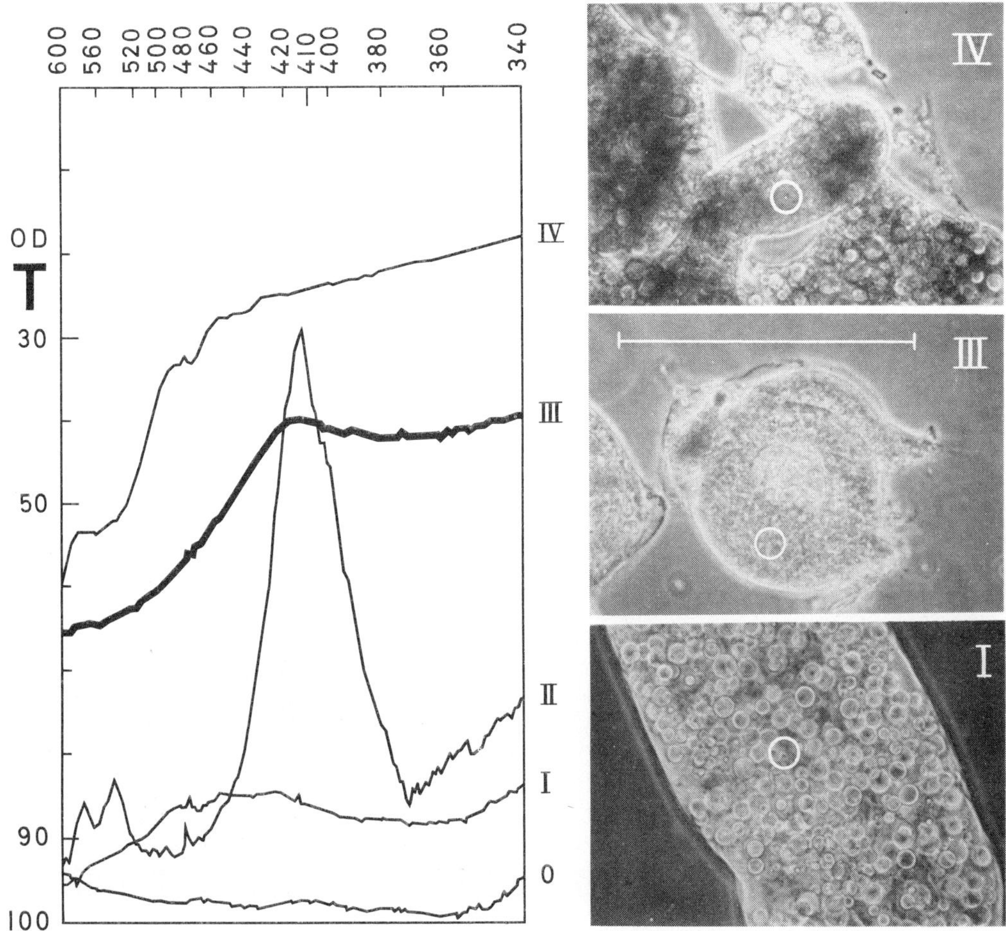

Fig. 3. The absorption spectra and the morphology of the tissues investigated spectrophotometrically.

Left) The absorption spectra of 0 = background, I = lateral fat body, II = human erythrocyte, III = oenocyte, IV = outer green fat body. Abscissa at the top indicates the wave length in nm. Ordinate, Transmission units.

Right) The morphology of the tissues and cells used for spectrophotometry. I = lateral fat body, III = oenocytes, IV = outer green fat body. The circle indicates the measured area, which corresponds to the diameter of an erythrocyte. The bar represents 0,1 mm.

CYTOCHEMICAL AND IMMUNOLOGICAL INVESTIGATIONS

The identification of haemoglobin in single cells, using spectrophotometric methods as described above, should also be possible by the application of cytochemical procedures. Most of the methods available, based on the reagens benzidine or one of its derivatives, are relatively unspecific. Results with reactions based on the use of benzidine are not very reproducible, and several cell types and organelles react positively, including nuclei of Malpighian tubules. The best results were obtained using the method of Owen, Silberman and Grot (1958) which gave a strongly positive reaction with oenocytes only.

In contrast to such nonspecific reactions, the immunological reaction of antibody and antigene is very highly specific. Histological preparations of the oenocytes and of the fat body showed that the fixation, necessary for the antibody incubation was not sufficient to immobilize the small haemoglobin molecule. It was not fixed in 50% acetic acid necessary for a rapid preparation of washed tissue. Fixations with alcohol gave better results, but the structure of the cells and tissues was drastically altered. Nevertheless, the preparations, fixed with alcohol, incubated with rabbit anti-haemoglobin-IgG, washed with PBS-buffer to remove excess of anti-haemoglobin-IgG and incubated with fluorescent goat anti-rabbit-IgG (Miles Laboratories, Frankfurt), showed a bright greenish fluorescence over the oenocytes, excluding the one proximal spherical cell. Only a very pale fluorescence over the fat body was visible. With the aid of optical filter kits, it was possible to remove from the oenocytes their yellowish to orange self-fluorescence. The oenocytes are thus the only cells which react with the anti-haemoglobin-IgG.

CONCLUSION

The data, which have been published up to now regarding the location of the haemoglobin synthesising tissue in Chironomus, indicate that haemoglobin is produced in the abdomen of the larva (Bergström, Laufer, Rogers, 1976), probably in the lateral fat body (Schin, Laufer, Carr, 1977). The results of the investigations and analyses presented in this paper provide strong evidence that the oenocytes synthesise haemoglobin and may indeed be the sole site of haemoglobin production in Chironomus larvae. It must be borne in mind that this can only be proven by cell culture of separated tissues and single cells. Only this method gives the opportunity to determine where haemoglobin is in fact synthesised and also to examine the functions of different cell types during haemoglobin synthesis. It is of interest to ask, how the oenocytes possibly interact with the fat body cells and what role, if any, the spherical oenocytes play in the haemoglobin synthesis. These investigations are in progress.

ACKNOWLEDGEMENTS

The author would like to express his gratitude to Professor Dr.W. Beermann for his interest and kind support. Thanks are due to Dr. H. Zacharias for his help and introduction into the use of the Zeiss-UMSP. The author also expresses his thanks to Mrs. K. Schenk for valuable, untiring technical assistance, to Mr. P. Hardy for linguistic aid, to Mr. K. Lamberty for the drawings and to Mrs. I. Darenberg for painstaking typing of this manuscript.

REFERENCES

Bergström, G., H. Laufer, and R. Rogers (1976). J.Cell Biol., 69, 264-274.

Braunitzer, G., G. Buse, and K. Gersonde (1974). In O. Hayaishi (Ed.) Molecular Oxygene in Biology, North Holland Publishing Comp.

English, D. S. (1969). J.Embryol.exp.Morph.,22, 465-476.

Firling, C. (1977). J.Insect Physiol., 23, 17-22.

Grossbach, U. (1977). In W. Beermann (Ed.) Biochemical Differentiation in Insect Glands, Vol. 8, Springer-Verlag Berlin, Heidelberg, New York.

Huber, R., O. Epp, and H. Formanek (1970). J.Mol.Biol., 52, 249-354.

Kleinschmidt, T., and G. Braunitzer (1978). Annalen d. Chem., 1060-1075.

Manwell, C. (1966). J.Embryol.exp.Morph., 16, 259-270.

Miall, L.C. and A.R. Hammond (1900). The Structure and Life-history of the Harlequin Fly Chironomus, Clarendon Press, Oxford.

Neumann, D. (1961). Zeitschr.f.Naturforsch., 16b, 820-824.

Owen, J. A., H.J. Silberman, and C. Grot (1958). Nature, London, 182, 1373.

Pelling, C. (1964). Chromosoma (Berl.), 15, 71-122.

Schaller, L. and D. S. English (1976). J.Heredity, 67, 300-302.

Schin, K., H. Laufer, and E. Carr (1977). J.Insect Physiol., 23, 1233-1242.

Shrivastava, H. N. and B. G. Loughton (1970). Can.J.Zool., 48, 563-568.

Thompson, P. E. and D. S. English (1966). Science, 152, 75-76.

Tichy, H. (1966). Anal.Biochem., 17, 320-326.

Tichy, H. (1970). Chromosoma (Berl.), 29, 131-188.

Tichy, H. (1975). J.Mol.Evol., 6, 39-50.

Tichy, H. (1976). Proc.of VI. Symposion on Chironomidae, Prag, in Press.

Weber, R. (1963). Koninkl.Nederl.Akademie v.Wetenschap. Proc.Ser.C/3.

Wielowiejski, H. v. (1886). Zeitschr.f.wiss.Zoologie, 43, 512-536.

Wülker, W., W. Maier, and P. Bertau (1969). Zeitschr.f.Naturforsch., 24b, 110-116.

Basic Patterns in Chromosome Evolution of the Genus Chironomus (Diptera)*

W. F. Wuelker

Biologisches Institut I (Zoologie) der Universität, Albertstr. 21a, D-7800 Freiburg, Federal Republic of Germany

ABSTRACT

Five of the six banding patterns, postulated by Keyl (1962) for chromosome arms A,E and F of the hypothetical Chironomus species, "which crossed the border between the thummi- and pseudothummi-complexes", could be found in several living species of both complexes. Moreover, three Chironomus species, collected in widely separated places, show the complete banding patterns of the hypothetical ancestral species in arms A,E and F. In contrast, chromosome arms B,C,D and G and other characters of the karyotypes differ clearly among these three species. Apparently, the evolution of these arms was less conservative than the evolution of arms A,E and F. Corresponding to the faunistic connections in the holarctic region, the Swedish Chironomus cfr.tenuistylus Brundin and the Californian Ch.spec.Apple Valley have remarkable similarities, whereas the African Ch.alluaudi Kieffer is more different. The phylogenetic consequences of these results are discussed.

KEYWORDS

Genus Chironomus - karyotypes - thummi- and pseudothummi-complexes-retained basic patterns - distribution.

* A detailed account of these results will be published in "Zeitschrift für zoologische Systematik und Evolutionsforschung", Verlag Paul Parey, Hamburg und Berlin.

Zur Atmungsintensitaet, Bewegungsaktivitaet und Herztaetigkeit nicht Dormanter und Dormanter Larven von Chironomus Plumosus

G. Adamek und J. Fischer

Zoologisches Institut der Universität Bern, Sahlistrasse 8, CH-3012 Bern, Switzerland

ABSTRACT

The oxygen consumption, movement activity and heart activity of non dormant and dormant larvae of Chironomus plumosus were investigated by means of a continuous flow polarographic respirometer. The oxygen consumption was correlated with the movement activity. On the other hand, a correlation of the oxygen consumption with the heart activity was not clearly detectable. The investigated activities of the non dormant and dormant larvae did not differ fundamentally.

KEYWORDS

Chironomus, dormancy, oxygen consumption, movement activity, heart activity.

Entwicklungshemmungen, die als Anpassung der Organismen an die jahreszeitlichen Schwankungen der Umwelt zu betrachten sind (heute allgemein als Dormanz bezeichnet), gehen mit mehr oder weniger tiefgreifenden Aenderungen des Stoffwechsels und des Verhaltens einher. Entsprechende Untersuchungen wurden bereits bei vielen Insekten angestellt; auch für mitteleuropäische Chironomus-Arten liegen einige Angaben vor. Bei der Dormanz dieser Arten handelt es sich um eine nicht obligatorische Entwicklungsruhe, die im vierten Larvenstadium durch Kurztag induziert und durch Langtag wieder aufgehoben werden kann (Fischer, 1974; Ineichen et al., 1979). Diese Form der Dormanz wird nach dem Müller'schen System als Oligopause bezeichnet (Müller, 1970).

In der folgenden Mitteilung werden bei nicht dormanten und dormanten Larven von Chironomus plumosus die Beziehungen zwischen Sauerstoffverbrauch, Bewegungsaktivität und Herztätigkeit untersucht. Die Daten wurden mit Hilfe eines polarographischen Durchfluss-Respirometers gewonnen, in welchem die Larven während der Messung durch ein Stereo-Mikroskop beobachtet werden können. Eine Beschreibung dieser Apparatur wird an anderer Stelle erfolgen (Adamek und Fischer, in Vorb.). Die Larven befanden sich bei der Untersuchung in einem Glasröhrchen, durch welches sauerstoffgesättigtes Wasser von 15°C strömte. In Ruhelage waren die Tiere meist ausgestreckt; hie und da blieben sie für kürzere Zeit in geknickter Position (Kopf und Abdomen gleich ausgerichtet) ruhig liegen. In Phasen des dorso-ventralen Schlängelns konnten Schlängelperioden von $\frac{1}{2}$ Sekunde (= 1 Schlängelbewegung) bis 10 Minuten beobachtet werden. Die Schlängelfrequenz ist nach Koidsumi (1931) temperaturabhängig; sie wies in unserem Falle im Verlaufe einer (5stündigen) Messung eine leicht abnehmende Tendenz auf. Mit unterschiedlicher Häufigkeit trat das von Lenz (1954) beschriebene "Abweiden" des Körpers auf, welches er als Folge einer Verknappung der Nahrung deutete. Bei genügend Spielraum bewegten sich die Larven - vor allem bei Versuchsbeginn sowie bei Störung durch starkes Licht oder durch plötzliche Aenderung der Durchflussgeschwindigkeit - spannerartig vorwärts, selten rückwärts. Den Larven wurde in dem Röhrchen so viel Spielraum gewährt, dass sie sich sowohl in Richtung Zufluss als auch in Richtung Abfluss wenden konnten. Zuweilen bauten sie mittels Speichelsekret röhrenartige Netze. Kotabgaben waren oft mit einem kurzen lebhaften Schlängeln verbunden. - Im folgenden werden die durch markante Bewegungen des Körpers charakterisierten Verhaltensweisen unter dem Begriff "Bewegungsaktivität" zusammengefasst, wobei das Abweiden des Körpers sowie das Schlängeln den weitaus grössten Teil dieser Aktivität ausmachte.

Die Herztätigkeit kann beobachtet werden, falls das 8. Abdominalsegment von oben oder von der Seite her sichtbar ist, und falls die Larven einigermassen ruhig sind. Bei sich stark bewegenden Larven konnte die Herztätigkeit nur selten registriert werden.

Es werden nun zwei Beispiele aufgeführt, bei denen gleichzeitig der Sauerstoffverbrauch, die Bewegungsaktivität und die Herztätigkeit registriert wurden. Die zwei Larven stammten aus dem gleichen Gelege, waren beide weiblich und wiesen praktisch den gleichen Entwicklungsstand auf (4. Stadium; Phase 5-6 bzw. 5). Die erste Larve wurde bei Langtag (18/6) gehalten; sie entwickelte sich dementsprechend subitan. Bei der zweiten Larve wurde durch Kurztag (6/18) eine Oligopause induziert; diese Larve wurde untersucht, nachdem sie 15 Tage lang in Phase 5 stehen geblieben war.

Bei den Sauerstoffverbrauchskurven (Abb. 1a und 2a) ist zunächst einmal auffällig, dass der Verbrauch bei Versuchsbeginn höher ist als gegen Versuchsende. Dieser "Overshoot" ist für alle derartigen Messungen typisch. Die Ursache für den anfänglichen Mehrverbrauch liegt wohl zum Teil darin, dass sich die Larven erst nach einiger Zeit an die neue Umgebung gewöhnt haben und deshalb besonders bewegungsaktiv sind. Es muss aber noch andere Gründe geben, denn Scharf (1972) stellte einen "Overshoot" auch bei narkotisierten Larven fest.

Der Sauerstoffverbrauch der dormanten Larve ist, gesamthaft gesehen, niedriger als jener der nicht dormanten Larve. Unter Berücksichtigung weiterer Messungen konnte ein reduzierter Sauerstoffverbrauch dormanter Larven statistisch gesichert werden (Adamek und Fischer, in Vorb.).

Vergleicht man in Abb. 1 und 2 die Bewegungsaktivität (b) mit dem

Sauerstoffverbrauch (a), so fällt auf, dass auf die Bewegungsaktivitäts-Maxima mit 18-19 Minuten Verspätung Sauerstoffverbrauchs-Maxima folgen. (Dies ist insoweit zu sehen, als beide Informationen vorhanden sind; man beachte die horizontalen Balken unter den Abbildungen 1b und 2b.) Diese Verzögerung ist zum Teil technisch bedingt. So muss zum Beispiel das Wasser zuerst von der Larve zur Messelektrode fliessen, was 7-8 Minuten benötigt. Ein Teil der Verzögerung wird jedoch durch das Tier selbst bewirkt. Die Sauerstoffaufnahme der Larve wird sowohl von der Diffusionskapazität der Haut, der Sauerstoffreserve des Gewebes und des Blutes, als auch von der Durchblutung abhängen. Die Verzögerung darf aber wohl nicht der im Mittel für 8-9 Minuten ausreichenden Sauerstoffreserve des Oxihämoglobins zugeschrieben werden (Walshe, 1950; Weber, 1965); eine Desoxigenierung des Hämoglobins unter den von uns gewählten Sauerstoff-Konzentrationen (8-9 mg O_2/l nach Verbrauch durch die Larve) kann wohl ausgeschlossen werden (vgl. Konstantinov, 1971; Kashirskaya, 1972; Platzer-Schultz, 1968).

Das Herz ist nur periodenweise in Aktion (Abb. 1c und 2c). Die mittlere Periodenlänge und der Anteil der Schlagperioden (Abb. 1b und 2b) ändert sich im Verlaufe der Messung, während die Herzschlagfrequenz ziemlich konstant in einer Grössenordnung von 100 Schlägen pro Minute bleibt. Eine Korrelation der Herztätigkeit mit der Bewegungsaktivität oder dem Sauerstoffverbrauch lässt sich auf Grund der vorliegenden Daten nicht eindeutig nachweisen.

Aus den Abb. 1 und 2 geht hervor, dass sich die Aktivitäten der dormanten Larve nicht grundlegend von jenen der nicht dormanten Larve unterscheiden. Im Gegensatz zu vielen anderen Insekten ist bei Chironomus plumosus die Dormanz also ein ausgesprochen unauffälliges Phänomen.

Die Arbeit entstand mit Unterstützung des Schweizerischen Nationalfonds, Gesuch Nr. 3.027.76.

LITERATUR

Fischer, J. (1974). Oecologia, 16, 73-95.
Ineichen, H., U. Riesen and J. Fischer (1979). Oecologia, 39, 161-183.
Kashirskaya, E.V. (1972). Biol. Nauki (Moskva), 15, 7-12.
Koidsumi, K. (1931). J. Soc. trop. Agricult. (Taihoku), 3, 354-364.
Konstantinov, A.S. (1971). Limnologica, 8, 127-134.
Lenz, F. (1954). Zool. Anz., 153, 197-204.
Müller, H.J. (1970). Nova Acta Leopoldina N.F., 35, 7-27.
Platzer-Schultz, I. (1968). Z. vergl. Physiol., 58, 229-240.
Scharf, B.W. (1972). Diss. math.-nat. Fak. Christian-Albrechts-Univ. Kiel.
Walshe, B.M. (1950). J.exp. Biol., 27, 73-95.
Weber, R.E. (1965). Diss. nat. Fak. Univ. Leiden.

ZU DEN ABBILDUNGEN

Abb. 1. Sauerstoffverbrauch, Aktivität und Herztätigkeit einer nicht dormanten ♀ Larve während einer fünfstündigen Messung (Abszisse: Messdauer in Stunden).

a) Sauerstoffverbrauch (mg O_2/g Trockengewicht/h).
V = Verzögerung der Sauerstoffverbrauchs-Registrierung. 1-10: Sauerstoffverbrauchs-Maxima. Gestrichelte Linien: Uebergangsphasen beim Umschalten vom "Kontrollweg" auf den "Versuchsweg" und umgekehrt.

b) Aktivitätsanteil (Säulen) und Anteil der Herztätigkeit (Kreise) in % innerhalb von 4-Minuten-Intervallen.
1-10: Aktivitäts-Maxima. Dicke horizontale Balken: Beobachtungsphasen.

c) Schlag- und Ruheperioden des Herzens in 4-Minuten-Intervallen.
Dicke Balken: Schlagperioden; dünne Linien: Ruheperioden. Balken + Linien: Zeit, während der die Herztätigkeit erfasst werden konnte.

Abb. 2. Sauerstoffverbrauch, Aktivität und Herztätigkeit einer dormanten ♀ Larve. Gleiche Darstellungsart wie Abb. 1.

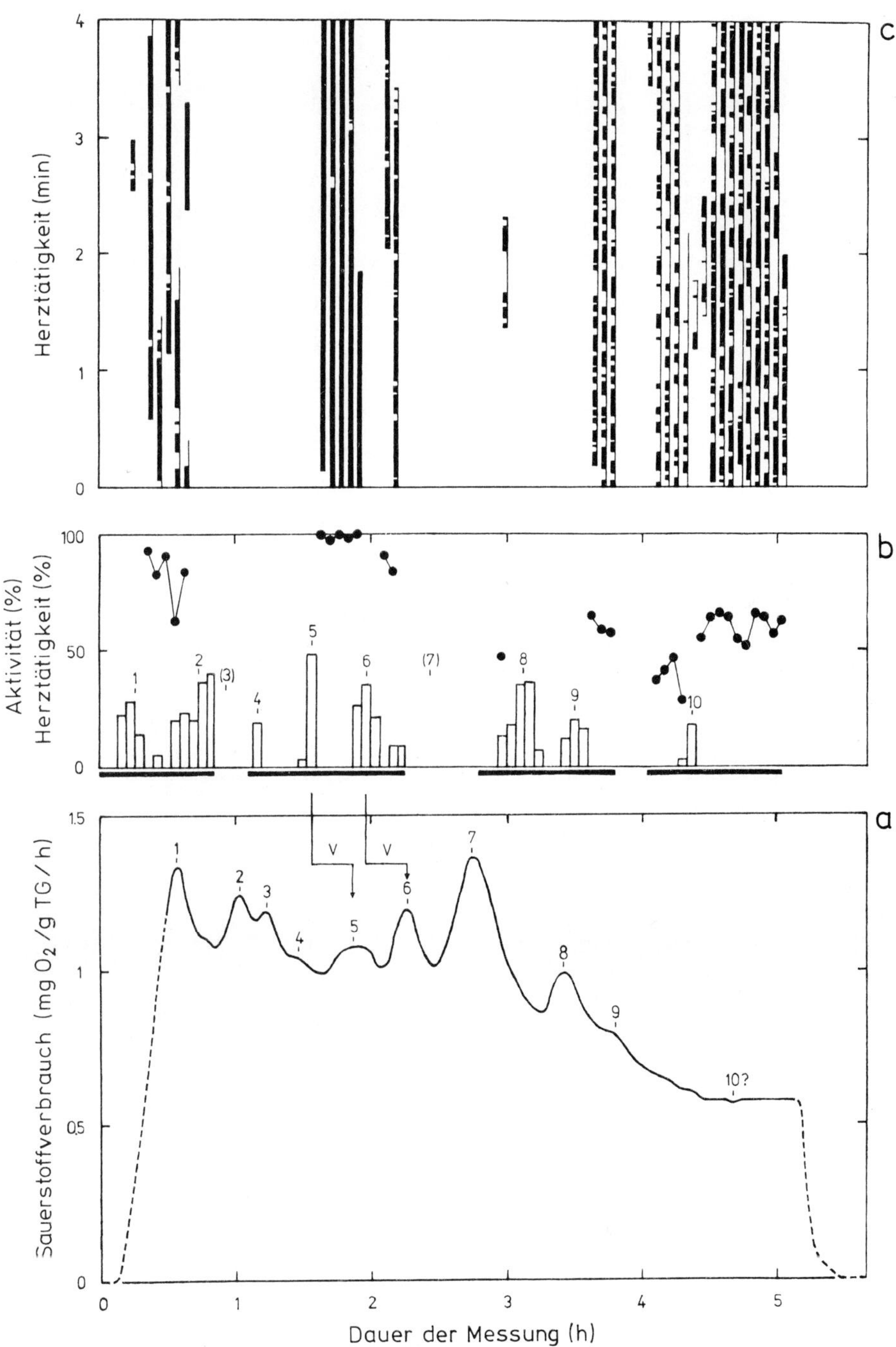

c
Herztätigkeit (min)
b
Aktivität (%)
Herztätigkeit (%)
a
Sauerstoffverbrauch (mg O_2/g TG/h)
V
V
10?
Dauer der Messung (h)

Abb. 1

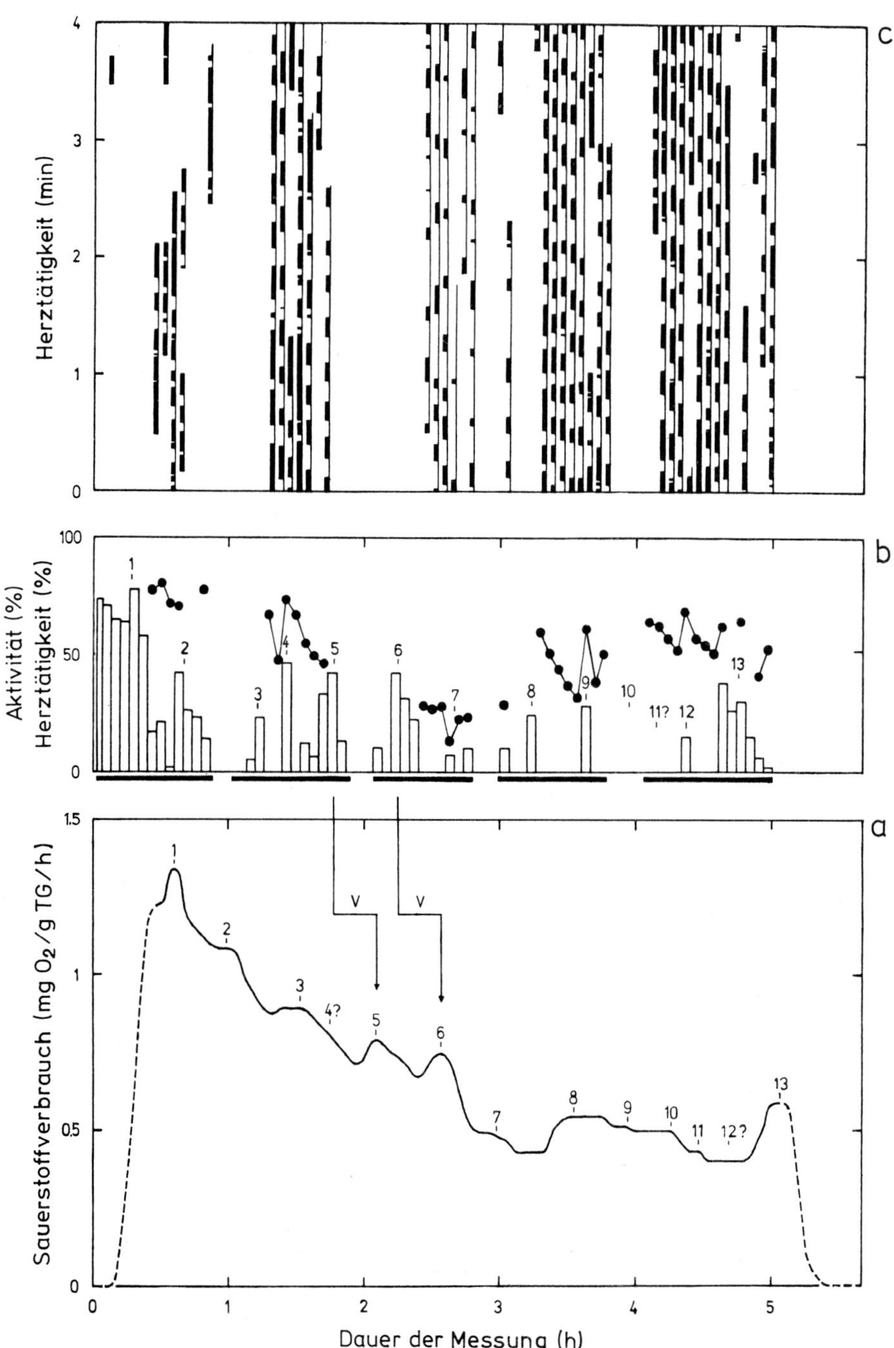
c
Herztätigkeit (min)
b
Aktivität (%)
Herztätigkeit (%)
a
Sauerstoffverbrauch (mg O_2/g TG/h)
V
V
Dauer der Messung (h)

Abb. 2

Do the Malpighian Tubules Persist Unchanged Throughout the Metamorphosis?

P. F. Credland

Department of Zoology, Bedford College, University of London, Regent's Park, London NW1 4NS, England

ABSTRACT

Present knowledge of the family Chironomidae is most unevenly distributed through the various branches of its biology. Many internal structures have not been studied for nearly 80 years and the ultrastructural techniques now available have been applied to very few organs and tissues in only one or two species. A new account of the Malpighian tubules in both larval and adult *Chironomus riparius* Mg. is presented and used to show why dependence on historical studies or assumed similarities with homologous structures in other insects is an unsatisfactory basis for statements concerning chironomid anatomy and ultrastructure.

KEYWORDS

Malpighian tubules; *Chironomus*; ultrastructure; metamorphosis; excretion.

INTRODUCTION

International Symposia on Chironomidae can only reflect the interests in the family shown by the scientific community as a whole. Taxonomy, ecology, genetic studies using larval salivary gland chromosomes and the occurrence and properties of haemoglobins have perhaps been the aspects of the biology of chironomids which have attracted the most attention. With a few notable exceptions, anatomy, including ultrastructural studies, and physiology have received scant coverage.

The anatomy of only a small number of chironomid species has been examined beyond the level required for taxonomic studies and in these few species, studies have usually been restricted to one or two organs or tissues. It is therefore necessary to rely very largely on extrapolations from other families of insects if remarks on the anatomy of chironomids are to be made. Furthermore, some of the older accounts of chironomid anatomy, such as the comprehensive work by Miall and Hammond (1900), are based upon observations made with techniques which have now been superseded or improved. They are often therefore incomplete.

Although there are numerous descriptions of the Malpighian tubules in insects (Stobbart and Shaw, 1974), the only comments on these excretory organs in chironomids were made by Miall and Hammond (1900). They state (p.70,71,108) that in the larva "there are four long Malpighian tubules, which enter the dilated beginning of the small intestine. They are lined by an epithelium of flattish cells with large nuclei, which often project into the lumen of the tubule. The Malpighian tubules persist unchanged throughout the metamorphosis, being we may suppose, still required for the elimination of the abundant waste material formed by the destruction of various larval tissues". To illustrate how these statements can be expanded by the use of modern techniques and to point out the risks of assuming that descriptions of homologous structures in other insects are equally applicable to chironomids, the Malpighian tubules of *Chironomus riparius* Meigen are now briefly described.

MATERIALS AND METHODS

Young, final-instar larvae, recognised by their head capsule size and the absence of swelling in their thoracic imaginal discs, and adults of *C. riparius* were taken from permanent laboratory cultures (Credland, 1973). The posterior part of the midgut with the hindgut and Malpighian tubules attached, was removed from each animal and fixed for 2 hours in cold 3% glutaraldehyde in 0.1M phosphate buffer (pH 7.2). The preparations were then washed overnight in fresh buffer, postfixed in 1% osmium tetroxide in 0.1M phosphate buffer for 1 hour and then dehydrated in graded ethanols. They were rinsed in 1:2 epoxypropane, infiltrated and embedded in TAAB resin. After polymerisation, sections were cut and stained in 1% uranyl acetate in 50% ethanol and lead citrate before examination in the transmission electron microscope. Some tubules were treated with lead nitrate in the primary fixative, rinsed in buffer, immersed in ammonium sulphide (Taylor, 1971b), and then prepared for electron microscopy in the usual manner except that neither secondary fixation nor staining of the sections was undertaken. Thick resin sections and wax-embedded material prepared by routine histological procedures were used for preliminary and correlative studies.

RESULTS

Both the larvae and adults possess four Malpighian tubules which enter the gut at the pylorus, the junction of the midgut and hindgut. From the junction they run anteriorly for about a third of their length and then turn sharply posteriorly to run alongside the gut into the penultimate segment of the body where they are anchored by filaments attached to the rectum or integument. The total length of each tubule in a fourth-instar larva is about 2.5 mm and its diameter about 0.05 mm. The adult tubules are of similar length but taper from about 0.035 mm in diameter distally to about 0.05 mm near the neck region. Fresh larval tubules are virtually colourless and translucent but adult tubules are usually white distally, the intensity of the whiteness decreasing in proximal regions.

The four tubules in each specimen are very similar in their general appearance and in ultrastructural detail. There is no clear structural division of each tubule into discrete regions characterised by different cell types, although tubules of adults and larvae have complex neck regions which are excluded from the following account. There is no evidence that either muscles or tracheae are associated with the tubules of either the adults or larvae.

Larval Malpighian Tubules

Two types of cell occur throughout the larval tubules distal to the neck region. Somewhat similar cells to these two types have been designated primary (Berridge and Oschman, 1969) or type 1 (Taylor, 1971a) and stellate (Berridge and Oschman, 1969) or type 2 (Taylor, 1971a, 1971b) in the tubules of other insects. As the secondary cell type is not stellate in shape in *C. riparius*, Taylor's (1971a, 1971b) terms are used in this description although there are differences of unknown significance from the cells given the same names in his study of *Carausius morosus*.

Type 1 cells. These cells are between 9 and 17 μm in height, from their underlying basement membrane to the tips of their apical folds. Although each tubule is circular in transverse section, the apices of the cells are irregular and the tubule lumen is crudely stellate in such a section.

The basal plasma membrane of each cell is deeply and tortuously infolded so that extracellular channels ramify through the basal cytoplasm (Fig. 1). The apical membrane is much more regularly folded to produce tightly packed microvilli or leaflets. Irregularly shaped mitochondria are associated with the basal folding lying among the folds and in a layer just apical to them. A few mitochondria occur in the central zone of each cell and a narrow layer occurs at the bases of the apical microvilli although mitochondria do not extend into the microvilli themselves. Each cell contains both rough and smooth endoplasmic reticulum, the latter sometimes extending into the apical microvilli. Golgi bodies are probably present in the central zone of each cell although profiles which could be positively identified have not been seen. Nuclei of type 1 cells are found in the central regions and an increase in cell height occurs in their vicinity.

Granular inclusions, some of which are probably glycogen rosettes, are found in increasing density in cells progressively nearer the proximal end of each tubule. Some similar material is also present in the lumen of the tubule. A wide variety of other inclusions, multilamellate and multivesicular bodies, vacuoles filled with dense material and a very few crystalline structures are also found in cells nearer the proximal end.

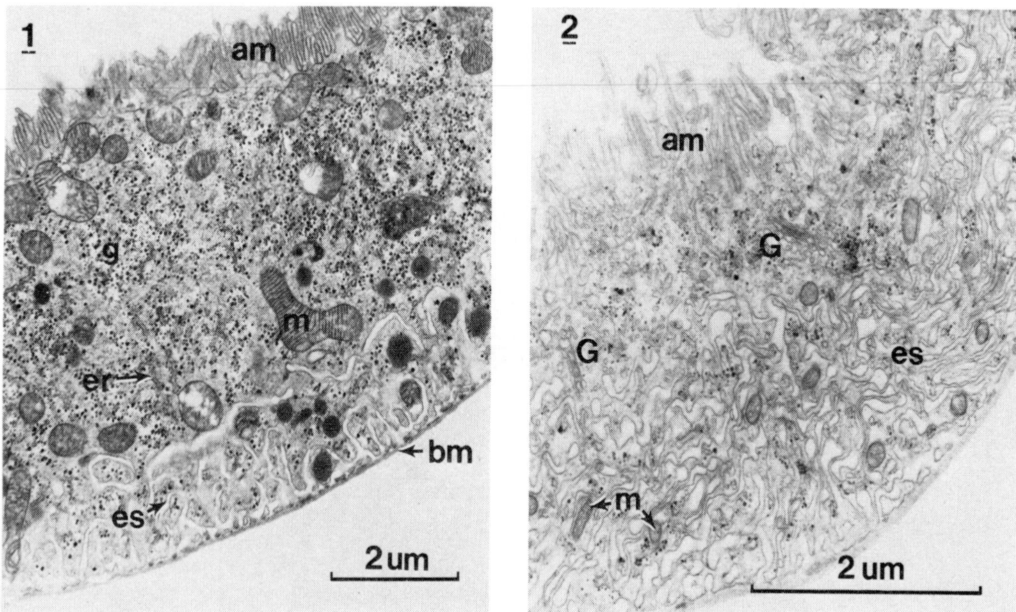

Fig. 1. Type 1 cell showing the folding of the basal plasma membrane to leave extracellular spaces (es) above the basement membrane (bm) of the tubule, the apical microvilli (am), mitochondria (m), pieces of endoplasmic reticulum (er) and abundant granular inclusions (g).

Fig. 2. Type 2 cell with few organelles but a number of Golgi bodies (G). Other labelling as in Fig. 1.

Type 2 cells. These cells occur irregularly along the tubule and although their apices reach the lumen in places, much of their cytoplasm extends in narrow strips between the basal faces of type 1 cells and the basement membrane. The maximum height of type 2 cells is only 2 to 3 μm. Few such cells seem to occur but as they do not stain with lead like the type 2A cells of the adult, an accurate estimate of their number has not been made. Because of their long processes, pieces of type 2 cells occur in most sections of larval tubules but, despite examination of more than 100 sections, nuclei have never been found in these cells.

The most characteristic features of the cells are the complexity of the basal infoldings which leave wider extracellular spaces than those in type 1 cells and extend almost to the apical membrane, the rarity of all organelles and the extreme irregularity of the apical microvilli which are also shorter than those of type 1 cells (Fig. 2). The few mitochondria which do occur are smaller and rounder than those found in type 1 cells and are irregularly distributed although more are found in association with basal foldings. The cells contain little endoplasmic reticulum and although groups of vesicles do occur below the apical microvilli, which may represent Golgi bodies, they are not as well defined as those in the type 2 cells of some other insects.

There are very few inclusions in the cells and those present are all finely granular.

Adult Malpighian Tubules

There are two cell types in each adult tubule distal to the neck region, which broadly resemble those in the larva. They are designated types 1A and 2A to distinguish them from the larval cells to which they most closely approximate in appearance. Variants of cell type 1A are found halfway along each tubule among the more common 1A cells. There is insufficient evidence at present to designate them as a third cell type.

Type 1A cells. These are the most common cells in the adult tubules. They are up to 20 μm in height and as the overall diameter of adult tubules is the same proximally or smaller distally than that of larval tubules, the lumen of adult tubules is smaller than that in larvae. In general form and in the distribution and nature of their organelles, the only ultrastructural differences between type 1 and 1A cells are that some apical microvilli of 1A cells appear to have swollen tips which are pinched off into the lumen, and the mitochondria of 1A cells are smaller, denser and have less prominent cristae (Fig. 3).

The fundamental difference between type 1 and 1A cells lies in the nature of their inclusions. The most common inclusions in type 1A cells are spherical vesicles about 0.7 μm in diameter each containing an electron-dense mass. This mass is diffuse in vesicles of distal cells, concentrates and then breaks up in cells of the proximal region into a mass of small granules which are apparently liberated into the lumen of the tubule. Other inclusions of the same general types as those found in type 1 cells occur in small numbers particularly in the proximal part of each tubule. A detailed account of the progressive changes in cell contents which occur down each adult tubule will be given elsewhere.

The variant on normal type 1A cells is similar in most respects but lacks the characteristic vesicles. Instead they contain a few dense bodies and large vesicles approximately twice the diameter (1.2 μm) of those in the normal cells. They also have fewer mitochondria, especially in central parts of the cell, and more irregular apical microvilli.

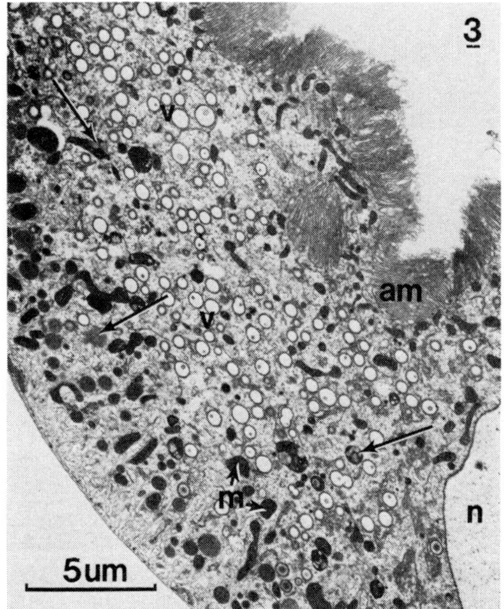

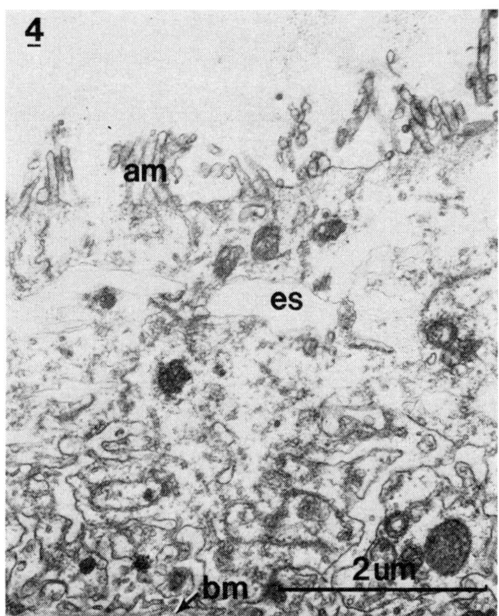

Fig. 3. Type 1A cell from about halfway along a tubule, with its characteristic vesicles (v), other inclusions (unlabelled arrows) and part of its nucleus (n). Other labelling as in Fig. 1.

Fig. 4. Type 2A cell. Labelling as in Fig. 1.

Type 2A cells. These are very similar to the larval type 2 cells but are somewhat taller, about 4 μm, where they extend from the lumen to the periphery of the tubule. They have extensive processes which run basal to parts of the type 1A cells. Ultrastructurally (Fig. 4), they are almost identical to type 2 cells and like them have wider extracellular channels than the type 1 or 1A cells. However, type 2A cells show an affinity for lead which is unique among the cells of the Malpighian tubules of *C. riparius*. Not only are the cells readily distinguished in whole mounts but also in the electron microscope the cells appear packed with lead although its precise distribution does vary among the type 2A cells examined. As the lead clearly penetrates the basement membrane to fill the extracellular channels in both larvae and adults (Figs. 5 and 6), lead uptake by type 2A cells must be a property of the cells themselves. This phenomenon would therefore indicate that they are physiologically distinct from the type 2 cells although they share so many ultrastructural characteristics.

DISCUSSION

The brief account of the structure of the cells in the Malpighian tubules of *Chironomus riparius* which has been given, is sufficient to allow a preliminary assessment to be made of their similarity to those in other insects and to expand considerably upon Miall and Hammond's (1900) original description. Any comparison must, however, be made in the realisation that the tubules of some insects such as *Rhodnius prolixus* are divided into discrete regions occupied by different cell types (Wigglesworth and Salpeter, 1962) whilst other are like *C. riparius* in not showing any regional specialisation.

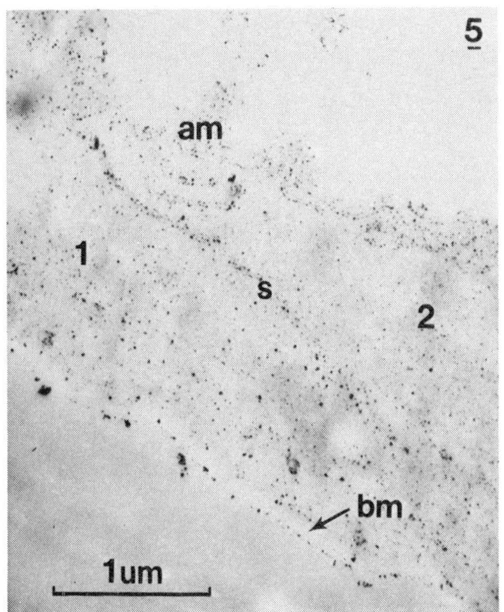

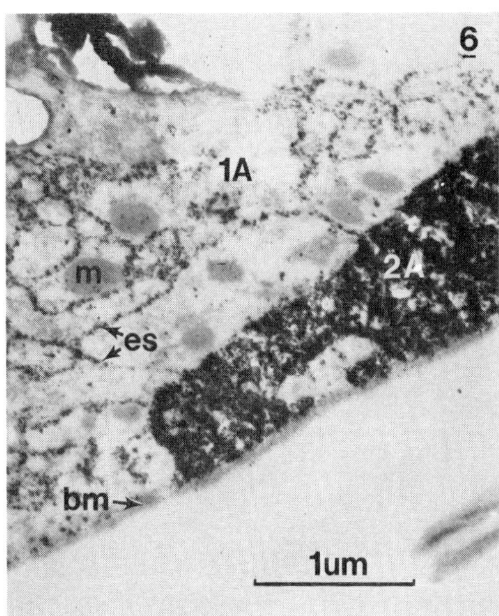

Fig. 5. Junction of a type 1 and a type 2 cell showing the intercellular space (s) lined with lead after fixation of the material in solution containing lead nitrate and precipitation of the lead with ammonium sulphide. Other labelling as in Fig. 1.

Fig. 6. A section prepared in the same way as Fig. 5 but showing parts of type 1A and 2A cells. The latter is packed with lead but elsewhere the lead is restricted to extracellular spaces. Labelling as in Fig. 1.

For the purposes of comparison it is convenient to consider each cell type in terms of its general form and proportions, its organelles and its inclusions.

The type 1 and 1A cells of *C. riparius* are very similar in general form to those of many other insects. For example, they all show basal infoldings and possess apical microvilli. The cells of *Periplaneta americana* (Wall, Oschman and Schmidt, 1975) and *Rhodnius* (Wigglesworth and Salpeter, 1962) are of similar size to those in *Chironomus*, but those in *Carausius morosus* (Taylor, 1971a), *Dissosteira carolina* (Tsubo and Brandt, 1962) and *Calliphora erythrocephala* (Berridge and Oschman, 1969) are sometimes nearly twice as tall.

The structure and distribution of the mitochondria is common to all the primary or type 1 cells previously examined in other insects which include not only those mentioned above but also the dipterans *Aedes aegypti*(Mathew and Rai, 1976; Cocke and others, 1979) and *Culex pipiens* (Suguri and others, 1969). The type 1 and 1A cells of *Chironomus* do not conform to this pattern as mitochondria do not appear in the apical microvilli of these insects. In other respects the organelles of type 1 and 1A cells of *C. riparius* are typical.

It is in their cellular inclusions that the type 1 cells of different insects show their greatest differences. It will be noted that the type 1 and 1A cells of *Chironomus* differ most in this way. The ultrastructure of the Malpighian tubules in the larvae of only two species of insect, *Aedes aegypti* (Cocke and others, 1979) and *Triatoma infestans* (Mello and Dolder, 1977) appear to have been looked at previously. All the remaining studies have been made on adults. There are no comparative studies of two stages in the life cycle of a single species except for *Triatoma* where no differences were noticed (Mello and Dolder, 1977). Only the type 1 cells of *Triatoma* contain the large numbers of small granules found in the larvae of *C. riparius*. In both cases there is evidence that glycogen comprises some or all of this material (Mello and Dolder, 1977; Credland, unpublished). Although numerous different inclusions occur in most insects studied, vesicles similar to those which make up most of the inclusions of type 1A cells in *Chironomus* are only found in large numbers in *Rhodnius* (Wigglesworth and Salpeter, 1962), *Triatoma* (Mello and Dolder, 1977), *Aedes aegypti* adults (Mathew and Rai, 1976) and the middle region of the tubules in *Periplaneta* (Wall, Oschman and Schmidt, 1975). It is notable that three of these four insects and *C. riparius* all contain either intrinsic or ingested haemoglobin and that Mathew and Rai (1976) noted the accumulation of inclusions after a blood meal. Whilst it is tempting to speculate that these vesicular inclusions are associated with haemoglobin metabolism it should be noted that apparently similar inclusions are found in *Periplaneta* and that Schin and others (1974) have reported haemoglobin degradation in the midgut of fourth-instar larvae and pharate adults of *Chironomus pallidivitatus*.

Type 2 or stellate cells have been identified in *Carausius* (Taylor, 1971b), *Calliphora* (Berridge and Oschman, 1969), *Aedes aegypti* (Mathew and Rai, 1976) and *Periplaneta* (Wall, Oschman and Schmidt, 1975) and similar cells may occur in other insects such as *Locusta migratoria* where they have been called mucocytes (Martoja, 1956). All these cells are similar in ultrastructure and are comparable with the type 2 and 2A cells of *Chironomus*. However, they are generally somewhat taller and contain more organelles and inclusions. Golgi bodies are usually numerous and prominent and nuclei have invariably been reported. Although nuclei have not been observed in either type 2 or 2A cells in *Chironomus*, this is more likely to be due to chance or their small size than their absence. The affinity of type 2 cells for lead is known (Berridge and Oschman, 1969; Taylor, 1971b) but the problem of the larval type 2 cells of *Chironomus* not staining whilst the adult 2A cells do so, still requires an explanation. The most reasonable hypothesis is that the basal plasma membrane undergoes an increase in its permeability during metamorphosis. This could be positively adaptive or a function of early cell degradation. As lead uptake varies among 2A cells in the same tubule when seen in thin sections, the latter idea is presently favoured. Whatever the explanation, there remains this clear distinction between the type 2 and 2A cells of *C. riparius* Malpighian tubules.

Thus, considering only their most fundamental features, it would appear that the type 1 and 1A cells of *Chironomus riparius* are similar to those of some other insects but differ markedly from others in the nature of their inclusions. The type 2 and 2A cells have conspicuously fewer organelles than their apparent homologues in other insects although they are similar in general form and the paucity of inclusions. With reference to Miall and Hammond's (1900) original description of the Malpighian tubules of *Chironomus*, it can be seen that they were essentially correct in their statements regarding larval tubules although apparently unaware of the two cell types that are present. However their assertion that the tubules "persist unchanged throughout the metamorphosis" is more questionable and certainly untrue if cellular inclusions are considered. It is, of course, likely that the change in inclusions is due to the "elimination of the abundant waste material formed by the destruction of various larval tissues". The change in lead uptake ability from type 2 to 2A cells does suggest that other changes do take place. One must therefore conclude that the tubules do not persist unchanged throughout the metamorphosis although the significance of the changes remains to be elucidated. Furthermore, the possibility of physiological discontinuity within or between the tubules of the larval and adult midges cannot be overlooked (Maddrell, 1978). Although Miall and Hammond (1900) may have been partially wrong, the challenge that they threw down in writing a single volume covering the complete anatomy of *Chironomus* using the best techniques available at the time remains to be taken up today.

REFERENCES

Berridge, M.J., and J.L. Oschman (1969). *Tissue & Cell*, 1, 247-272.
Berridge, M.J., and J.L. Oschman (1972). *Transporting Epithelia*. Academic Press, New York.
Cocke, J., A.C. Bridges, R.T. Mayer and, J.K. Olsen (1979). *Life Sci.*, 24, 817-832.
Credland, P.F. (1973). *Freshwater Biol.*, 3, 45-51.
Maddrell, S.H.P. (1978). *J. exp. Biol.*, 75, 133-145.
Martoja, R. (1956). *Bull. Soc. zool. Fr.*, 81, 172-173.
Mathew, G., and K.S. Rai (1976). *Ann. ent. Soc. Am.*, 69, 659-661.
Mello, M.L.S., and H. Dolder (1977). *Protoplasma*, 93, 275-288.
Miall, L.C., and A.R. Hammond (1900). *The Structure and Life History of the Harlequin Fly (Chironomus)*. Clarendon Press, Oxford.
Schin, K., J.J. Poluhowich, T. Gamo, and H. Laufer (1974). *J. Insect Physiol.*, 20, 561-571.
Stobbart, R.H., and J. Shaw (1974). In M. Rockstein (Ed.), *The Physiology of Insecta*, Vol. 5, 2nd ed. Academic Press, New York. pp. 361-446.
Suguri, S., Y. Tongu, K. Itano, D. Sakumoto, and S, Inatomi (1969). *Jap. J. sanit. Zool.*, 20, 1-6.
Taylor, H.H. (1971a). *Z. Zellforsch. mikrosk. Anat.*, 118, 333-368.
Taylor, H.H. (1971b). *Z. Zellforsch. mikrosk. Anat.*, 122, 411-424.
Tsubo, I., and P.W. Brandt (1962). *J. Ultrastruct. Res.*, 6, 28-35.
Wall, B.J., J.L. Oschman, and B.J. Schmidt (1975). *J. Morph.*, 146, 265-306.
Wigglesworth, V.B., and M.M. Salpeter (1962). *J. Insect Physiol.*, 8, 299-307.

The Activities of Glycerinaldehyde 3 Phosphate Dehydrogenase, Lactate Dehydrogenase and Phosphoenol Pyruvate-Carboxykinase in Chironomid Larvae and Chaoborus Cristallinus Larvae

C. Frank

Institut für Tierphysiologie und Angewandte Zoologie der Freien Universität Berlin, Haderslebener Straße 9, D 1000 Berlin 41, Federal Republic of Germany

ABSTRACT

The activities of glycerine aldehyde phosphate dehydrogenase measured in the extracts of Chironomus plumosus, Microtendipes spec., Endochironomus spec., Polypedilum nubeculosum, Glyptotendipes paripes and Chaoborus cristallinus larvae indicate a low rate of glycolysis, only Prodiamesa olivacea larvae show a range like Molluscs or Tubificids. In C. plumosus a seasonal effect on the activities of GAPDH was assumed. Lactate dehydrogenase activities in % of GAPDH varies from 1.2 - 88.9 % in C. plumosus larvae. In Chaoborus cristallinus, an average of 21 % of GAPDH activity during different seasons is shown. PEPCK activities are very low and it may be reasonable to assume that there is no succinate or propionate production ability in the larvae tested in this study.

KEYWORDS

Glycolysis; anaerobic energy production, seasonal effect.

INTRODUCTION

Recent studies were conducted in the physiology of the anaerobic metabolism of nonparasitic invertebrates. These studies attempted to describe the eco-physiological adaptation mechanism of facultative anoxia. Alternatives to lactate formation have been described first in different parasites (Zoeten et al., 1969), later in Molluscs (Hochachka and Mustafa, 1972; de Zwaan and Wijsman, 1976). Polychaetes (Zebe, 1975), Oligochaetes (Schöttler and Schroff, 1976) and in Chironomids (Wilps and Zebe, 1976; Frank, 1977). Chironomid larvae have a different distribution depending on O_2-saturation of the water, so it was the aim of this study to find some links in the method of energy production during anoxia in different Chironomid species. The estimation of activity of key enzymes should account for the potential of anaerobic energy production and the relative activities of related enzymes may indicate the production of other endproducts than lactate.

MATERIAL AND METHODS

Animals

The larvae were caught in various lakes of West Berlin with an Ekman-Birge bottom sampler and kept in Petri dishes with tap water at 4 - 8° C in darkness.

Extraction and Estimation of Enzyme Activity

The animals were cleaned with cellulose, were weighed , homogenised in 2 ml 0,9 % NaCl, 4 x 15" in an Potter Elvehjem homogenisator, 30' zentrifuged at 50000 xg.

1. Glycerine aldehyde 3 phosphate dehydrogenase
   E.C. 1.2.1.12.
2. Lactate dehydrogenase
   E.C. 1.1.1.27.
3. Phosphoenol pyruvate carboxykinase
   E.C. 4.1.1.32.

The enzyme assays were performed from the clear supernatant, 1 and 2 according to Bergmeyer (1974), 3 according to Mustafa and Hochachka (1973), two determinations, 2 - 26 larvae fourth stage.

RESULTS

Glycerine aldehyde 3 phosphate dehydrogenase (GAPDH) shows the lowest values in larvae of Chironomus plumosus (2574 µmoles/g.d.w./h.) and increases over Microtendipes spec., Endochironomus spec., Polypedilum spec., Glyptotendipes to 60258 µmoles/g.d.w./h. in Prodiamesa olivacea (Tab. 1).

TABLE 1 Enzyme Activities of various Chironomid Larvae and Chaoborus cristallinus Larvae in µmoles/g.d.w./h and Percent of GAPDH Activity

Enzymes	GAPDH	LDH	PEPCK	Number of Individuals
Chironomus plumosus	2576,9	2299,7 88,9 %	7,08 0,27 %	10
Microtendipes	3555,3	3396,6 95,5 %	25,37 0,71 %	8
Endochironomus	6705,1	6292,3 93,8 %	47,77 0,71 %	6
Polypedilum nubeculosum	9560,1	4441,6 46,5 %	NN	6
Glyptotendipes paripes	11035,5	1264,3 11,5 %	27,73 0,25 %	8-10
Prodiamesa olivacea	60258	2524,8 24,7 %	2,94 0,03 %	2
Chaoborus cristallinus	10222	2524,8 24,7 %	2,94 0,03 %	26

Lactate-dehydrogenase shows a different pattern in the Chironomid larvae from 1264,3 µmoles/g.d.w./h in Glyptotendipes and 6292,3 µmoles/g.d.w./h in Endochironomus. In % of GAPDH-activity the values varied between 11,5 and 95,5 %. Phosphoenole-pyruvate carboxykinase has a low activity with 2,94 to 47,77 µmoles/g.d.w./h (0,03 to 0,71 % of GAPDH-activity). Compared with the values of the Chironomid larvae the activities of Chaoborus cristallinus larvae lie between Glyptotendipes and Prodiamesa. The comparison of GAPDH values from different seasons shows an increase in the larvae of C. plumosus and a decrease in Chaoborus cristallinus (Tab. 2).

TABLE 2 Activity of Glycerinealdehyde 3 Phosphate Dehydrogenase GAPDH (µmoles/g.d.w./h) at different Sampling Dates

	27.3.79	2.5.79	11.7.79
Chironomus plumosus	1576,8	2577	13466,3
Chaoborus cristallinus	23019	10222,6	7452,3

Considering an average water temperature of 4,6 and 12° C at the sampling date, a correlation of r = 0,9862 (C. plumosus) and r = 0,8038 (Chaoborus cristallinus) was found. This may be interpreted as a developmental-physiological influence on the enzyme activities. There is no seasonal aspect of LDH activities in C. plumosus larvae, but in Chaoborus cristallinus larvae the absolute activities decrease, in % of GAPDH stay within the same range (Tab. 3).

TABLE 3 Activity of Lactate Dehydrogenase (µmoles/g.d.w./h) and in Percent of GAPDH at different Sampling Dates

Sampling Date	27.3.79	2.5.79	11.7.79	
Chironomus	1308	2299	130,3	
plumosus	82,96	88,9	1,21	% of GAPDH
Chaoborus	5120	2524	1221	
cristallinus	22,4	24,7	16,4	% of GAPDH

DISCUSSION

Pette (1965) pointed out that certain enzymes in different tissues show great absolute differences but have constant proportions. Therefore, GAPDH activities can be used to estimate the rate of capacity of the Emden-Meyerhof pathway. The activities of LDH and PEPCK show possible metabolic specification. The glycolytic capacity of the examined larvae is much lower than that of the muscles of crustaceans vertebrates und Tubifex (Gäde and Zebe, 1973; Schöttler and Schroff, 1976), an exception is Prodiamesa olivacea with 60236 µmoles/g.d.w./h.

The metabolic activity in the larvae agrees with the oxygen demand in the habitat of the larvae (Reiss, 1969; Saether, 1975). Zebe and McShan (1957) recorded that activities of LDH in the same range as in this investigation do not show sufficient lactat production during anoxia. It has been shown by Ranson and colleagues (1968) and Frank (1977) that lactate is only a product of short term anoxia. The function of LDH could be changing during the season and this may explain the variation in % of GAPDH from 1.21 % to 88,9 % of activity. The low activities of LDH in Prodiamesa olivacea and Glyptotendipes paripes could be explained by the assumption of another possibility of anoxic energy production. As these different values could be a reaction to various oxygen concentrations in the sediment water interface or more a developmental phenomenon might be proven experimentally. The activities of PEPCK are too low for a possible anoxic energy production via succinate to propionate. This pathway appears to be energetically more efficient than straightforward glycolysis (de Zwaan and Wijsman, 1976; Gnaiger, 1977). The enzyme activities of Chaoborus cristallinus which lives in the same biotop show also only a low possibility of lactate formation for energy production during anoxia. Ransom and colleagues (1968) found that Chaoborus punctipennis excrete more than 30 % of volative fatty acids during short-term anaerobiosis.For Chironomus thummi and C. plumosus, ethanol could be detected as the main end-product of long-term anaerobiosis (Wilps and Zebe, 1976; Frank, 1977). To what extend this way of energy production is realised in all Chironomid larvae which endure facultative anoxic conditions or the energetically more favourable way of production of volative fatty acids will be discussed in subsequent publications.

REFERENCES

Bergmeyer, H. U. (1974). Methoden der enzymatischen Analyse. Verlag Chemie, Weinheim/Bergstraße.

Brand, T. (1972). Parasitenphysiologie. Gustav Fischer Verlag, Stuttgart.

Frank, C. (1977). Ökologie und anaerober Stoffwechsel der Larven von Chironomus plumosus L. (Diptera, Nematocera). Dissertation Tübingen.

Gäde, G., and E. Zebe (1973). Über den Anaerobiosestoffwechsel von Molluskenmuskeln. J. comp. Physiol. 85, 291-301

Gnaiger, E. (1977).Thermodynamic consideration on invertebrate anoxibiosis. In: Application of calorimetry in life sciences (eds. L. Lamprecht, B. Schaarschmidt) pp 281-303, Berlin, Walter de Gryter.

Hochachka, P. W., and T. Mustafa (1972). Invertebrate facultative anaerobiosis. Science, 1978, 1056-1060.

Mustafa, T., and P. W. Hochachka (1973). Enzymes in facultative anaerobiosis of molluscs. II. Basic catalytic properties of phosphoenolpyruvate-carboxykinase in oyster adductor muscle. Comp. Biochem. Physiol., 45B, 639-655.

Pette, D. (1965). Plan und Muster im zellulären Stoffwechsel. Naturwissenschaften, 52, 597-616.

Ransom, J. D., F. L. Rainwater, and C. G. Beames (1968). A note on the metabolism of two Diptera larvae, Chaoborus punctipennis and Chironomus plumosus. Proc. Okla. Acad. Sci., 49, 215-217.

Reiss,F. (1968). Ökologische und systematische Untersuchungen an Chironomiden (Diptera) des Bodensees. Ein Beitrag zur lakustrischen Chironomidenfauna des nördlichen Alpenvorlandes. Arch. Hydrobiol., 64, 176-323.

Saether, O.A. (1975). Nearctic Chironomids as indicators of lake typology. Verh. int. Ver. Limnol., 19, 3127-3133.

Schöttler, V., und G. Schroff (1976). Untersuchungen zum anaeroben Glykogenabbau bei Tubifex tubifex M.. J. comp. Physiol., B, 108, 243-254.

Wilps, H.,and E. Zebe (1976). The endproducts of anaerobic carbohydrate metabolism in the larvae of Chironomus thummi thummi. J. comp. Physiol., B, 112, 263-272.

Zebe, E. (1975) In-vivo studies on glucose degradation in Arenicola marina (Annelida, Polychaeta). J. comp. Physiol. B, 101, 133-146

Zebe, E., C. McShan, and Witt (1957). Lactic and α-Glycerophosphate Dehydrogenases in Insects. J. Gen. Physiol. 40, 779-790.

Zoeten. L. W., de; D. Posthuma, and J. Tipker (1969). Intermediary metabolism of the liver fluke Faciola hepatica. Hoppe-Seylers. Z. Physiol. Chem, 350, 683-690.

Zwaan, A., de,and T.C.M. Wijyman (1976). Anaerobic metabolism in Bivalvia. Characteristics of anaerobic metabolism. Comp. Biochem. Physiol. 54 B, 313-324.

Circadian Eclosion Rhythm in *Chironomus Thummi:* Ecological Adjustment to Different Temperature Levels and the Role of Temperature Cycles

A. Kureck

Zoologisches Institut der Universität, Lehrstuhl: Physiologische Ökologie, Weyertal 119, D-5000 Köln 41, Federal Republic of Germany

ABSTRACT

The circadian eclosion rhythm of *Ch. thummi* is synchronized with the photoperiod. The pattern, however, is modified by the temperature level. The midges emerge from cold water near noon, from warmer water in the evening. Temperature cycles can synchronize eclosion in constant light. Under light-dark conditions, however, they hardly affect the pattern as long as their amplitude is below 4° C. With much higher amplitudes the phase as well as the level of the temperature cycle can modify the eclosion time, but the influence of the photoperiod is never completely overruled.

KEYWORDS

Chironomidae, circadian rhythm, pupal eclosion, photoperiod, daily temperature cycle, temperature level, ecology, Zeitgeber.

INTRODUCTION

In temperate regions most chironomids emerge after sunset (Coffman, 1974; Jónasson, 1961; Koskinen, 1968; Palmén, 1955; Remmert, 1962; Wool and Kugler, 1969), but arctic as well as spring species prefer a time nearer noon, which usually is the warmest part of the day (Kureck, 1966; Oliver, 1968; Remmert, 1965). Danks and Oliver (1972) attributed this difference to different timing mechanisms. They suggested that arctic midges respond directly to the temperature cycle, whereas in the other species endogenous rhythms, synchronized with the light-dark cycle (LD) control eclosion.

Fischer and Rosin (1968), on the other hand, observed that the eclosion of *Chironomus nuditarsis* changed with the level of constant temperatures. This phenomenon also occurs in *Ch. thummi* and was recently studied in some detail (Kureck, 1979). *Ch. thummi* emerged in the evening if the water temperature was above 16° C, but it switched to the early afternoon if the water was cooler than 14° C. At moderate temperatures of about 15° C one part of the population eclosed in the evening, the other part during the day, but no intermediate eclosion peak appeared. Thus, there were two alternative eclosion times for high and low temperatures. Both were controlled by endogenous circadian rhythms entrained by the photoperiod. A temperature cycle was not required to produce the diurnal eclosion peak under cold conditions. Synchronization with the light-dark cycle and information about the temperature level was sufficient to produce the appropriate pattern also under constant temperature conditions.

Constant temperature conditions, however, rarely occur in the natural environment. Daily cycles of temperature variation are the rule in the shallow waters preferred by Ch. thummi. Can these cycles affect the eclosion rhythm under constant light or under LD-conditions? This paper deals with this question.

METHODS

Chironomus thummi K. (sensu Strenzke)[1] was reared for many generations in the laboratory. For details of the procedure and the set-up see Kureck (1979). Generally the experimental conditions were kept constant throughout the development from the egg to the adult stage. Light intensity at the water surface was 500 to 700 lux (white fluorescent light). Darkness began and ended with 20 minutes of twilight. The daily temperature cycles in the water followed a sinusoidal function. Room temperature was always 20° C. Males and females were counted separately in all experiments. The males predominated during the first days of emergence, but there were no significant differences between males and females in the daily pattern of eclosion. Therefore the sexes are not shown separately in the following graphs.

RESULTS

The influence of temperature on the eclosion pattern was studied in three types of experiments.

1. Constant temperatures under LD 12:12 conditions,
2. Temperature cycles under constant light (LL), and
3. Temperature cycles under LD 12:12 conditions.

Figure 1 shows examples of the different eclosion times under constant temperature conditions. Midges reared at 12° C emerged during the day, those reared at 25° C preferred the night, especially the sampling interval beginning with dusk. In LD 12:12 the eclosion peaks were not as distinct as in some longer photoperiods (Kureck, 1979), but the equal length of day and night facilitated a combination with warm and cold phases of equal length.

In constant light and a temperature cycle between 14° and 18° C, the midges emerged mainly near the temperature minimum. A minor peak appeared near the temperature maximum (Fig. 2, left side). The lower part of the thermocycle was also preferred if its mean was 4° C higher, but a larger proportion of individuals emerged outside the main peak and the minor peak disappeared (Fig. 2 middle). At an even higher temperature level (minimum 22°, maximum 26° C), the temperature cycle hardly ever synchronized the population and the midges emerged troughout the day (Fig. 2, right side).

Obviously, the synchronizing effect of the thermocycle decreased with increasing temperatures. Whether the thermocycle entrained the endogenous rhythms or whether it controlled the development and the eclosion directly, has not yet been tested.

---

[1]For taxonomy see Miehlbradt and Neumann (1976)

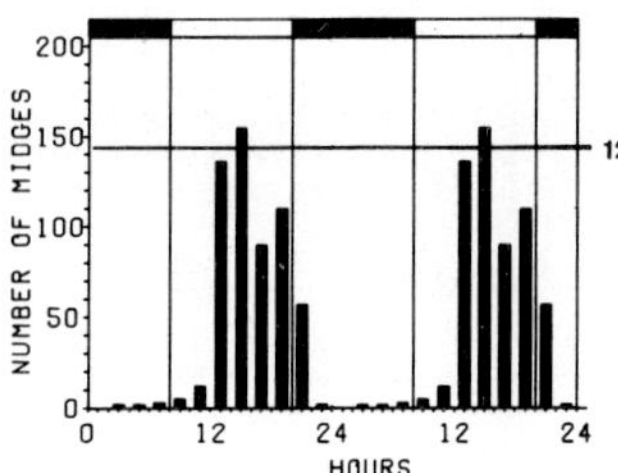

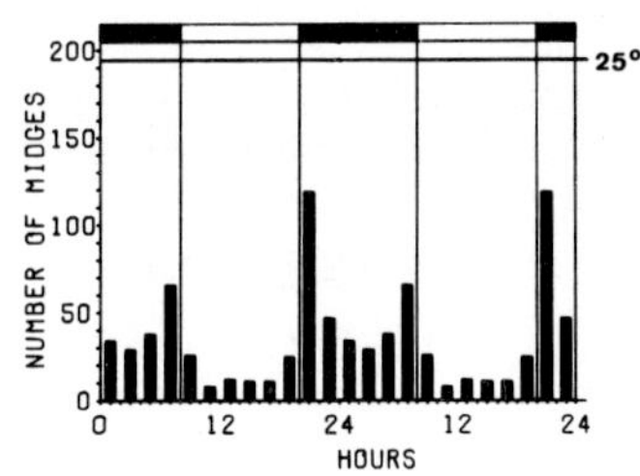

Fig. 1. Eclosion patterns under constant temperature conditions. Left 12° C, right 25° C. Pooled data from several consecutive days. Each 24-h plot is shown twice for better visual comparison. The black horizontal bars mark the dark phases. The thickness of the vertical lines indicates the duration of twilight.

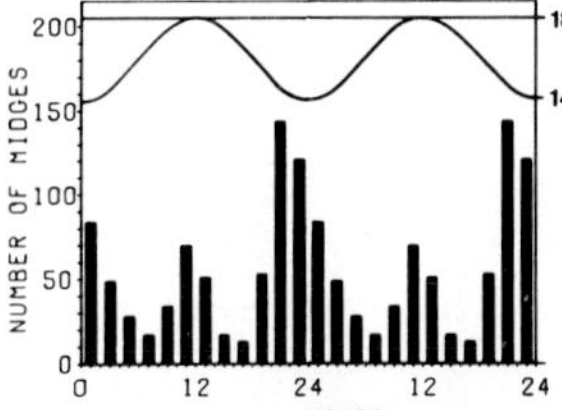

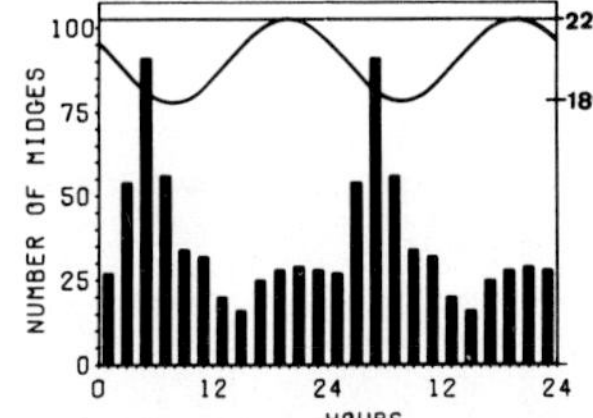

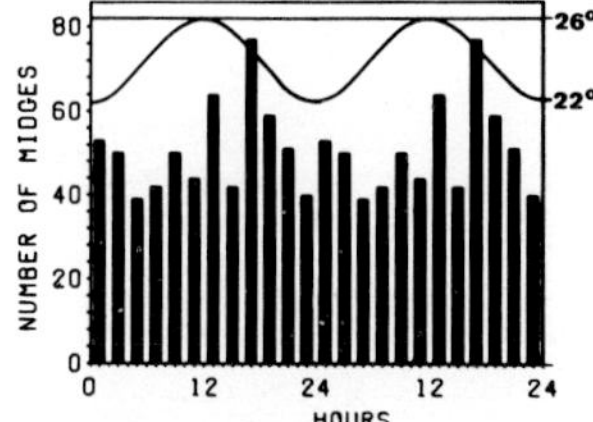

Fig. 2. Eclosion patterns in constant light (550 lux) and sinusoidal temperature cycles of equal amplitudes at different levels. Mean temperatures: 16° (left), 20° (middle), and 24° C (right). Plotted as Fig. 1.

When thermo- and photoperiods were combined the eclosion peaks were always related to dusk, quite independent of the phase relationships of the two cycles (Fig. 3). However, a greater proportion of midges emerged outside the main peak if the nights were warmer than the days (Fig. 3, right side). With the cooler temperature cycles (mean 16° C), generally more adults emerged during the day than during the night, whereas nocturnal emergence prevailed during the warmer temperature cycles (mean 24° C). This difference was obviously due to the change of the mean temperature level since the same patterns were recorded at constant temperatures of 16° and 25° C (Kureck, 1979). The eclosion rhythm was therefore controlled by the photoperiod and the temperature level, and was only slightly affected by the phase of the temperature cycle.

However, the influence of the thermocycle grew with its amplitude. One example is given in Fig. 4 for an amplitude of 10° C and a mean of 12° C. Four different phase relationships between thermo- and photoperiod resulted in four different eclosion patterns. The emergence times were not related to a certain phase of the thermocycle, but appeared near the maximum (Fig. 4 A) and near the minimum (Fig. 4 C) as well as with increasing and decreasing temperatures (Fig. 4 B, D).

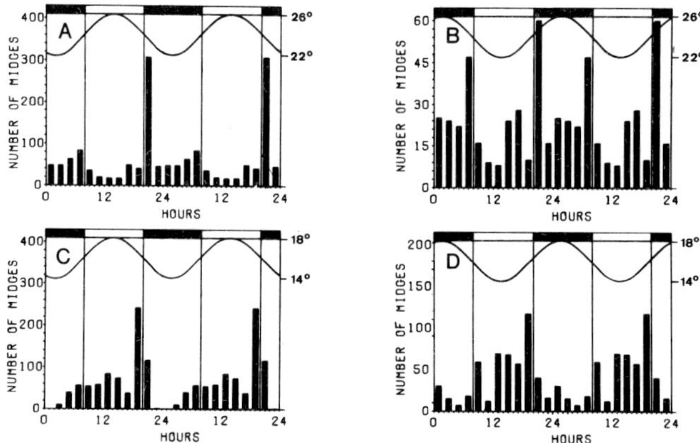

Fig. 3. Eclosion of Ch. thummi in temperature cycles combined in two phase relations with the light-dark cycle. The temperature maxima of the warmer and the cooler cycle coincided either with noon (A, C) or with midnight (B, D).

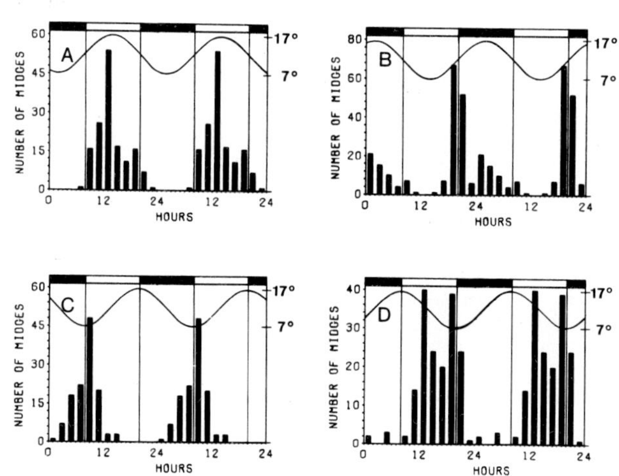

Fig. 4. Effect of a temperature cycle with a higher amplitude (10° C) on the eclosion in LD 12:12. The temperature maxima coincided with noon (A), midnight (B), dusk (C) and dawn (D).

Generally, daylight emergence prevailed, as observed in the case of a constant temperature equal to the mean of the cycle. The patterns in Fig. 4 A an 4 D are similar to the one observed at 12° C (Fig. 1). Only in one combination more midges emerged during the night, but even in this case the peak appeared in the last sampling interval of the light phase, just before dusk (Fig. 4 B).

DISCUSSION

Daily eclosion patterns are often regarded as specific for a taxonomical group. This has been proved in the case of the intertidal midge *Clunio*, where the differnt patterns found in the various strains are inherited adaptations to the local conditions (Heimbach, 1978; Neumann, 1966). However, the variable patterns in *Chironomus* show, that one should be careful in the interpretation of "specific" patterns.

Modifying influences of the temperature on daily rhythms have also been observed in some other insects (Bodenheimer and Klein, 1930; Cardé and others, 1975; Corbet, 1957; Edwards, 1964; Hamilton, 1971; Kureck, 1969; Nielsen and Nielsen, 1962; Syrjämäki, 1966; Truman, 1973; White, 1968). It is likely that similar phenomena will be found in more species, although this flexibility is no common feature. It has, for example, not been observed in the very well studied eclosion rhythm of *Drosophila* (Pittendrigh, 1954). Also in some midges, among them *Chironomus halophilus*, the daily pattern of eclosion was not modified by temperatures between 10° and 22° C (Palmén, 1955).

Within the genus *Chironomus*, variable eclosion patterns were hitherto found only in two polyvoltine species. They enable these insects to use the warmest part of the day for take off, if the mean temperatures are low, without abandoning possible advantages of nocturnal activity at other times of the year.

The advantages of nocturnal or crepuscular emergence of midges have been discussed, among others, by Fischer and Rosin (1968) and Palmén (1955). It possibly reduces the predation by fish, insects and birds. On cool days, however, the air temperature can drop below the threshold for flight activity during twilight, whereas the afternoon can still be warm enough. It might then be advantageous to emerge during the day, especially in seasons and places where predation is less severe.

Even under these conditions eclosion is coupled to the light-dark cycle and not directly stimulated by increasing temperatures. This mechanism has some advantages. The endogenous circadian rhythms, constituting a basic property of most organisms, are maintained. To some extent they enable the insects to "predict" the daily changes in the environment, and to react in time. The photoperiod is generally the strongest and also the most reliable Zeitgeber (time cue) for circadian rhythms. Temperature cycles, on the other hand, are more variable since they are affected by the weather and local conditions such as shading and wind breaks. Especially in the water they are also modified by currents, depth and stratifications. This can greatly reduce the temperature amplitudes and can delay the phase of the temperature cycle in the water. For emerging midges, however, the air temperature may be more important than the water temperature, especially on cool days. The orientation towards the photoperiod enables them to sense the warmest part of the day, even if the temperature cycle in the water is very weak or phase shifted.

The modifying effect of extreme temperature cycles under LD-conditions, as shown in Fig. 4, cannot be explained. More experiments are necessary, to elucidate the role of such cycles. They possibly are outside the physiological range of the species. Wilmers (1978) measured the temperatures in a 1.2 m deep pool on a clear, warm summer day. The temperature amplitude at the surface was 7° C; in a depth of 50 cm it did not exceed 1.8° C. At the substrate of most natural waters the amplitude of the daily temperature cycle will be so small that it will not have any significant effect on the timing of eclosion.

For the surprising fact that the midges reared under constant light conditions emerged near the temperature minimum, no explanation can be offered yet. The results show, however, that the temperature cycle cannot synchronize the eclosion of Ch. thummi with the warmest part of the day. This in fact is achieved by coupling the endogenous circadian rhythm to the light-dark cycle and by the temperature dependent selection of the appropriate pattern. Therefore a mere coincidence of temperature- and eclosion- maxima, as in Fig. 4 A, does not necessarily mean that temperature is the controlling factor.

With lower temperatures the synchronizing effect of the temperature cycle increased, and a minor second peak appeared near the temperature maximum. Further experiments in constant light with temperature cycles near the threshold for development are planned to elucidate, whether a different phase of the temperature cycle is selected, when temperatures are extremly low.

REFERENCES

Bodenheimer, F. S. and H. Z. Klein (1930). Über die Temperaturabhängigkeiten von Insekten. II. Die Abhängigkeit der Aktivität bei der Ernteameise Messor semirufus E. André von der Temperatur und anderen Faktoren. Z. vergl. Physiol., 11, 345-385.

Cardé, R. T., A. Comeau, T. C. Bakker, and W. L. Roelofs (1975). Moth mating periodicity: Temperature regulates the circadian gate. Experientia, 31, 46-48.

Coffman, W. P. (1974). Seasonal differences in the diel emergence of a lotic chironomid community. Ent. Tidskr., 95 (Suppl.), 42-48.

Corbet, P. S. (1957). The life history of the emperor dragonfly, Anax imperator Leach (Odonata: Aeschnidae). J. Anim. Ecol., 26, 1-69.

Danks, H. V., and D. R. Oliver (1972). Diel periodicities of emergence of some high arctic Chironomidae (Diptera). Can. Ent., 104, 903-916.

Edwards, D. K. (1964). Activity rhythms of lepidopterous defoliators. II. Halisidota argentata Pack. (Arctiidae) and Nepytia phantasmaria Stkr. (Geometridae). Can. J. Zool., 42, 939-958.

Fischer, J., and S. Rosin (1968). Einfluß von Licht und Temperatur auf die Schlüpfaktivität von Chironomus nuditarsis Str.. Rev. Suisse Zool., 75, 538-549.

Hamilton, W. J. III (1971). Competition and thermoregulatory behavior of the Namib Desert tenebrionid beetle genus Cardiosis. Ecology, 52, 810-822.

Heimbach, F. (1978). Sympatric species, Clunio marinus Hal. and Cl. balticus n. sp. (Dipt., Chironomidae), isolated by differences in diel emergence time. Oecologia (Berl.), 32, 195-202.

Jónasson, P. M. (1961). Population dynamics in Chironomus anthracinus Zett. in the profundal zone of Lake Esrom. Verh. int. Ver. Limnol., 14, 196-203.

Koskinen, R. (1968). Seasonal and diel emergence of Chironomus salinarius Kieff. (Dipt., Chironomidae) near Bergen, Western Norway. Ann. Zool. Fenn., 5, 65-70.

Kureck, A. (1966). Schlüpfrhythmus von Diamesa arctica (Diptera, Chironomidae) auf Spitzbergen. Oikos, 17, 276-277.

Kureck, A. (1969). Tagesrhythmen lappländischer Simuliiden (Diptera). Oecologia (Berl.), 2, 385-410.

Kureck, A. (1979). Two circadian eclosion times in Chironomus thummi (Diptera), alternately selected with different temperatures. Oecologia (Berl.), 40, 311-323.

Miehlbradt, J., and D. Neumann (1976). Reproduktive Isolation durch optische Schwarmmarken bei den sympatrischen Chironomus thummi und Ch. piger. Behaviour, 58, 272-297.

Neumann, D. (1966). Die lunare und tägliche Schlüpfperiodik der Mücke Clunio. Steuerung und Abstimmung auf die Gezeitenperiodik. Z. vergl. Physiol., 53, 1-61.

Nielsen, H. T., and E. T. Nielsen (1962). Swarming of mosquitoes. Laboratory experiments under controlled conditions. Ent. Exp. Appl., 5, 14-32.

Oliver, D. R. (1968). Adaptations of arctic Chironomidae. Ann. Zool. Fenn., 5, 111-118.

Palmén, E. (1955). Diel periodicity of pupal emergence in natural populations of some chironomids (Diptera). Ann. Zool. Soc. Vanamo, 17, 1-30.

Pittendrigh, C. S. (1954). On temperature independence in the clocksystem controlling emergence-time in *Drosophila*. Proc. Nat. Acad. Sci. USA, 40, 1018-1029.

Remmert, H. (1962). Der Schlüpfrhythmus der Insekten. 73 pp. Wiesbaden.

Remmert, H. (1965). Über den Tagesrhythmus arktischer Tiere. Z. Morph. Ökol. Tiere, 55, 142-160.

Syrjämäki, J. (1966). Dusk swarming of *Chironomus pseudothummi* Strenzke (Diptera, Chironomidae). Ann. Zool. Fenn., 3, 20-28.

Truman, J. W. (1973). Temperature sensitive programming of the silkmoth flight clock: A mechanism for adapting to the seasons. Science, 182, 727-729.

White, T. C. R. (1968). Hatching of eggs of *Cardiaspina densitexta* (Homoptera, Psillidae) in relation to light and temperature. J. Insect Physiol., 14, 1847-1859.

Wilmers, F. (1978). Temperaturen in und an einem künstlichen Teich. Verh. Ges. f. Ökologie, Kiel 1977, 413-426.

Wool, D., and J. Kugler (1969). Circadian rhythm in chironomid species (Diptera) from the Hula Nature Preserve, Israel. Ann. Zool. Fenn., 6, 94-97.

The Relation of Dry Weight and Temperature to Respiration in Some Benthic Chironomid Species in Lough Neagh

M. P. Ripley

Limnology Laboratory, New Univ. Ulster, Traad Point, Ballyronan, Co. Derry, N. Ireland

ABSTRACT

The oxygen consumption rates of 4th instar larvae of Chironomus plumosus, Chironomus anthracinus, Procladius crassinervis, and Glyptotendipes sp. from Lough Neagh have been measured. Measurements have been made at a range of naturally occurring temperatures on acclimated larvae in a constant pressure respirometer. Body weight and temperature have a clear effect on respiration. The data are analysed, the suitability of several models, and the likely contribution of chironomid respiration to oxygen depletion in Lough Neagh is briefly discussed.

KEYWORDS

Chironomids; metabolic rate; temperature; dry weight; respiration; benthic oxygen demand.

INTRODUCTION

The experiments described in the present paper represent the first results of a project designed to discover the reasons for the relative success of certain benthic chironomid species in L. Neagh. Carter (1977) discusses the oxygen conditions in the lough, which have become worse with the eutrophication that has occurred, and play a major part in determining the succession of chironomids. Thus a detailed knowledge of the oxygen consumption rates is a necessity for a study of this nature. While the literature contains oxygen consumption values for the species in this study, these figures have been obtained under markedly different conditions and therefore are not necessarily valid for use in Lough Neagh (Johnson and Brinkhurst, 1971; Edwards, 1958; Walshe, 1968; McFarlane and Mc Lusky, 1972). There is also some suggestion in the literature (Young, 1979) that certain components of models relating to metabolic rate vary with habitat within one system. The wide range of temperatures under which experiments have been run have enabled this hypothesis to be tested. It therefore becomes important to compare animals taken from one specific site, so that these studies can be used to investigate metabolic adaptations to particular conditions. Data from this study may also be used for production studies on the lough as well as increasing our knowledge of the extent to which benthic fauna contribute to the oxygen depletion of the water column and sediments.

METHODS

Lough Neagh is a shallow and eutrophic lake (mean depth 8m.) which only very rarely stratifies. All the animals used in this study were taken from one 8m. depth site, where the substrate consists of fine mud. The animals from the respirometry experiments were taken using an Ekman grab and separated from the mud using a I80μ sieve and Mg SO_4 (Jónasson, I955; Healey and Russell-Smith, I970). Wet weights of the experimental animals were converted to dry weight using regressions prepared each month, as the percentage dry matter varies seasonally (Carter, I978). If the animals were not used immediately for experiments run at lough temperature, then they were acclimated to the experimental temperature for at least 24 hours for each one degree change in temperature, in well fed and oxygenated conditions (Johnson and Brinkhurst, I97I).

Animals were wet weighed and placed into the respiratory chambers of a Gilson Respirometer (Gilson, I963) on the day before the experiment. The chambers contained 2ml autoclaved mud, to reduce bacterial respiration, and 2ml lake water so that the animals were free to live naturally in the chambers. The mud, which had been disturbed and autoclaved, appeared to provide a substrate of normal texture with an oxidised layer, and feeding matter for the animals. The overnight acclimation was important to ensure that the extra activity associated with burrowing and the shaking of the machine did not influence the results. The experiments were run in the morning so that if there were any circadian rhythm effects, by picking consistently on only one part of the cycle, these effects would not influence the results (Shirley, Denoux and Stickle, I978; Duval and Green, I976). The results were analysed using the method of Gregory and Winters (I965) allowing for the combined effects of pressure and temperature on the solubility of oxygen.

RESULTS AND DISCUSSION

The values for metabolic rate have proved to be higher than those presented in the literature for similar species (Johnson and Brinkhurst, I97I; Edwards, I958; Walshe, I968; McFarlane and Mc Lusky, I972). This is mainly due to the fact that active metabolism has been measured here rather than the basal metabolism advocated by Krogh (I9I6) which can lead to much higher metabolism occurring (Ryabushko, I975). This has also led to a greater variation in results due to the inherent variation in activity displayed by the animals. Attempts to minimise certain components of this variation have been made, such as bacterial respiration, circadian rhythms and non-acclimation to the chambers. A large range of temperatures have also been studied to ensure that a full picture of temperature response can be shown.

Metabolic Rate and Temperature

The results are plotted against temperature in Fig. I and conform to the theoretical curve Fig. 2. This has been derived from the experimental results shown here and represents the average curve shown by all 4 species. The position and scale of the curve varies with each species. Zone B in Fig.2 conforms to the zone of temperatures through which the lake passes relatively quickly between the two relatively stable temperature regimes of winter and summer. The position of the Zone B varies, a major factor in its positioning being the depth of the habitat.

For an animal adapted to a site it would be expected to acclimate to the two alternate stable temperature regimes, winter and summer. Acclimation to a particular temperature consists of a deviation from the physiological prediction of metabolism, and often consists of a zone of zero Q_{IO} (Precht, I973). This may be because of opp-

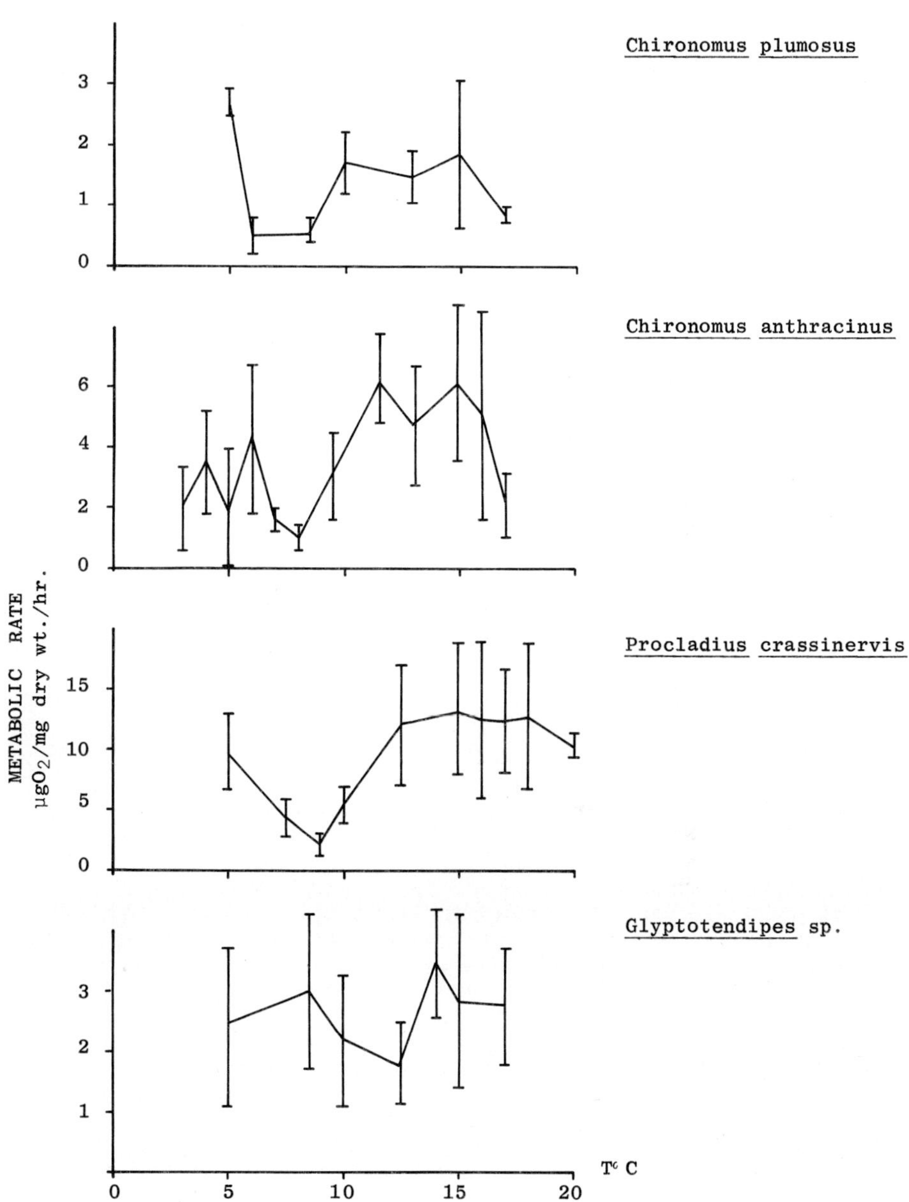

Fig. I. Respirometry results plotted against temperature

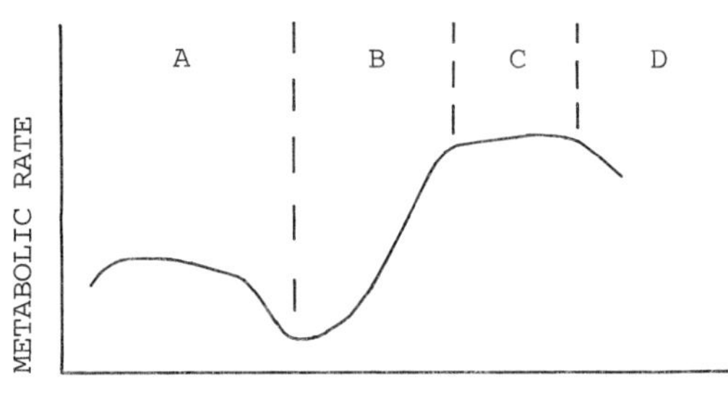

Fig. 2. Theoretical effects of temperature on metabolism

osing and balancing changes brought about by the differing effects of temperature on various enzyme processes and the hormones controlling them (Rao, 1962).

If zone B in Fig. 2 corresponds to a zone of non-acclimation, deviations from this projected line represent acclimation. Zone B for all the species has been tested against the three main families of models in the literature.

1/ The Van't Hoff or Q_{10} equation

$$M=a.b^T \quad \text{where } M=\text{Metabolic Rate}, \; T=\text{Temperature} \qquad (1)$$

This is derived from the theoretically sounder equation of Arrhenius. The Krogh curve is also derived from this.

2/ The Arrhenius equation.

$$M=a.e^{\mu/RT} \quad \text{where } \mu=\text{activation energy/cal}, \; R=\text{gas constant/cal per mole} \qquad (2)$$

which is derived from the laws of chemical reactions.

3/ The Power law.

$$M=a.T^b \quad \text{where } a,b \text{ are constants} \qquad (3)$$

which is derived from the laws of theoretical effects of temperature on physical processes such as viscosity and diffusion.

The best fit to the data is provided by the Arrhenius equation (Table I). The activation energy derived from this model can be considered as a measure of the habitat temperature to which the animals are adapted (Young, 1979). The lower the average temperature to which the animal is adapted, the lower the activation energy is. The species adapted to the lowest temperature is C. plumosus which predominates in the deeper parts of the lough (Carter, 1978) and this has the lowest activation energy. C. anthracinus predominates in the next warmest zone (8m) and has a medium activation energy and P. crassinervis is well distributed in the lough and thus is adapted to a warmer mean temperature and the highest activation energy. According to this analysis however, Glyptotendipes sp. having a low activation energy, is also adapted to the profundal zones, which contradicts other evidence presented here.

Deviations from the predicted Arrhenius line (Equ'n 2) occur at approximately the winter and summer temperature ranges, (Zones C and A respectively). Zone C corresponds to a Q_{10} of approximately zero and the onset of this summer acclimation also is related to the mean summer habitat temperature of the species (Table I). Again Glyptotendipes sp. deviates from the theoretical prediction and emerges as a warmer habitat species than the other 3 species. The onset of the winter zone (Zone A) shows the same habitat temperature distribution as the summer zone (Zone C), with Glyptotendipes sp. again showing as a warm water species.

Table I Relationship of Respiration rate and Temperature for some Chironomids

	Onset of summer acclimation/°C.	Onset of winter acclimation/°C.	Activation energy μ/Cal.	r^2
C. plumosus	IO.25	6	36.5	.622
C. anthracinus	II.5	7.5	49.9	.774
P. crassinervis	I3	8.5	57.8	.829
Glyptotendipes sp.	I4	IO	34.9	.329

The effect of winter acclimation is different from that of summer acclimation in that Q_{IO} does not display a zero value but varies from a negative value to a positive value. Cold temperature acclimation in poikilotherms might involve a heightened protein synthesis and a corresponding rise in metabolic rate (Percy, I974; Bullock, I955), thus the rise in metabolic rate here is therefore not likely to be an experimental artefact, rather a true representation of tissue adaptation to cold temperatures, if it follows this response pattern.

Zone D (Fig. 2) represents a temperature range in which the chironomids are not able to function normally shown by the metabolism dropping with a negative Q_{IO}. It is not necessarily a zone of lethal temperature, rather a sub-optimal temperature range. The temperature at which it occurs, exists only for short periods in the lough at the bottom depth where the chironomids live.

Metabolic Rate and Weight

The relationship of metabolic rate and weight is not as clear as that for temperature. The results have been tested against the power law model as reviewed by Hemmingsen (I960); $M=aW^b$ where M=Metabolic rate (4)

W=Weight

a and b are constants

Table 2 Relationship between Respiration and Dry Weight for some Chironomids

	b	r^2
C. plumosus	-0.85	0.I8
C. anthracinus	-0.86	0.34
P. crassinervis	-I.52	0.36
Glyptotendipes sp.	-0.89	0.46
Inter-specific relation for summer mean weight and metabolic rate	-0.83	0.97

It can be seen that the figuresfor b (Equ'n 4, Table2), are distinctly lower than those reviewed by Hemmingsen (I960). It is suggested that there are two possible reasons for this.

I/ That most authors take a large sample of animals at one time which consists of one cohort of only a narrow size range, and the regression is statistically less valuable than these figures taken over a wider weight range. The inter-specific relation of metabolic rate with weight also produces similar figures which confirms

that the effect is one of weight rather than experimental artefact, as it includes a far wider weight range than any one single species (0.5 mg to 6 mg, mean summer dry weight).
2/ These are figures for active animals rather than basally metabolising animals. As smaller individuals have a higher metabolic rate than larger ones (Banse, 1979), an increase in activity will produce a relatively higher increase in metabolism for smaller individuals. Thus the slope of the power relation will steepen with activity (Fig. 3). The fact that the results shown in Table 2 are markedly lower than in the literature therefore is an indication of the higher activity levels under which these experiments were run. The difference in slopes between these results and those in the literature is therefore a measure of the difference between normal and basal metabolic efficiency, for different sized individuals.

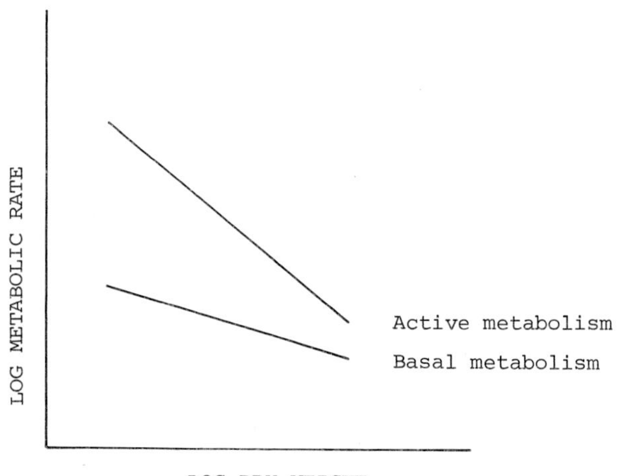

Fig. 3 Comparison of active and basal metabolism.

The Role of Chironomid Respiration in Benthic Oxygen Demand

Core respiration has been measured since the beginning of May, 1979 at the same site as the chironomids have been sampled from (pers. comm. B. Rippey). The results of this and a derived figure for the respiration of the total biomass of chironomids are presented in Fig. 4. It can be seen that the respiration of the total biomass of chironomids is virtually constant and thus does not vary with the same factors as does the core respiration. The contribution varies from c. 15% to c. 40% of the core respiration. This suggests that at certain times of the year the chironomids contribute significantly to the total benthic oxygen demand while at others their contribution is minor. In late summer, when the biomass is much higher and the temperature is still high, one may expect a higher percentage contribution.

Figures from a continuous oxygen monitor during a period of rapid oxygen depletion in early July 1977 show a benthic oxygen demand for a half metre column above the surface of the mud of 34 mg $O_2/m^2/hr$ (FBIU Annual Report 1977). Of this 40% is estimated to be due to the biological and chemical oxygen demand of the water. Taking the water oxygen demand into account, the percentage of the true oxygen demand that the chironomids could be responsible for is 25%, which is more significant than estimated above. The remaining fraction of oxygen demand is probably accounted for by the population of remaining zoobenthos (mainly tubificids), bacteria and the chemical oxygen demand of the sediments (Graneli, 1977).

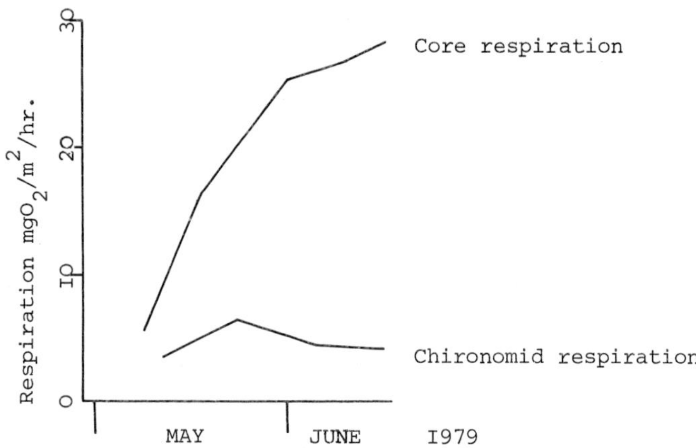

Fig. 4. Comparison of core and chironomid respiration

ACKNOWLEDGEMENT

The author would like to express his gratitude to the Natural Environment Research Council for their Research Grant Number GT4/78/ALS/32, to the staff of the New University of Ulster's Limnology Laboratory and to Prof. B. Wood and Dr. T. E. Andrew who kindly read the manuscript.

REFERENCES

Banse, K. (1979). On weight dependence of net growth efficiency and specific respiration rates among field populations of invertebrates. Oecologia , 38, 111-126.

Bullock, T. H. (1955). Compensation for temperature in the metabolism and activity of poikilotherms. Biol. Rev., 30, 311-342.

Carter, C. E. (1977). Recent history of chironomid fauna of Lough Neagh, from the analysis of remains in sediment cores. Freshwat. Biol., 7, 415-423.

Carter, C. E. (1978). The fauna of the muddy sediments of Lough Neagh, with particular reference to eutrophication. Freshwat. Biol., 8, 547-559.

Duval, W. S. and G. H. Green (1976). Diel feeding and respiratory rhythms in zooplankton. Limnol. Oceanogr., 21, 823-829.

Edwards, R. W. (1958). Relation of oxygen consumption to body size and temperature in the larvae of Chironomus riparius. J. Exp. Biol., 35, 383-395.

F.B.I.U. Annual Report (1977)

Gilson, W. E. (1963). A differential respirometer of simplified and improved design. Science, 141, 531-532.

Graneli, W. (1978). Sediment oxygen uptake in S. Swedish lakes. Oikos, 30, 7-16.

Gregory, K. F. and H. C. Winter (1965). Data reduction with constant pressure respirometers. Analyt. Biochem., 11, 519-531.

Healey, I. N. and A. Russell-Smith (1970). The extraction of fly larvae from woodland soils. Soil Biol. Biochem., 2, 119-129.

Hemmingsen, A. M. (I960). Energy metabolism as related to body size and respiratory surfaces, and its evolution. Reports of the Steno Memorial Hospital, 9 (2), I-IIO.

Johnson, M. G. and R. O. Brinkhurst (I97I). Production of benthic macro-invertebrates of the Bay of Quinte and Lake Ontario. J. Fish. Res. Bd. Can., 28, I699-I725.

Jonasson, P. M. (I955). The efficiency of sieving techniques for sampling freshwater bottom fauna. Oikos, 6, I83-207.

Krogh, A. (I9I6). The respiratory exchange of animals and man. Longmans, Lond.

McFarlane, A. and D. S. Mc Lusky (I972). Oxygen consumption of chironomid larvae from Loch Leven in relation to temperature. Comp. Biochem. Physiol., 43A, 99I-IOOI

Percy, J. A. (I974). Thermal adaptation in the boreo-arctic echinoid, Strongylocentropus droebachiensis. III Seasonal acclimation and metabolism of tissues in vitro. Physiol. Zool. ,47 (I), 59-67.

Precht, R. (I973). Temperatur und Leben. Springer Verlag, Berlin.

Rao, K. P. (I962). Physiology of acclimation to low temperature in poikilotherms. Science, I37, 682-683.

Ryabushko, V. I. (I975). Influence of environmental factors on the respiration of the sea urchin, Strongylocentropus droebachiensis. Biologiya Morya, 5, 23-28.

Shirley, T. C., G. J. Denoux and W. B. Stickle (I978). Seasonal respiration in the Marsh Periwinkle, Littorina irrorata. Biol. Bull., I54, 322-334.

Walshe, B. M. (I948). Oxygen requirements in chironomid larvae. J. Exp. Biol., 25, 35-44.

Young, S. R. (I979). Respiratory metabolism of Alaskozetes antarcticus. J. Insect Physiol., 25, 36I-369.

SECTION II

SYSTEMATICS AND DISTRIBUTION

Methods and Principles of Phylogenetic Biogeography

L. Brundin

Swedish Museum of Natural History, S 10406 Stockholm, Sweden

ABSTRACT

Phylogenetic biogeography in the sense of the present author is intended to be the biogeographic implication of Hennig's phylogenetic systematics s.str. Hennig's method for reconstruction of nature's hierarchy by simultaneous cross-reference to extant vicariance patterns forms the basis for the causal study of biotic history in time and space. Further insight is obtained by known paleogeographic events and by fossils. Essential for a successful reconstruction of the history of a group is the integration of a wide hierarchic and global geographic perspective and consistent exploitation of available means to investigate dispersal whenever we are faced with sympatry between closely related groups. A critical approach to the still controversial problem of dispersal is feasible by investigation of the causal connection between sympatry, subordinate vicariance, hierarchic structure, and the geographic distribution of the involved monophyletic groups as exponents of comparative apomorphy/plesiomorphy. Important here is the evolutionary "law" based on experience that dispersal followed by speciation, just as any speciation by a peripheral isolate, will give rise to peripheral apomorphy, not to peripheral plesiomorphy. What matters foremost are the results of dispersal, not the relation between apomorphy/plesiomorphy and aptness to disperse or to keep a certain range. Directions of dispersal and areas of origin of incipient ancestral species are the corollaries of dispersal and hence indispensable concepts of phylogenetic biogeography. Several examples of the application in practice of our means to investigate dispersal and its corollaries can be given. It is also possible to demonstrate that dispersal can be established without reference to sympatry - Croizat's panbiogeography, as symbolized by the vicariance paradigm of Croizat, Nelson, and Rosen (1974), does not signify the harmonic integration of all biogeographic aspects that would be the embodiment of a biogeographic synthesis. The model suffers from defective methodology for investigation of dispersal that hampers estimation of areas of origin and the history of generalized distribution patterns before their subdivision into smaller areas of vicariance. There is a marked tendency to use the major distribution patterns simply as starting points and to concentrate the biogeographic analyses on the history of their subdivision. In its present form the vicariance model signifies a clear underrating or concealment of the role that has been played by dispersal.

Phylogenetic biogeography in the sense of the present author is symbolized by a more harmonic and dynamic model that may be called the vicariance/dispersal paradigm. It is based on the following fundamental considerations: (1) The gradual subdivision by local formation of the ranges of ancestral species via the appearance of barriers, a biotic process that is immobile in space, (2) also fundamental has been the gradual widening of the ranges of incipient ancestral species via the disappearance of barriers, a biotic process that is mobile in space and (3) these processes have been each others corollaries, and a free appraisal of their influence, based on experience of particular cases, is a distinctive feature of phylogenetic biogeography.

KEYWORDS

Phylogenetic biogeography; Systematics; Dispersal; Sympatry; Distribution pattern.

REFERENCE

Croizat, L., G. Nelson and D.E. Rosen (1974). Centers of origin and related concepts. Syst. Zool 23 (2), 265 - 285.

Taxonomic Problems in Holarctic Chironomidae (Diptera)

B. Lindeberg

Zoological Museum, University of Helsinki, P. Rautatiekatu 13, SF-00100 Helsinki 10, Finland

ABSTRACT

Problems associated with the taxonomic status of distant populations of closely related chironomid species are discussed. Some of the recently published data are reviewed, and personal observations presented.

KEYWORDS

Chironomidae; Holarctic taxonomy; sibling species; dispersal; barriers.

INTRODUCTION

Problems of international taxonomy have been discussed in several recent papers. I shall not give a full review of the opinions expressed since the ideas put forward by the Becks (Beck and Beck, 1966) at the first Symposium on Chironomidae, but content myself with choosing some examples from certain recent revisions and presenting some findings of my own.

Some 15 years ago I felt very pessimistic about how to solve taxonomic problems in distant populations, for instance when comparing related forms from Europe and America. This was mainly due to my studies on species that were structurally very similar. If work on sibling species is carried out under strictly sympatric and synchronous conditions there is a firm theoretical basis, but the treatment of allopatric populations showing differences of various magnitudes appeared almost impossible. Since that time, however, the situation has improved considerably, and the prospects are now better.

RESULTS AND DISCUSSION

The study of variation is important for the analysis of sympatric sibling species, and an understanding of the variation between populations is necessary in comparisons of material from different localities. Information on the limits of variation is needed from both small areas and large regions.

I have been able to study several good samples of Tanytarsus gracilentus from different parts of the Holarctic. Many of the localities are widely separated. The work will be continued, enlarged, and, I hope, concluded.

For the examination of geographic variation in a restricted area, I have chosen Paratanytarsus penicillatus, which is actually a group of four closely related species. I have copious samples from many localities, particularly in northern Fennoscandia. One small sample from northern Canada is very important for the present discussion.

Tanytarsus gracilentus is predominantly a high arctic species with no close relatives. I have repeatedly examined hypopygia of specimens mounted on slides, and made a number of drawings to facilitate simultaneous comparisons. I have become accustomed to the characteristic features of each population and, for instance, if I examine specimens from Baffin Land, western Greenland and Iceland at random, I can now place every one correctly.

Most, but not all, populations are very homogeneous. The Cornwallis Island population is distinctly heterogeneous. There are specimens that roughly resemble those from Baffin Land, and ones that are closely similar to those from British Columbia. Moreover, certain characters seem to vary discontinuously. For a while, such an observation suggested the presence of two species. But the idea had to be discarded because in two other heterogeneous populations (Ellesmere I., Peary Land) the different variants of characters were independently combined in different specimens. This is perhaps an indication of polymorphism, but no grounds for splitting up Tanytarsus gracilentus can be proposed.

My observations on the Paratanytarsus penicillatus aggregate can be summarized as follows:

Three species at most have been found in the same lake; there is one such a case. One species has pelagic swarming behaviour, and can also be distinguished by morphology. The two others frequently occur in the same lake. They are univoltine, with periods of emergence that are well separated in the south of Finland, but near each other or slightly overlapping in the north.

A fourth species is distinct for many reasons. It lives in habitats with poorer oxygen conditions (in bogland waters, for instance), whilst the others prefer oligotrophic lakes. This one happens to be P. penicillatus s. str.; it could be identified with the original type specimens from England.

One of the four species, which is on the wing later in the season, has been studied in greater detail than the others. There are abundant quantitative data and qualitative observations, and in this species also, variation is of a kind that seems to suggest the presence of polymorphism. It is interesting that the Canadian sample mentioned earlier corresponds to this particular form. The specimens even display features of hypopygial variation which resemble those from northern Fennoscandia.

The Canadian and European populations must be called by the same name. There is no other alternative, and this example shows that the identification of distant populations is not impossible even in cases where sibling species are involved.

Tanytarsus gracilentus and Paratanytarsus penicillatus are high boreal or arctic species, and similar problems will certainly arise with other such species. With species from more temperate latitudes taxonomic questions are another matter, and more difficult.

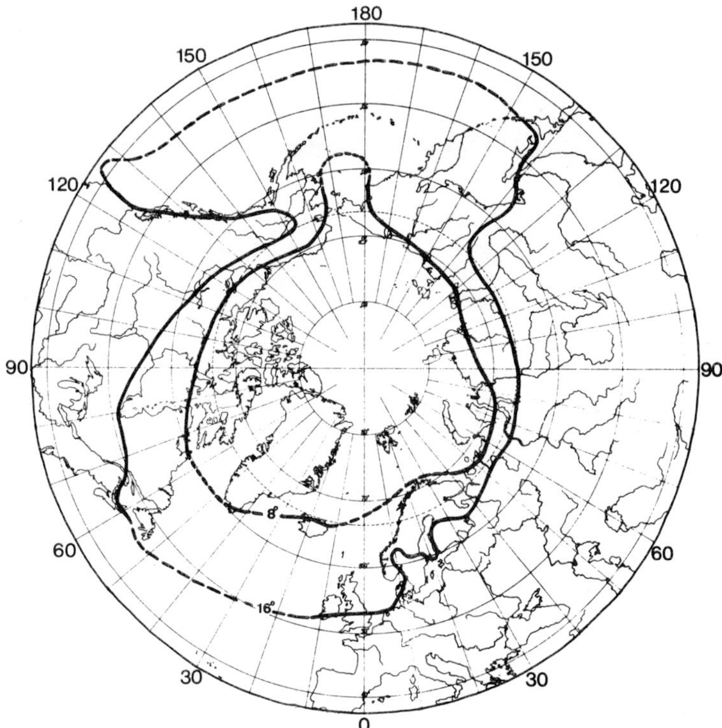

Fig. 1. Northern 8°C and 16°C July mean isotherms.

I shall not discuss past climatology, but will take an example from present conditions. The map (Fig. 1) shows two mean isotherms for July, 8°C and 16°C. The tree-line of boreal forests coincides roughly with the 10°C isotherm. The Bering Strait area is interesting, and not everyone perhaps has realized how extremely cold its climate is, considerably colder than that of northern Norway. The strait itself is not broad, some 90 km, and hardly an important barrier to the dispersal of arctic Chironomidae.

It is different with the species requiring a milder climate and a longer growing season. For such species the Bering Strait is an effective barrier, and has been so for a long time in the past. Therefore, the probability of species common to Europe and America decreases with decreasing latitude.

One more detail can be seen from the map and the 16°C isotherm. It would be very interesting to know the fauna of northern Japan, for instance. It is tempting to speculate that Europe and Japan will prove to have more species in common than central Europe and America, or even Japan and America.

An example may indicate such a trend. There are 11 species of Corynoneura and Thienemanniella in Japan (Sasa and Yamamoto, 1977). Seven of them were described by Tokunaga and four were described from Europe by Edwards. No Japanese species have so far been reported from Europe, but M. Hirvenoja and I have identified C. longipennis Tokunaga in Finland. Moreover, C. tenuistyla Tokunaga and C. lacustris Edwards are very similar, and Hirvenoja, having seen the type of the former, has found it practically impossible to distinguish them. So 5 or 6 of the Japanese species may occur in Europe. Reiss (1977) has reported that 84.5 per cent of the species found in Mongolia and the Baikal area occur in Europe.

European names of Heterotrissocladius were formerly used in the Nearctic. Saether's (1975) revision changed the situation, and only H. marcidus is accepted. All European species except H. maari have a sister species in the Nearctic.

Of the 28 Nearctic species of the subgenus Orthocladius 20 are from that region only (Soponis, 1977). It can be noted that most of them are not markedly arctic species. Of the eight remaining, three live in Spitzbergen and four or five in Sweden, but not in central Europe. These are predominantly arctic or montane species.

It would be very useful to have a good paper on the Chironomidae of the Aleutian Islands. This area has a moderate climate, heavy rainfall, and a long growing season, which begins in early May and ends in late September. Interesting biogeographical results have been published about this chain of islands, such as Lindroth's (1963) study of the ground-beetles. American and Soviet collectors should make some excursions in the area.

REFERENCES

Beck, W. M., and C.E. Beck (1966). The Chironomidae of Florida: a problem in international taxonomy. Gewässer Abwässer, 41/42, 129-135.

Lindroth, C. H. (1963). The Aleutian islands as a route for dispersal across the north Pacific. Proc. 10th Pacific sci. congr., Bishop Museum Press. pp. 121-131.

Reiss, F. (1977). Verbreitungsmunster bei paläarktischen Chironomidenarten (Diptera, Chironomidae). Spixiana, 1, 85-97.

Saether, O. A. (1975). Nearctic and Palaearctic Heterotrissocladius (Diptera: Chironomidae). Bull. Fish. Res. Board Can., 193, 1-67.

Sasa, M., and M. Yamamoto (1977). A checklist of Chironomidae recorded from Japan. Jap. J. Sanit. Zool., 28, 301-318.

Soponis, A. R. (1977). A revision of the Nearctic species of Orthocladius (Orthocladius) van der Wulp (Diptera: Chironomidae). Mem. Ent. Soc. Can., 102, 1-187.

Modern Approaches to the Congruence Problem in Chironomid Systematics

C. J. Webb

Department of Zoology, University of Bristol, Bristol, England

ABSTRACT

A serious problem in chironomid systematics is the difficulty of identifying larvae. This paper reports the value of modern ultrastructural and biochemical characters for improving the congruence of larval and adult classifications.

KEYWORDS

Chironomidae; systematics; congruence problem; ultrastructure of larval head capsule; protein electrophoresis.

INTRODUCTION

On grounds of their ubiquity, abundance and diversity, dipterous flies of the family Chironomidae represent one of the most important groups of aquatic macro-invertebrates in Great Britain (Pinder, 1977; Wilson and McGill, 1977). Despite this, progress in their investigation has undoubtedly been hampered by systematic problems, important among which is the incongruity between the classification systems of different life-history stages (Pinder, 1977, 1978). Thus, while some 450 British species of chironomid have been described (Kloet and Hincks, 1975), the majority of these are recognised solely on the basis of adult male characters and only a small proportion of them can be positively identified as larvae (Pinder, 1978). This situation has arisen because the larval morphology of traditional study often fails to provide adequate diagnostic features and because alternative modern characters such as polytene chromosomes, although of proven value (Acton, 1956; Keyl and Keyl, 1959), have been employed rather rarely.

The aim of the present communication is to indicate that the diagnostic value of a well-known and well-used feature of larval morphology (ventromental plates) may be extended when studied by a novel technique, and to illustrate the scope of modern, biochemical characters for improving congruence between the classificatory schemes of imagoes and immature stages.

TAXONOMIC IMPLICATIONS OF VENTROMENTAL PLATE MICROARCHITECTURE

The head capsules of many chironomid larvae contain some sort of lobe or plate-like structure on each side of the ventral, sclerotised 'toothplate', which, in accordance with varying views on the homologies of this part of the head capsule, have been termed 'paralabial' (Bryce, 1960; Bryce and Hobart, 1972), 'hypostomial' (Smith, 1972) or 'ventromental' (Saether, 1971; Cranston, 1977) plates. These structures are best developed in the subfamily Chironominae where they also appear to be striated to some extent when viewed with the light microscope. Indeed, the presence of striated ventromental plates has been, and is still used as one of the main features for distinguishing larvae of the Chironominae from those of other subfamilies, while the size, shape and striation pattern of ventromental plates are often of use in assigning larval chironominids to lower systematic categories (Bryce, 1960: Bryce and Hobart, 1972; Cranston, 1977).

Despite this taxonomic importance, very little is known about striated plates, a situation which stimulated the author and his colleagues J.D. McGill and R.S. Wilson to investigate their structure and function. During the course of this investigation, applications of the previously unemployed techniques of scanning electron microscopy and thin resin sectioning indicated that in several cases striated plates have a hitherto unsuspectedly complicated ultrastructure. For example, plates of *Microtendipes pedellus* (Degeer) observed with the light microscope *in situ* (Fig. 1a) or dissected from the head capsule (Fig. 1b), appear as near quarter *annuli*, the anterior part of which is radially striated. Use of the scanning electron microscope reveals that the plates of this species are gently concave and have an outer (ventral) surface which is fairly smooth while the inner (dorsal) surface has a complex topography (Figs. 1c and 1d). Thus the inner surface curves dorsally along the posterio-anterior axis of the plate in two concave sections. The posterior section is unsculptured while the anterior one bears a series of radially arranged ridges and furrows (Figs. 1e and 1h) which correspond to striae visible in the light microscope. However, the ridges terminate on either side of a sharp fold at the anterior margin of the plate (Figs. 1f and 1g) in an elaborate system of apertures and protruberances (Figs 1i and 1j) which are not readily visible by light microscope.

The microarchitecture of striated plates from specimens of different genera is often markedly different, a point illustrated in Fig. 2 which compares the appearance of striated plates from species of *Polypedilum*, *Cryptochironomus*, *Glyptotendipes*, *Paratendipes*, *Endochironomus*, *Micropsectra* and *Chironomus*. Nevertheless, the organisation of plates from some genera, for example *Chironomus* and *Cryptochironomus*, is more similar than that of others and this may be an indication of affinity. Certainly within genera, plates of different species often have a similar basic organisation, although in all cases examined so far the detailed ultrastructure of plates from different species is characteristic. For example, the microarchitecture of plates from *Chironomus riparius* Meigen, *C. salinarius* Kieffer and *C. plumosus* (L.) is quite distinct (Figs. 2g - 2l).

An assessment of the taxonomic value of a character may be aided if information is available on its functional significance (Cain, 1959). Thus, features which are highly functional are often of use in the delimitation of biospecies - fundamentally adaptive units, while functional characters may have less value for the deduction of phylogenetic relationships since they can be subject to convergence. Studies of the relationships of striated plates to other features of head capsule anatomy have led the author and his colleagues to believe that the microarchitecture of striated plates has a role in the production of silk or mucus threads of a specific quality which may enable a larva to handle sediment particle of a certain type and therefore adapt it to a particular ecological niche. If this is the case the microarchitecture of striated plates may well be a source of characters of use in species diagnosis.

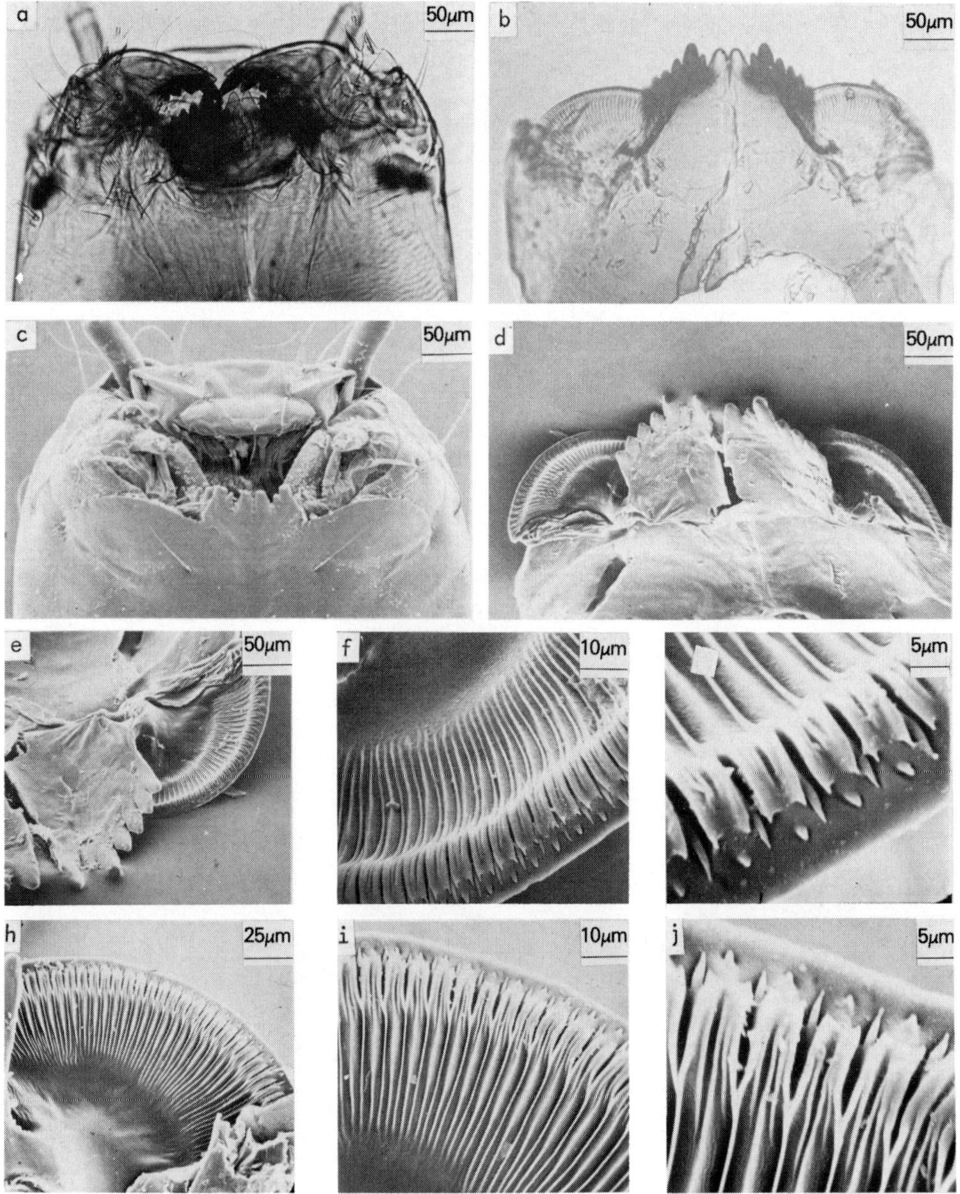

Fig. 1. Light and scanning electron micrographs of the head capsule and ventromental plates of Microtendipes pedellus.

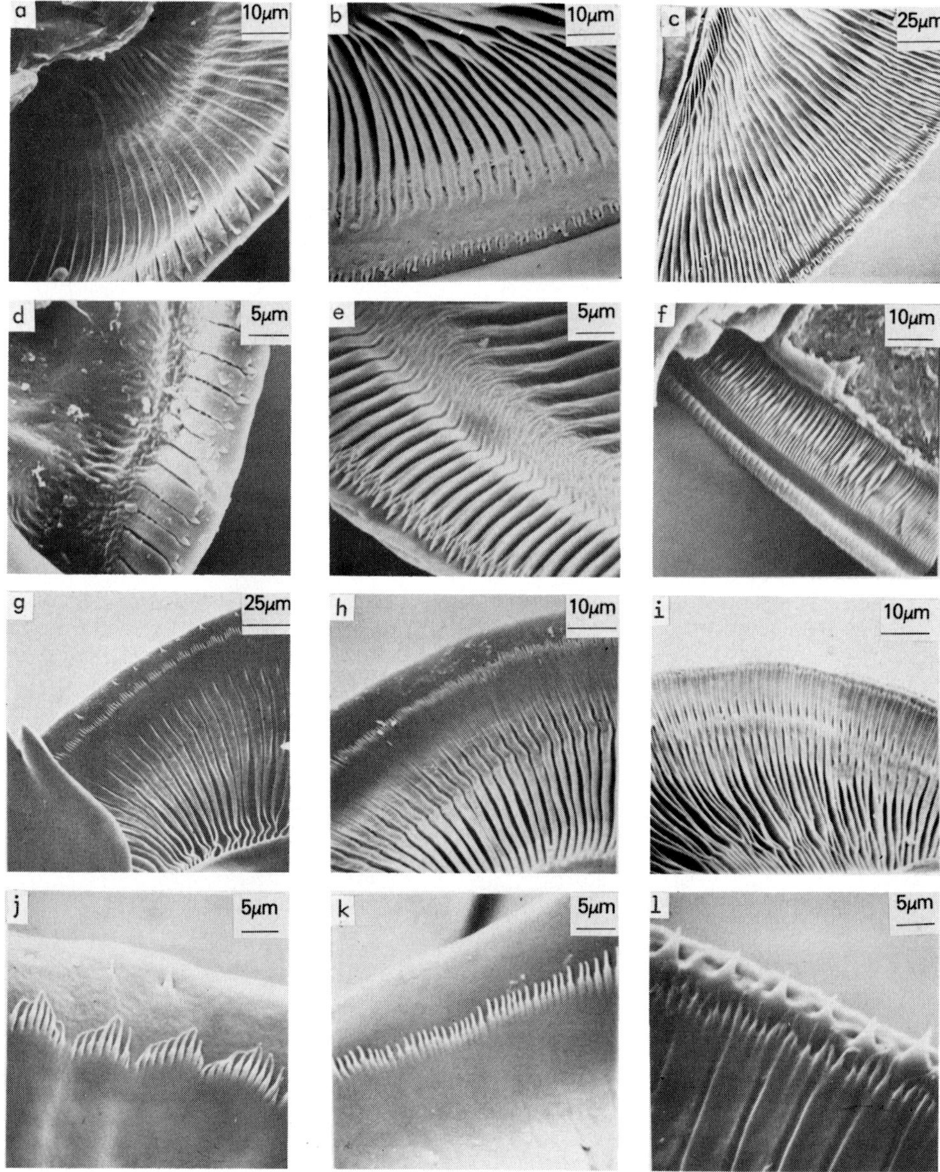

Fig. 2. Scanning electron micrographs of the dorsal surface of ventromental plates of a) Polypedilum sp., b) Cryptochironomus sp., c) Glyptotendipes sp., d) Paratendipes sp., e) Endochironomus sp., f) Micropsectra sp., g) and j) Chironomus riparius, h) and k) Chironomus salinarius, i) and l) Chironomus plumosus.

BIOCHEMICAL CHARACTERS IN ONTOGENY AND SYSTEMATICS

Chemical features of organisms have been used by systematists since the turn of this century. However, it is only in recent years that a distinct and rapidly expanding field of biochemical systematics has emerged for the increased use of biochemical characters, particularly large 'information-containing' or 'semantotrophic' molecules such as nucleic acids and proteins, has been the result of advances made in the modern discipline of molecular biology (Alston and Turner, 1963; Sneath, 1968). For example, in the last two decades it has become apparent that the properties of protein molecules of an individual more or less directly reflect the structural organisation of its actual genetic material and therefore that the comparison of these molecules between organisms can have significance for their classification (Sibley, 1962).

The ideal method for comparing homologous protein molecules is to determine their respective amino-acid sequences, but this is a complicated and time-consuming procedure and a simpler means of comparison, electrophoretic separation, is often adopted (Avise, 1974). Electrophoresis is the movement of charged particles in a supporting medium under the influence of an electric field (Smith, 1968). The electrophoretic mobility of a protein is a function of its net electric charge, size and shape, and proteins which migrate at different rates usually differ by at least one amino-acid and are the products of different gene loci, or of different alleles at the same locus (Shaw, 1971; Avise, 1974).

Electrophoretic data have been employed in systematic investigations of many organisms and successfully applied to a wide range of taxonomic problems (Wright, 1974). They may be of special value in chironomid systematics by providing a source of diagnostic characters common to larvae and imagoes which are morphologically and ecologically very distinct. Thus, there are indications that homologous enzymes from different life-history stages of certain holometabolous insects, including some chironomid species, have a similar electrophoretic mobility (Rothen, Scholl and Rosin, 1975; Avise and McDonald, 1976).

The electrophoretic behaviour of five glucose-metabolising enzymes in homogenates of different life-history stages of *Chironomus riparius* reared from single egg masses was investigated by the author. The enzymes, phosphoglucose isomerase (PGI), arginine kinase (AK), myokinase (AMPK) pyruvate kinase (PK) and phosphoglucose mutase (PGM) were studied by thin layer horizontal starch gel electrophoresis in a Tris-EDTA-borate buffer (Smithies, 1959) and were revealed by the filter paper staining technique of Scopes (1968). No differences were detected in the electrophoretic behaviour of PGI, AK, AMPK, and PGM throughout the ontogeny of *C. riparius*, although an extra zone of PK activity occurred in extracts of pupae and adults of this species (Figs. 3a and 3b).

While the electrophoretic behaviour of enzymes studied is similar throughout the life-history of *C. riparius*, investigations indicate that the same enzyme obtained from equivalent developmental stages of different species can behave differently on electrophoresis (Fig. 3c). The use of biochemical characters for species diagnosis is illustrated by the work of Rothen, Scholl and Rosin (1975) who were able to recognise different life-history stages of nine species of *Chironomus* on the basis of the electrophoretic behaviour of five glucose-metabolising enzymes. However, it should be noted that while studies on a wide range of animals have indicated that different species often show major differences at 20-50% of their loci, there is no strict rule relating the genetic similarity of two populations with their taxonomic status (Ayala, 1975). For example, very low levels of genetic differentiation are characteristic of populations which are reproductively isolated as a result of changes in chromosome structure and number (Nevo and Shaw, 1972), a point worth noting since chromosome rearrangements have played an important role in the evolution of a number of chironomid species (White, 1973).

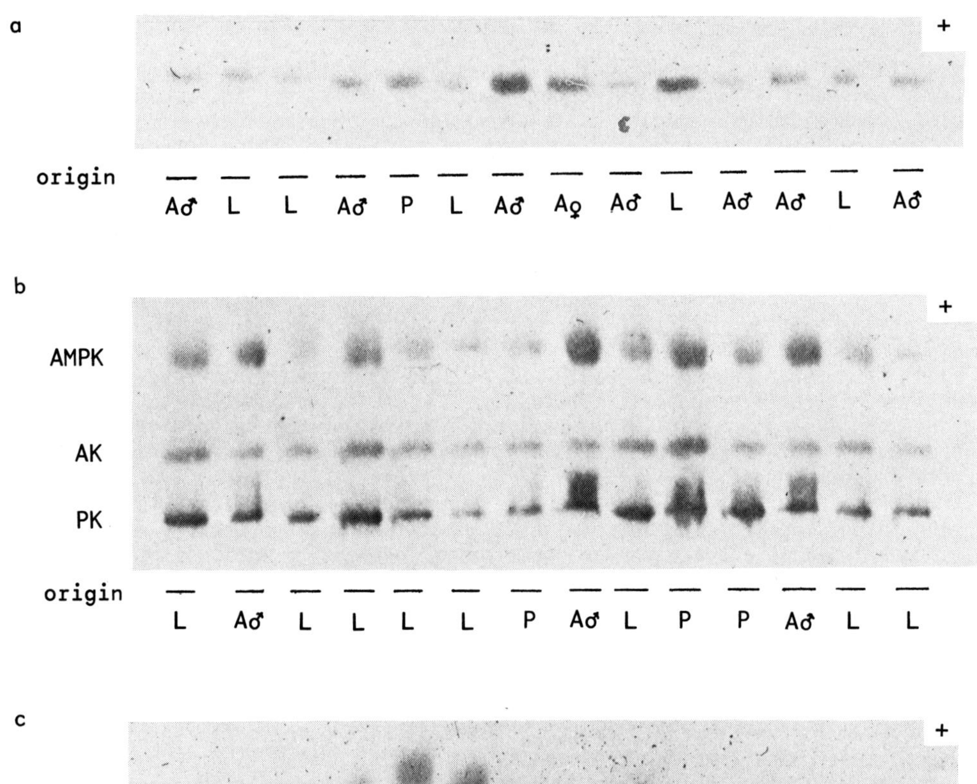

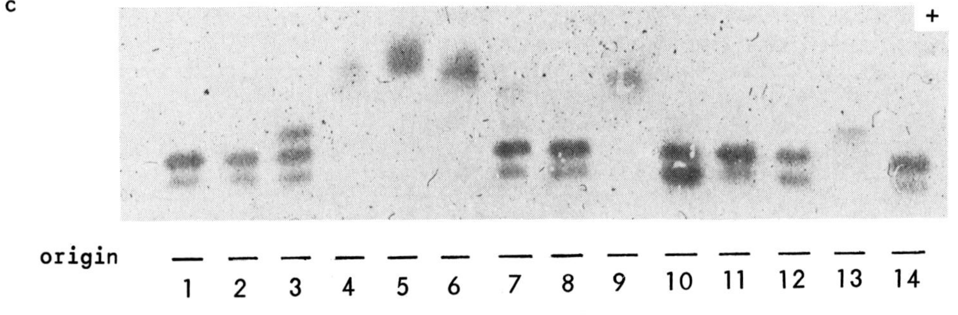

Fig. 3. Electrophoretic behaviour of chironomid glucose-metabolising enzymes. a) PGM and b) AMPK, AK and PK from larvae (L), pupae (P) and adults (A) of *Chironomus riparius*, c) PGM from larvae of *Chironomus plumosus* (1,2,3, 7,8,10,11,12,14), *Cryptochironomus* sp. (4,5,6,9) and *Polypedilum* sp. (13).

CONCLUSION

It is not the purpose of this paper to suggest that biochemical characters or the aspects of larval ultrastructure described provide a complete or exclusive solution to the congruence problem but rather to demonstrate that progress in this difficult area of chironomid systematics can be made by the use of such modern approaches.

ACKNOWLEDGEMENT

The author is indebted to Miss L. Clarke for preparing the manuscript and to Mr K. Wood for photographic assistance. This work was carried out during the tenure of a N.E.R.C. Research Fellowship.

REFERENCES

Acton, A. B. (1956). The identification and distribution of the larvae of some species of Chironomus (Diptera). Proc. Roy. Ent. Soc. (A), 31, 161-164.

Alston, R. E., and B. L. Turner (1968). Biochemical Systematics. Prentice-Hall Inc., Englewood Cliffs, N.J.

Avise, J. C. (1974). Systematic value of electrophoretic data. Syst. Zool., 23, 465-481.

Avise, J. C., and J. F. McDonald (1976). Enzyme changes during development of holo- and hemi-metabolic insects. Comp. Biochem. Physiol., 53B, 393-397.

Ayala, F. J. (1975). Genetic differentiation during the speciation process. In T. Dobzhansky, M. K. Hecht, and W.C. Steere (Eds.), Evolutionary Biology, Vol. 8. Plenum Press, N.Y. and London. pp. 1-78.

Bryce, D. (1960). Studies on the larvae of the British Chironomidae (Diptera), with keys to the Chironominae and Tanypodinae. Trans. Soc. Br. Ent., 14, 19-62.

Bryce, D. and A. Hobart (1972). The biology and identification of the larvae of the Chironomidae (Diptera). Entomologists' Gaz., 23, 175-217.

Cain, A. J. (1959). Function and taxonomic importance. In A.J. Cain (Ed.), Function and Taxonomic Importance. Systematics Association, London.

Cranston, P. S. (1977). A provisional key to the genera of the larvae of British Chironomidae. Unpublished manuscript.

Keyl, H.-G. and I. Keyl (1959). Die cytologische Artdifferenzierung der Chironomiden. 1. Bestimmungstabelle für die Gattung Chironomus auf Grund der Speicheldrüsen-Chromosomen. Arch. Hydrobiol., 56, 43-57.

Kloet, G.S. and W.D. Hincks (1975). A checklist of British insects, 2nd ed. Part 5: Diptera and Siphonaptera. Handbk. Ident. Br. Insects, 11, 139 pp.

Nevo, E. and C.R. Shaw (1972) Genetic variation in a subterranean mammal, Spalax ehrenbergi. Biochem. Gen., 7, 235-241.

Pinder, L. V. C. (1977). The Chironomidae and their ecology in chalk streams. Freshwater Biological Assn., 45th Annual Report, 62-69.

Pinder, L. V. C. (1978). A Key to the adult males of British Chironomidae. Freshwater Biological Assn., Scient. Publs. No. 37.

Rothen, R., A. Scholl, and S. Rosin (1975). Artdiagnose durch Enzymelektrophorese bei Chironomus. Rev. Suisse Zool., 82, 699-704.

Saether, O. A. (1971). Notes on the general morphology and terminology of the Chironomidae (Diptera). Can. Ent., 103, 1237-1260.

Scopes, R. K. (1968). Methods for starch-gel electrophoresis of sarcoplasmic proteins. Biochem. J., 107, 139-150.

Shaw, C. R. (1971). The extent of genetic divergence in speciation. Rapp. P.-V. Reun. Cons. perm. int. Explor. Mer, 161, 143-146.

Sibley, C. G. (1962). The comparative morphology of protein molecules as data for classification. Syst. Zool., 11, 108-118.

Smith, I. (Ed.) (1968). Chromatographic and electrophoretic techniques. 2nd ed. Heinemann, London.
Smith, V. G. F. (1972). Studies on the Chironomidae (Diptera), with a report on the fauna of a new reservoir. Ph.D. Thesis, University of Liverpool.
Smithies, O. (1959). An improved procedure for starch-gel electrophoresis. Further variations in the serum proteins of normal individuals. Biochem. J., 71, 585-587.
Sneath, P. H. A. (1968). Forward. In J.G. Hawkes (Ed.), Chemotaxonomy and Serotaxonomy, Systematics Association Special Volume 2. Academic Press, London and New York. pp. xv-xvi.
White, M. J. D. (1973). Animal Cytology and Evolution. 3rd ed. Cambridge University Press, Cambridge.
Wilson, R. S. and J. D. McGill (1977). A new method of monitoring water quality in a stream receiving sewage effluent, using chironomid pupal exuviae. Water Res., 11, 959-962.
Wright, C.A. (Ed.) (1974). Biochemical and immunological taxonomy of animals. Academic Press, London and New York.

Nostococladius, a New Subgenus of *Cricotopus* (Diptera : Chironomidae)

P. Ashe and D. A. Murray

Zoology Department, University College, Dublin, Belfield, Dublin 4, Ireland

ABSTRACT

Cricotopus (Nostococladius) lygropis Edw. n. subgen. has recently been found in material collected from the River Flesk, Killarney, S.W. Ireland. Male and female imagines, pupae and larvae have been obtained. Detailed descriptions of the larval and pupal stages are given. Larvae of the new subgenus have been found living within colonies of the blue-green alga Nostoc parmelioides Kutz. N. parmelioides is recorded from Ireland for the first time.

KEYWORDS

Chironomidae; Nostococladius; new subgenus; Nostoc parmelioides; Ireland.

INTRODUCTION

During an intensive study of the Chironomidae of the River Flesk, S.W. Ireland (Fig. 1, grid reference V 987 902), larvae, pupae and adults of Cricotopus lygropis Edw. have been obtained. This species was described by Edwards (1929) based on a single female. Brundin (1947) gives a description of male imagines which he ascribed to Paratrichocladius cfr. lygropis. Hirvenoja (1973), using Edwards' type female and Brundin's tentatively associated male imagines, placed C. lygropis into a distinct group, the lygropis group, of the subgenus Cricotopus. Based on the distinctive immature stages, it is necessary to erect a new subgenus for the species. Because of the ecology of the larva, i.e. found living within colonies of Nostoc, it is here proposed to assign the name Nostococladius to the new subgenus. The terminology used follows that of Saether (1976).

NOSTOCOCLADIUS SUBGEN. NOV.

Type of the subgenus: Cricotopus lygropis Edw.

Cricotopus lygropis Edwards 1929 : 325.
Paratrichocladius cfr. lygropis (Edw.), Brundin 1947 : 16.
Cricotopus (Cricotopus) lygropis Edw., Hirvenoja 1973 : 212.

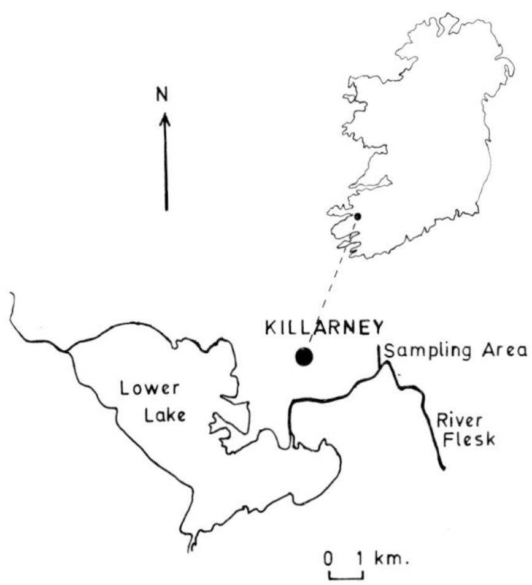

Fig. 1. Killarney Area, Ireland, showing sampling location.

Imagines

General description as in Hirvenoja (1973), male and female genitalia as in Fig.2.

Pupa

Total length 5.4 - 6.2 mm.

Cephalothorax. Frontal plate devoid of setae. Thoracic horn 14 - 54 μ long, 12 - 21 μ wide, devoid of spines. Precorneal setae present but weakly developed (Fig. 3A). Thorax pale apart from the darkened base of the wing sheaths. Three

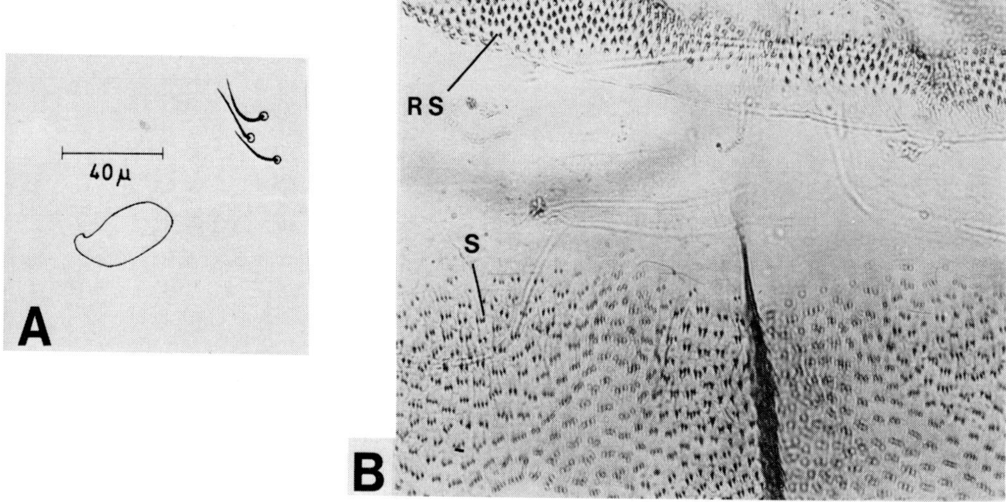

Fig. 3. Cricotopus (Nostococladius) lygropis Edw., subgen. nov., pupa. A, thoracic horn and precorneal setae. B, recurved spines (RS) of tergite II and the shagreen (S) of tergite III.

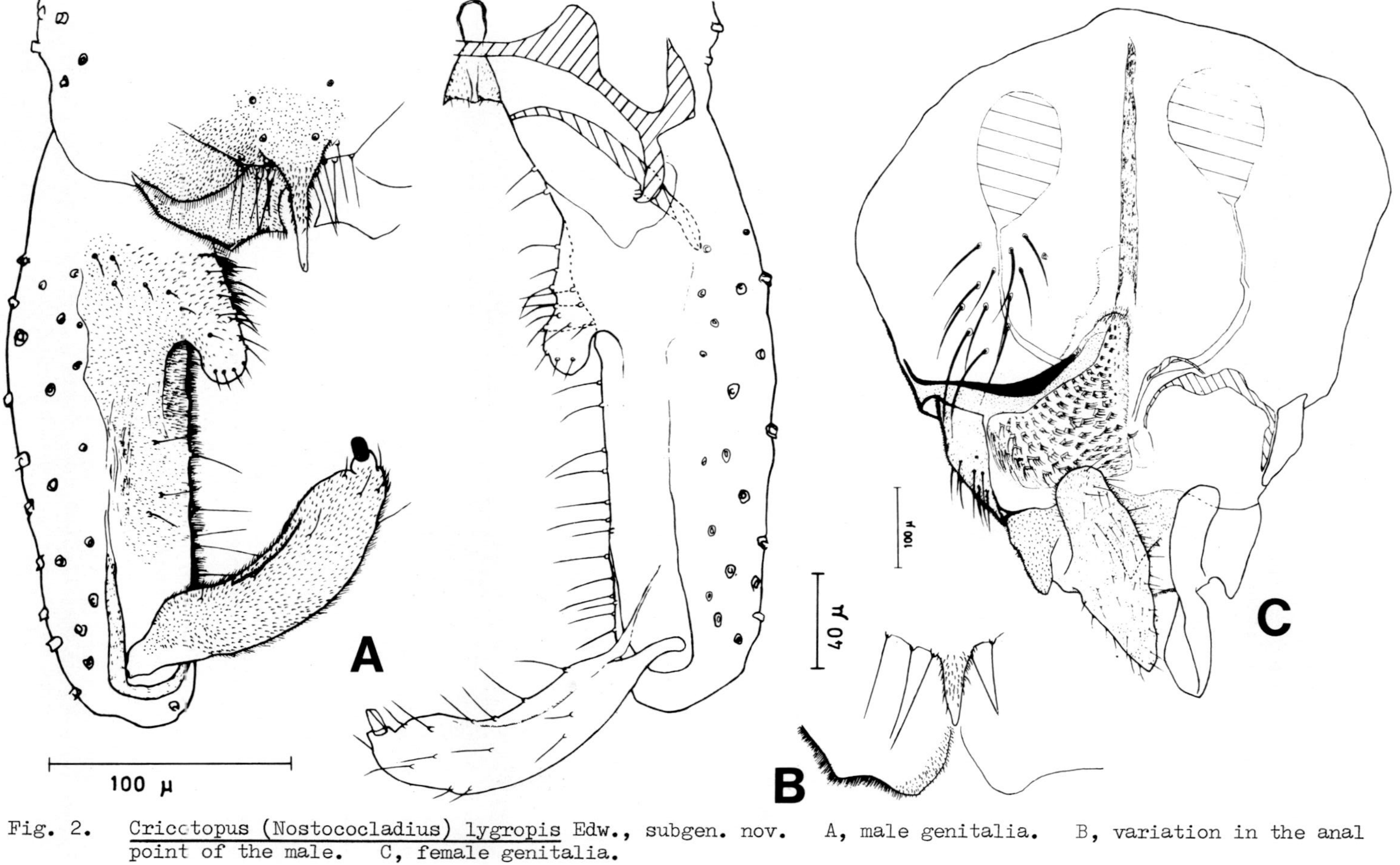

Fig. 2. Cricotopus (Nostococladius) lygropis Edw., subgen. nov. A, male genitalia. B, variation in the anal point of the male. C, female genitalia.

dorsocentral setae and one supra-alar seta present on each side of the thorax.

Abdomen. Abdominal segments pale brown. Tergite 1 with weakly developed shagreen, tergites II - VII with a characteristic continuous shagreen pattern over most of the surface (Fig. 3B), tergite IX with shagreen in the oral half. Pedes spurii A and B absent. Pleurites VI - VIII darkened. Anal lobes drawn out into a point, anal macrosetae absent (Fig. 4 A, B). Gonopodial sheaths in the male, in contrast to the female, extend well beyond the anal lobes. One seta is present on the inside of each anal lobe in the female, two such setae in the male.

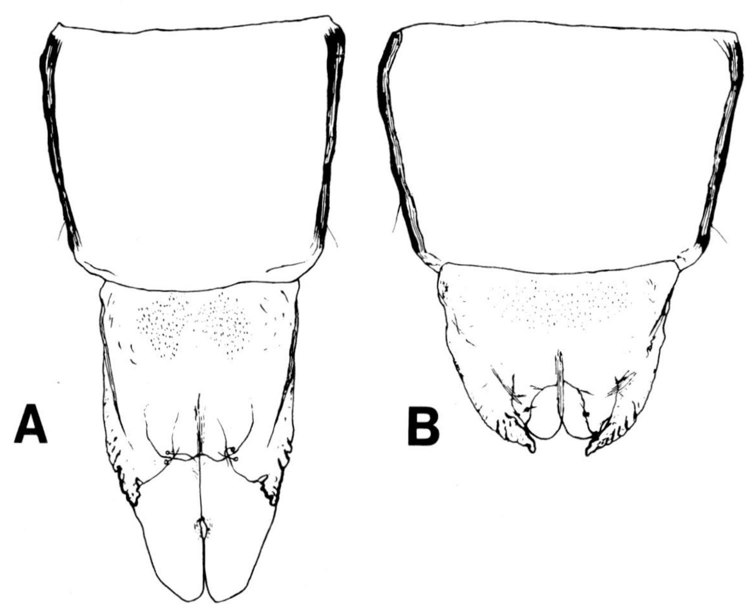

Fig. 4. Cricotopus (Nostococladius) lygropis Edw., subgen. nov., tergites VIII - IX of pupa. A, male. B, female. (Shagreen, present on tergite VIII is not illustrated).

Larva (Fourth Instar).

Total length 6.0 - 6.4 mm.

Head. Dark brown to black. Head capsule length 0.51 - 0.54 mm. Antenna 5 - segmented and reduced (Fig. 5A). Lengths of antennal segments (µ): 28 - 30, 12 - 14, 4.7 - 5.8, 2.8, 2.3. Antennal ratio 1.28 - 1.36. Ring organ in apical half of the first segment. Antennal blade slightly higher than segments 2 - 5 combined, Lauterborn's organs absent. S_1 setae of labrum bifid, S_{11} and S_{111} simple (Fig. 5B). Pecten epipharyngis with a reduced middle spine, the two lateral spines are of equal length and slightly broadened (Fig. 5B). Premandibles 39 µ broad, 51 - 58 µ long with two apical teeth. Mandibles with four teeth, both the seta interna and the seta subdentalis present (Fig. 5D). Mandible 135 - 152 µ long. Maxilla as in Fig. 5C. Mentum with a broad middle tooth and five or six lateral teeth (Fig. 5E).

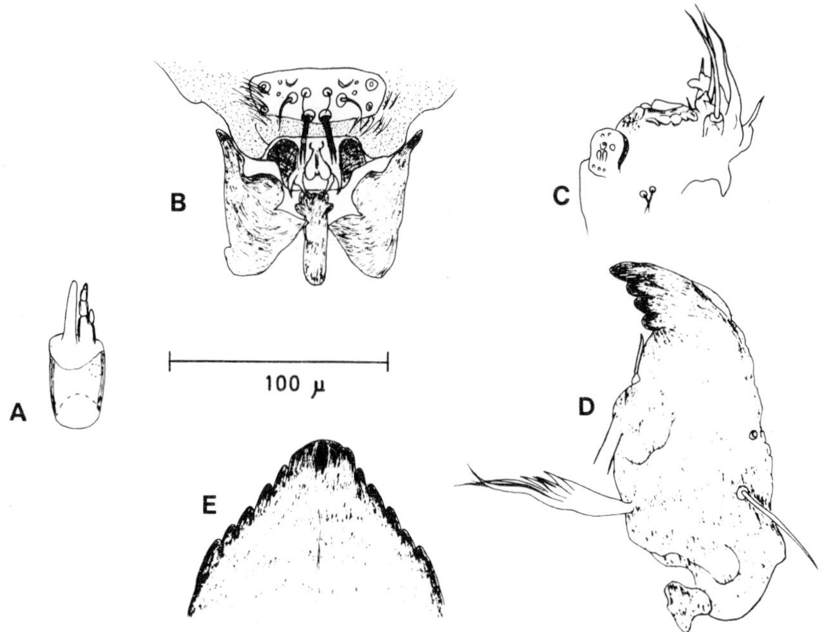

Fig. 5. Cricotopus (Nostococladius) lygropis Edw., subgen. nov., larva. A, antenna. B, labrum. C, maxilla. D, mandible. E, mentum.

Abdomen. In living material the abdominal segments of the larvae are yellow and the thoracic segments purple. Very few setae are present and lateral brush - hairs (Borstenbüschel of Hirvenoja, 1973 : 67) are absent. Anal tubules present. Procerci very short with seven setae. Procerci 8 - 9 µ high. Parapods well developed.

Material of C. (N.) lygropis, larvae, pupal exuviae and adults (on slides and in alcohol), is deposited in the National Museum, Natural History Division, Kildare St., Dublin 2 (Reg. No. N.M.I. 218 : 1979).

ECOLOGY AND DISTRIBUTION

This species is previously only known with certainty from England (Edwards, l.c., Fittkau and Reiss, 1978), but it is probably also present in Sweden (Brundin, l.c.). Larvae and pupae have been found living exclusively within colonies of the blue-green alga Nostoc parmelioides Kutz. in the River Flesk near Killarney, S.W. Ireland. An examination of the gut contents show that the larvae feed on the alga. Pupal exuviae have also been found in the River Maine, a river approximately 14 km. to the north of Killarney. The emergence period extends from April to October. N. parmelioides is recorded from Ireland for the first time.

The occurrence of chironomid larvae within colonies of the blue-green alga Nostoc in North America was noted by Johannsen (1937) who recorded larvae as "Spaniotoma sp. G". Wirth (1957) described two species of Cricotopus, C. nostocicola and C. fuscatus from California and states (loc. cit.) that the larva of these species are indistinguishable from those of "Spaniotoma sp. G".

Brock (1960) described in detail the ecology of *C. nostocicola* and *C. fuscatus*. The description of the immature stages of *C. nostocicola* and *C. fuscatus* differs in some respects from *Nostococladius* - in the Nearctic material thoracic horns were not observed. In addition, the presence of dorsally directed black spines on tergite IX of the pupa differs markedly from *C. (N.) lygropis*. A re-examination of the Nearctic material seems desirable.

The type material of *lygropis* was obtained by Edwards (loc. cit.) from Rydal, Westmoreland, in England. Recently Holmes and Whitton (1975) recorded *Cricotopus* species living in *Nostoc* in streams in the north-east of England but it is not known if these belong to *Nostococladius*. The occurrence of "*Cricotopus* sp." larvae in similar habitat is also known for North Germany (Reiss and Fittkau, pers. comm.).

SYSTEMATIC PLACEMENT OF *NOSTOCOCLADIUS* SUBGEN. NOV.

In the light of the present descriptions of the juvenile stages it is necessary to revise Hirvenoja's (loc. cit. p.66) provisional phylogenetic placement of the *lygropis* group. When the juveniles were unknown *lygropis* was tentatively placed within the subgenus *Cricotopus s. str*. However, it is now clear, because of the even distribution of shagreen on the pupal abdominal tergites and the "buckelförmig" appendage 1 of the adult, that the placement of *lygropis* within *Cricotopus s. str*. is no longer tenable. Likewise it is apparent that the group cannot be placed within *Isocladius* because of the absence of pupal anal macrosetae and the presence of the anal point in the male hypopygium. The unique apomorphy for *lygropis* is the arrangement of the pecten epipharyngis. In *Cricotopus* s. str. all three spines are of similar size, in *Isocladius* the two lateral spines are reduced while in *lygropis* the median spine is reduced.

Based on these observations the *lygropis* group sensu Hirvenoja merits the status of subgenus here established as *Nostococladius*. A full phylogenetic placement of the subgenus within *Cricotopus s. lat*. v.d. Wulp must, however, await examination of the Nearctic material.

ACKNOWLEDGEMENTS

The authors wish to express their thanks to Prof. O. A. Saether, Zool. Museum, Bergen, Norway; to Dr. H. Heuff, Forest and Wildlife Service, Bray, Co. Wicklow for identifying *Nostoc parmelioides*. Thanks are also due to Mr. M. Foster for aid in preparation of the figures.

REFERENCES

Brock, E.M. (1960). Mutualism between the midge *Cricotopus* and the alga *Nostoc*. *Ecology* *41* : 474 - 483.

Brundin, L. (1947). Zur Kenntnis der schwedischen Chironomiden. *Ark. Zool.* *39*: 1 - 95.

Edwards, F.W. (1929). British non-biting midges (Diptera, Chironomidae). *Trans. R. ent. Soc. Lond.* *77* : 279 - 430.

Fittkau, E. J. and F. Reiss (1978). Chironomidae. In J. Illies (Ed.), *Limnofauna Europea*, Gustav Fischer Verlag, Stuttgart. pp. 404 - 440.

Hirvenoja, M. (1973). Revision der Gattung *Cricotopus* van der Wulp und ihrer Verwandten (Diptera, Chironomidae). *Ann. Zool. Fenn.* *10* : 1 - 363.

Holmes, N. J. and B. A. Whitton (1975). Notes on some macroscopic algae new or seldom recorded for Britain. *Vasculum* *60* (3) : 47 - 55.

Johannsen, O.A. (1937a). Aquatic Diptera III Chironomidae : Subfamilies Tanypodinae, Diamesinae and Orthocladiinae. Mem. Cornell Univ. agric. Exp. Stn. 205 : 3 - 84.

Saether, O.A. (1976). Revision of Hydrobaenus, Trissocladius, Zalutschia, Paratrissocladius and some related genera (Diptera : Chironomidae). Bull. Fish. Res. Bd. Can. 195 : 1 - 287.

Wirth, W. W. (1957). The species of Cricotopus midges living in the blue-green alga Nostoc in California (Diptera : Tendipedidae). Pan - Pacif. Ent. 33 : 121 - 126.

Preliminary Notes Concerning the Revision of the Genus Dicrotendipes Kieff.

R. Lichtenberg

Naturhistorisches Museum Wien, 2. Zoologische Abt. Burgring 7, P.O. Box 417, A-1014 Wien, Austria

ABSTRACT

Up to now we know about 40 to 50 species of the genus Dicrotendipes from the palaearctic, nearctic, ethiopian and neotropical region. The revision will start with the palaearctic species.

Nearly one third of the species or socalled varieties - still mentioned by Goetghebuer (1937) and Lenz (1957) in Lindner: "Die Fliegen der palaearktischen Region" - are now considered as synonyms or are uncertain species. Goetghebuer (1937) separates Limnochironomus and Dicrotendipes. Freeman (1955, 1957) places Limnochironomus into the synonymy of Dicrotendipes.

The genus Dicrotendipes had been described by Kieffer (1913) from Eastern Africa. As character separating this genus from all other genera he mentions the appendices inferiores of the male hypopygium, which are bifurcated. In 1920 Kieffer described the genus Limnochironomus and named as character of the genus the long, narrow and strongly curved appendices inferiores, which have a simple or an incompletely bi- or trifid end.

Regarding the hypopygia indeed two forms can be distinguished: those with simple or incomplete bi- or trifid appendices inferiores and those with a bifurcation of the appendices inferiores. Considering the synonymy of Limnochironomus and Dicrotendipes as correct, the bifurcation of the appendices inferiores as to be seen in Dicrotendipes pallidicornis, Dicrotendipes peringueyanus, Dicrotendipes pilosimanus and Dicrotendipes fusconotatus can be interpreted as a continuation of a tendency towards bifurcation. This tendency is indicated frequently in species with simple appendices inferiores at least by the position of bristles.

The geographic distribution of Dicrotendipes in Europe shows, that species with bifurcated appendices inferiores seem to have their distribution in southern and southeastern regions of Europe. A possible contradiction may be found in the fact, that Dicrotendipes pallidicornis has been collected in England recently.

Three Female Chironomid Genitalia (Diptera)

O. A. Saether

Freshwater Institute, Winnipeg, Man., Canada and Museum of Zoology, University of Bergen, N-5014 Bergen/U., Norway

ABSTRACT

The female genitalia of *Habrobaenus hudsoni* Sæth., *Omisus pica* Town., and *Polypedilum* (*Tripodura*) *pardus* Town. are described for the first time. *Habrobaenus* Sæth. has long gonocoxites IX (as in *Cardiocladius* Kieff.) and undivided tergite IX and gonapophyses VIII. The genitalia and immatures of *Omisus* Town. indicate close relationship with *Lauterborniella* Bause not, as stated previously, with *Microtendipes* Kieff. *P. pardus* essentially is a typical member of the subgenus *Tripodura* Town.

KEYWORDS

Chironomidae, female genitalia, phylogenetic placement, *Habrobaenus*, *Omisus*, *Polypedilum*.

INTRODUCTION

Sæther (1977a) completed a comparative morphological study of the female genitalia, gave a generic key to females, and discussed the phylogenetic implications. The hierarchy were further discussed by Sæther (1979). Since the publication of the first paper, Rodova (1978) has presented a generic and specific key to several female Chironomini. The male and the pupa of the genus *Habrobaenus* Sæth. were described by Sæther (1977b). The genus *Omisus* Town. (Townes 1945 p. 27, Beck and Beck 1970 p. 29) is of importance in understanding the relationships of the more plesiomorphic genera of the tribe Chironomini. However, its female was not available at the time of the comparative study. The present paper describe the genitalia of the tentatively associated female of *Habrobaenus hudsoni* Sæth., of the associated female of *Omisus pica* Town., as well as that of *Polypedilum* (*Tripodura*) *pardus* Town.

The general terminology follows that of Sæther (1974, 1976, 1977a).

HABROBAENUS SÆTHER, 1977b P. 2354
(Fig. 1 A - D)

The female described is from the same sample as some males of *Habrobaenus hudsoni*. The characteristic features such as strong pulvilli, no trace of acrostichals, antepronotal lobes meeting at a point only, and the strong punctation of microtrichia on the wing membrane, tell that the female can belong only to *Habrobaenus* or *Parachaetocladius* (Wülk.). Unfortunately, the same samples contain also pupae and males of *Parachaetocladius*. However, although the males of *Parachaetocladius* and *Habrobaenus* are very similar (Sæther, 1969 fig. 49 - 51, 1977b fig. 1), *Parachaetocladius* according to the diagnosis (Sæther, 1969 p. 96) has preepisternals and anepisternals which both are lacking in *Habrobaenus*.

Generic Diagnosis of Female Genitalia

Gonocoxapodeme VIII broad, but not well delineated. Gonapophysis VIII undivided, apparently two-layered, rounded. Apodeme lobe indistinct, but relatively large, oval. Tergite IX medium large, undivided caudally, transversely divided by a sclerotized apodeme at basal third; area basad of apodeme rectangular, void of setae, but covered with microtrichia; area apicad of apodeme pointed, triangular, with numerous setae. Gonocoxite IX conspicuously long, lobelike, reaching level of base of cerci. Coxosternapodeme curved, normal. Segment X and postgenital plate normal. Cerci relatively short, broad.

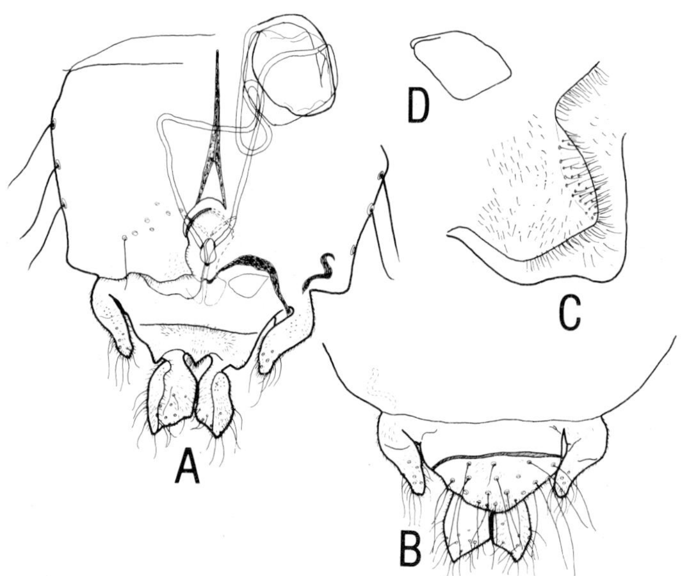

Fig. 1. *Habrobaenus hudsoni* Sæth., female genitalia. A, ventral view. B, dorsal view. C, dorsomesal lobe. D, apodeme lobe.

Labia relatively long, bare. Seminal capsules large, oval or nearly circular, void of microtrichia. Spermathecal ducts looped without bulbs before separate openings.

Systematics

Sæther (1977b) based on the male and the pupa and the trends used in Sæther (1976) regarded *Habrobaenus* as a possible sistergroup of *Trissocladius* Kieff. However, judging on the female genitalia the phylogenetic placement is more ambiguous. In the key to female Orthocladiinae in Sæther (1977a p. 87) the female would key to couplet 34. Since tergite IX is relatively large and triangular and the wing membrane has coarse punctation of microtrichia the key do not lead further. Disregarding the coarse punctation the key lead to couplet 35. Also this couplet causes problems since both gonapophysis VIII and tergite IX are undivided and the latter is relatively large and triangular. Emphasizing tergite IX the key leads to couplet 36 with the *Hydrobaenus lugubris* Fries group, while regarding the undivided gonapophysis VIII as more important leads to couplet 38 with *Eukiefferiella* Thien. If the triangular shape of tergite IX is disregarded in couplet 34, however, the key leads to couplet 56 with *Cardiocladius* Kieff. Lastly, if the presence of a hind tibial comb in couplet 9 is disregarded, the female keys to couplet 17 with *Baeoctenus* Sæth.

In the scheme of argumentation (Sæther, 1977a fig. 36) the genus apparently is synapomorphous for trends 73, 71 and 69. For trends 67 and 68 no judgments can be made and the genus could belong with "Cardiocladiini" (*Cardiocladius, Tokunagaia* Sæth. and *Eukiefferiella*). If the dorsomesal lobe is regarded as secondarily fused with the ventrolateral lobe and the anal macrosetae of the pupa as secondarily lost, the trends could lead to the same result as stated originally, i.e. to the *Hydrobaenus* group of genera where the genus might form a possible sister group of *Trissocladius*. It is, however, necessary to know the larva in order to follow the synapomorphic diagram. The general appearance of the male and the pupa suggest that the genus is related to *Trissocladius*. Such a relationship, however necessitates that apparent plesiomorphies in reality are secondarily changed apomorphies. Without these suppositions the genus appear related to *Cardiocladius*.

Description of Female *Habrobaenus hudsoni* Sæth. (Fig. 1 A - D)

Generally as in male except larger size (wing lenght 2.21 mm), higher chaetotaxy, and below measurements.

Antenna with 6 flagellomeres. AR 0.29. Temporal setae 14. Coronal suture undivided, 97 mµ long. Clypeus with 11 setae. Thorax with 20 dorsocentrals. Wing with 25 setae on R, 16 on R_1, 28 on R_{4+5}, and 18 on squama.

Sternite VIII with 13 median and 3 larger setae to each side. Tergite VIII with 35 setae. Tergite IX with 24 setae. Gonocoxite IX with 10 setae. Cercus 93 mµ long. Notum 121 mµ long. Seminal capsules 116 mµ long, 93 mµ wide.

Material examined: Female, Swift Creek, Kershaw Co., U.S. Hwy 521 south of Camden, South Carolina, 12 XII 1976, P. L. Hudson.

OMISUS TOWNES, 1945 P. 27

(Fig. 2 A - F)

Generic Diagnosis of Female Genitalia

Gonocoxapodeme VIII strong, nearly straight, ends on gonapophysis VIII. Gonapophysis VIII with well developed dorsomesal lobe and very small and far lateral ventrolateral lobe. Apodeme lobe weak, but relatively long. Tergite IX undivided; occassionally with median reticulation, paler mesocaudal area, and setae concentrated on lateral halves, i.e. indications of division. Gonocoxite IX with a few short and a few longer setae. Segment X with setae. Postgenital plate well developed, apically truncate to broadly rounded. Cerci of moderate size.

Labia bare. Seminal capsules ovoid; with triangular, weakly sclerotized, caudolateral neck. Spermathecal ducts straight.

Systematics

Sæther (1977a, fig. 62) tentatively placed *Omisus* together with *Microtendipes* Kieff. primarily on the base of the immatures as described by Beck and Beck (1970). However, judging from the female genitalia and a reexamination of the immatures, *Omisus* clearly is most closely related to *Lauterborniella* Bause sensu Townes (i.e. including *Zavreliella* Kieff. as a subgenus). The ventrolateral lobe in fact, appear intermediate between that of *L.* (*Z.*) *varipennis* (Coq.) as illustrated in Sæther (1977a, fig. 73 D, F) and that of *L.* (*Z.*) *marmorata* (v.d. Wulp) as illustrated by Rodova (1978, fig. 41).

In the key to female Chironomini *Omisus* tentatively is placed in couplet 22 with *Microtendipes*. It should be deleted from that couplet and second part of couplet 26 should be changed to:

Five or six flagellomeres, when six hind tibia with one spur.

Couplet 33 should be changed to:

33a.	Four flagellomeres	*Pedionemus* Subl.
	Five or six flagellomeres	33b
33b.	Six flagellomeres	*Omisus* Town.
	Five flagellomeres	*Polypedilum* Kieff., pro parte.

The scheme of argumentation for the Chironominae (Sæther, 1977a p. 131 - 139) is in error in trends 53 as the thoracic horn of the pupa of *Lauterborniella* may have only two branches. *Omisus* apparently have 4 (perhaps 6 ?) branches. Trends 53, 54, 47, 48, 41, 42 and 45 show *Omisus* as the plesiomorphic sister genus of *Lauterborniella*. The median notch on mentum in some larval specimens of *Omisus* pica town. mentioned by Sæther (1977a p. 135) should probably not be regarded as a reduced tooth. The larval pecten epipharyngis not described by Beck and Beck (1970) is illustrated in fig. 2 F. It consists of 3 toothed scales and *Omisus* thus is synapomorphous for trends 47. Beck and Beck (1970) give the number of pupal L-setae on segments V - VIII as 3 - 3 - 4 - 5. The specimens seen (including one of Beck and Beck) all has L-setae as 3 - 4 - 4 - 5.

Possible synapomorphies for *Lauterborniella* and *Omisus* are the median reticulation of tergite IX in *Lauterborniella* and in some specimens of *Omisus* (Fig. 2 C), the oval patches on pupal abdominal tergites (on II - VI in *Lauterborniella*, II - V in

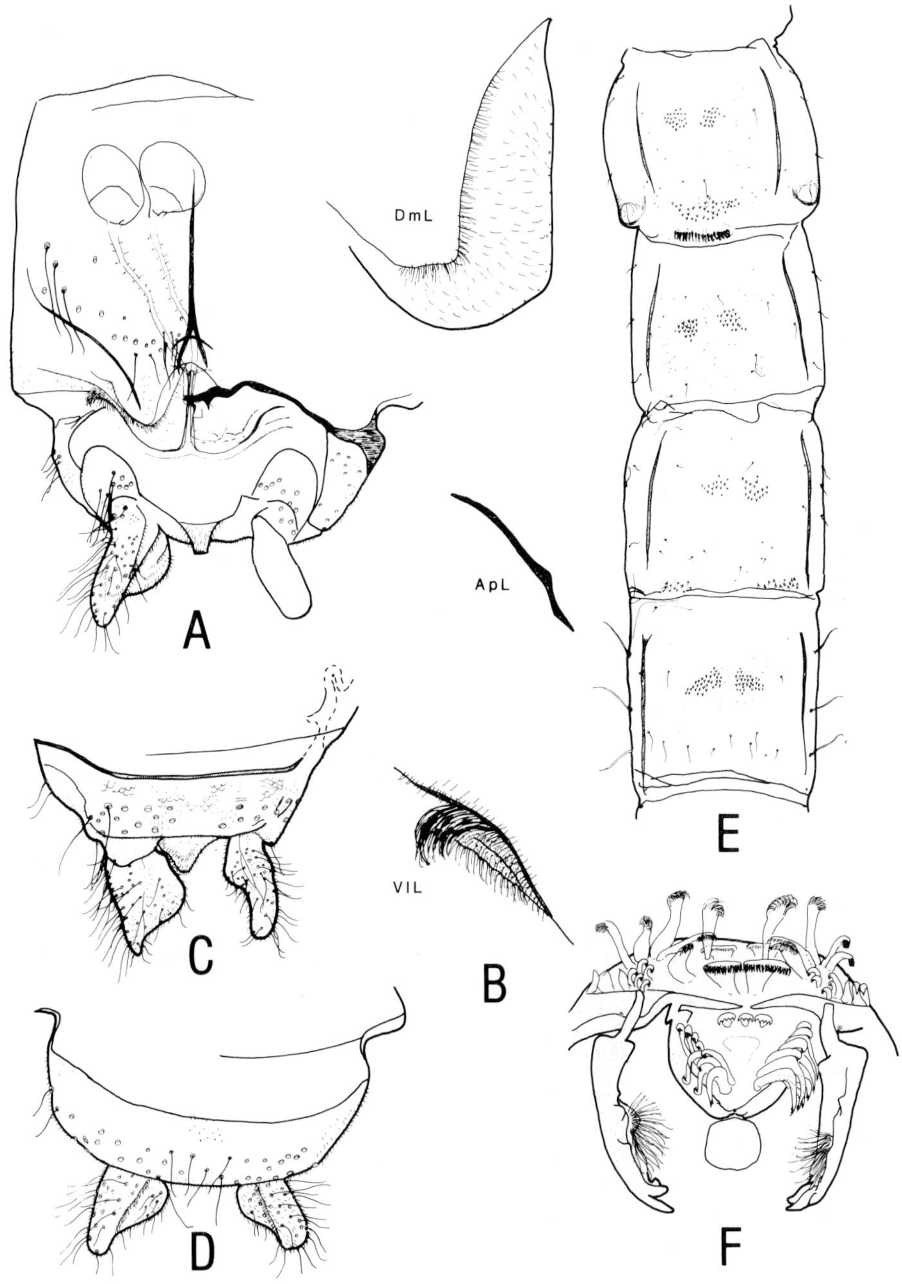

Fig. 2. *Omisus pica* Town. A - D, female genitalia; A, ventral view; B, gonapophysis VIII, dorsomesal lobe (DmL), apodeme lobe (ApL), and ventrolateral lobe (VlL); C - D, ventral view. E, pupa, tergites II - V. F, larval labrum.

Omisus (Fig. 2 E), and possibly the alternating Lauterborn organs (see Sæther 1977a p. 136), and the mentum with the second lateral teeth longer than adjacent teeth. (The same configuration of mentum, however, is found in the related *Pagastiella* Brund. and *Polypedilum* Kieff.) Symplesiomorphies for *Omisus* and *Lauterborniella* as compared to their sistergroup are the small ventrolateral lobe and the large Lauterborn organs.

Description of Female Genitalia of *Omisus pica* Town. (Fig. 2 A - D)(n=2)

Sternite VIII with 44 - 47 setae. Tergite VIII with 29 - 32 setae. Gonocoxite IX with 3 short and 2 - 4 longer setae. Segment X with 9 - 11 setae on each side. Cercus 176 - 187 mμ long. Notum 191 - 218 mμ long. Seminal capsules 101 - 116 mμ long, 81 - 89 mμ wide.

Material examined: Two females, one with associated pupa, emergence traps, Long Bay, South Indian Lake, Manitoba, 17 - 20 VI and 27 - 29 VI 1977, B. Bilyj; male reared from larva, Lake Susan, Lake Co, Florida, 14 VII 1961, W. M. and E. C. Beck.

POLYPEDILUM (*TRIPODURA*) *PARDUS* Town. (n=1)
(Fig. 3 A - D)

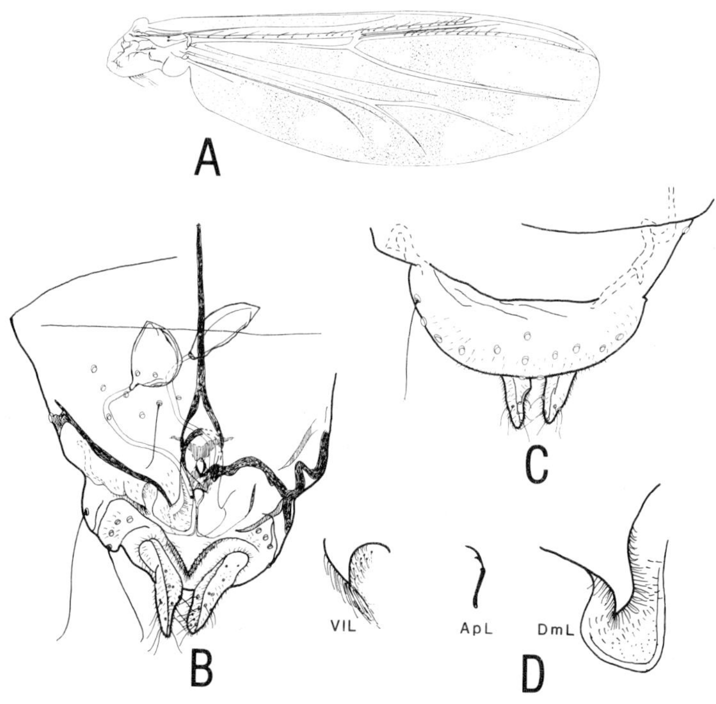

Fig. 3. *Polypedilum* (*Tripodura*) *pardus* Town., female. A, wing. B - D, female genitalia; B, ventral view; C, dorsal view; D, gonapophysis VIII, dorsomesal lobe (DmL), apodeme lobe (ApL), and ventrolateral lobe (VlL).

The illustrated female is easily identifiable by means of the characteristic and distinct wing pattern. The genitalia conforms with the generic and subgeneric diagnoses for *Polypedilum* and *Tripodura* Town. given by Sæther (1977a p. 165). They resemble the genitalia illustrated for *P.* (*I.*) *simulans* (Town.) (Sæther, 1977 a fig. 76 E - F) except that the microtrichia of the ventrolateral lobe are directed more caudad.

Sternite VIII has 17 setae, tergite VIII about 23, tergite IX 13, gonocoxite IX 2, and segment X 5 setae to each side. The cercus is 81 mμ and notum 121 mμ long. The seminal capsules are 51 mμ long, 39 mμ wide.

The exquisite wing coloration reminds of *Lauterborniella perpulcher* (Mitch.) (Townes 1945 p. 22), a species which probably do not belong in *Lauterborniella* and perhaps could be placed in an emended *Polypedilum*.

Material examined: Female, Tinker Creek, Savannah River Plant, Aiken Co., South Carolina, 8 VIII 1977, P. L. Hudson.

ACKNOWLEDGEMENTS

I am much indebted to Mr. P. L. Hudson, Southeast Reservoir Investigations, Clemson, S. C., for the females of *Habrobaenus hudsoni* and *Polypedilum* (*Tripodura*) *pardus*; to Mr. B. Bilyj, Freshwater Institute, Winnipeg, Man., for the females of *Omisus pica*; to Dr. W. M. Beck, Tallahassen, Fla., for a male of *O. pica* reared from larva; and to my wife, Mrs. U. Sæther,for making the drawings.

REFERENCES

Beck, W. M. and Beck, E. C. (1970). The immature stages of some Chironomini (Chironomidae). *Q. Jl Fla Acad. Sci 35*, 29 - 42.

Rodova, R. A. (1978). *Opredelitelj samok komarov-zvonzov Tribyj Chironomini* (*Diptera, Chironomidae*). (Determination key for female midges of the tribe Chironomini (Diptera, Chironomidae.) (In Russian.) *Inst. Akad. Nauk SSSR*, 145 pp.

Sæther, O. A. (1969). Some Nearctic Podonominae, Diamesinae, and Orthocladiinae (Diptera: Chironomidae). *Bull. Fish. Res. Bd Can. 170*, 154 pp.

Sæther, O. A. (1974). Morphology and terminology of female genitalia in Chironomidae (Diptera). *Ent. Tidskr. Suppl. 95*, 216 - 224.

Sæther, O. A. (1976). Revision of *Hydrobaenus, Trissocladius, Zalutschia, Paratrissocladius* and some related genera. (Diptera: Chironomidae). *Bull. Fish. Res. Bd Can. 195*, 287 pp.

Sæther, O. A. (1977a). Female genitalia in Chironomidae and other Nematocera: morphology, phylogenies, keys. *Bull. Fish. Res. Bd Can. 197*, 209 pp.

Sæther, O. A. (1977b). *Habrobaenus hudsoni* n. gen., n. sp. and the immatures of *Baeoctenus bicolor* Sæther (Diptera: Chironomidae). *J. Fish. Res. Bd Can. 34*, 2354 - 2361.

Sæther, O. A. (1979). Hierarchy of the Chironomidae with special emphasis on the female genitalia. *Ent. scand. Suppl. 10*, 17-26.

Townes, H. K. (1945). The nearctic species of Tendipedini (Diptera; Tendipedidae (=Chironomidae)). *Am. Midl.Nat. 34*, 1 - 206.

A Checklist of the Chironomidae (Diptera) of the Killarney Valley Catchment Area Ireland

D. J. Douglas* and D. A. Murray**

*Science Dept., Regional Technical College, Dundalk, Co. Louth, Ireland
**Zoology Dept., University College, Belfield, Stillorgan Rd., Dublin 4, Ireland

ABSTRACT

A study of the Chironomidae (Diptera) of the Killarney Valley catchment area dur- the period 1971 to 1974 gives a list of one hundred and forty two species. Twenty three of these are new records to the Irish fauna. A taxonomic list of the species with appended notes on distribution and time of capture is given.

KEYWORDS

Chironomidae; Diptera; Irish fauna; checklist; Killarney.

INTRODUCTION

This paper records the species of Chironomidae taken in the Killarney Valley catchment area and is based on collections taken during the period October 1971 to September 1974. Earlier studies on the Irish Chironomidae indicate that some two hundred and forty species are known to occur in Ireland (Fahy and Murray, 1972; Murray 1972, 1974). Prior to this investigation, however, only thirty six species were recorded from the Killarney region. This region, which proved so fruitful to taxonomists in other arthropod groups e.g. Bullock (1928), Halbert (1935) etc., has long been neglected by chironomid specialists. Twenty species were recorded by Edwards (1929) including one *Stenochironomus hibernicus* Edw. described on material collected in the Killarney region. The remaining fifteen species were recorded from L. Kilbrean, some four km. north east of Killarney town, by Bracken and Murray (1973).

During this investigation comparative studies were carried out on the biota of the three main lakes i.e. Upper Lake, Muckross Lake and Lough Leane and the rivers Flesk and Laune. In addition, material was obtained from a number of other locations in the catchment area. Approximately one thousand quantitative larval collections were taken using Eckmann grabs. A large amount of this quantitative larval material was retained alive for rearing purposes. In other areas only qualitative sampling was carried out. Adult chironomids were obtained by net sweeps, and by the use of both floating and submerged insect emergence traps on the lakes. Representative samples were mounted according to the methods of Schlee (1966).

Collections were made from a total of forty two locations. A list of these locations together with their Irish grid reference number is given (Table 1). The approximate positions of the locations are shown (Fig. 1).

TABLE 1 Location of Sampling Stations

Location	Map Ref.	Location	Map Ref.
Lough Leane		Muckross Lake	
1 Laune Exit	900910	17 Camilan Bay	943859
2 Fossa	907913	18 Colleen Bawn	950857
3 Mahony's Point	932912	19 Kilbeg Bay	960860
4 Victoria Bay	946900	20 Dundag Bay	964858
5 Ross Bay	945890	21 Goleen Bay	963853
6 Castlelough a	966866	22 Dinis	939850
7 Castlelough b	975873	23 Open Water	950850
8 Bog Bay	963866		
9 Juniper Bay	949863	24 Doolough	949861
10 Peninsula Bay	940860		
11 Brickeen	937858	Upper Lake	
12 Glena Bay	930858	25 Tunnel	918818
13 O'Sullivans	915888	26 S/W Shore	891817
14 Inishfallen	933893	27 Open Water	910821
15 Open water	930883		
16 Cow Island	925897	28 L. Guitane	025847
29 L. Reagh	820808	36 Station 3	978900
30 Cushvalley L.	875863	37 Station 4	965894
31 L. Kilbrean	003933		
River Laune		Torc Cascade	
32 Station 1	891912	38 Station 1	962847
33 Station 2	880920	39 Station 2	964835
		40 Station 3	959830
River Flesk		41 Station 4	965824
34 Station 1	036876		
35 Station 2	987904	42 Owenreagh R.	875798

CHECKLIST

Tanypodinae

Ablabesmyia longistyla Fitt. Loc. 2,3,4,6,20,24,35; July to September

A. monilis (L.) Loc. 5,6,11,18,20,27,35; May to September.

A. phatta (Egg.) Loc. 6,20; July to September.

Arctopeolpia griseipennis (v.d. Wulp) Loc. 2,3,4,6,11,13,19,20,31,33,35; March to September

Clinotanypus nervosus Meig. Loc. 20; July

Conchapelopia melanops (Weid.) Loc. 4,10,20,36; July, August, October.

C. pallidula (Meig.) Loc. 20,32,33,35,37,39; July to October.

C. viator (Kieff.) Loc. 33,35; June, July, August.

*Guttipelopia guttipennis** (v.d. Wulp) Loc. 24; May, June.

Larsia atrocincta var. Innaren (Goetgh.) Loc. 20; July, September.

Macropelopia goetghebueri (Kieff.) Loc. 9,20,28; May, July, October.

M. nebulosa (Meig.) Loc. 35; July.

M. notata (Meig.) Loc. 4,19,32; August, September.

Natarsia nugax (Walk.) Loc. Bracken and Murray (1973).

Nilotanypus dubius (Meig.) Loc. 35; August.

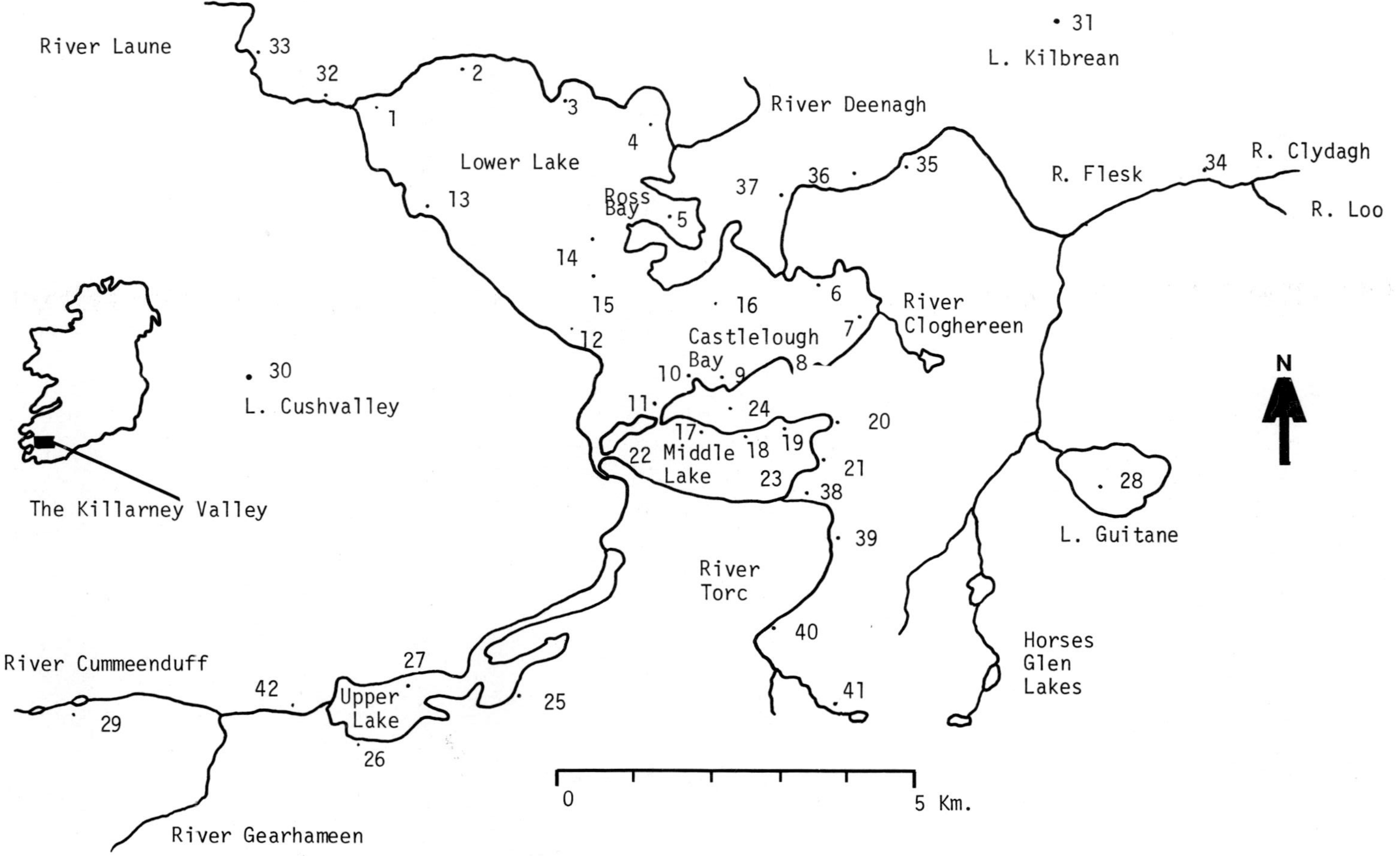

Fig. 1. Location of sampling stations in the Killarney area.

Paramerina cingulata (Walk.) Loc. 8; July.
P. divisa (Walk.) Loc. 36; July.
Procladius choreus (Meig.) Loc. 5; March, April.
*P. barbatus** Brund. Loc. 11,13; April.
*P. signatus** Zett. Loc. 6; September.
P. cfr. crassinervis Zett. Loc. 6,11,20,24; April, June, July.
*Psilotanypus albinervis** Kieff. Loc. 6,9,24; June, July, August.
P. flavifrons Edw. Loc. 6,7; June.
*Rheopelopia maculipennis** (Zett.) Loc. 35; June, July, August.
*Tanypus punctipennis** Meig. Loc. 5; July.
Thienemannimyia northumbrica (Edw.) Loc. 6,11,20,32; July to September.
T. pseudocarnea Murr. Loc. 35,36; July, August.
Zavrelimyia hirtimana (Kieff.) Loc. 9; May.
Buchonomyiinae
Buchonomyia thienemanni Fitt. Loc. 35; July.
Diamesinae
Potthastia gaedii (Meig.) Loc. 12,20,23,27,33,36; August, September.
Protanypus morio (Zett.) Loc. 13,15,16,23,28; February to May, July and October.
Prodiamesiinae
Prodiamesa olivacea (Meig.) Loc. 20,30,37; July.
Orthocladiinae
Acricotopus lucens Staeg. Loc. 11; December.
Brillia longifurca Kieff. Loc. 37; August.
B. modesta (Meig.) Loc. 18,24,35; May, July, September.
Cardiocladius fuscus Kieff. Loc. 11,15,23; June, July.
Corynoneura lobata Edw. Loc. 20,21; June and October.
Cricotopus (Cricotopus) bicinctus Meig. Loc. 6; July.
C. (C.) festivellus Kieff. Loc. 26,35; May, August.
*C. (C.) fuscus** (Kieff.) Loc. 11,14,31; May, June, July.
C. (C.) pulchripes Verral Loc. 42; July.
C. (C.) tibialis (Meig.) Loc. 6,20; June, July, August.
C. (C.) tremulus (L.) Loc. 35,36,42; March, May, August.
C. (C.) trifascia Edw. Loc. 1,6,24,34,35,36; July, September.
C. (Isocladius) sylvestris (Fab.) Loc. 20; October.
C. (I.) trifasciatus (Panz.) Loc. 11; June.
*C. (Nostococladius) lygropis** Edw. Loc. 35; July.
Epoicocladius flavens (Mall.) Loc. 20; May, June, August.
*Eukiefferiella bavarica** Goetgh. Loc. 35,40; July to September.
E. calvescens Edw. Loc. 40; March.
E. clypeata Kieff. Loc. 35; August.
*Eurycnemus crassipes** (Panz.) Loc. 36; July.
*Gymnometriocnemus brumalis** Edw. Loc. 8; January and March.
Heleniella ornaticollis (Edw.) Recorded by Edwards (1929).
Heterotanytarsus apicalis (Kieff.) Edwards (1929), Bracken and Murray (1973).
Heterotrissocladius grimshawi (Edw.) Edwards (1929).
H. marcidus (Walk.) Edwards (1929).
Limnophyes gurgicola Edw. Loc. 40; March.
L. minimus (Meig.) Loc. 7; April.
Metriocnemus fuscipes (Meig.) Loc. 20; January.
Nanocladius (Nanocladius) bicolor (Zett.) Loc. 15; July.
Orthocladius (Orthocladius) frigidus (Kieff.) Loc. 36,39,40; July, August.
O. (O.) oblidens Walk. Loc. 20,24; January, July.
Orthosmittia albipennis (Goetgh.) Edwards (1929).
Paracladius conversus (Walk.) Loc. 6; July.
Parakiefferiella bathophila Kieff. Loc. 26; May.
P. coronata Edw. Loc. 20; July.
Parametriocnemus stylatus (Kieff.) Loc. 17,35; March, August.

Paraphaenocladius impensus (Walk.) Loc. 11; May.
Paratrichocladius rufiventris (Meig.) Loc. 11,14; May.
Pogonocladius consobrinus (Holm.) Loc. 13; April.
Psectrocladius (Mesopsectrocladius) barbatipes Kieff. Loc. 18,20,25; June, July.
P. (Monopsectrocladius) calcaratus Edw. Loc. 6,11,20,28; June, July, October.
P. (Psectrocladius) barbimanus (Edw.) Loc. 20; July.
P. (P.) fennicus Stora Loc. 11,20; June, July.
P. (P.) psilopterus Kieff. Loc. 11; May, June.
P. (P.) sordidellus (Zett.) Loc. 20; August.
"Psectrocladius" turfaceus Kieff. Loc. 20; August.
Rheocricotopus chalybeatus Edw. Loc. 35; July.
*Smittia aquatilis** Goetgh. Loc. 29; Known only from larvae.
S. pratorum Goetgh. Loc. 20; January.
Synorthocladius semivirens (Kieff.) Loc. 3,11,20,29; July.
Thienemanniella flavescens Edw. Edwards (1929).
T. morosa Edw. Edwards (1929).
Chironominae
Chironomini
Chironomus anthracinus Zett. Loc. 11,13,14,15,16,17; March to May.
Cryptocladopelma viridula (L.) Loc. 11; July.
Demeijerea rufipes L. Loc. 6; July.
Demicryptochironomus vulneratus (Zett.) Loc. 6,9,13; April, May June.
Dicrotendipes lobiger (Kieff.) Loc. 25; May.
D. nervosus (Staeg.) Loc. 15,36; February, March, May, September.
D. notatus (Meig.) Loc. 5,15,35; February, May, August.
D. pulsus (Walk.) Loc. 14,15,18,20,25; May, June.
Endochironomus albipennis (Meig.) Loc. 4,5,6,9,21; May to July.
E. tendens Fab. Loc. 5,23; July.
Glyptotendipes gripekoveni Kieff. Loc. 20,26; May, June.
G. pallens (Meig.) Loc. 6; June.
G. viridis Macq. Loc. 6; June, July.
Kribioxenus brayi Goetgh. Loc. 5; July.
Microtendipes chloris (Meig.) Loc. 11,14,25; May.
M. pedellus (de Geer) Loc. 6,14,20,25,35; May, July.
*M. rydalensis** (Edw.) Loc. 35; June.
M. tarsalis Walk. Loc. 6; July.
Pagastiella orophila Edw. Loc. 20; July, August.
Parachironomus arcuatus Goetgh. Loc. 20; July, August.
*P. frequens** Joh. Loc. 6,7; July.
*P. parilis** Walk. Loc. 9; May.
*P. subalpinus** Goetgh. Loc. 6; June, July.
P. swammerdami Krus. Bracken and Murray (1973).
P. tenunicaudatus Mull. Loc. 6; June.
Paratendipes albimanus Meig. Loc. 35; August.
*Phaenopsectra coracina** (Zett.) Loc. 10,12,13,17,21,27; March, April
P. flavipes (Meig.) Loc. 9; May.
P. punctipes (Weid.) Loc. 20; July.
Polypedilum (Pentapedilum) nubens Edw. Loc. 20,21; June, July.
P. (P.) sordens (v.d. Wulp) Loc. 6,9,11,18,20,28; May, June, July, October.
P. (P.) tritum (Walk.) Loc. 18; July.
P. (Polypedilum) acutum Kieff. Loc. 6,20; July, August.
P. (P.) albicorne (Meig.) Loc. 11; May.
*P. (P.) arundinetum** Goetgh. Loc. 9; June.
P. (P.) nubeculosum (Meig.) Loc. 9; June.
P. (P.) pedestre (Meig.) Loc. 36; August.
P. (Tripodura) bicrenatum Kieff. Loc. 6; June.
P. (T.) pullum (Zett.) Loc. 20; June.
Stenochironomus gibbus Fabr. Loc. 9,17; May, June.

S. hibernicus Edw. Edwards (1929).
Stictochironomus pictulus (Meig.) Loc. 12,17; May, June.
S. rosenschöldi (Zett.) Loc. 9,23; May.
*Xenochironomus xenolabis** Kieff. Loc. 6; September.
Pseudochironomini
Pseudochironomus prasinatus (Staeg.) Loc. 1,2,6,7,11,20,21,25,36; June, July.
Tanytarsini
Cladotanytarsus mancus (Walk.) Edw. Loc. 6,20; May, June.
Micropsectra fusca Meig. Loc. 13; April.
Paratanytarsus inopertus (Walk.) Edw. Loc. 20; July.
P. laccophilus Edw. Loc. 6; July.
P. tenuis Meig. Loc. 20; September, October.
*Rheotanytarsus pentapoda** Kieff. Loc. 33,34,37,40; July, August.
*Stempellina bausei** (Kieff.) Loc. 7; August.
Stempellinella brevis (Edw.) Edwards (1929).
Tanytarsus bathophilus Kieff. Loc. 11; May.
T. gregarius Kieff. Loc. 7, 10,12,13,15,17,23,24; March, April.
T. lestagei Goetgh. Loc. 8,10,28; August, October.
*T. medius** Reiss and Fittkau Loc. 20,25; May, August.
*T. quadridentatus** Brund. Loc. 6; June.
T. signatus v.d. Wulp. Edwards (1929).

SPECIES IDENTIFIED

A total of one hundred and thirty species including twenty four species recorded by Edwards (1929) and Bracken and Murray (1973) were taken during this survey. There are, however, a further twelve species, recorded by these workers which were not encountered during this survey. The number of chironomid species known to occur in the Killarney region now stands at one hundred and forty two. One hundred and six species are recorded from the Killarney region for the first time and twenty three constitute additions to the Irish faunal list. In the list above, these new records are denoted by an asterisk*. The locations (abbreviated as Loc.) where the species were recorded are given and the month or months of capture are noted. The location numbers correspond to those in Table 1 and Fig. 1.

The majority of species were taken during the months from May to August. Some species were taken continuously; others were taken sporadically. It is difficult to state whether such records indicate the occurrence of more than one emergence period or are due to shortcomings in the sampling programme.

It should be borne in mind that although this survey extended over a three year period and collections were made, as far as possible, on at least a regular monthly basis, it would have been impossible to make extensive regular collections at all forty two locations due to the size of the area under investigation. The list, therefore, is incomplete and recent additional records for the area will be presented in another paper (Murray and Ashe, in prep.).

ACKNOWLEDGEMENT

Sincere thanks are extended to the officials and staff of the Bourn Vincent Memorial Park Killarney for the use of boats and permission to collect throughout the National Park. Sincere thanks also to Mr. P. Ashe for constructive comments.

REFERENCES

Bracken, J.J. and Murray, D.A. (1973). Insect emergence data from four small lakes in the South and Southwest of Ireland. *Irish Fish. Invest.*, Ser. A. 11, 3-17

Bullock, E. (1928). *Corixa dentipes* Thoms. in the Killarney District. *Ent. Mo. Mag.* LXIV, 117.

Edwards, F.W. (1929). British non-biting midges. *Trans. Ent. Soc. Lond.*, 77 (2), 279-430

Fahy, E. and Murray, D.A. (1972). Chironomidae from a small stream system in Western Ireland with a discussion of species composition of the group. *Ent. Tidskr.*, 93, 148-155.

Halbert, J.N. (1935). A list of Irish Hemiptera (Heteroptera and Cicadina). *Proc. Roy. Ir. Acad.*, XLII, B, No. 8, 211-318.

Murray, D. A. (1972). A list of the Chironomidae known to occur in Ireland with notes on their distribution. *Proc. Roy. Ir. Acad.*, 72 B (16), 275-293.

Murray, D.A. (1974). Notes on some Chironomidae (Diptera) from the Killarney area, Ireland. *Ent. Tidskr. Suppl.*, 95, 177-181.

Murray, D.A. (1976) *Buchonomyia thienemanni* Fitt. (Diptera Chironomidae), a rare and unusual species recorded from Killarney, Ireland. *Entomol. Gaz.*, 27, 179-180.

Schlee, D. (1966). Präparation an Chironomiden (Diptera). *Gewasser u. Abwässer*, 41/42, 169-193.

Preliminary Investigations on the Chironomidae (Insecta, Diptera) from Some Lotic Environments in Iran

C. Dowling

Zoology Department, University College Dublin

ABSTRACT

The Chironomid fauna of the rivers Karun and Zayanderud in Iran was investigated by a study of drifting pupal exuviae. A total of sixty-one taxa is recorded. The Tanypodinae, Orthocladiinae and Chironominae are well represented. The fauna is dominated by the Orthocladiinae. Some rare and interesting types are recorded and notes are given on taxonomic difficulties encountered.

KEYWORDS

Chironomidae, Iran, lotic environments, exuviae, distribution.

INTRODUCTION

During the course of a water quality survey on the rivers Karun and Zayanderud in Iran in the period August 1978 to November 1978, a number of drift collections were made. Much of the material collected was composed of chironomid pupal exuviae and results obtained from the examination of this material form the basis of the present paper. In many cases it is not possible, at the present time, to identify pupal exuviae to species level and since very few imagines or mature pupae were obtained, the taxonomic list presented here remains, regrettably, incomplete.

METHODS

Pupal exuviae were collected by the use of drift nets placed in the rivers for periods of 30 to 60 minutes. The collected material was preserved in 70% alcohol.

THE RIVERS

The Karun and Zayanderud, deep, fast-flowing rivers for most of their length, both rise in the Zagros mountains in western Iran (Fig. 1). The Karun flows south/ south-west and enters the Persian Gulf below the town of Abadan. It rapidly descends from 3,500 m.a.s.1. to 100 m. at Gotvand, where it is joined by it's main

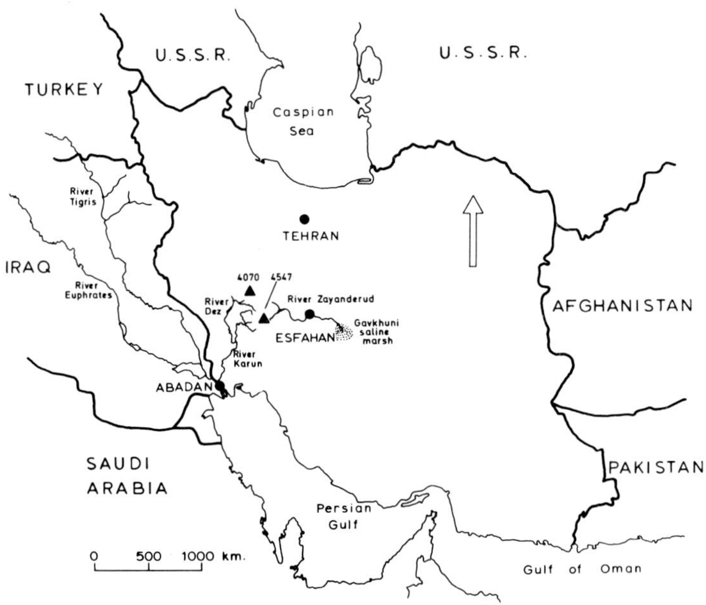

Fig. 1. Location map, the rivers Karun and Zayanderud, Iran.

	Karun	Zayanderud
Catchment area km^2	60,000	32,000
Altitude m.a.s.l.	0-3,500	200-3,000
Temperature °C	13-31	5-26
pH	5.5-8.6	6.5-8.6
Dissolved oxygen mg/l	0.2-14	3-13
Suspended solids mg/l	1-11,250	1-180
Total dissolved solids mg/l	230-1170	175-6300
Conductivity umhos/cm^2	320-2,100	200-19,000
Total Hardness mg/l ($CaCO_3$)	-	145-470
Alkalinity mg/l (HCO_3)	30-300	56-260
Calcium mg/l	42.5-260	44-52
Chloride mg/l	28-465	11-5,325
Magnesium mg/l	9.6-158	6.2-763
Sodium mg/l	18 - 290	6.5-2,645
Salinity °/oo	0.04-1.1	0.05-9.6

Table 1. Physico-chemical characteristics of the Rivers Karun and Zayanderud, Iran.

tributary, the river Dez. The Karun and it's tributaries form the largest river system in Iran, and are a major source of water for Khuzestan Province. Flow is regulated by a number of dams at the headwaters of the Karun and Dez.

The Zayanderud rises around 3,000 m.a.s.l., flows eastwards through the province of Esfahan and drains into the Kavkhuni saline marsh, east of the city of Esfahan. Flow is regulated by a series of dams below the headwaters.

The main physical and chemical characteristics of the Karun and Zayanderud are summarised (Table 1). An increasing gradient in dissolved solids along the Zayanderud is evident. East of the city of Esfahan, the surrounding area becomes semi-arid, and there is a natural ingress of salts into the river, causing a striking increase in all major ions. Before the saline marsh a salinity of 9 $^{o}/oo$ was recorded in the river.

TANYPODINAE
Ablabesmyia cf longistyla
Ablabesmyia sp 1
Conchapelopia sp
Macropelopia cf afghanistani
Psilotanypus sp
Rheopelopia cf maculipennis
Tanypus sp

BUCHONOMYIINAE
Buchonomyia cf thienemanni

DIAMESINAE
Potthastia gaedi

ORTHOCLADIINAE
Cardiocladius sp
Cricotopus bicinctus
Cricotopus ornatus
Cricotopus sylvestris
Cricotopus trifascia
Cricotopus vierrensis
Eukiefferiella cf calvescens
Eukiefferiella cf coerulescens
Eukiefferiella cf lobifera
Eukiefferiella cf minor
Eukiefferiella sp 1
Euorthocladius sp
Heleniella sp
Limnophyes sp
Nanocladius cf spiniplennis
Orthocladius cf saxicola
Parametriocnemus sp
Psectrocladius cf edwardsi/limbatellus
Rheocricotopus cf chalybeatus
Rheocricotopus sp 1
Thienemanniella sp
Orthocladiini sp 1
Orthocladiini sp 2
Orthocladiini sp 3
Orthocladiini sp 4

CHIRONOMINAE
Beckidia sp
Chironomus sp
Cryptochironomus sp 1
Cryptochironomus sp 2
Cryptotendipes sp holsatus type
Demicryptochironomus sp
Harnischia sp
Limnochironomus sp
Paracladopelma sp
Pentapedilum sp 1
Pentapedilum sp 2
Polypedilum sp
Robackia sp
? Stenochironomus sp ?
Stictochironomus sp
Genus near Stictochironomus
Chironomini sp 1
Micropsectra sp 1
? Micropsectra sp 2 ?
Paratanytarsus sp
Rheotanytarsus cf additus
Rheotanytarsus cf distinctissimus
Rheotanytarsus cf reissi
Tanytarsus sp 1
Tanytarsus sp 2

Table 2. Chironomidae from Iran.

RESULTS AND DISCUSSION

A total of 61 taxa is identified (Table 2). The Tanypodinae, Orthocladiinae and Chironominae are well represented.

Tanypodinae. The Tanypodinae are represented by 6 genera and at least 7 species. Within the genus Ablabesmyia 3 types are recognised; the larger, darker specimens are most easily related to Ablabesmyia longistyla Fitt; a smaller, paler type also appears close to A. longistyla; a third is a very small, pale type, (length 4 to 4.2 mm.). This species appears similar to the monilis group on the ratio of the gonopodial sheaths to the anal lobe length, but is closer to the longistyla group on the position of the LS setae on abdominal segment VII. (Fig. 2). The Conchapelopia species differs from the known exuviae (Fittkau, 1962), particularly on the structure of the thoracic horn (Fig. 2d). It is worth noting that 4 new species of Conchapelopia have recently been described from Nepal (Murray, 1976), whose pupae are as yet unknown. The Macropelopia species belongs to the nebulosa group and appears similar to Macropelopia afghanistani (Kownacki et al, 1976).

Buchonomyiinae. Exuviae of Buchonomyia were collected from the river Zayanderud. These appear similar to B. thienemanni Fitt. (Ashe, pers. comm.). Only 2 species of Buchonomyia are known. B. thienemanni has been recorded in Germany (Fittkau, 1955), Ireland (Murray, 1976) and England (Wilson, pers. comm.). B. burmanica Brundin and Saether, is recorded from Burma but it's pupal stage is as yet unknown.

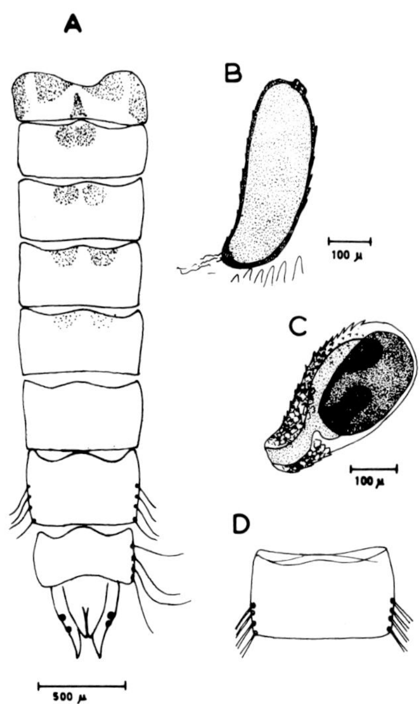

Fig. 2. Ablabesmyia sp 1 a-b: a) Abdomen, b) Thoracic horn
Conchapelopia sp c-d: c) Thoracic horn, d) Segment VII.

Orthocladiinae. Five species of the genus Cricotopus are recorded. C. ornatus Meig. is a halobiont (Hirvenoja, 1973), and was found at the lowermost station on the Zayanderud. C. bicinctus (Meig.), C. sylvestris (Fab.), and C. vierrensis Goetgh. were also found at this station but occurred in other areas.

The genus Eukiefferiella is represented by 5 species, all confined to the upper reaches of both rivers. Eukiefferiella sp 1 (Fig. 3 a-c), shows similarities to both E. calvescens Edw. (presence of spines at the base of the anal macrosetae) and E. bavarica Goetgh. (shape of anal lobe and position of fourth setae; ventral hook rows discontinuous), (Lehmann, 1972). Orthocladius cf saxicola appears similar to O. saxicola (Kieff.) except that the thoracic horn has spines along its entire length, (Fig. 3d), whereas O. saxicola (Kieff.) has spines only on the distal one-third (Thienemann, 1944).

Orthocladiini sp 1 is a large (6 to 7 mm.) brown species with strong spines on the dorso-anal edge of segments II-VIII, (Fig. 4a-b). Orthocladiini sp 2 has spines dorsally on II-VIII, and ventrally on (III) IV-VIII. The anal spines on tergite VIII are split into two groups and placed at the lateral corners, (Fig. 4c-d).

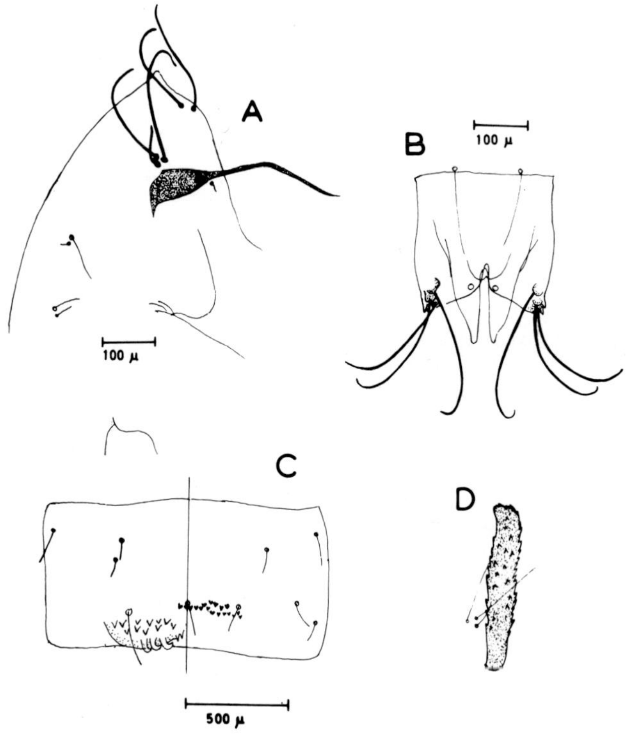

Fig. 3. Eukiefferiella sp a-c: a) Cephalothorax: b) Segment IV: c) Anal lobe: Orthocladius cf Saxicola: d) Thoracic horn.

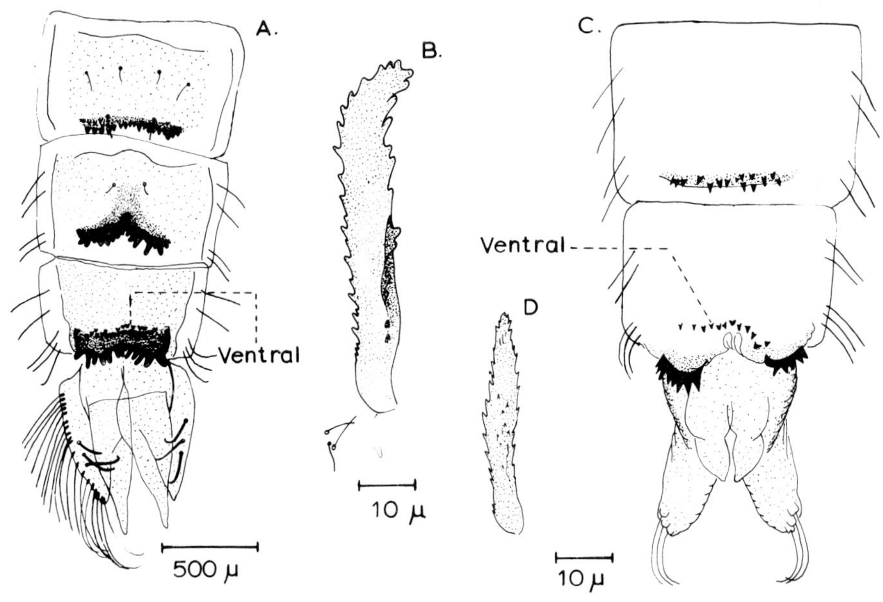

Fig. 4. Orthocladiini sp 1 a-b: a) Abdomen. b) Thoracic horn.
Orthocladiini sp 2 c-d: c) Abdomen. d) Thoracic horn.

Chironominae. Within the Chironominae 16 and 8 types are recorded for the Chironomini and Tanytarsini respectively. At least 2 species of the genera Cryptochironomus and Pentapedilum are present. The Robackia species shows some differences from the known exuviae (Saether, 1977). The dorsal chagrin is strong and extensive; tergite 11 has a small oral group of weak spines; tergite 1 and 11 have discontinuous rows of weak spines caudally and there is no evidence of spines on tergite 111.

At least 3 species are recorded for the genus Rheotanytarsus. R. additus Joh. is recorded previously from Java and Sumatra, (Johannsen, 1933; Zavrel, 1934). Rheotanytarsus cf reissi was difficult to place as it appeared to show characters in common with both R. reissi Lehmann and R. nigricauda Fitt. (Lehmann, 1970). There are no spines apparent on the thoracic horn and the additional setae on the anal lobe are absent.

The present records of the Chironomidae from Iran increase the knowledge of the distribution of a number of Palaearctic genera. Iran lies in the transitional zone of the Oriental, Palaearctic and Ethiopian regions and as such contains elements of the fauna of these regions.

ACKNOWLEDGEMENTS

The Chironomid material on which this paper is based was obtained during a water quality survey by Environmental Engineers, Tehran, whose assistance is gratefully acknowledged. Thanks are extended to P. Ashe, P. Langton, and D. Murray for help with exuval identification and to H. J. Egglishaw and B. Sandford for additional material.

REFERENCES

Brundin, L., and O. A. Saether (1978). Buchonomyia burmanica sp.n. and Buchonomyiinae, a New Subfamily among the Chironomidae (Diptera). Zoologica Scripta., 7, 269-275.

Fittkau, E. J. (1955). Buchonomyia thienemanni n. gen. n.sp. Chironomidestudien IV (Diptera, Chironomidae). Beitr. Ent. 5, 403-414.

Fittkau, E. J. (1962). Die Tanypodinae (Diptera, Chironomidae). Abh. Larvalsyst. Insekten. Berlin, 1-453.

Hirvenoja, M. (1973). Revision der Gattung Cricotopus van der Wulp und ihrer verwandten (Diptera, Chironomidae). Ann. Zool. Fenn. 10, 1-363.

Johannsen, B. A. (1933). Chironomidae from the Malayan Subregion of the Dutch East Indies. Tropische Binnengewasser III, Supple. -Bd. XI des Archiv f. Hydrobiol. 503-552.

Kownacki, A., J. Wojtusiak, and R. Zurek. (1976). New and Rare species of Rotatoria, Cladocera and Chironomidae for the aquatic fauna of Afghanistan. Acta. Hydrobiol. 18 (3), 291-304.

Lehmann, J. (1970). Revision der europalischen Arten der Gattung Rheotanytarsus Bause (Diptera, Chironomidae). Zoologischer Anzeiger Bd. 185, Heft 5/6, 343-378.

Lehmann, J. (1972). Revision der europaischen Arten der Gattung Eukiefferiella Thienemann. Beitr. Ent. Bd. 22:11, 347-405.

Murray, D. A. (1976). Buchonomyia thienemanni Fitt. (Diptera, Chironomidae) a rare and unusual species recorded from Killarney, Ireland. Entomologist's Gaz. 27, 179-180.

Murray, D. A. (1976). Four new species of Conchapelopia Fittkau from Nepal. Ent. Scand. 7, 293-301.

Saether, O. A. (1977). Taxonomic studies on Chironomidae: Nanocladius, Pseudochironomus, and the Harnischia complex. Bull. Fish. Res. Bd. Can. 196, 1-143.

Thienemann, A. (1944). Bestimmungstabellen fur die bis jetzet bekannten Larven und Puppen der Orthocladiinae. Arch. Hydrobiol. 39, 551-664.

Zavrel, J. (1934). Tanytarsuslarven und -puppen aus Niederlandisch-Indien. Arch. fur Hydrobiol. Suppl.-Bd. XIII. Band V, 139-165.

Ein Zoogeographischer Vergleich der Chironomiden der Westpalaearktis und der Aethiopis

E. J. Fittkau

Zoologische Staatssammlung, Maria-Ward-Str. 1 b, D-8000 München 19, Federal Republic of Germany

ABSTRACT

A comparison of the chironomid fauna of the western Palaearctic and the Aethiopian faunal region demonstrates: Africa contains a relatively low number of species. The majority of genera belongs to phylogentic more recent groups. Phylogenetic old taxa are limited in their distribution to the regions of Southern Africa with temperate climatic conditions. Diamesinae are almost missing in Africa. Orthocladiinae are highly represented belonging to the same genera as in the Palaearctic. There is a high number of African endemic genera of Chironomini; Pseudochironomini, abundant in the Neotropic, are missing.

KEYWORDS

Zoogeographical comparison, Chironomidae, Diptera, Western Palaearctic faunal region, Aethiopian faunal region.

Jeder Versuch, die Chironomiden in zoogeographische Betrachtungen einzubeziehen, wird durch die derzeit noch unzureichende taxonomische und faunistische Kenntnis dieser Tiergruppe belastet und ist mit entsprechenden Vorbehalten zu werten. Neuere taxonomische Studien, die Artidentität bei Chironomiden über Faunenregionen hinweg nachweisen, ermutigen jedoch zum Vergleich von Chironomidenfaunen benachbarter Kontinente. Derartige zoogeographische Gegenüberstellungen mögen wiederum Anlaß zu kritischen taxonomischen Revisionen geben.

Grundlagen für den vorliegenden zoogeographischen Vergleich der Chironomiden der Westpalaearktis und der Aethiopis sind der Katalog der afrikanischen Chironomiden von Freeman and Cranston (198o), die Beschreibung der Chironomiden eines zentralafrikanischen Fließgewässers (Lehmann, 1979), und die Auflistung der Chironomiden in der zweiten Auflage der Limnofauna Europaea(Fittkau und Reiss, 1978). Schon seit der Revision der afrikanischen Chironomiden südlich der Sahara durch Freeman (1955-1958) ist die Taxonomie der von Afrika beschriebenen Arten besser geklärt als die des westpalaearktischen Gebietes, wo weiterhin hunderte unsichererArten in vielen noch nicht revidierten

Gattungen mitgeschleppt werden müssen. Der Katalog der afrikanischen Chironomiden erhält seinen besonderen Wert dadurch, daß man bemüht war, alle Arten in ein modernes Gattungskonzept einzufügen. Insgesamt sind 38o Arten in 93 Gattungen aufgeführt. Nur 35 Arten, von Kieffer und von Goetghebuer beschrieben, konnten nicht sicher zugeordnet werden. Der Beitrag von Lehmann vermittelt erstmals eine Vorstellung von der Chironomidenfauna eines Baches im montanen Regenwald des östlichen Kongo. Während eines ganzen Jahres wurde dort mit Emergenzfallen quantitativ Bachfauna gefangen. Die Hälfte, 23 der 46 im Kalengo nachgewiesenen Chironomiden, hat Lehmann als neue Arten beschrieben. Einschließlich dieser Taxa beträgt die Zahl der aus der Aethiopis sicher bekannten Chironomidenarten derzeit 4o3. Dejoux (1973) hat gezeigt, daß weite Teile Afrikas, insbesondere das äquatoriale Waldgebiet, bisher schlecht besammelt worden und von dort noch viele neue Arten zu erwarten sind. Das Ergebnis der Arbeit Lehmanns bestätigt einerseits diese Erwartung, andererseits wird mit ihr auch weiterhin die Erfahrung belegt, daß die Mehrzahl der aus Afrika schon bekannten Arten weit verbreitet ist.

Außerhalb der äquatorialen Urwaldgebiete scheinen die Chironomiden schon relativ gut bekannt zu sein. Die intensiven Aufsammlungen von Dejoux im Tschad und in Westafrika, vgl. Dejoux(1974),haben erstaunlich wenige neue Arten erbracht und deutlich gemacht, daß die afrikanischen Chironomidenarten in der Regel Verbreitungsareale besitzen, die vom südlichen Afrika bis in die Sahelzone oder bis nach Israel und ausnahmsweise sogar bis nach Mitteleuropa reichen. Lehmann (1979) vermutet, daß einige der Kalengo-Arten ganz nahe mit europäischen Formen verwandt oder mit ihnen identisch sind. So wird von ihm _Nanocladius angustistilus_ Freeman als ein Synonym der europäischen Art _Eukiefferiella calvescens_ Edwards aufgefaßt. Aufgrund der guten Bearbeitung der afrikanischen Arten und deren meist ausgedehnter Verbreitung glaube ich annehmen zu dürfen, daß inzwischen wenigstens die Hälfte der Chironomidenfauna der Aethiopis bekannt ist, und sie folglich kaum mehr als 8oo Arten umfaßt.

Für den Vergleich mit der Westpalaearktis wird die Zusammenstellung der europäischen Chironomiden in der Limnofauna Europaea herangezogen. Obwohl in der 2. Auflage (Fittkau und Reiss, 1978)128 Arten neu aufgenommen wurden, schrumpfte der Artenbestand Europas gegenüber der 1968 erschienenen 1. Auflage von 1523 auf 14o4 Arten in 175 Gattungen. Da noch verschiedene artenreiche Gattungen zu revidieren sind, z.B. _Limnophyes_, _Metriocnemus_, _Smittia_ und _Procladius_, und außerdem weitere neue Arten auch in Zukunft noch in Europa zu entdecken sein werden, könnte der derzeitige Bestand von ca. 14oo Arten in der westlichen Palaearktis den gegebenen Verhältnissen entsprechen. Die Artenzahl für die Gesamtpalaearktis ist auf etwa 2ooo anzusetzen und gleicht in ihrem Umfang vermutlich der Chironomidenfauna der Nearktis.

Die Chironomiden der Orientalis sind noch zu mangelhaft bekannt, als daß sie bei diesem Vergleich mit herangezogen werden könnten. In dem ersten Dipterenkatalog dieser Region führen Sublette and Sublette (1973) 424 Arten in 49 Gattungen auf. Die Hälfte der Arten bleibt jedoch taxonomisch ungeklärt. Auf die Zusammensetzung der neotropischen Chironomidenfauna und deren geographische Beziehungen zu anderen Kontinenten ist bereits an anderer Stelle eingegangen worden (Fittkau und Reiss, 1979). Die Zahl der im tropischen Südamerika vorkommenden Arten wird auf wenigstens 1500 geschätzt. Hinzuzurechnen sind noch mehrere hundert Arten aus den andinen und chilenisch-patagonischen

Gebieten.

Der für Afrika geschätzte Artenbestand von ca. 8oo Arten erscheint gegenüber Europa und auch den anderen erwähnten Faunengebieten verhältnismäßig klein. Afrika südlich der Sahara umfaßt eine Fläche von etwa 2o Mill. km^2. Die westliche Palaearktis, die zum Vergleich herangezogen wird, ist nur halb so groß. Beide Kontinentteile sind topographisch und klimatisch vergleichbar stark differenziert. Es ist nicht möglich, in diesem Zusammenhang näher auf eine Erklärung dieses Artendefizits einzugehen. Wahrscheinlich haben Klimaveränderungen über große Zeiträume hinweg immer wieder zur Austrocknung großer Gebiete und damit zu gravierender Einschränkung aquatischer Lebensräume und zur Vernichtung ihrer Faunen in Afrika geführt.

Aber nicht nur ein quantitativer Unterschied im Artenangebot zeichnet sich zwischen den beiden Faunenregionen ab. Die prozentualen Anteile der einzelnen Unterfamilien sind unterschiedlich groß, ferner weichen die Verteilung der Arten auf die Gattungen und das Verhältnis der Zahl der Gattungen zur Zahl der Arten voneinander ab (vgl.Tab.1).

Tabelle 1 Anzahl der Gattungen und Arten der Chironomiden Afrikas, der Westpalaearktis und des tropischen Südamerika und die prozentuale Verteilung der Arten auf die Unterfamilien. ( ) Zahl der Gattungen, die in Afrika, Europa und im tropischen Südamerika vorkommen und in Europa bzw. in Afrika fehlen.

Chironominae	Aethiopis (Afr.südl.Sahara)			W-Palaearktis (Europa)			Neotropis (Trop.Subtr.SA)		
Tanypodinae	(3)	17/58	14.3	(11)	26/95	11.o	(6)	12/66	13.1
Podonominae	(2)	2/3	o.7	(5)	5/6	o.4	-	-	-
Aphroteniinae	(1)	1/2	o.5	-	-	-	-	-	-
Telmatogetoninae	-	1/3	o.7	-	2/3	o.2	-	2/4	o.8
Diamesinae	-	1/2	o.5	(12)	13/84	6.o	(1)	1/1	o.2
Orthocladiinae	(3)	29/1o8	27.o	(37)	63/653	47.6	(6)	15/41	8.2
Chironominae	(17)	42/227	56.3	(4o)	65/3o1	34.5	(37)	55/391	77.7
Chironomini	(17)	36/184	81.o	(25)	44/294	61.2	(37)	5o/239	61.1
Tanytarsini	-	6/43	19.o	(14)	2o/2o7	38.6	-	5/1o9	27.9
Pseudochironomini	-		-	(1)	1/1	o.2	(12)	12/43	11.o
	(26)	93/4o3		(1o5)	175/14o4		(5o)	85/5o3	

Tanypodinae: Der Anteil mit 14.3 % am Gesamtartenbestand ist hoch und deckt sich mit den Werten der südamerikanischen Tropen. Nur 3 der 17 Gattungen kommen nicht in Europa vor, zwei davon sind endemisch, die dritte ist auch aus der Nearktis bekannt. Podonominae, Aphroteniinae, Telmatogetoniinae: Zu bemerken ist, daß die Podonominae in Europa stärker vertreten sind als in Afrika und daß die Aphroteniinae in der Westpalaearktis fehlen. Das Vorkommen der Podonominae und Aphroteniinae in der Aethiopis ist auf das südliche Afrika beschränkt. Diamesinae: Die geringe Präsenz dieser Unterfamilie mit nur o.5 % kennzeichnet ganz allgemein die afrikanische Chironomidenfauna. Die beiden einzigen bekannten Arten gehören zur relativ apomorphen Gattung Diamesa. In Europa sind die Diamesinae mit 84 gut definierten Arten in 13 Gattungen vertreten. Das nahezu völlige Fehlen in der Aethiopis dürfte für eine genaue Analyse der Entstehung der Chironomidenfauna dieses Kontinents wichtige Hinweise liefern. Orthocladinae: Mit 27 % bleibt ihr Anteil an der Gesamtchironomidenfauna klein. Kleiner als in Europa ist auch das Verhältnis der Zahl der Gattungen zur Zahl der Arten (1:3,7 in Afrika, 1:10 in Europa). Nur drei der 29 Gattungen sind endemisch. Zumindest bei zweien dieser Endemiten handelt es sich um südafrikanisch verbreitete plesiomorphe und monotypische Elemente. Alle anderen Gattungen sind stammesgeschichtlich jungen Gruppen zuzuordnen, die zumindest in der Holarktis meist weit verbreitet sind. Gegenüber der Neotropis, wo ihr Anteil nur 8.2 % ausmacht, ist die Zahl der afrikanischen Orthocladiinae hoch. Wie Lehmann (1979) gesagt hat, ist selbst in den äquatorialen Gebieten ihre Anzahl groß. Im Bach Kalengo, Ostzaire, in 1800 m Höhe mit einer Jahresdurchschnittstemperatur von 18°C, waren 52.2 % der Arten Orthocladiinae und nur 36.9 % Chironominae. Zum Vergleich die Zahlen vom Great Berg River, Kap-Provinz, Südafrika, die Scott (1958) ermittelt hat: 46 % Orthocladiinae und 41 % Chironominae. Methodisch vergleichbar durchgeführte Untersuchungen wie am Kolengo brachten von zwei deutschen Mittelgebirgsbächen (Ringe, 1974) 58.9 bzw. 67.8 % Orthocladiinae und 32.9 bzw. 24.8 % Chironominae. Chironominae: Nur in dieser Unterfamilie ist die Zahl endemischer oder nicht in Europa ebenfalls verbreiteter Gattungen hoch. Sie gehören alle zu den Chironomini. Der Anteil der Tanytarsini an der Unterfamilie mit 19 % ist halb so groß wie der in der Westpalaearktis. Nur 6 der 20 europäisch verbreiteten Tanytarsini-Gattungen kommen auch in Afrika vor. Aufschlußreich für die in der Neotropis anders verlaufene Evolution der Chironomiden ist der hohe Anteil von 11 % der Pseudochironomini an der dortigen Fauna. Aus Afrika ist noch keine Pseudochironomus bekannt. Die einzige europäische Art dieses Tribus scheint nearktischen Formen nächst verwandt zu sein.

Bei besserer systematischer und auch phylogenetischer Kenntnis der afrikanischen Chironomiden dürfte die Analyse der aufgezeigten oder auch nur angedeuteten Unterschiede in den Chironomidenfaunen der aethiopischen und der westpalaearktischen Faunenregion einen wesentlichen Beitrag zum Verständnis der Besiedlungsgeschichte der Tierwelt Afrikas und auch der Evolution der Chironomidae erbringen.

REFERENCES

Dejoux, C.(1973). Données faunistiques nouvelles concernant les Chironomides (Diptères, Nématocères) de la region éthiopienne. Cah.O.R.S.T.O.M. Ser. Hydrobiol. 7, 77-93.

Dejoux, C.(1974) Contribution à la connaissance des Chironomides de l'Afrique de l'Ouest. Ent. Tidskr. Suppl. 95, 84-90.

Fittkau, E.J. and F. Reiss (1978). Chironomidae. In J.Illies (Ed.), Limnofauna Europaea, 2nd ed. G. Fischer, Stuttgart and Swets and Zeitlinger B.V., Amsterdam. pp. 404-440.

Fittkau, E.J. and F. Reiss (1979). Die zoogeographische Sonderstellung der neotropischen Chironomiden, Diptera. Spixiana 2 (3). In press.

Freeman, F. (1955-1958). A study of the Chironomidae (Diptera) of Afrika South of the Sahara. Bull. Br. Mus. nat. Hist. Ent. 4, 1-67. 4, 287-368. 5, 323-426. 6, 263-363.

Freeman, F. and Cranston, P.S. (198o). Family Chironomidae. In Catalogue of the Diptera of Africa. In press.

Lehmann, J. (1979) Chironomidae (Diptera) aus Fließgewässern Zentralafrikas (Systematik, Ökologie, Verbreitung und Produktionsbiologie) Teil I: Kiwu Gebiet, Ostzaire, Spixiana, Suppl. 3, pp. 1-144.

Ringe, J. (1944) Chironomiden-Emergenz 197o in Breitenbach und Rohrwiesenbach. Schlitzer Produktionsbiologische Studien (1o). Arch. Hydrobiol.Suppl. 45, 212-3o4.

Scott, K. M. F. (1958) Hydrobiological studies on the Great Berg River Western Cape Province. III. The Chironomidae. Trans.R. soc. S.Afr. 35, 277-298.

Sublette, J.E. and M.S.Sublette (1973). Family Chironomidae. In M. Delfinado and E. D. Hardy (Eds.), Catalogue of the Diptera of the Oriental region, Vol.1 Honolulu, Hawaii. pp. 289-422.

Zur Zoogeographie der Chironomidenfauna (Diptera, Insecta) Nordkoreas

F. Reiss

Zoologische Staatssammlung, Maria-Ward-Str. 1 b, D-8000 München 19, Federal Republic of Germany

ABSTRACT

Preliminary investigation of the first chironomid material collected in North Korea shows the presence of 70 species and 34 genera. The low representation of species within the Orthocladiinae (1o %), together with the relatively high proportion of species in the Harnischia complex, is very striking. An exclusively Palaearctic representation is apparent at the generic level. East and west Palaearctic, Holarctic and Panpalaeotropical faunal elements are evident at the species level together with numerous not definable new species. An unexpected high proportion of the North Korean chironomid fauna (34%) has its distribution in or beyond the Palaearctic. From the present material North Korea shares only two species in common with Japan.

KEYWORDS

Chironomidae; Diptera; zoogeography; North Korea; comparsion palaearctic fauna.

Sieht man von den über 17o nachgewiesenen Arten der japanischen Inseln und Einzelfunden im Amurgebiet (Shilova, 1976) ab, so ist die kontinentale Chironomidenfauna der südöstlichen paläarktischen Region bis heute unbekannt geblieben.

In den Jahren 1971 (Mitte Mai - Mitte Juni) und 1972 (Anfang August - Mitte September) führte das Ungarische Naturhistorische Museum Budapest zwei zoologische Sammelreisen nach Nordkorea durch, bei denen auch mehrere tausend Chironomiden-Imagines gesammelt wurden. Für die Überlassung des Materials zur Bearbeitung möchte ich hier herzlich danken.

Aufgrund der nordkoreanischen Tiere ist es nun erstmals möglich, der Frage nach der West-Ost-Differenzierung der paläarktischen Chironomidenfauna auf einer maximalen Distanz von 12 000 km nachzugehen. Die Fauna Japans eignet sich für diese Frage weniger, da sie sich einerseits als Inselfauna in einem nicht kalkulierbaren Ausmaß von der kontinentalen Fauna unterscheidet, und zum anderen die aus Japan beschriebenen Taxa, vor einem Vergleich mit westpaläarktischen Taxa, fast ausnahmslos einer kritischen Typenrevision bedürfen (vgl. Sasa and Yamamoto, 1977:3o1).

Die Landesnatur Nordkoreas ist in vieler Hinsicht der von Mittel-und Osteuropa vergleichbar, so daß das Angebot an aquatischen Biotopen ähnlich ist. Da das Vorkommen von Chironomidenarten, auch großräumig, in erster Linie von ökologischen und nicht von historisch-zoogeographischen Faktoren bestimmt wird (Reiss, 1978), ist eine wesentliche Voraussetzung für einen Faunenvergleich von Europa und Nordkorea gegeben. Abweichend vom feuchtgemäßigten Cfa-Klima großer Teile Europas ist das boreale Dwa-Klima Nordkoreas mit warmen Sommern (August-Monatsmittel 22.6°C) und sehr kalten trockenen Wintern (Januar-Monatsmittel -21°C). Die ursprüngliche Vegetation Nordkoreas war ein geschlossener sommergrüner Mischwald, im küstennahen Bereich ein Laubwald. In mittleren und tiefen Lagen mußte der Primärwald landwirtschaftlichen Nutzungsflächen weichen. Korea ist seit 5ooo Jahren Kulturland! Die resultierende Bodenerosion führte in den meist kurzen und gewundenen Flüssen zu einer hohen Schwebstoffracht, die sicher, analog zu europäischen Verhältnissen, zur frühzeitigen Vernichtung der suspensoidempfindlichen potamalen Faunenelemente führte. In jüngster Zeit dürfte der massive Einsatz von DDT großflächig eine starke Reduktion der Entomofauna bewirkt haben, so etwa in den Bergen der Umgebung der Hauptstadt Pyongyang ("a strong smell (!) of DDT can be felt everywhere"; vgl. Mahunka and Steinmann, 1971:24).

Trotz der anthropogenen Veränderungen scheinen lokal ursprüngliche aquatische Biotope erhalten geblieben zu sein, so etwa in Kum-gan san (Berggebiet bei Wonsan) oder in den nordöstlichen Gebirgen und Hochgebirgen, in denen sich auch die höchste Erhebung des Landes, der Vulkan Pektusan (2744 m),befindet. Chironomiden enthaltende Proben liegen nur bis in eine maximale Höhe von 17oo m vor.

Erwähnenswert ist, daß auch während der Maximalvereisung nur der nordöstliche Landesteil vergletschert war, und die koreanische Halbinsel während der Mindeleiszeit mit den japanischen Inseln über die heutige Koreastraße hinweg in Landesverbindung stand. Sehr jung, nämlich postglazial, ist das westlich angrenzende Gelbe Meer, so daß Korea auch nach Westen mit Nordchina bis in jüngste Zeit Landkontakt hatte.

In dem vorliegenden Material konnten bisher 7o Chironomidenarten aus 34 Gattungen nachgewiesen werden (Tabelle 1). Die Proben sind noch nicht vollständig ausgewertet und die gefundenen Taxa nicht gänzlich bestimmt. Besonders in der Unterfamilie der Orthocladiinae sind weitere Gattungen und Arten zu erwarten, so daß sich die im folgenden aufgeführte prozentuale Verteilung der Arten auf die Unterfamilien zugunsten der Orthocladiinen verschieben wird. Dennoch dominieren unter den 7o Arten mit bisher 8o % klar die Vertreter der Unterfamilie Chironominae. Orthocladiinae- und Tanypodinae-Arten sind einstweilen mit jeweils 1o % vertreten. Die Unterfamilien Diamesinae, Podonominae und Telmatogetoninae sind in dem Material nicht vertreten, jedoch vom Biotopangebot her aus Nordkorea zu erwarten.

Innerhalb der Chironominae dominiert in auffallender Weise der Harnischia-Gattungskomplex mit 13 Arten aus 9 Gattungen. Fast ein Fünftel aller nachgewiesenen Chironomidenarten (19 %) gehört hierher.

Mit lo Arten (14 %) ist auch die Gattung Polypedilum sehr reich vertreten. Andererseits konnten andere artenreiche Gattungen, zum Beispiel Microtendipes, Parachironomus, Micropsectra oder Rheotanytarsus bisher nicht nachgewiesen werden. Vermutlich ist das Fehlen der genannten und weiterer Gattungen auf methodische Gründe beim Sammeln und nicht auf zoogeographische Phänomene zurückzuführen.

Ein zoogeographischer Vergleich der koreanischen Fauna läßt sich vorläufig nur mit der Westpaläarktis und der ostsibirischen Fauna (Baikalseegebiet, Westmongolei und Amurgebiet)durchführen, nicht jedoch mit der Fauna der orientalischen Faunenregion. Auch sie bedarf, wie die Fauna Japans, vor dem Versuch eines ernsthaften Vergleichs, einer kritischen systematischen Revision, für die der Katalog von Sublette and Sublette (1973) die Grundlage ist.

Ein unerwartet hoher Anteil von 34 % der nordkoreanischen Arten ist paläarktisch oder darüber hinaus weit verbreitet. Dies bedeutet, daß Nordkorea mit Europa über ein Drittel der Arten gemeinsam hat. Von diesen Arten sind 6 (9 % der Gesamtfauna) auch aus der Nearktis bekannt und damit holarktisch verbreitet (Tabelle 1). Eine Art, Paracladopelma nereis (Townes), konnte aus Nordkorea erstmals für die Paläarktis nachgewiesen werden. Drei Arten, Dicrotendipes p. pilosimanus (Kieff.), Microchironomus tener (Kieff.) und Polypedilum nubifer (Skuse) (syn. pharao), gehören dem panpaläotropischen Verbreitungstyp an (Reiss, 1977) und kommen auch in der Äthiopis, Orientalis und Australis vor.

Ein Vergleich der koreanischen Chironomidenfauna mit der Ostsibiriens (Baikalseegebiet und Westmongolei, Amurgebiet und Kamtschatka ; Reiss, 1977 und Shilova, 1976) bringt zur Zeit noch nicht das zu erwartende Ergebnis. Der Anteil gemeinsamer Arten (11 %) ist niedriger, nicht gleich oder höher, als der Vergleichswert von Europa. Berücksichtigt man jedoch die hohe Zahl von über 14oo aus Europa bekannten Arten gegenüber den nur loo Arten aus dem ostsibirischen Vergleichsgebiet, so sind zukünftig noch viele gemeinsame Arten zu erwarten.

Eine Aussage über ostpaläarktisch verbreitete Arten ist bei der geringen faunistischen Kenntnis weiterhin gewagt. Vermutlich gehört zu diesem Verbreitungstyp die Art Saetheria reissi Jackson, die bisher nur von Irkutsk bekannt war, nunmehr jedoch recht frequent in den nordkoreanischen Proben auftritt.

Erstaunlich gering ist die nachweisbare faunistische Gemeinsamkeit zwischen Japan und Nordkorea. Nur 2 weit verbreitete gemeinsame Arten sind bekannt: Tanypus punctipennis (Meig.) und Polypedilum nubeculosum (Meig.). Eine dritte Art, Stenochironomus sp.K2, ist eventuell mit der aus Japan beschriebenen Art nelumbus Tok. identisch. Ich bin aber sicher, daß eine systematische Revision der japanischen Arten eine größere Zahl paläarktisch weit verbreiteter Arten aufdecken wird.

Über die faunistische Eigenständigkeit der Chironomiden Nordkoreas, das zoogeographisch zur mandschurischen Faunenprovinz gehört, kann man zur Zeit nur Spekulationen äußern. Morphologisch auffällige, in der Holarktis unbekannte Taxa sind zum Beispiel Cladopelma sp.K1, Harnischia sp.K1, Paracladopelma sp.K2, Polypedilum sp.K3, Xenochironomus sp.K2, Chironomini gen.K1 und gen.K2. Möglicherweise sind es mandschurische Faunenelemente, sofern sie nicht darüber hinaus in der

Ostpaläarktis verbreitet sind oder es sich um bisher nicht erfaßte Arten der Orientalis handelt.

Trotz aller Unsicherheit, mit der ein großräumiger Faunenvergleich über die Paläarktis hinweg belastet sein muß, wenn er, wie in diesem Falle, nur drei, mehrere tausend Kilometer voneinander entfernte Untersuchungsgebiete berücksichtigt, läßt sich doch eine wesentliche Tendenz erkennen: Das paläarktische Arboreal hat in seiner West-Ost-Erstreckung einen unerwartet hohen Anteil gemeinsamer Arten, der im Vergleich mit Europa nach Osten geringer wird, in Ostsibirien noch über 8o % und sogar am äußersten Südostrand, in Nordkorea, noch immer mindestens ein Drittel beträgt.

Tabelle 1 Liste der bisher unterschiedenen Chironomiden-Taxa aus Nordkorea

Die eingeklammerten Zahlen entsprechen den Fundorten bei Mahunka and Steinmann (1971) sowie Papp and Horvatovich (1972). o Paläarktisch weit verbreitete Arten. + Holarktisch verbreitete Arten.

Tanypodinae (7 Arten)

o Ablabesmyia monilis (L.) (218)
Procladius (mindestens 2 Arten) (19,49,87,142,15o,181,234)
o Rheopelopia ornata (Meig.) (234,243)
o Tanypus punctipennis (Meig.) (19,234)
Thienemannimyia sp.K1 (234)
o Trissopelopia ?flavida (Kieff.) (1oo)

Orthocladiinae (7 Arten)

Cricotopus (mind.4 Arten) (19,28,49,93,1o9,137,177,181,2o1,225,227)
Limnophyes sp. (218)
Orthocladius sp. (36,1o9)
Paratrichocladius sp.K1 (1o9)
sowie noch weitere unbestimmte Taxa.

Chironominae (Chironomini) (43 Arten)

+ Chernovskiia ?orbicus (Townes) (19)
Chironomus (4 Arten) (19,49,87,93,1o9,142,181,193,227,248)
Cladopelma sp.K1 (28,1o9,181,193,227)
Cladopelma sp.K2 (87)
Cryptochironomus sp. (218)
Cryptochironomus sp. (49,181)
o Demicryptochironomus vulneratus (Zett.) (218)
+ Dicrotendipes nervosus (Staeg.) (234)
o Dicrotendipes p. pilosimanus (Kieff.) (93,181,225,227,234)
Einfeldia sp. (87)
o Endochironomus impar (Walk.) (198,2o1,218)
Glyptotendipes sp. (28,29,49)
Harnischia sp.K1 (93)
o Microchironomus tener (Kieff.) (19,28,29,87,137,181,227,234)
Paracladopelma sp.K1 (19)
Paracladopelma sp.K2 (19,27,29)
+ Paracladopelma nereis (Townes) (225) (Erstnachweis für Paläarktis)
o Paratendipes nubilus (Meig.) (142,181,227,229,234)
+ Polypedilum cultellatum Goetgh. (177,218)

+ Polypedilum ?nubeculosum (Meig.) (19,29,234,248)
o Polypedilum nubifer (Skuse)(syn.pharao Kieff.) (28)
o Polypedilum pedestre (Meig.) (93,1oo,225)
+ Polypedilum scalaenum Schr. (13,19,142,181,227,234)
Polypedilum (Tripodura) sp.K1 (234)
Polypedilum sp.K2 (181)
Polypedilum sp.K3 (19,15o,225,234)
Polypedilum sp.K4 (87)
Polypedilum (Tripodura) sp.K5 (229)
o Robackia pilicauda Saeth. (225)
?o Saetheria reissi Jackson (93,1o9,181,193)
Stenochironomus sp.K1 (225,234)
Stenochironomus sp.K2 (1oo,156,234)
Stenochironomus sp.K3 (181)
o Stictochironomus pictulus (Meig.) (193)
Stictochironomus sp.K1 (87)
Xenochironomus sp.K1 (19,225,227,234)
Xenochironomus sp.K2 (145)
Chironomini gen.K1 (142,15o,156,225,234)
Chironomini gen.K2 (142)

Chironominae (Tanytarsini) (13 Arten)

Cladotanytarsus sp.K1 (87)
Cladotanytarsus sp.K2 (19,87,15o,181,227,234)
o Paratanytarsus confusus Palmen oder inopertus (Walk.) (13)
o Paratanytarsus laccophilus Edw. (198,2o9,218)
Paratanytarsus sp.K1 (1oo)
o Tanytarsus chinyensis Goetgh. (19,1o9)
o Tanytarsus fimbriatus Reiss und Fittkau (142,181)
o Tanytarsus heusdensis Goetgh. (1o9)
Tanytarsus sp.K1 (eminulus-Gruppe)(13,225,234)
Tanytarsus sp.K2 (eminulus-Gruppe) (19)
Tanytarsus sp.K4 (44,49)
Tanytarsus sp.K5 (1o9)
Tanytarsus sp.K6 (1o9)

REFERENCES

Mahunka, S., and H.Steinmann (1971). Zoological collectings by the Hungarian Natural History Museum in Korea. 1. A report on the collecting of the first expedition. Fol.ent.Hung. (ser.n.),24,21-46.

Papp, J., and S.Horvatovich (1972). Zoological collectings by the Hungarian Natural History Museum in Korea. 2. A report in the collecting of the second expedition. Fol.ent.Hung.(ser.n.),25,187-227.

Reiss, F. (1977). Verbreitungsmuster bei paläarktischen Chironomidenarten (Diptera, Chironomidae). Spixiana,1,85-97.

Reiss, F. (1978). Sich abzeichnende Verbreitungsmuster in der paläarktischen-paläotropischen Chironomidenfauna (Dipt.). Mitt. dt. Ges. allg. angew. Ent.,1,72-76.

Sasa, M., and M.Yamamoto (1977). A checklist of Chironomidae recorded from Japan. Jap. J. sanit. Zool.,28, 3o1-318.

Shilova, A.I. (1976). Khironomidy Rybinskogo Vodokhranilishcha. (Chironomiden des Rybinsker Stausees). Izd. Nauka, Leningrad 1976, 249 p.

Sublette, J.E., and M.S.Sublette (1973). Family Chironomidae. In M.Delfinado, and E.D.Hardy (Eds.), Catalogue of the Diptera of the Oriental Region,Vol.1, Honolulu,Hawaii. pp. 289-422.

SECTION III

ECOLOGY

Spatial Distribution of Chironomidae in an English Chalk Stream

L. C. V. Pinder

Freshwater Biological Association, East Stoke, Wareham, Dorset, England

ABSTRACT

The chironomid fauna of gravel is described from 5 sites along the course of a southern English chalk stream, the River Frome. The distribution of chironomid larvae in relation to the nature of the substratum is considered in more detail at one of these sites and at an additional site on a major tributary, the Tadnoll Brook.

The major substrata in this system are submerged macrophytes, principally *Ranunculus penicillatus* var. *calcareus* (R. W. Butcher), C. D. K. Cook, gravel and soft deposits of sand with varying amounts of organic detritus. The first two are dominated by the subfamily Orthocladiinae whilst in the latter Chironominae predominate.

The majority of species occur throughout the system, although some tend to be relatively more abundant close to the source and others become more common downstream. *Diamesa insignipes* K. was found only at the most upstream station.

KEYWORDS

Longitudinal distribution; substratum type; gravel; sand; organic detritus; *Ranunculus penicillatus* var. *calcareus* (R. W. Butcher) C. D. K. Cook.

INTRODUCTION

The earliest detailed studies of the chironomid fauna of chalk streams in S. England were those of Ford (1959) and Hall (1951, 1961). Little has been published on the subject since then apart from a list of species taken from a single site (Pinder, 1974) and a brief review of the topic (Pinder, 1977). The work presented here forms part of a more detailed study of the life cycles and ecology of some of the more abundant chalk stream species. The ecology of chalk streams is discussed in general terms by Westlake and colleagues (1972).

SAMPLING SITES

Samples were taken from 5 sites on the River Frome (Fig. 1) spaced more or less equal distances apart between a point close to the source (site 1), where, under conditions of low flow, the stream is little more than 1.5 m wide and only *c*.20 cm deep, and one 35 Km downstream (site 5) where the width is 10-15 m and the maximum depth *c*.2 m. At all of these sites the river bed consists mainly of gravel and,

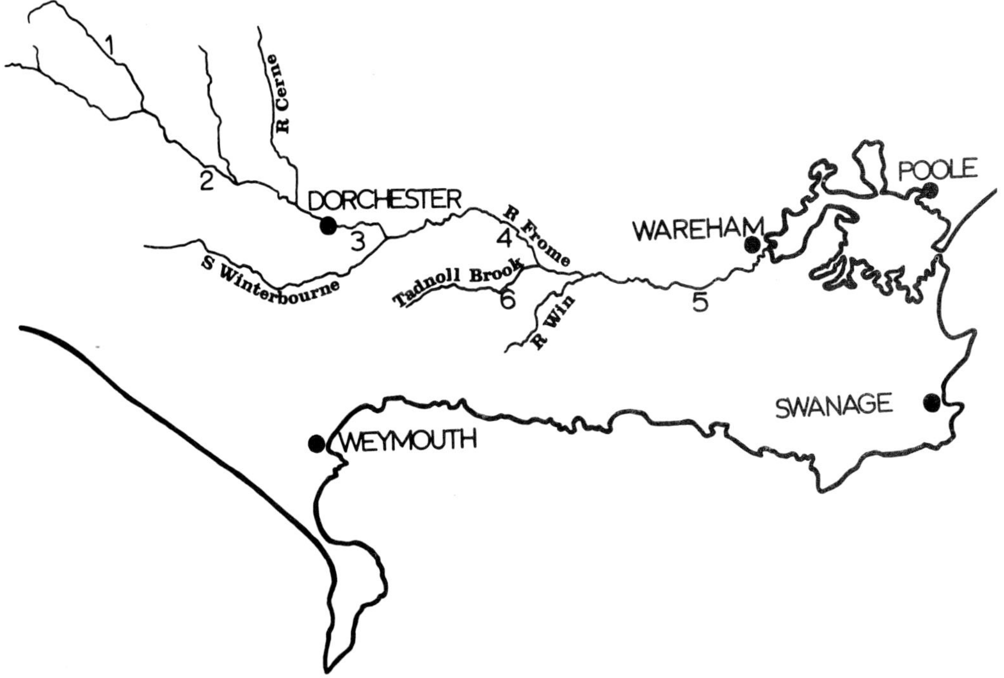

Fig. 1. The R. Frome catchment, showing sampling sites (1-6).

except at site 1, there are dense stands of *Ranunculus penicillatus* var. *calcareus* (R. W. Butcher) C. D. K. Cook. Beds of soft sediment, sand and organic detritus also accumulate in areas where current velocity is reduced, notably close to the margins and in the shelter of weed beds. The distribution of species in relation to these three major types of substratum was studied at site 5 and at an additional site (site 6) on a major tributary, the Tadnoll Brook, where the current velocity is relatively low and soft sediments predominate.

The physical and chemical characteristics of the Frome system are described in detail by Casey and Newton (1973) and site 6 is described more fully by Pinder (1974).

METHODS

The comparisons between the major substrata are based on two sets of samples taken at site 5 in May and September 1977. A longitudinal survey of the gravel fauna was carried out in May, July and September of the following year. In all cases 15 replicate samples were taken. Data on the preferences of certain species for particular types of soft sediment are drawn from a 2 year study of the fauna of the Tadnoll Brook carried out in 1970 and 1971, during which samples were taken every two weeks.

Gravel cores were obtained using an open-ended steel cylinder which was pushed into the river bed to a depth of 10-15 cm. Large stones were removed by hand whilst

TABLE 1 Taxa recorded from Gravel Samples in May (M), July (J) and September (S), 1978. Numbers indicate Relative Abundance; 0 = absent, 1 = < 6% of Total Larvae, 2 = 6-10%, 3 = 11-20%, 4 = 21-30%, 5 = 31-40%, 6 = 41-50%, 7 = >50%

	SITE 1 M J S	SITE 2 M J S	SITE 3 M J S	SITE 4 M J S	SITE 5 M J S
TANYPODINAE					
Thienemannimyia gp.	0 2 0	0 0 0	1 0 1	1 1 1	2 1 0
DIAMESINAE					
Diamesa insignipes K.	1 4 1	0 0 0	0 0 0	0 0 0	0 0 0
Potthastia gaedii (Mg.)	1 0 0	1 0 1	1 0 1	2 5 1	4 7 2
P. longimana K.	0 0 0	0 0 0	0 0 0	0 0 1	0 0 0
PRODIAMESINAE					
Prodiamesa olivacea (Mg.)	0 0 1	0 2 1	0 0 0	1 1 1	0 1 1
ORTHOCLADIINAE					
Brillia sp.	1 2 0	0 0 1	0 0 1	0 0 0	0 0 0
Cricotopus (*C.*) *bicinctus* (Mg.)	0 0 0	0 0 1	0 0 1	0 1 1	0 0 2
**Cricotopus* (*C.*) sp. A	0 0 1	0 3 1	0 1 1	0 0 0	0 0 1
Cricotopus (*C.*) *trifascia* Edw	0 0 0	0 0 1	0 0 3	0 0 1	0 0 1
Cricotopus (*I.*) *trifasciatus* (Panz.)	0 0 0	0 0 1	0 0 1	0 1 0	0 0 0
Eukiefferiella brevicalcar (K.)	2 0 0	0 0 0	1 0 0	0 0 0	0 0 0
E. calvescens (Edw.)	5 7 4	4 3 3	0 3 2	1 1 1	1 1 1
E. claripennis (Lund)	6 0 2	4 5 1	1 4 1	1 1 1	1 1 1
E. clypeata (K.)	1 0 1	1 1 1	1 0 1	1 2 7	1 2 6
E. discoloripes Goet.	1 0 0	0 0 0	0 0 0	0 0 0	0 0 0
E. gracei (Edw.)	1 0 1	3 0 1	5 0 1	1 1 1	2 1 1
E. ilkleyensis (Edw.)	0 0 0	2 0 1	2 0 2	1 2 2	0 1 1
E. minor (Edw.)	0 0 0	1 0 0	1 0 0	0 1 1	0 0 0
**Eukiefferiella* sp. C	0 0 0	1 0 0	0 1 0	1 1 1	1 2 1
Heterotrissocladius marcidus (Walk.)	0 0 0	0 1 0	0 0 0	0 0 0	0 0 0
Nanocladius rectinervis (K.)	0 0 3	0 0 1	1 0 1	0 0 0	1 1 0
Orthocladius (*E.*) *rivulorum* (K.)	0 0 0	0 0 0	2 0 0	0 0 0	1 0 0
Orthocladius (*E.*) *thienemanni* K.	1 0 1	1 1 1	3 0 3	1 4 3	5 1 2
**Orthocladius* (*O.*) sp. A	0 0 1	0 0 7	1 0 4	0 1 1	0 0 1
Rheocricotopus sp.	1 0 4	0 0 1	0 1 1	1 1 1	1 1 1
Synorthocladius semivirens (K.)	0 0 0	1 0 1	1 0 1	1 1 0	0 0 1
Corynoneura spp.	0 0 1	1 1 1	1 2 1	0 1 0	1 0 1
Epoicocladius flavens (Mall.)	0 0 0	1 0 0	0 0 0	0 1 1	0 1 0
Parametriocnemus stylatus (K.)	0 0 0	0 1 1	0 1 1	4 0 0	1 1 2
Thienemanniella spp.	1 2 4	2 1 1	1 3 1	3 1 1	1 1 2
CHIRONOMINAE					
Cryptochironomus sp.	0 0 0	1 0 0	0 0 0	1 1 1	1 0 1
Demicryptochironomus vulneratus (Zett.)	0 0 0	1 0 0	1 4 0	1 1 1	1 0 1
Microtendipes sp.	0 0 0	0 0 0	0 0 0	1 0 0	0 0 1
Paracladopelma camptolabis (K.)	0 0 0	0 2 1	0 0 0	1 1 1	0 0 1
Polypedilum convictum (Walk.)	1 0 1	2 1 1	1 0 1	4 0 1	1 1 0
P. cultellatum Goet.	1 0 0	0 1 1	0 1 1	4 1 1	1 1 0
Stictochironomus sp.	0 0 0	0 0 0	0 0 0	0 1 0	0 0 1
Cladotanytarsus sp.	0 0 0	1 1 1	0 0 0	2 1 1	1 1 1
Micropsectra aristata Pinder	0 0 0	0 0 1	1 3 0	0 0 0	0 1 0
Micropsectra sp.	1 0 1	0 1 1	1 0 1	0 0 0	1 1 0
Tanytarsus arduennensis Goet.	0 0 0	1 0 0	1 0 0	1 0 0	0 0 0
T. brundini Lind.	0 0 0	1 0 0	0 0 0	0 0 0	1 0 0
Tanytarsus sp.	0 0 0	0 1 1	1 0 0	0 0 0	1 0 0

* corresponding with Cranston's (1979) terminology.

smaller particles and the overlying water column were pumped into a sieve of 250 μm aperture. Samples of soft sediment from site 5 were taken using a corer of 3.5 cm internal diameter. *Ranunculus calcareus* was sampled using a 25 cm square, metal quadrat from within which the vegetation was cut and removed by hand. Larvae were removed by washing the plant material several times in buckets of water, the washings being filtered through a sieve of 250 μm aperture, until all of the animals appeared to have been removed.

In the earlier study on the Tadnoll Brook a corer of 5.5 cm internal diameter was used, with cores being taken in clusters of 5. Fifteen such samples (i.e. 75 cores) were taken on each occasion, 5 from each of the margins and 5 from the central region. A subjective assessment of the composition of each sample, based on the presence or absence of various types of material was made before washing through a sieve (aperture size 250 μm). The following categories of material were recognized: gravel, sand, coarse detritus (i.e. containing recognizable fragments of vegetation), fine detritus and clay. Clay and gravel occurred rarely and were not considered in the subsequent analysis. The data were bulked for periods when a particular species was abundant and analyses of variance were computed on the numbers of animals occurring in samples of each type, using log. transformed data. When the variance ratio proved significant the mean numbers of larvae in samples of different compositions were compared by estimation of the least significant difference ($P = < 0.05$) (Snedecor and Cochran, 1967).

RESULTS

Table 1 shows the taxa recorded from gravel samples taken from the 5 sites used in 1978 with an indication of their relative abundance at each site. Most taxa appeared to be widely distributed throughout the system although *Diamesa insignipes* occurred only at site 1. *Eukiefferiella claripennis* and *E. calvescens* were relatively more abundant towards the source, whereas *Potthastia gaedii*, *Eukiefferiella* Sp. C, *E. clypeata* and *Orthocladius thienemanni* were more common at the downstream sites. One species, *Orthocladius* sp. A tended to be more common at the intermediate sites 2 and 3. The mean densities of larvae at each site with 95% confidence limits (log. transformed data) are shown in Table 2 together with the percentage contributed by each of the dominant taxa.

TABLE 2 Mean Densities of Chironomid Larvae, with 95% Confidence Intervals (log. transformed) at each Site in May, July and September, 1978. The Most Abundant Taxa are listed, with the Percentage Contribution of each to the Total

	MAY	JULY	SEPTEMBER
SITE 1	2040 m^{-2} (1358-3063)	48 m^{-2} (14-99)	188 m^{-2} (80-381)
	E. claripennis (47.5%)	*E. calvescens* (55%)	*E. calvescens* (23.5%)
	E. calvescens (35.7%)	*D. insignipes* (30%)	*Thienemanniella* (23.5%)
SITE 2	710 m^{-2} (514-986)	102 m^{-2} (24-256)	5273 m^{-2} (3801-7063)
	E. claripennis (28.1%)	*E. claripennis* (37.1%)	*Orthocladius* sp.A (51.3%)
	E. calvescens (20.1%)	*E. calvescens* (15.7%)	*E. calvescens* (14.7%)
SITE 3	1085 m^{-2} (648-1824)	131 m^{-2} (81-216)	6273 m^{-2} (4818-8165)
	E. gracei (33.7%)	*E. claripennis* (20.6%)	*Orthocladius* sp.A (28.5%)
	O. thienemanni (18.7%)	*D. vulneratus* (20.6%)	*O. thienemanni* (17.6%)
		E. calvescens (14.7%)	*C. trifascia* (16.5%)

TABLE 2 (cont'd)

	MAY	JULY	SEPTEMBER
SITE 4	1443 m^{-2} (966-2159) *P. convictum* (38.2%) *P. cultellatum* (33.6%) *P. stylatus* (21.2%) *Thienemanniella* (15.9%)	2131 m^{-2} (955-4773) *P. gaedii* (35.6%) *O. thienemanni* (21.1%)	4798 m^{-2} (3352-6847) *E. clypeata* (50.3%) *O. thienemanni* (11.8%)
SITE 5	1795 m^{-2} (1341-2403) *O. thienemanni* (39.4%) *P. gaedii* (27%)	977 m^{-2} (495-1920) *P. gaedii* (55%)	5670 m^{-2} (4438-7244) *E. clypeata* (42.9%)

Table 3 lists the taxa recorded from gravel, soft sediments and *R. calcareus* at site 5 in 1977. Thirty taxa were found in gravel, 17 in soft sediments and 23 on *R. calcareus*. The mean densities of larvae on each of the substrata, together with

TABLE 3 Taxa taken in Samples from the Three Major Types of Substratum in the River Frome, at SITE 5. Numbers indicate the Relative Abundance of Taxa in each Sample. 0 = Absent, 1 = <6% of total larvae in sample, 2 = 6-10%, 3 = 11-20%, 4 = 21-30% 5 = 31-40%, 6 = 41-50%, 7 = >50%

	GRAVEL		SOFT SEDIMENT		RANUNCULUS	
	MAY	SEPT	MAY	SEPT	MAY	SEPT
TANYPODINAE						
Thienemannimyia gp.	1	0	0	0	0	0
DIAMESINAE						
Potthastia gaedii (Mg.)	1	1	0	0	0	0
PRODIAMESINAE						
Prodiamesa olivacea (Mg.)	0	0	1	0	0	0
ORTHOCLADIINAE						
Brillia sp.	0	1	0	0	1	0
Cricotopus (*C.*) *bicinctus* (Mg.)	1	1	0	0	2	1
**Cricotopus* (*C.*) sp. A	0	0	0	0	1	2
C. (*C.*) *trifascia* Edw.	1	1	0	0	0	1
C. (*Isocladius*) *trifasciatus* (Panz)	0	0	0	0	0	1
Eukiefferiella brevicalcar (K.)	0	1	0	0	0	0
E. calvescens (Edw.)	1	5	1	1	1	4
E. claripennis (Lund)	1	1	0	1	3	2
E. clypeata (K.)	1	2	0	0	1	1
E. gracei (Edw.)	7	1	0	0	1	1
E. ilkleyensis (Edw.)	1	1	0	0	7	3
E. minor (Edw.)	1	1	0	0	1	3
**Eukiefferiella* sp. C	1	3	0	0	1	1
Nanocladius rectinervis (K.)	0	1	1	0	0	1
Orthocladius (*E.*) *rivulorum* K.	1	0	0	0	0	0
O. (*E.*) *thienemanni* K.	4	1	0	3	1	1
Rheocricotopus sp.	1	1	0	0	0	1
Synorthocladius semivirens (K.)	0	1	0	0	0	1
Corynoneura sp.	0	1	1	0	0	0
Parametriocnemus stylatus (K.)	0	1	0	0	0	1
Thienemanniella sp.	0	2	2	0	2	5
CHIRONOMINAE						
Cryptochironomus	0	1	2	1	0	0
Demicryptochironomus vulneratus (Zett.)	0	1	1	1	0	0
Microtendipes sp.	0	1	0	0	1	0

TABLE 3 (cont'd)

	GRAVEL		SOFT SEDIMENT		RANUNCULUS	
	MAY	SEPT	MAY	SEPT	MAY	SEPT
Paracladopelma camptolabis (K.)	0	1	0	3	0	0
Paratendipes albimanus (Mg.)	0	0	1	0	0	0
Polypedilum convictum (Walk.)	1	0	6	1	1	0
P. cultellatum Goet.	1	1	2	5	1	0
Cladotanytarsus sp.	0	0	0	1	0	0
Micropsectra aristata Pinder	1	1	1	1	1	0
Micropsectra sp.	0	0	1	0	0	0
Rheotanytarsus sp.	1	0	0	0	1	0
Tanytarsus arduennensis Goet.	0	1	0	1	0	0

* corresponding with Cranston's (1979) terminology.

their 95% confidence limits (log. transformed) are shown in Table 4, which also lists the dominant taxa with the percentage contribution of each to the total. Whereas soft sediments were dominated by the subfamily Chironominae, the gravel and *R. calcareus* were dominated by Orthocladiinae. Several species were abundant in samples from both gravel and *R. calcareus*, notably *Eukiefferiella* sp. C, *E. calvescens* and *Thienemanniella* spp.. In contrast *E. gracei*, which was the dominant gravel species in May, occurred rarely in *R. calcareus* samples, where *E. ilkleyensis* dominated.

TABLE 4 Densities of Chironomid Larvae, with 95% Confidence Intervals/Log. Transformed, in Different Substrata. Dominant Taxa are listed, with the Percentage contributed by each to the Total

	MAY 1977	SEPTEMBER 1977
GRAVEL	3668 m^{-2} (3214-4188) *E. gracei* (51.2%) *O. thienemanni* (27.8%) *P. gaedii* (5%)	2432 m^{-2} (1422-4157) *E. calvescens* (38.3%) *E.* sp. C (12.3%) *Thienemanniella* sp. (8.8%) *E. clypeata* (8.3%)
SOFT SEDIMENTS	1691 m^{-2} (1040-2566) *P. convictum* (44.8%) *P. cultellatum* (10.3%) *Thienemanniella* sp. (10.3%) *Cryptochironomus* sp. (6.9%)	1910 m^{-2} (1351-2702) *P. cultellatum* (31.6%) *P. camptolabis* (15.8%) *O. thienemanni* (10.6%)
R. calcareus	15421 m^{-2} (12314-19302) *E. ilkleyensis* (57.2%) *E. claripennis* (11.4%) *Thienemanniella* sp. (8.2%) *C. bicinctus* (6.2%)	3121 m^{-2} (2451-3977) *Thienemanniella* sp. (30.8%) *E. calvescens* (23.5%) *E.* sp. C (13.9%) *E. ilkleyensis* (10.6%)

Table 5 compares gravel samples taken at site 5 in May and September of 1977 and 1978. *Orthocladius thienemanni* and *Thienemanniella* spp. were more or less equally represented in both years. In contrast, *Eukiefferiella gracei*, *E. calvescens* and *Eukiefferiella* sp. C were much more abundant in 1977, whilst the opposite was true of *Potthastia gaedii* and *E. clypeata*.

TABLE 5 Comparison between the Dominant Taxa in Gravel Samples from Site 5 in 1977 and 1978. Percentages indicate the Proportion contributed by each Taxon to the Total

		1977	1978
MAY	*E. gracei*	51.2%	5.2%
	O. thienemanni	27.8%	39.4%
	P. gaedii	5%	27%
SEPTEMBER	*E. clypeata*	8.3%	42.9%
	E. calvescens	38.3%	4.1%
	E. sp. C	12.3%	2.4%
	Thienemanniella	8.8%	6.8%

TABLE 6 Distribution of Major Taxa in Soft Sediments at Site 6 (Tadnoll Brook)

	More abundant in sandy sediments	More abundant in sediments with organic detritus	Equally abundant in both types of sediment
TANYPODINAE		*A. trifascipennis* *M. nebulosa* *P. choreus*	
DIAMESINAE	*P. gaedii*		
PRODIAMESINAE	*Odontomesa fulva*	*P. olivacea*	
ORTHOCLADIINAE		*H. marcidus*	
CHIRONOMINAE	*P. camptolabis*(1) *P. cultellatum* *Cladotanytarsus* sp.		*P. camptolabis*(2) *P. albimanus* *Micropsectra* spp. *Tanytarsus* spp.

(1) Late summer generation.
(2) Spring and early summer generations.

Most of the common species in the Tadnoll Brook (site 6) showed a clearly defined preference for either sandy sediments or for those containing quantities of organic detritus (Table 6). *Paracladopelma camptolabis* larvae were more abundant in sandy deposits in the late summer, but in spring and early summer they were equally abundant in both sandy and organic sediments. No such change in distribution was noted for any other species.

DISCUSSION

The list of taxa recorded in this study is relatively short, comprising only 45 species. Undoubtedly a complete species list would be considerably longer, indeed Pinder (1974) recorded 75 species from a single site on the Tadnoll Brook. However, most of the common species at each site are probably included, since gravel samples inevitably also contain a certain amount of fine sediment, and most of the species typical of *R. calcareus* also occur to some extent on gravel.

A number of studies have included lists of chironomid larvae, but, because of the varying degrees to which different authors have taken the identification of their material, comparisons are difficult to make. Thienemann (1954) concluded that in mountain streams Orthocladiinae constitute *c.* 80% of the total number of species with Chironominae making up only *c*. 10%. Gradually the relationship alters with decreasing altitude until, in lowland rivers, Chironominae predominate with *c*. 55% of the total and Orthocladiinae *c*. 30%. On this basis the fauna of the River Frome has more in common with that of a mountain stream than a lowland river. In noting a similar situation in the Danish stream, Linding Å, Lindegaard-Petersen (1972) attributed it to the low summer temperatures of Linding Å. Summer temperatures in the Frome are also low, though not as low as in Linding Å, as they are in chalk streams in general (Westlake and colleagues, 1972). An additional and more important factor contributing to the abundance of Orthocladiinae in the Frome is the nature of the dominant substrata. The relatively high current velocities which occur in chalk streams (Westlake and colleagues, 1972; Casey & Newton, 1973) favour the establishment of a bed composed of gravel, rather than fine particles, and the clarity of the water together with an abundance of major plant nutrients (Westlake and colleagues, 1972) encourages the establishment of extensive growths of submergent macrophytes. Both of these types of substratum favour Orthocladiinae rather than Chironominae as is shown by Table 3, in which 68% of the taxa in gravel samples and 78% of those on *R. calcareus* were Orthocladiinae whilst only 38% of those in soft sediments belonged to this family.

The reason for the change in the distribution of *P. camptolabis* in late summer is not clear. At about this time, however, the populations of Tanypodinae, mainly *A. trifascipennis*, *M. nebulosa* and *P. choreus* which are low during the first half of the year, build up rapidly in the organic rich deposits. A probable explanation is that the numbers of *P. camptolabis* are reduced in these areas as a result of competition with, or direct predation by, Tanypodinae.

A good deal of overlap was found to exist between the faunas of different substrata, and the relative abundance of particular species may vary quite considerably between seasons, from one year to another, and between sites. Nevertheless, it is possible to identify groups of species which are characteristic of a particular substratum type, as follows:

R. calcareus; *Eukiefferiella ilkleyensis*, *E. calvescens*, *E. claripennis*, *Cricotopus* sp. A, *C. bicinctus*, *C. trifasciatus*, *Thienemanniella* sp. (mainly *T. vittata* (Edw.)), *Rheotanytarsus curtistylus* (Goet.).

Gravel; *Eukiefferiella gracei*, *E. calvescens*, *E. claripennis*, *E. clypeata*, *Orthocladius thienemanni*, *Diamesa insignipes* (site 1 only).

Sandy sediments; *Potthastia gaedii*, *Cladotanytarsus* sp. (principally *C. vanderwulpi* (Edw.)).

Detritus rich sediments; *Apsectrotanypus trifascipennis*, *Macropelopia nebulosa*, *Procladius choreus*, *Prodiamesa olivacea*, *Heterotrissocladius marcidus*.

Soft sediments generally; *Paratendipes albimanus*, *Micropsectra* spp. (including *M. aristata*), *Tanytarsus* spp. (including *T. arduennensis* and *T. brundini*).

ACKNOWLEDGEMENTS

Thanks are due to Mrs A Matthews and Mr J A B Bass for assistance in collecting and sorting the samples, and to Miss J Harrison for typing the manuscript. The work was partially supported by the Department of the Environment (Contract No. DGR 480/309).

REFERENCES

Casey, H., and P. V. R. Newton (1973). The chemical composition and flow of the River Frome and its main tributaries. *Freshwat. Biol.*, 3, 317-333.

Cranston, P. S. (1979). The Biosystematics of British Aquatic Orthocladiinae (Diptera: Chironomidae). *PhD Thesis*, University of London.

Ford, J. B. (1957). A study of the biology and distribution of mud-dwelling chironomid larvae in a chalk stream. *PhD Thesis*, University of Southampton.

Hall, R. E. (1951). Comparative observations on the chironomid fauna of a chalk stream and a system of acid streams. *J. Soc. Br. Ent.*, 3, 253-262.

Hall, R. E. (1961). The Chironomidae of three chalk streams in southern England. *Proc. 11th. int. congr. Ent.*, Vienna 1960, 1, 178-181.

Lindegaard-Petersen, C. (1972). An ecological investigation of the Chironomidae (Diptera) from a Danish lowland stream (Linding Å). *Arch. Hydrobiol.*, 69, 465-507.

Pinder, L. C. V. (1974). The Chironomidae of a small chalk stream in southern England. *Ent. Tidskr.*, 95, 195-202.

Pinder, L. C. V. (1977). The Chironomidae and their ecology in chalk streams. *Rep. Freshwat. biol. Ass.*, 45, 62-69.

Snedecor, G. W., and W. G. Cochran (1967). *Statistical Methods*. Ames, Iowa.

Thienemann, A. (1954). Chironomus. Leben, Verbreitung und wirtschaftliche Bedeutung der Chironomiden. *Binnengewässer*, 20, 1-834.

Westlake, D. F., H. Casey, H. Dawson, M. Ladle, R. H. K. Mann and A. F. H. Marker (1972). The chalk stream ecosystem. In Z. Kajak and A. Hillbricht-Ilkowska (Eds), *Proceedings of the IBP-UNESCO Symposium, Kazimierz Dolny, Poland. 6-12 May 1970*. Warszawa-Krakow, 615-635.

Taxonomic Composition of Chironomidae (Diptera) in a Sand-Bottomed Stream of Northern Florida

Annelle R. Soponis

Laboratory of Aquatic Entomology, Florida A and M University, Tallahassee, Florida 32307, U.S.A.

ABSTRACT

Drift nets were placed in the stream for 24 hour periods twice each month. Pupal exuviae and larvae were examined. Results of 6 months of sampling are given. Five major taxa of Chironomidae were found: Chironomini (dominant), Orthocladiinae, Tanytarsini, Tanypodinae, and Diamesinae. Forty-two genera were identified. Future work is outlined.

KEYWORDS

Chironomidae. Florida. Sand-bottomed stream. Drift. Emergence.

INTRODUCTION

This investigation began as one way to add names to the species list of the Chironomidae of Florida. About 180 species are recorded for the state (Beck and Beck, 1959, and subsequent works), but as many as 400 species have been estimated for Florida. Where could 200 unrecorded species be found? A clue to the answer to this question was found in the literature.

Beck and Beck (1974) reported unusual distributions for chironomids based on collections from the Blackwater River Basin in Florida. They concluded that the Blackwater was not unique or misplaced geographically. Rather, these unusual distributions had remained unrecorded because the microhabitats of the species had not been searched at the right time. They suggested that searches of other habitats with this concept in mind would yield similar results.

One habitat that attracted the attention of the author was the sand-bottomed stream. The sand-bottomed stream "is the most widely distributed and most frequently encountered type of stream in the state (Florida). It has been the most typical feature of the area and is the one disappearing most rapidly with the alteration of drainage patterns" (Beck 1965, 116). It was surprising then, to learn that little work has been published on the chironomid composition of these streams.

Turkey Creek is a typical sand-bottomed stream. It was selected for study because of its small size, easy accessibility, and close proximity to Tallahassee. Initially only benthic samples of larvae were collected for identification. However, it soon became apparent that species could be determined more readily from pupal exuviae collected in the drift. Two nets were placed in the stream for 24 hour periods twice each month.

Based on drift samples and general collections from February through July, 1979, 42 genera of chironomids have been identified from Turkey Creek. Chironomini are dominant in both numbers of individuals and numbers of genera. Orthocladiinae and Tanytarsini are also well represented. Other taxa found in fewer numbers are Tanypodinae and Diamesinae. These results should be regarded as tentative until more sampling is done. Future work includes determination of specimens to species and identification of larvae to instar.

STUDY AREA

Turkey Creek ($30^{o}29'$N, $84^{o}35'$W) is a small, spring-fed tributary of Rocky Comfort Creek in Gadsden County, Florida (T1N, R4W, LG32). The stream (Fig. 1) meanders through forest for 6.28 km from the headwaters to the sampling site. Then, in .36 km it joins Rocky Comfort which empties into Lake Talquin. These waters are part of the Ochlockonee River Basin.

The sampling site is located at a bridge on State Highway 65B about 14.48 km south of Quincy. At the bridge the upstream drainage area of Turkey Creek is 12.38 km^2 (USGS). The stream averages about 4 m in width at the sampling site. During floods the width can reach 20 m. The average depth of the stream is about 15 to 30 cm. During floods the depth can reach 2.5 m.

Velocity readings taken during the study period (Table 1) ranged from 0.07 m/sec to 0.34 m/sec. Three estimates of discharge have been made for Turkey Creek (USGS): Sept. 9, 1958, 0.08 m^3/sec; Nov. 13, 1958, 0.09m^3/sec; Sept. 23, 1976, 0.04 m^3/sec.

The bottom is sand of predominantly (55%) medium particle size (>.25 mm, <.50 mm). Fine particle-sized sand (>.106 mm, <.25 mm) is next most abundant (34%). The stream bed is free from vegetation except for occasional plants along stream margins. Sand bars are common along the length of the stream, often with pool areas behind. The pools are flushed by periodic flooding of the stream.

Dominant plants of the surrounding forest are the same as those listed for Rocky Comfort Creek by Pescador and Peters (1974). In addition, leaves of the southern magnolia, *Magnolia grandiflora* Linnaeus, are commonly found in the stream.

Table 1 Flow (m/sec) and Temperatures (^{o}C) recorded for Turkey Creek on Sampling Dates in 1979.

	II/11	II/27	III/19	III/28	IV/17	IV/28	V/21	V/29	VI/13	VI/26	VII/10	VII/30
Net 1	0.13	0.18	0.31	0.27	0.07	0.28	0.08	0.11	0.32	0.34	0.30	0.16
Net 2	0.21	0.24	0.24	0.20	0.07	0.08	0.25	0.13	0.21	0.18	0.23	0.15
^{o}C	11.5	12.0	20.0	20.1	19.0	19.9	20.0	19.5	20.0	23.0	23.0	23.8

METHODS

Two nets were placed in the stream for 24 hour periods twice each month. Net 1 was positioned near the bank (1 m away). Net 2 was positioned near the middle of the stream (2 m from bank). Both nets were suspended from a log placed across the stream. This allowed part of the net to remain above the water surface so that floating exuviae could be trapped. Initially nets were placed upstream of the bridge. However, after spring flooding in April, water was too slow and deep at the upstream site. In May, nets were placed downstream of the bridge where water was more shallow.

Drift nets consisted of an aquatic net bag (Ward's No. 10W0616, 34 mesh to 2.5 cm) fitted onto a 30.48 cm diameter hoop of the standard insect aerial net. Frequently nets placed in 20 cm or less of water would, by the end of the 24 hr period, be almost completely submerged. The current excavated a hole in the sand allowing the nets to sink.

Temperature and flow were recorded twice each month (Table 1). Temperature was taken with a standard laboratory thermometer or field thermometer to the nearest 0.1^{o}C. Current was recorded with an Inter Ocean Flow Meter (TKS USA model 313). Measured to the middle of the meter, the meter was held about 15 cm below the surface of the water.

Nets were emptied into a container and preserved with ethanol in the field. Samples were sorted by the author by hand under a dissecting microscope. Care was taken to be as thorough as possible. Specimens were slide-mounted in Euparol according to standard techniques. A total of 849 pupal exuviae and 1354 larvae were collected in the drift during the 6 month sampling period.

RESULTS

Forty-two genera of Chironomidae (Table 2) have been identified from Turkey Creek. Genera not found in the drift were collected with dip nets from pool areas.

The numbers of larvae and pupal exuviae from nets 1 and 2 were each plotted against flow. No relationship was detected between numbers and flow.

The density of drift (Table 3) was estimated as the numbers of chironomids per volume of water passing through the net in 24 hours (volume=velocity x net area). Total area of the net was used.

Two nets were placed in the stream in order to determine whether or not position affected the numbers of specimens found in the drift. A t-test was used to compare the 6 month means of numbers of larvae and pupal exuviae in nets 1 and 2. The difference ($P>.1$) between the nets was not significant. Totals of both nets were combined and are here referred to as drift.

The Chironomini are the most abundant taxon represented in the drift comprising 35% of pupal exuviae and 64% of larvae. Orthocladiinae (27% pupal exuviae, 21% larvae) and Tanytarsini (26% pupal exuviae, 9% larvae) are well represented. Tanypodinae also comprise a regular part of the drift (11% pupal exuviae, 5% larvae). Diamesinae were not abundant during the sampling period (1% pupal exuviae, <1% larvae).

Peak emergence of all taxa occurred in May (Figs. 2,5) with sharp declines by July. Chironomini and Orthocladiinae had moderate to large emergences throughout the sampling period.

Peak numbers (354) of larvae were found in the drift in June (Fig. 2). These were largely Chironomini (Fig. 6), followed by Orthocladiinae. Larvae of Tanypodinae were not abundant in the drift. Larvae of Tanytarsini became more numerous in the drift during May and June.

TABLE 2 Taxonomic Composition of the Chironomidae of Turkey Creek by Genera and Major Taxa. (* not found in drift)

Tanypodinae

- Ablabesmyia
- Conchapelopia
- Clinotanypus *
- Djamalbatista *
- Guttipelopia *
- Paramerina
- Procladius *
- Larsia

Diamesinae

- Odontomesa
- Pagastia

Orthocladiinae

- Brillia
- "Cordites"
- Corynoneura
- Cricotopus
- Eukiefferiella
- Limnophyes
- Nanocladius
- Orthocladius
- Parakiefferiella
- Parametriocnemus
- Rheocricotopus
- Thienemaniella

Chironominae

Chironomini

- Chironomus
- Cryptochironomus
- Cryptotendipes *
- Dicrotendipes *
- Einfeldia *
- Glyptotendipes
- Paracladopelma *
- Parachironomus
- Paratendipes *
- Paralauterborniella
- Phaenopsectra *
- Polypedilum
- Robackia
- Stenochironomus
- Stictochironomus
- Tribelos

Tanytarsini

- Cladotanytarsus
- Paratanytarsus
- Rheotanytarsus
- Tanytarsus

TABLE 3 Density of Drifting Chironomids in Turkey Creek from February through July, 1979. (numbers/24 hr per m^3/sec)

	Net 1		Net 2	
	Pupal Exuviae	Larvae	Pupal Exuviae	Larvae
High	18,793	9,000	8,555	9,800
Low	365	384	200	800
Avg.	2,550	3,566	2,500	4,557

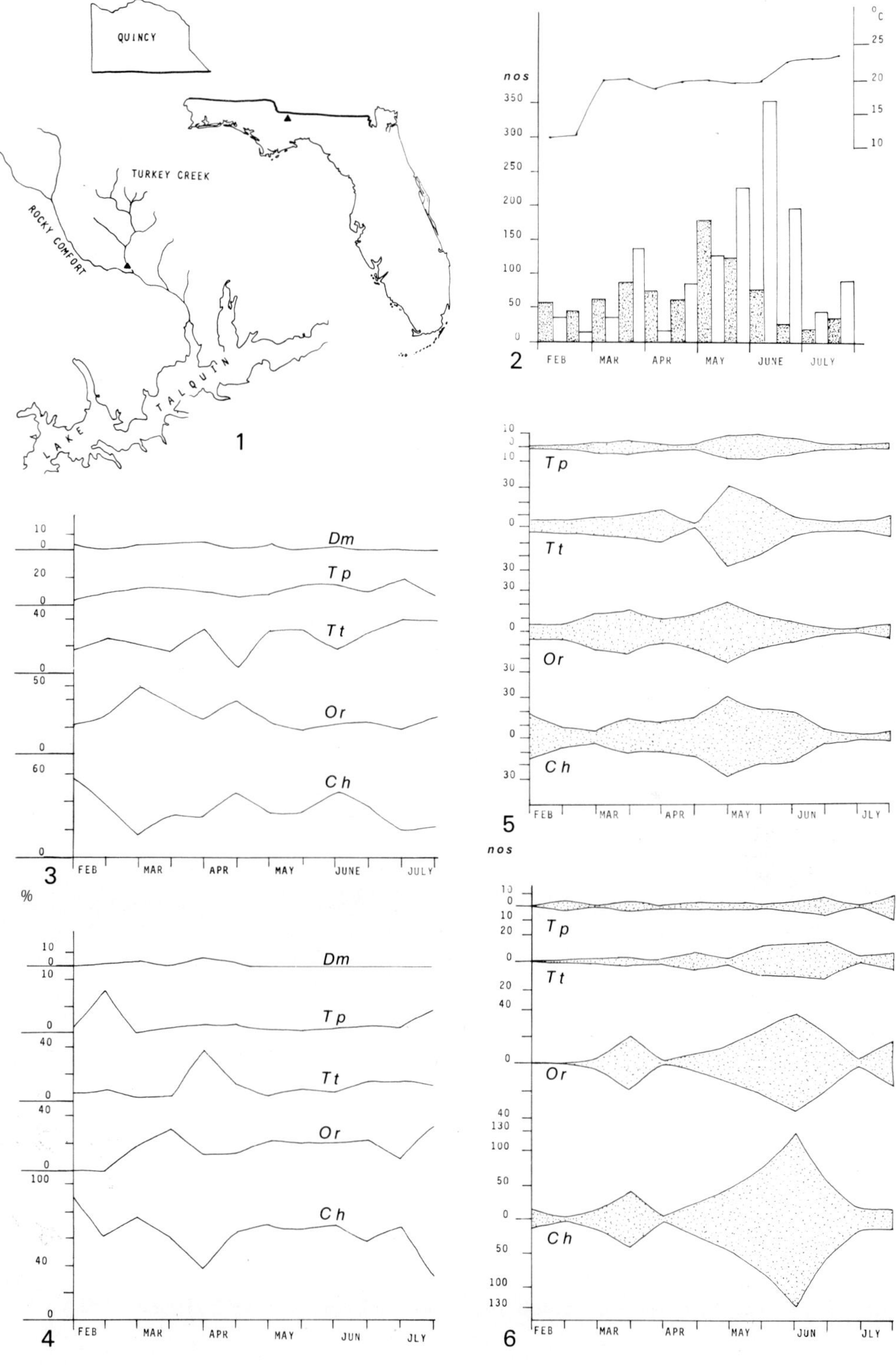
QUINCY
TURKEY CREEK
ROCKY COMFORT
LAKE TALQUIN
1
nos
°C
2
FEB MAR APR MAY JUNE JULY
Dm
Tp
Tt
Or
Ch
3
%
4
5
6

Fig. 1. Map of Turkey Creek with inset of state map. Dark triangle marks sampling site.

Fig. 2. Total numbers of larvae (light bars) and pupal exuviae (dark bars) in drift of Turkey Creek from February through July, 1979. Water temperature plotted above.

Fig. 3. Percentage composition of pupal exuviae in the drift by major taxon.

Fig. 4. Percentage composition of larvae in the drift by major taxon.

Fig. 5. Composition (total numbers) of pupal exuviae in the drift by major taxon.

Fig. 6. Composition (total numbers) of larvae in the drift by major taxon.

Abbreviations: Ch: Chironomini; Dm: Diamesinae; Or: Orthocladiinae; Tp: Tanypodinae; Tt: Tanytarsini

DISCUSSION

In recent years several reports on the drift of chironomids in streams have appeared (Ali and Mulla, 1978; Coffman, 1973,1974; Cowell and Carew, 1976; Wartinbee, 1979; Wartinbee and Coffman, 1976; Wilson, 1977; Wilson and Bright, 1973). The data on Turkey Creek in the present form cannot be compared to many of these studies. However, a comparison of the chironomid composition of Turkey Creek can be made with that reported for Linesville Creek, Pennsylvania (Coffman, 1973).

The Chironomini dominate the fauna in Turkey Creek whereas the Orthocladiinae dominate the fauna in Linesville Creek. It appears that the Tanypodinae and the Tanytarsini comprise a similar makeup in both streams. The numbers of genera of Chironomini, Tanypodinae, and Diamesinae found in Turkey Creek compare favorably with the numbers reported from Linesville Creek. Diamesinae are represented by two genera in both habitats, but higher numbers are recorded for Linesville Creek. However, Diamesinae are winter active and the data for Turkey Creek do not include the winter months.

Only half the number of genera reported for the Tanytarsini and Orthocladiinae in Linesville Creek occur in Turkey Creek. These results may be real, or they may change with further investigation. The Orthocladiinae are generally more active in the winter, and again, these data here do not include the winter months. The low numbers of Tanytarsini reported may be due to the author's present taxonomic ignorance of the group.

Based on the 6 month sampling period, emergence of all taxa occurs earlier in Turkey Creek than in Linesville Creek. Before generalizations can be made, yearly samples must be taken.

A high faunal diversity is indicated for Turkey Creek based on the 42 genera presently reported. The contention that sand-bottomed streams are biological deserts is not supported by the data presented here.

The high numbers of larvae found in the drift in May and June cannot be explained at present. Larvae must be identified to instar; specimens must be determined to species; and sampling must continue into the fall and winter months.

In conclusion, the Chironomidae of Turkey Creek constitute an interesting and diverse fauna. Much work remains to be done before information can be gained about the life histories of the chironomid species inhabiting sand-bottomed streams. This work should, however, provide insights into the dynamics of one of Florida's more interesting habitats.

ACKNOWLEDGMENT

I would like to thank the following people: D. Towns for stimulating discussions about streams; B. T. Kidd for assistance with field work; W. M. Beck, Jr. and D. R. Oliver for help with difficult identifications; W. M. Beck, Jr. and B. C. Cowell for constructive comments on the typescript; and C. L. Russell and C. A. Starling for technical assistance.

This material is based upon work supported by the National Science Foundation under Grant No. R1M78-17403, A. R. Soponis, Principal Investigator. This research is also supported by a research program (FLAX 79009) of the SEA/CR, USDA, to Florida A and M University, W. L. Peters, Research Leader.

REFERENCES

Ali, A. and M. S. Mulla (1978). Mosq. News, 38, 122-126.
Beck, E. C. and W. M. Beck, Jr. (1959). Bull. Fla. State Mus., 4, 85-96.
Beck, W. M. ,Jr. (1965). Bull. Fla. State Mus., 10, 91-126.
Beck, W. M. ,Jr. and E. C. (1974). Entomol. tidskr., 95, 18-20.
Coffman, W. P. (1973). Arch. Hydrobiol., 71, 281-322.
Coffman, W. P. (1974). Entomol. tidskr., 95, 42-48.
Cowell, B. C. and W. C. Carew (1976). Freshwater Biol., 6, 587-594.
Pescador, M. L. and W. L. Peters (1974). Bull. Fla. State Mus., 17, 151-209.
Wartinbee, D. C. (1979). Freshwater Biol., 9, 147-156.
Wartinbee, D. C. and W. P. Coffman (1976). Am. Midl. Nat., 95, 479-485.
Wilson, R. S. (1977). Freshwater Biol., 7, 9-17.
Wilson, R. S. and P. L. Bright (1973). Freshwater Biol., 3, 283-302.

Chironomids and Particles : Microorganisms and Chironomid Distribution in a Peaty Upland River

R. J. Toscano and A. J. McLachlan

Dept. of Zoology, The University, Newcastle-upon-Tyne NE1 7RU, England

ABSTRACT

Quantitative samples of chironomid larvae and bottom sediments were taken at eight sites along the River North Tyne in May and August 1979. Numbers of bacteria in sediment samples at each site were estimated, using epifluorescence microscopy. In the lower reaches, the size of the larval chironomid community was closely related to the weight of particulate material present, as suggested in previous studies. In the peaty headwaters, however, low numbers of larvae were found, despite an apparent abundance of particles. In these headwater sites, the nutritional quality of the particulate material, as indicated by bacterial numbers, was very low. It is suggested that in the upper reaches, particle food quality rather than quantity may be an important factor limiting the density of the larval chironomid community.

KEYWORDS

Chironomids, Bacteria, Particles, Peat, Epifluorescence microscopy.

INTRODUCTION

In many freshwater ecosystems, terrestrially derived organic matter forms a major part of the diet of the invertebrate community (Hynes, 1975). It has become apparent that this material is made available as food to detritivores largely through the activities of microorganisms, particularly bacteria and fungi (Barlocher & Kendrick, 1973; Kaushik & Hynes, 1971; Mackay & Kalff, 1973). Recently, Ward & Cummins (1979) showed that the growth pattern of larvae of the midge *Paratendipes albimanus* was related to seasonal change in the microbial biomass of its food in a stream. Studies on a Northumberland bog lake (McLachlan & Dickinson, 1977) showed that larvae of *Chironomus lugubris* were attracted to sediments containing the highest numbers of bacteria.

The larval chironomid community of the River North Tyne has received attention in recent years. Brennan, McLachlan & Wotton (1978) concluded that in the lower reaches, the size of the larval community was limited by the amount of particles available for both feeding and tube building. However, Walentowicz & McLachlan (in press and personal communication) have shown that this relationship may break down in the upper reaches, where large quantities of peat particles are eroded into the water. This leads to the deposition of bottom sediments which have a high organic content, but are very poor in organic nitrogen. Walentowicz & McLachlan have suggested that in these humic headwater streams, larval chironomid densities may be limited by the low nutritional quality of the detrital food. This apparently food limited environment provides an excellent opportunity to study the effects of spatial changes in microbial abundance, and hence detrital food quality, on larval chironomid distribution. In the present study we have attempted to measure changes in particle quantity and microbial quality along the length of the North Tyne river. In doing this, we hoped to assess the relative importance of particle amount and nutritional quality in determining the density of the larval chironomid community. This paper is a preliminary report based on the first few months sampling in a three year programme.

THE STUDY AREA

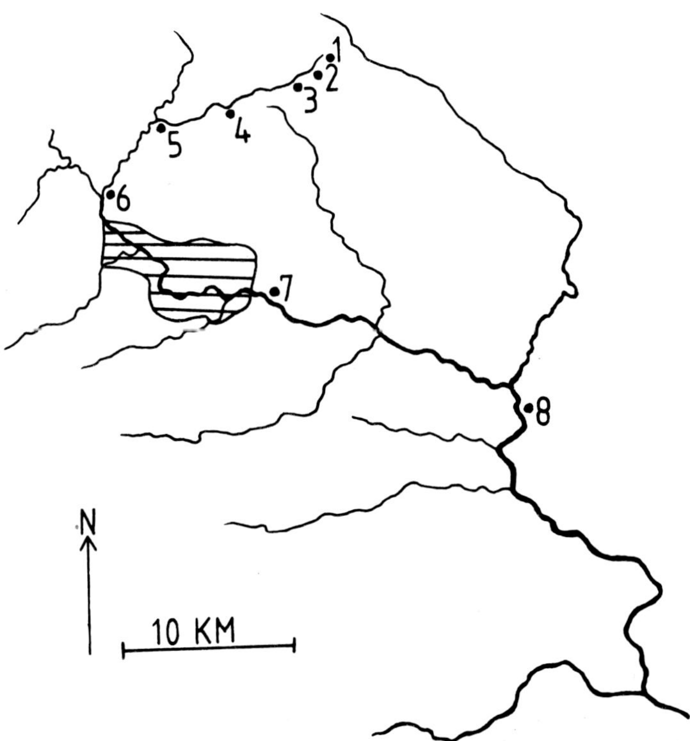

Fig. 1. Map of the River North Tyne, showing the location of the sampling sites 1-8. The area to be flooded to form Kielder Water is shaded.

The River North Tyne is located in Northumberland in the North of England. In its upper reaches it drains extensive areas of moorland peat, the lower regions of which have been drained and planted with coniferous forest. In its lower reaches, it develops into a typical northern salmonid river, with long stretches of slowly flowing water, broken at frequent invervals by riffle sections. The river undergoes frequent heavy spates, which have a scouring effect. This prevents the accumulation of particulate material and the growth of macrophytes, and restricts the development of stone surface animal communities. A dam is at present under construction, and the resulting Kielder Water will flood an estimated 1000-2000 hectares of the surrounding land.

Eight sampling sites were chosen (Fig. 1), taking in the full spectrum of changes from the source to the main river. Site 7 was situated immediately downstream of the dam construction area, in order to make it possible to monitor changes associated with the construction and filling of the reservoir.

MATERIALS AND METHODS

Field Sampling

A sampler (Fig. 2), based on a design by Coffman, Cummins & Wuycheck (1971), was used to collect quantitative samples of both fauna and bottom sediments simultaneously.

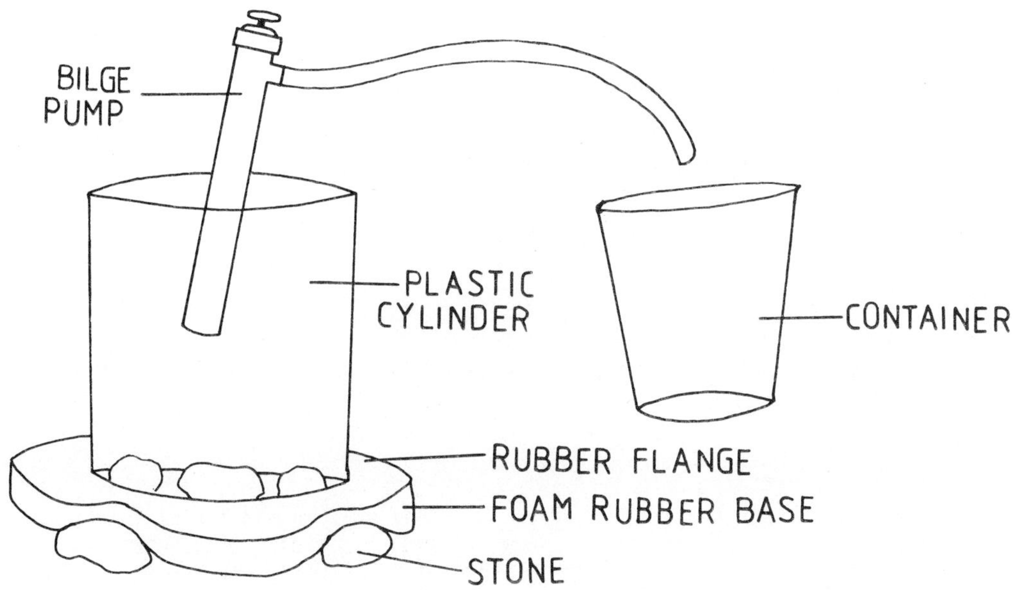

Fig. 2. Diagram of the sampler used to collect quantitative samples of fauna and sediments.

The sampler consisted of an open plastic cylinder, covering an area of 500 cm^2, and surrounded at its base by a 10 cm wide rubber flange, with a 10 cm thick layer of foam rubber attached to its underside. During sampling, this device was located on the stream bottom and held in position by placing weights on the rubber flange. The foam base formed a seal around the sampling area, preventing material from entering or escaping. Epilithic material, fauna, water and sediments were then transfered to a container, using a bilge pump and a soft brush to scrub stone surfaces. A 100 ml subsample was then removed from the resulting sample and fixed in a solution of 0.5% glutaraldehyde in 0.1M cacodylate buffer, for later microbial counts and particle weight analysis. The remaining sample was poured through a 212um mesh sieve, and the material retained preserved in 5% formalin for later examination of fauna. Using this method, it was possible to determine larval chironomid numbers, weight of particles and numbers of micro-organisms in each sample. Samples were collected in May and August, 1979, with a minimum of five replicate samples taken at each site on each occasion.

Analysis of Field Samples

Counts of microorganisms in sediment samples were done using epifluorescence microscopy This technique makes it possible to obtain direct counts of micro-organisms associated with inert particulate material.

A part of each sediment subsample from each site was pooled to provide a single subsample for direct counts. Particles were stained with a 10 mg/l solution of acridine orange, following principally the method of Jones & Simon (1975), with the following modification; samples were sonified at 16 Khz for 30 secs. in order to disperse aggregates. All glassware used during staining was autoclaved prior to use and all solutions used were first sterilised by filtering them through 0.22um pore diameter 'Millipore' membranes. Preparations were examined under oil immersion using a 'Reichert Zetopan' microscope, fitted with a mercury HBO 200N light source and the following filter combination; blue barrier filters GGI and OG515 and blue exciter filters FITC 490 and BG 38. One slide was prepared from the pooled sample from each site on each occasion. A minimum of thirty fields were counted on each slide, and the mean numbers of cells per field and the 95% confidence limits determined. Very few fungi were found during the study period, and therefore no attempt has been made to quantify fungal densities.

After bacterial counts, the remaining sediment subsamples were each dried at 60° C and weighed separately, to provide an estimate of the weight of particles present at each site.

Faunal samples were sorted and chironomid larvae counted and classified as far as subfamily or tribe. Each sample was then weighed wet to provide an estimate of chironomid biomass.

RESULTS

The results obtained for bacterial numbers, particle weights and larval chironomid numbers on both sampling occasions are shown in Fig. 3. Figure 3(a) shows the number of bacteria per gram of sediment at each site. In May, numbers show a rapid downstream increase from Site 1 to Site 4, after which the values fluctuate. A similar trend is apparent in August, although values are much higher throughout in this month and differences between the sites are less pronounced.

Figure 3(b) illustrates the weight of deposited fine particulate material present per square metre of stream bottom at each site. Large quantities of particles are present upstream at Site 1 in both May and August, but on both occasions there is a steady downstream decrease in weight of particles as far as Site 3, after which the values again fluctuate.

The number of chironomid larvae per square metre at each site is shown in Fig. 3(c). In May, very few larvae are present in the headwaters, but numbers then show a steady downstream increase, reaching a peak of 2280 m^{-2} at Site 5. In August, numbers are much higher throughout, but a downstream increase in abundance over the first five sites is again apparent. It is notable that at Site 7, which is immediately downstream of the dam construction area, numbers of larvae are very low for both months.

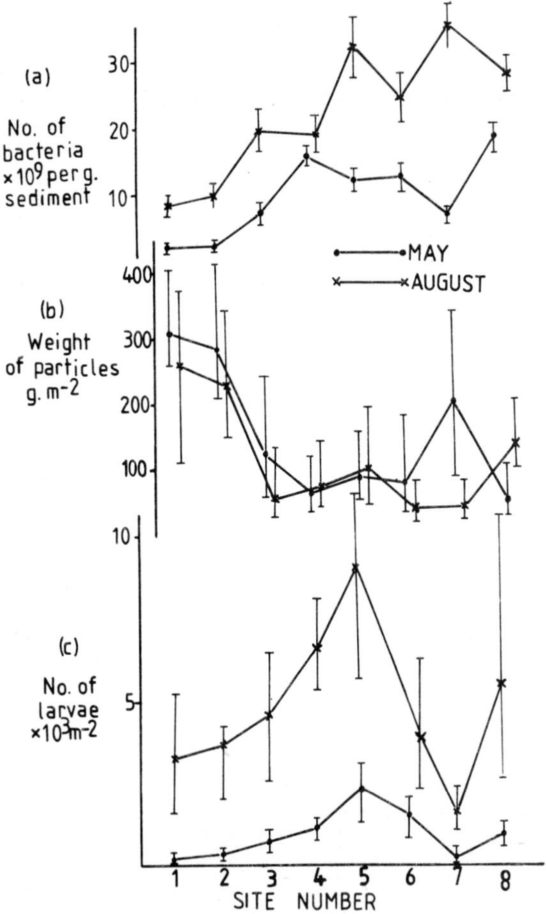

Fig. 3. (a) Numbers of bacteria present in sediment samples at each site in May and August. The mean numbers of cells from thirty replicate counts from one sub-sample and 95% confidence limits, are indicated.

(b) Weight of deposited fine particulate material (particles < 750um diameter) per square metre of stream bottom at each site. Each point is the mean, ± log transformed 95% confidence limits, of five replicate sample units.

(c) Mean number of larvae per square metre of stream bottom at each site, ± log transformed 95% confidence limits, based on five replicate sample units.

The results on particle weight, bacterial numbers and larval numbers show a pattern of distribution along the length of the river. At the downstream sites 4, 5, 6 and 8, larval densities to be related to the total weight of particles present. In the headwaters, particularly at Sites 1 and 2, the availability of particles is much greater than downstream, but larval densities are comparatively low. At these sites, the nutritional quality of the particulate material, reflected in the bacterial numbers, is also low. Downstream increase in particle food quality from Sites 1 to 3 are reflected by a corresponding increase in larval numbers. This data suggests that there is a trend along the length of the river system, from the headwaters, where food quality limits larval abundance, to the lower reaches, where food quality is relatively high and particle availability is the principal factor limiting larval densities.

The low larval numbers recorded at Site 7 are of some interest. This site was situated immediately downstream of the dam construction works, where the deleterious effects of large inputs of inorganic material are to be expected. It seems likely that the low larval densities recorded at Site 7 may have been due to a periodic blanketing out of the stream bottom by large amounts of silt. It will be interesting to monitor changes at this site on completion and filling of the reservoir.

DISCUSSION

It is apparent from the results presented here that considerable spatial variations in microbial abundance may occur over relatively short distances in upland streams and rivers. Ward & Cummins (1979) have defined the 'food quality' of detrital material as its microbial biomass per unit of detritus, food quality improving with an increase in numbers of microorganisms. It therefore seems likely that the spatial variations in bacterial abundance observed in this study can be taken to indicate variations in detrital food quality. Our data, along with that of Walentowicz & McLachlan (in press and personal communication), suggest that in the upper reaches of peaty rivers, detrital food quality is very poor, and this may account for the low density of larval chironomids there. Downstream increases in larval numbers appear to correspond to an improvement in food quality, up to a point at which total particle availability becomes the main factor limiting larval density, as suggested by Brennan, McLachlan & Wotton (1978).

A similar downstream improvement in detrital quality has been noted in the River Duddon by Minshall & Minshall (1978). In the North Tyne, there is a change in the nature of the allochthonous material entering the river, from peat in the headwaters, to conifer needles and deciduous leaves further downstream. Leaves probably provide a higher quality food, and this may account for much of the downstream improvement in food quality. This type of downstream change may be widespread in many river systems, although changes may not perhaps be as clear as they are in the low nutrient peaty waters of the upper North Tyne.

ACKNOWLEDGEMENTS

The authors would like to thank Mr. Alan Sanderson for his assistance with the field work. The study was sponsored by a Ridley Fellowship from the University of Newcastle-upon-Tyne.

REFERENCES

Barlocher, F., and B. Kendrick (1973). Fungi and food preferences in Gammarus pseudolimnaeus (Amphipoda). Oikos, 24, 295-300.

Brennan, A., A.J. McLachlan, and R.S. Wotton (1978). Particulate material and midge larvae (Diptera: Chironomidae) in an upland river. Hydrobiologia, 59, 67-73.

Coffman, W.P., K.W. Cummins, and J.C. Wvycheck (1971). Energy flow in a woodland stream ecosystem: I Tissue support structure of the autumnal community. Arch. Hydrobiol., 68, 232-276.

Hynes, H.B.N. (1975). The stream and its valley. Verh. Int. Verein. Limnol., 19, 1-15.

Jones, J.G., and B.M. Simon (1975). An investigation of errors in direct counts of aquatic bacteria by epifluorescence microscopy, with reference to a new method for dyeing membrane filters. J. Appl. Bact., 39, 317-329.

Kaushik, N.K., and H.B.N. Hynes (1971). The fate of the dead leaves that fall into streams. Arch. Hydrobiol., 68, 465-515.

Mackay, R.J., and J. Kalff (1973). Ecology of two related species of caddis fly larvae in the organic substrates of a woodland stream. Ecology, 54, 499-511.

McLachlan, A.J., and C.J. Dickinson (1977). Microorganisms as a factor in the distribution of Chironomus lugubris Zetterstedt in a bog lake. Arch. Hydrobiol., 80, 133-146.

Minshall, G.W., and J.N. Minshall (1978). Further evidence on the role of chemical factors in determining the distribution of benthic invertebrates in the River Duddon. Arch. Hydrobiol., 83, 324-355.

Walentowicz, A.T., and A.J. McLachlan. Chironomids and particles: A field experiment with peat in an upland stream. Proceedings of the VIIth International Chironomid symposium.

Ward, G.M., and K.W. Cummins (1979). Effects of food quality on growth of a stream detritivore Paratendipes albimanus (Meigen) (Diptera: Chironomidae). Ecology, 60, 57-64.

Chironomids and Particles: a Field Experiment with Peat in an Upland Stream

A. T. Walentowicz and A. J. McLachlan

Dept. of Zoology, The University, Newcastle-upon-Tyne NE1 7RU, England

ABSTRACT

Some preliminary results are presented of the effects on a larval chironomid community after artificial peat introduction to a small moorland stream. Sediments and larvae were collected above and below the point of introduction. Differences in sediment nitrogen content were recorded. Peat particles were used in both feeding and tube-building especially by the Tanytarsini. This, in an environment possibly limited by available particles, may be important. Quantitative differences in numbers of larvae above and below the peat input were recorded. Below the point, large increases in deposited material especially at reduced flow rates, produced conditions suitable for Tanytarsini species but had an adverse effect on the Orthocladiinae. This may be connected with changes in type and quantity of available particles.

KEYWORDS

Stream; particles; peat; larvae; feeding; tube-building.

INTRODUCTION

Much current research on running waters has concentrated on feeding and the source of organic particles. There is now evidence that many streams and rivers rely upon organic matter produced in the terrestial environment (Minshall, 1967; Boling, 1975). For example the role of autumn-shed leaves is now well documented (Kaushik & Hynes, 1971; Winterbourne, 1976).

Upland streams often flow for considerable distances through areas devoid of trees. These same areas are frequently the sites of peat deposits. This material may be eroded into streams thus providing a supply of organic particles. These under suitable conditions may be important in the biology of stream dwelling organisms.

Apart from food, particles are required for other functions as in tube-building. This is important in the Chironomidae and the Trichoptera. From a community study in an upland river, Brennan (1978) suggested that particle quantity may limit larval chironomid density. Other work by the present authors on the same river system suggests that in addition to particle quantity, larval densities are related to some aspects of particle 'nutritional' quality. Maximum densities and biomass of larvae frequently occurred when organic nitrogen content of the sediment particles was greatest. Further, in the headwater streams particle quality appeared more important than quantity in influencing larval densities.

The role of peat in a bog lake was examined by McLachlan and Dickinson (1977). Chironomus lugubris ZETTERSTEDT larvae were common on the sheltered shore, appearing to select particles here as a result of their 'palatibility' rather than for any value in tube-building.

In the present study, an approach based on experiments in the field has been used to obtain information on peat particles in the biology of a larval chironomid community. The results described here are preliminary observations of an experiment in which peat was introduced into a small upland stream having no such natural input. This work forms part of a larger project which is the first attempt to assess the value of peat in running waters.

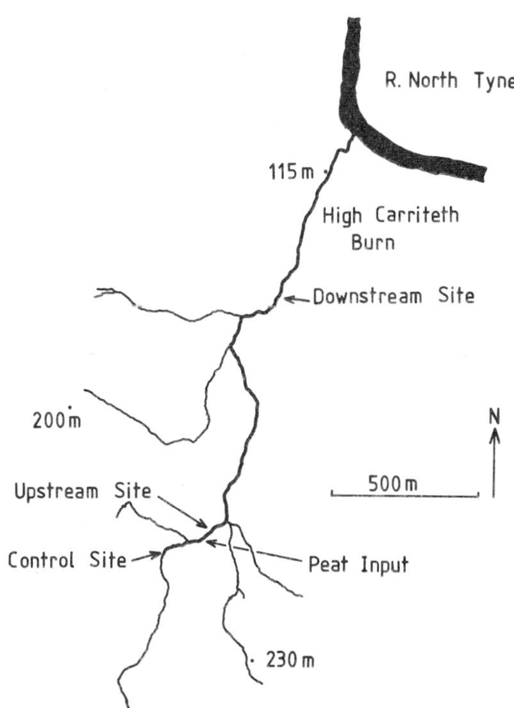

Fig. 1. The experimental stream with the three sampling sites and point of peat introduction. Altitude in metres is indicated at three points.

DESCRIPTION OF STUDY AREA

The High Carriteth Burn was chosen as it has no natural peat input and is of a suitable small size. It is also in an area where many of the streams are receiving peat inputs. It is about 2 kilometres in length, flowing in a northerly direction to enter the river North Tyne above Bellingham, Fig. 1. The geology of the area is characterised by rocks of the Scremerston Coal Group. Impermeable sandstones are dominant giving rise to acid podsols (Warn, 1975). The pH of the stream varies between 5 and 6.

Three sampling sites were established, a CONTROL SITE above the peat input point, an UPSTREAM SITE immediately below and a DOWNSTREAM SITE 1 kilometre away, Fig. 1. The CONTROL and UPSTREAM sites are identical with a bed of rock, stones, coarse gravel and small amounts of sand. The mean width is about 1 metre. The DOWNSTREAM site is 2 to 3 metres wide with a similar bed except for greater amounts of sand. Agricultural use has resulted in increased drainage and some changes in the typical moorland vegetation of the surrounding land.

METHODS

Field Methods

Fresh peat from neighbouring sites was introduced two to three times a week over a period of 124 days. Inputs commenced on 18.3.77 after two earlier faunal collections. Approximately 150 kilograms per week were used, amounting to a total of 2800 over the experimental period. Despite several spates which would rapidly remove the material, this method ensured that particles were continually entering the stream.

Sediments and chironomid larvae were collected with a riffle sampler similar to that used by Coffman (1971). This had a sample area of 30 x 30 square centimetres. By means of a flange and foam rubber base it could be held in place on the stream bed whilst a sample was removed. Large stones were removed and scrubbed in water with a soft brush. The remaining material was stirred vigorously whilst being removed with a bilge pump. This fraction and the stone washings were combined. Seven samples were taken in this way, three combined and passed through a 1 millimetre mesh screen to remove larger particles and animals. The filtrate was retained for particle analysis in the laboratory. The remaining four samples were washed through a 0.25 millimetre mesh screen, the residue preserved in 5 per cent formaldehyde for later faunal analysis.

Larval collections began in February and finished in September at the CONTROL and DOWNSTREAM sites. Two collections were taken prior to peat introduction in March and two after inputs finished in July. The UPSTREAM site was sampled from May to September only.

Laboratory Methods

Larvae were sorted under a binocular microscope and separated into major taxonomic groups. When large amounts of sediment and/or large numbers of larvae were present subsampling was used following the method of Brennan (1978). Depending on the number of larvae present, one, two or three subsamples were removed for an estimate of the total.

The sediments were oven-dried at 60 degrees centigrade for 24 hours. This treatment was carried out immediately on return from the field. Prior to chemical analysis the dried sediment was ground to pass a 0.25 millimetre mesh screen and thoroughly mixed.

Total organic nitrogen was determined by digestion (sulphuric acid, hydrogen peroxide mixture) followed by measurement of ammonium nitrogen using the manual indo-phenol blue method (Allen and colleagues, 1974). Organic content was determined by ashing at 550 degrees centigrade for three hours.

RESULTS AND DISCUSSION

Percentage total organic nitrogen for small particles is shown in Fig. 2. Low values at the UPSTREAM site are associated with the peat input. Between May and August much reduced flow rates resulted in large quantities of peat accumulating

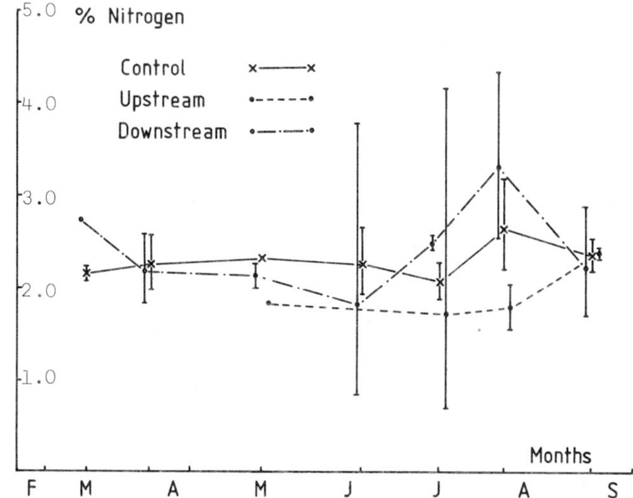

Fig. 2. Total organic nitrogen in percentage, ash-free dry weights for sediment particles. Figures are means (n = 2) with derived 95% confidence limits.

here. Peat is noted for its low nitrogen content. Thus the UPSTREAM site has been subject to a large input of low nitrogen value particles. When inputs ceased at the end of July values increased to reach those of the CONTROL site by the end of the experiment.

The CONTROL and DOWNSTREAM sites have similar profiles until June after which those at the DOWNSTREAM have increased. By the end of the experiment in September all three sites have similar values. Particulate material reaching the DOWNSTREAM site would have been in the stream longer than that arriving at the CONTROL site. The increase in nitrogen values could have resulted from longer exposure to decomposing organisms.

Total numbers of larvae at the three sites are shown in Fig. 3. At the CONTROL and DOWNSTREAM sites maximum numbers are occurring when nitrogen values of the sediments are at their highest. Over the summer period there is a down stream increase in larval numbers, Fig. 3 and Table 1. The Tanytarsini and Orthocladiinae are the major groups of larvae present. In Table 1 percentage contribution to total numbers by these groups together with total larval numbers on four sampling occasions over the summer have been combined. The CONTROL site shows the 'normal' stream condition with Orthocladiinae predominant whilst at the UPSTREAM site this is reversed. At the DOWNSTREAM site the 'normal' condition is maintained. Figures 4 and 5 show clearly that Tanytarsini larvae at the UPSTREAM site were using peat particles for

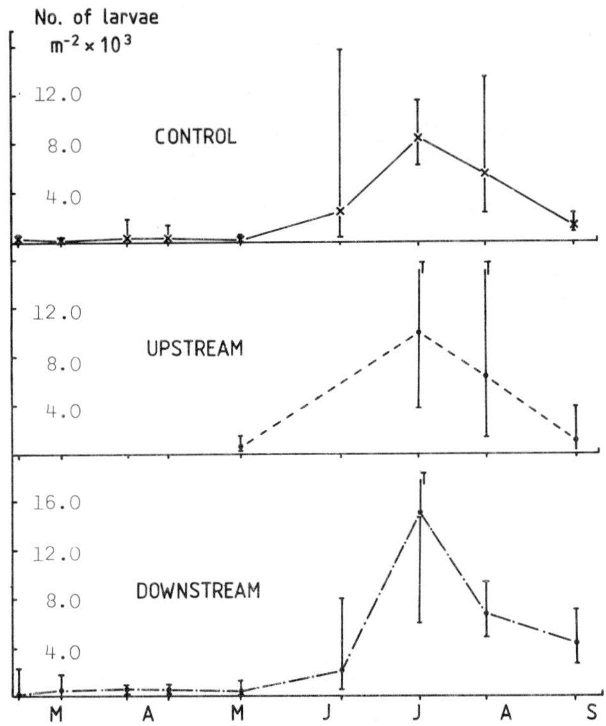

Fig. 3. Total numbers of chironomid larvae per square metre at each site. Figures are derived means (n = 4) with 95% confidence limits.

TABLE 1 Total Larval Numbers and Percentage Contribution

Site	No. of larvae.m with 95% C.L.	% Tanytarsini ± 95% C.L.	% Orthocladiinae ± 95% C.L.
CONTROL	4218 1962 9069	30.7 ± 1.1	38.4 ± 1.0
UPSTREAM	5396 2521 11547	44.7 ± 3.5	32.8 ± 2.8
DOWNSTREAM	7443 3631 15258	37.3 ± 2.8	47.7 ± 3.2

Figures for total numbers are real means with derived confidence limits. Those for percentages are derived means with derived limits. N = 16 in all cases.

both tube-building and feeding.

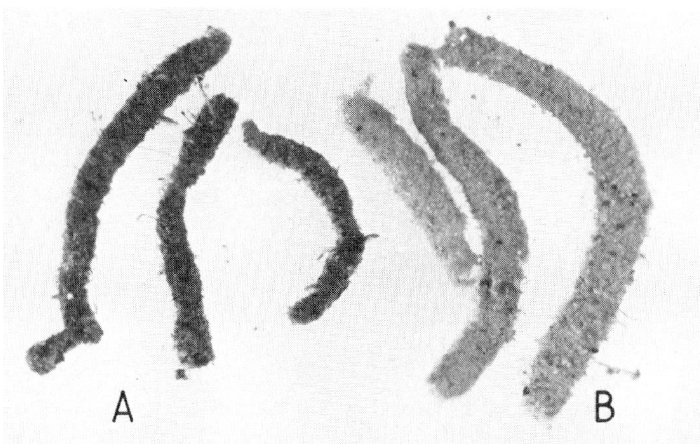

Fig. 4. Tanytarsini larval tubes from, A. the UPSTREAM site and B. the CONTROL site.

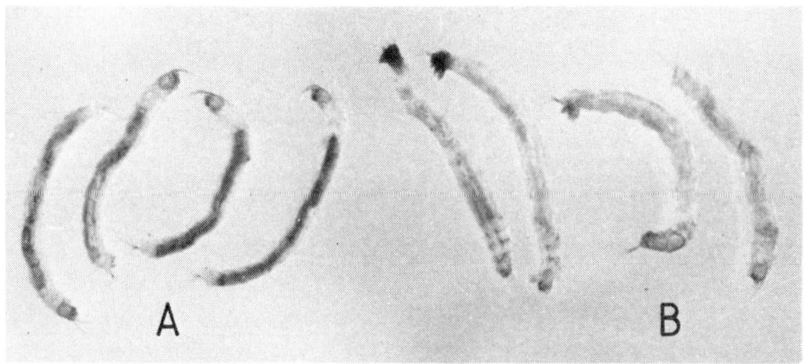

Fig. 5. Tanytarsini larvae from, A. the UPSTREAM site and B. the CONTROL site.

Brennan (1978) has shown that a relationship exists between particle quantity and larval densities. He suggested an upper limit could be expected when the amount and type of particulate material begins to alter the environment. This would lead to changes in the dominant larval types. The results presented here substantiate these ideas. At the UPSTREAM site an upper limit has been reached for some Orthocladiinae whilst the increased quantities of particles have favoured development of a predominantly Tanytarsini community.

The higher nitrogen content of particles at the DOWNSTREAM site would benefit both groups of larvae. Also, because of dilution particles would be arriving here in smaller quantities. This small increase in particle quantity would have been useful to both larval groups.

Thus at the UPSTREAM site the increase in particle quantity had enhanced conditions for Tanytarsini larvae at the expense of some Orthocladiinae. Particle quantity and quality were suitable for both groups of larvae at the DOWNSTREAM site. This may have contributed in producing the highest larval densities here.

ACKNOWLEDGEMENTS

We would like to thank Mr. C. Allgood on whose land the stream was situated and Mr. G. Howson for photographic assistance. Thanks also to all those who helped carry peat. This programme was supported by the Natural Environment Research Council, grant number GR 3 2575.

REFERENCES

Allen, S.E., Grimshaw, H.M., Parkinson, J.A. and C. Quarmby (1974). Chemical Analysis of Ecological Materials. Blackwell Scientific Publications.

Boling, R.H. Jr., Goodman, E.D., Van Sickle, J.A., Zimmer, J.O., Cummins, K.W., Petersen, R.C., and S.R. Reice (1974). Toward a model of detritus processing in a woodland stream. Ecology, 56 141-151.

Brennan, A, McLachlan, A.J., and R.S. Wotton (1978). Particulate material and midge larcae (Chironomidae: Diptera) in an upland river. Hydrobiol, 59, 67-73.

Coffman, W.P., Cummins, K.W., and J.C. Wuycheck (1971). Energy flow in a woodland stream ecosystem: 1. Tissue support trophic structure of the autumnal community. Arch. Hydrobiol, 68, 232-276.

Kaushik, N.K., and H.B.N. Hynes (1971). The fate of dead leaves that fall into streams. Arch. Hydrobiol, 68, 465-515.

McLachlan, A.J., and C.H. Dickinson (1977). Micro-organisms as a factor in the distribution of Chironomus lugubris ZETTERSTEDT in a bog lake. Arch. Hydrobiol, 80, 133-146.

Minshall, G.W. (1967). Role of allochthonous detritus in the trophic structure of a woodland springbrook community. Ecology 48, 139-149.

Warn, C.R. (1975). Rocks and scenery from Tyne to Tweed. Frank Graham, Newcastle-upon-Tyne.

Winterbourne, M.J. (1976). Fluxes of litter falling into a small beech forest stream. New Zeal. J. Mar. & Freshwat. Res., 10, 399-416.

Effect of Thermal Pollution on the Chironomid Fauna in an Urban Channel

T. Koehn and C. Frank

Institut für Tierphysiologie und Angewandte Zoologie der Freien Universität Berlin, Haderslebener Straße 9, 1000 Berlin 41, Federal Republic of Germany

ABSTRACT

The influence of thermal pollution from a power station on the chironomid community of a waste-water polluted urban channel was investigated. In the part of the channel most affected by sewage *Chironomus thummi* is the dominant species comprising at least 99 % of all chironomid species, with a maximum abundance of 44 099 ind./m². There is an increase in species diversity below the power station as an effect of selfpurification of the water. The differences in the abundance and length of generations do not show a correlation to increased water temperature. The aberrations of the labial plates are due to industrial effluents, such may be heavy metals.

KEYWORDS

Channel; thermal pollution; sewage; *Chironomus thummi*; deformations of labial plates; species diversity.

INTRODUCTION

During the last decades, the problem of water pollution has become more and more serious. It is realised that thermal pollution is not only waste of energy but can create a lot of problems for biocoenoses, e.g. oxygen depletion. Dusoge and Wiśniewski (1976) found a decrease in the stability of benthos communities as well under the effect of pollution as under the effect of heating and the combined effect of both heating and pollution. Fey (1978) showed that aquatic insects emerged earlier under the effect of higher water temperature as a result of the lack of a diapause or the shortening of the diapause. This study should show the effect of thermal pollution on the chironomid community of a polluted urban channel. It was supposed that there might be a difference in the length of generations above and below the power plant. The whole channel is to be dredged and renewed by 1981, so this study can be an inventory of the present situation.

DESCRIPTION OF STUDY AREA

The Teltowkanal is located in the southern part of West-Berlin and in the GDR. The channel was opened in 1906, has a maximum depth of 2.5 m and is approximately 27.5 m wide. The water flows with a speed of 0.1 to 0.2 m/s. Currently, only the eastern part of the channel up to the power plant Lichterfelde is used for shipping traffic. The channel is polluted by more than 300 inlets including industrial effluents. At point A in Fig. 1 biologically cleared effluents from a sewage treatment plant are pumped in at a rate of 1.24 m^3/s, at point B effluents from an irrigated sewage field are pumped in at a rate of 1.3 m^3/s. To increase the oxygen content of the water an enrichment device was installed below inlet A. The West-Berlin power plants Rudow with 3.5 m^3/s cooling water intake, Steglitz with 0.07 m^3/s intake, and Lichterfelde with 4.35 m^3/s intake stress the channel. The power plant Rudow has an output of 175 MW, the power plant Steglitz (not continuously in use) has 75 MW, and Lichterfelde 450 MW.

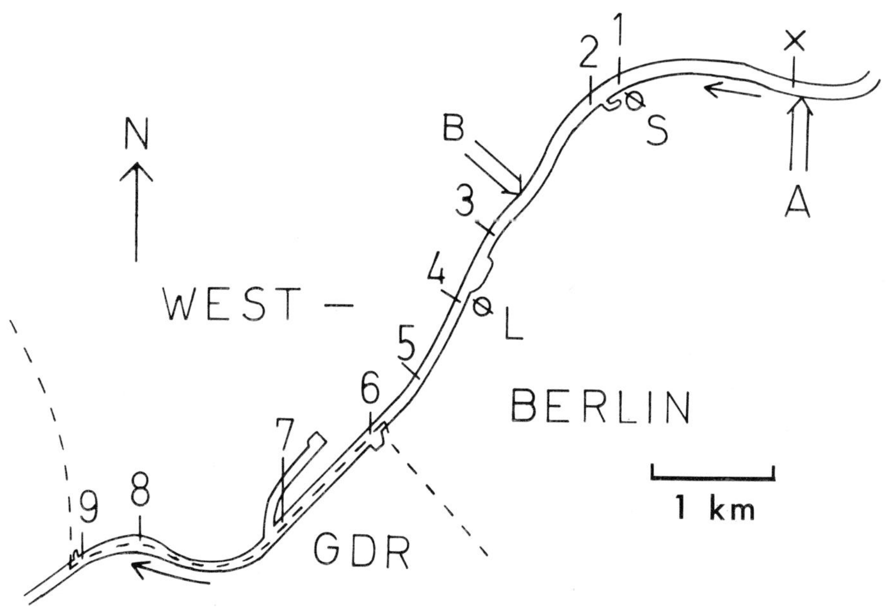

Fig. 1 Study area. A, B = sewage inlets; x = oxygen enrichment device; S, L = power plants Steglitz and Lichterfelde; 1 - 9 = sampling stations

The 9 sampling stations are located within a distance of 7.2 km. The investigation was carried out between 3. November 1978 and 17. July 1979.

MATERIAL AND METHODS

The samples were taken with an EKMAN-BIRGE bottom sampler with a surface of 205 cm^2. Parallel samples were taken, the number of chironomid larvae differed by about 20 %. The samples were sieved through two sieves with mesh sizes of 1 and 0.3 mm. The chironomidae were identified after Bryce and Hobart (1972), Keyl (1959), Lenz (1962), and Mason (1973). The phases of the 4th instar of the genus Chironomus were determined according to Wülker and Götz (1968). The number of oligochaeta was estimated. The chemical analyses were made according to the Deutsche Einheitsverfahren zur Wasser-, Abwasser- und Schlammuntersuchung (1975).

RESULTS AND DISCUSSION

The Teltowkanal is polluted by discharges from a sewage treatment plant, heated water from power plants, and industrial waste water.

Chemical and Physical Characterization

During the study period temperatures varied between 3.6 °C and 28 °C. Surface and bottom temperatures differ up to 1 °C. At low air temperatures the warm water can be detected at the surface for 1.5 km downstream from the power plant. In December 1978 and January 1979 the Teltowkanal did not freeze in contrast to most other Berlin waters at air temperatures of -20 °C. The power plant Steglitz increases the water temperature up to 5.5 °C, the power plant Lichterfelde up to 12.9 °C.

TABLE 1 Surface Temperatures of the Teltowkanal in °C

Date	Sampling stations								
	1	2	3	4	5	6	7	8	9
3.Nov.78	12.2	17.7	11.8	21.5	--	--	--	--	--
12.Dec.78	6.0	6.0	6.5	16.9	15.5	--	9.8	--	9.2
24.Jan.79	4.0	4.0	3.6	16.5	14.3	14.1	11.1	8.1	--
12.Mar.79	7.5	8.5	7.0	14.5	12.1	12.1	9.5	9.2	9.1
4.Apr.79	9.0	14.5	9.6	18.5	18.3	17.2	15.3	13.6	13.7
10.Apr.79	8.5	9.5	9.5	17.5	16.5	15.0	13.0	12.0	14.0
1.May 79	--	--	15.3	25.3	22.9	16.8	--	--	--
15.May 79	15.5	18.0	16.0	24.3	24.8	23.2	22.5	23.0	23.5
19.Jun.79	19.6	19.7	19.3	25.4	24.5	24.0	23.0	22.0	21.5
5.Jul.79	20.2	20.0	19.8	27.0	26.9	26.6	26.0	24.8	24.4
17.Jul.79	19.0	19.0	19.0	25.7	25.5	25.0	23.5	23.3	23.5

Light penetration is between 0.3 and 0.7 m.

The oxygen content above the sediment is between 2.55 and 9.56 mg/l, the saturation is between 31 and 116 %. The oxygen content is up to 50 % higher at the surface than at the bottom. To increase the supply of oxygen air is pumped into the water.
Nitrogen and phosphorous content is increased by the inlets A and B, at sampling station 5 the mean total nitrogen content without organic nitrogen was 10.11 mg/l during the summer of 1977, ortho-phosphate content was 1.48 mg/l (Sen. Bau. Woh., 1978).
At sampling station 1 the sediment contains approx. 40 % sand and 60 % silt, the sediment of the other stations is 100 % silt (sapropel). The water content increases below station 5, and traces of oil were often found.
The chemical parameters show that the Teltowkanal has to be considered as strongly polluted.

Bottom Fauna

The chironomid community is sympatric with the following species:

Oligochaeta
- *Limnodrilus hoffmeisteri* Clap.
- *Tubifex tubifex* Müll.
- *Stylaria lacustris* L.

Hirudinea
- *Haemopis sanguisuga* L.
- *Helobdella stagnalis* L.

Isopoda
- *Asellus aquaticus* L.

The oligochaeta have a maximum of approx. 200 000 ind./m² (4. April 1979, station 3). At sampling stations 1 to 4 *Chironomus thummi* is the dominant species composing 99 %, the highest abundance was 44 099 ind./m² at station 3 on the 12. March 1979.

Table 2 shows the total number per m² of chironomidae during the study period.

The total number of the chironomidae increases from sampling station 1 and reaches the maximum of 134 036 ind./m² at station 3 and decreases continuously to station 9. *Ch. thummi* is an indicator for organically polluted sewage channels (Scharf, 1972). This is emphasized by the fact that *Ch. thummi* is the dominant species at the sampling stations most polluted by sewage. It is an extreme biotop with high individual abundance but with a few species. Dusoge and Wiśniewski (1976) found that in the Narew River *Ch. thummi* and *Procladius sp*. are most adapted to the combined effect of increased water temperature and water pollution. 700 m below the power plant at station 5 the species diversity increased and *Ch. plumosus*, *Cryptochironomus defectus*, *Parachironomus cryptotomus*, *Glyptotendipes paripes*, and *Tanypus sp*. become more abundant. It is supposed that the temperature increase has a positive effect on selfpurification. The oxygen content does not decrease because the coolingsystem water may be enriched with oxygen during the cooling process (LAWA 1977). The chemical results show an accelerated self-purification in the 1.3 km between the stations 3 and 5. Ortho-phosphate decreases more than 50 %, while nitrite and nitrate increase. It has to be taken into account that there may be oxygen depletion connected with fish mortality, and that the water quality is still bad in the lower part of the channel.

TABLE 2 Total Numbers and Percentages of Chironomidae per m² found in Teltowkanal between 12. December 1978 and 17. July 1979

Sampling stations	Abundance	Chironomus thummi KIEFF.	Chironomus plumosus L.	Cryptochironomus defectus	Parachironomus cryptotomus	Glyptotendipes paripes EDW.	Tanypus sp.	Procladius sp.	Psectrotanypus	Prodiamesa olivacea MEIG.	Σ
1	N	33 986	-	49	-	98	-	-	-	-	34 133
	N%	99,57	-	0,14	-	0,29	-	-	-	-	100
2	N	58 093	-	-	-	-	-	-	-	-	58 093
	N%	100	-	-	-	-	-	-	-	-	100
3	N	132 715	98	-	-	978	-	-	-	245	134 036
	N%	99,01	0,07	-	-	0,73	-	-	-	0,18	99,99
4	N	61 810	-	-	-	-	-	-	-	-	61 810
	N%	100	-	-	-	-	-	-	-	-	100
5	N	36 382	2 396	2 836	2 054	245	147	-	-	-	44 060
	N%	82,57	5,33	6,44	4,66	0,55	0,33	-	-	-	99,99
6	N	1 320	1 027	245	-	-	196	-	-	-	2 788
	N%	47,35	36,84	8,79	-	-	7,03	-	-	-	100,01
7	N	440	1 223	49	-	-	49	-	-	-	1 761
	N%	24,99	69,45	2,78	-	-	2,78	-	-	-	100
8	N	-	538	147	-	-	734	49	49	-	1 517
	N%	-	35,46	9,69	-	-	48,38	3,23	3,23	-	99,99
9	N	-	98	-	-	49	-	-	-	-	147
	N%	-	66,67	-	-	33,33	-	-	-	-	100
Ind./ Species	N	324 746	5 380	3 326	2 054	1 370	1 126	49	49	245	338 345
	N%	95,98	1,59	0,98	0,61	0,40	0,33	0,01	0,01	0,07	99,98

Thermal Effects on Zoobenthos

Fey (1978) found that the length of generation of the Trichoptera Hydropsyche pellucidula is shortened by temperature increase in winter. Scharf (1972) discovered in laboratory studies that Ch. thummi has a diapause in the mean of the 4th instar at water temperatures of 10 °C. At 15 °C one generation had a length of 34.8 days, at 20 °C 20.6 days, and at 25 °C 15.5 days. The Teltowkanal population at sampling station 3 had a diapause in winter as well, the

larvae were developped approx. until phase 6 of the 4th instar. The winter generation had almost a length of 6 months. No significant differences in the age structure of the populations at different stations could be found. Very often few larvae were found, and drift has to be considered. At low temperatures the ages do not deviate very much in one population but with higher temperatures this deviation is much greater. The generations may overlap. There are no significant differences in the phases in the 4th instar between male and female larvae. Parasites mermithidae were scarcely found.
The decrease of the abundances of the larvae below the power plant may have different causes: Zhitenjowa (1972) found a decrease of the biomass of chironomidae and oligochaeta at temperatures of 26 °C and higher. The preferred temperature of Ch. thummi is 15.4 °C (Scharf, 1972). Fish were seen at station 4; Hadderingh (1975) found that the number of oligochaeta in the outlet of a power plant was reduced by fish that were about 100 times more abundant in the outlet than in the intake.
Up to station 3 the sediment is whirled up by ships which could enrich the sediment with oxygen.
Below station 5 in a part of the canal with no shipping more than 2 300 migratory diving ducks (Aythya fuligula, A. ferina) overwintered, most of them leaving the channel in March 1979 (Witt, personal communication). Diving ducks feed on benthos, therefore oligochaeta were scarce. Willy (1970) found that Aythyinae may clear out the whole benthos.

Morphological Aberrations

The larvae of Ch. thummi and Ch. plumosus show unsymmetrical deformations and gaps of the labial plates. (Fig. 2)

TABLE 3 Mean Percentages and Standard Deviations of Deformed Labial Plates of Ch. thummi

Sampling station	$\bar{x}$	$\pm$	s
1	32.2	$\pm$	18.8
2	25.4	$\pm$	11.2
3	27.0	$\pm$	7.6
4	37.6	$\pm$	27.0
5	27.2	$\pm$	4.2

The percentages do not differ significantly.

A correlation between the higher water temperature and the deformations of the labial plates could not be found in spite of the highest rate of aberrations of station 4. Those aberrations are caused by industrial effluents (Hare and Carter, 1976). The Teltowkanal is polluted by heavy metals as well. A possible correlation between the aberrations and the content of heavy metals shall be investigated.

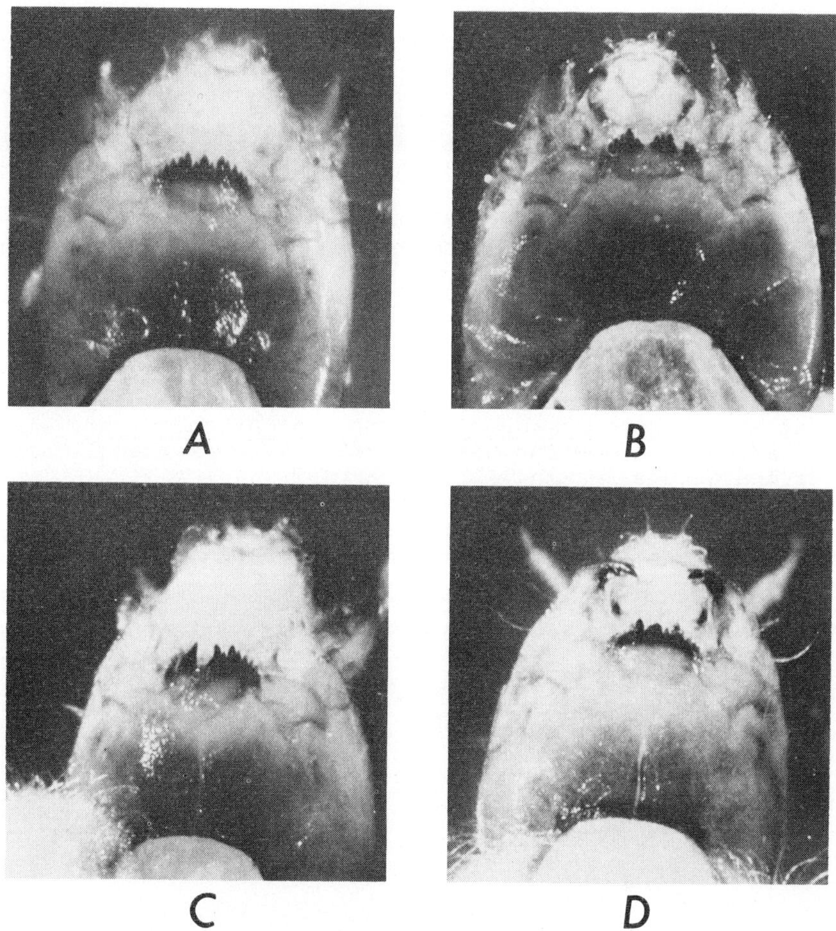

Fig. 2. Labial plates of Ch. thummi, A normal; B, C, D deformed.

REFERENCES

Bryce, D., and A. Hobart (1972). The biology and identification of larvae of the chironomidae. Entomologist's Gazette, 23, 175-216.

Deutsche Einheitsverfahren zur Wasser-, Abwasser- und Schlamm-Untersuchung (1975). 3. Aufl. Verlag Chemie, Weinheim.

Dusoge, K., and R. J. Wiśniewski (1976). Effect of heated waters on biocenosis of the moderately polluted Narew River. Pol. Arch. Hydrobiol., 23, 539-554.

Fey, J. M. (1978). Die Beeinflussung der Lenne durch die Abwärme des Kohlenkraftwerkes Elverlingsen. Natur- u. Landschaftsk. Westf., 14, 53-60.

Hadderingh, R. H. (1975). Effects of cooling water discharge on the macroinvertebrates and fish populations around Flevo power station. Verh. Internat. Verein. Limnol., 19, 2214-2218.

Hare, L., and J. C. H. Carter (1976). The distribution of Chironomus (s.s.)? cucini (salinarius group) larvae (Diptera: Chironomidae) in Parry Sound, Georgian Bay, with particular reference to structural deformities. Can. J. Zool., 54, 2129-2134.

Keyl, H. G., and I. Keyl (1959). Die cytologische Diagnostik der Chironomiden. I. Arch. f. Hydrobiol., 56, 1/2, 43-57.

LAWA (1977). Grundlagen für die Beurteilung der Wärmebelastungen von Gewässern. Teil 1, 2 verb. Aufl. Länderarbeitsgemeinschaft Wasser Mainz.

Lenz, F. (1962). Die Metamorphose der Tendipedidae. In E. Lindner, Die Fliegen der palaearktischen Region. 13c. Schweizerbarth'sche Verlagsbuchhandlung, Stuttgart.

Mason, W. T. jr. (1973). An introduction of the identification of chironomid larvae. Analytical Control Laboratory, National Environmental Research Center, US Environmental Protection Agency, Cincinnati, Ohio.

Scharf, B. (1972). Experimentell-ökologische Untersuchungen zur Einnischung von Chironomus thummi thummi und Ch. th. piger. Diss. Kiel.

Senator für Bau- und Wohnungswesen (1978). Gewässerkundlicher Jahresbericht des Landes Berlin, Abflußjahr 1977.

Willy, W. (1970). Zugverhalten, Aktivität, Nahrung und Nahrungserwerb auf dem Klingnauer Stausee häufig auftretender Anatiden, insbesondere von Krickente, Tafelente und Reiherente. Orn. Beob., 67, 141-217.

Wülker, W., and P. Götz (1968). Die Verwendung der Imaginalscheiben zur Bestimmung des Entwicklungszustandes von Chironomus-Larven. Z. Morph. Tiere, 62, 363-388.

Zhitenjowa, T. S., and J. I. Nikanorow (1972). Der Einfluß des vom Konakowschen Wärmekraftwerk abfließenden Warmwassers auf die biologischen Prozesse im Iwanjkowo-Stausee. Verh. Internat. Verein. Limnol., 18, 833-836.

An Assessment of the Importance of the Chironomidae (Diptera) in Biological Surveillance

D. L. Morris and M. P. Brooker

UWIST Field Centre, Newbridge-on-Wye, Powys, Wales

ABSTRACT

The Chironomidae are often numerically abundant in collections of aquatic invertebrates yet their specific identification is generally omitted in surveillance studies. This paper uses data collected from the R. Wye catchment to explore the influence of different levels of taxonomic penetration of the Chironomidae on community analyses often used in biological survey. The implications of the temporal distribution of the Chironomidae to surveillance sampling strategy is also considered.

KEYWORDS

Aquatic macroinvertebrates, chironomids, biological surveillance, community analyses, sampling strategy.

INTRODUCTION

Benthic macroinvertebrates are widely used for the biological surveillance of water quality in rivers and surveys are generally designed to describe the spatial distribution and actual or relative abundance of these organisms. Interpretation of survey data is often based on computed summary indices such as the Shannon-Weiner diversity index (H), Jaccard similarity index (I) and the Spearman correlation coefficient (r_s) (Hellawell, 1978), the values of which may depend on the seasonal timing and procedures of sampling and on the degree of taxonomic penetration (Edwards, Hughes and Read, 1975; Hellawell, 1978; Hughes, 1978; Murphy, 1978). The chironomids often form a high proportion of benthic macroinvertebrate associations (Lindgaard-Petersen, 1972) but their identification, and hence information content, has often been neglected in biological surveys (Morgan and Egglishaw, 1965; Armitage, MacHale and Crisp, 1974). The present study utilises data on the spatial and temporal distribution of the Chironomidae in the Wye catchment to compare the effects of different levels of identification in this family on the values and interpretation of summary statistics derived from general survey data and on alternative temporal sampling strategies.

STUDY SITES AND METHODS

The River Wye, which is 250km long and has a total catchment area of 4183km^2, rises at Plynlimon (677m O.D.) in mid-Wales and joins the Severn estuary at Chepstow. Water quality varies from nutrient-poor upland reaches, which drain impervious Ordovician and Silurian mudstones and shales, to nutrient-rich lowland areas draining calcareous sediments of Carboniferous origin: there are few sources of industrial or domestic pollution. The substratum varies from unstable cobbles and coarse gravel in the upper reaches to consolidated cobbles in the slower flowing lowland areas where substantial summer growths of *Ranunculus* spp. occur (Brooker, Morris and Wilson, 1978).

Samples of benthic invertebrates were collected from fourteen sites (see Fig. 1, Brooker and Morris, 1980) in the Wye catchment, twelve on the main river, one on the impounded River Elan (W4) and one on the River Irfon (W7). Invertebrates were collected using a modified cylinder sampler with a surface area of $0.05m^2$ and a mesh aperture of 440μm. Four replicate samples were taken across the width of a riffle at each site in March and September 1975 and July and September 1976 and 1977.

Three sites (W2, W3 and W5) in the upper catchment were studied more intensively during the period March 1975 to February 1978, between four and fifteen replicate samples being taken from each site as often as weekly during the summer months (May - September) but less often at other times.

Summary statistics of invertebrate associations have been computed from pooled survey data collected in July and September 1976 and 1977. The use of these statistics, the Jaccard similarity index, Shannon-Weiner index and Spearman rank correlation coefficient, which utilise simple presence-absence, quantitative and ranked quantitative data respectively, have been described by Hellawell (1978).

RESULTS

Seasonal changes in the total number of taxa, which were generally identified to species but included a variety of taxonomic levels, collected at W2, W3 and W5, those sites in the upper reaches which were sampled intensively, were generally similar with major peaks recorded during the period June - September (Fig. 1a). Both W2 and W5 were richer in taxa than W3 but at all sites the number of chironomid taxa, 48, 33 and 48 respectively, formed a substantial proportion of the total taxa collected. Chironomid taxa were generally most abundant during May to September (Fig. 1a) and were principally represented by *Eukiefferiella* spp. (8 taxa) and *Cricotopus* spp. (8 taxa).

Temporal changes in total benthic density at W2, W3 and W5 were similar to changes in the numbers of taxa with major peaks recorded during June and July: densities were generally substantially higher at W5, reaching peak densities of $12395m^{-2}$, compared with the two upstream sites W2 (Fig. 1b) and W3. The Chironomidae were generally absolutely and relatively more abundant at W5 (23% of fauna overall) than at W2 (16%) and W3 (12%) and were principally represented by *Eukiefferiella* spp. (W2, 17%; W3, 42%; W5, 47%) and *Cricotopus* spp. (W2, 33%; W3, 2%; W5,21%).

A total of 227 invertebrate taxa were recorded from all general surveys of the Wye catchment, 77 (34%) of which were chironomids. However, few taxa (84) were recorded in March 1975: of these 26% were chironomids. Most chironomid taxa (47) were recorded from W12 and fewest (22) from W3. The most frequently represented genera were the *Eukiefferiella* spp. (9 taxa) and *Cricotopus* spp. (11 taxa).

The Chironomidae also formed a substantial proportion of total invertebrate density in the Wye catchment, representing between 11 and 40% overall at different sites, and was generally the most abundant insect family. The chironomids formed a smaller proportion of the overall fauna in the March survey (11%) than in July (27%) or September (17%) collections.

The Orthocladiinae, particularly the genera *Eukiefferiella* (maximum density: $1604m^{-2}$, W6) and *Cricotopus* (maximum density: $1545m^{-2}$, W11) were generally the most abundant chironomids throughout the catchment and represented between 27% (W12) and 83% (W5) of all chironomids collected. Of the *Eukiefferiella* spp.

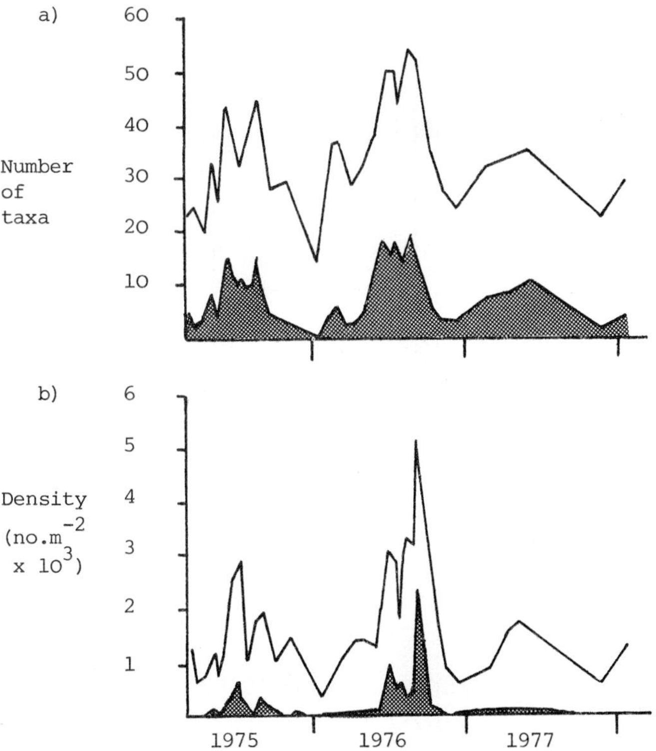

Fig. 1. Seasonal changes in a) the number of taxa and b) the estimated mean density of total invertebrates and chironomids (shaded) at W2.

E. clypeata (Kieffer) and *E. discoloripes/veralli* were the most abundant and were recorded at all sites: *E. brevicalcar* (Keiffer), *E. minor* (Edwards) and *E. ilkleyensis/devonica* were generally restricted to the middle and lower catchment (W3a - W9) and *E.* sp. 9 (cfr. *similis*) was recorded only at W4 and W8-W13 (Fig. 2). The most abundant *Cricotopus* spp., *C. bicinctus* (Meigen) and *C. (trifascia?)*, were distributed throughout the catchment but *C. (Isocladius) 'sylvestris'* grp. and some of the unidentified, but morphologically distinct, *Cricotopus* spp. were not generally recorded upstream of W3a (Fig. 2). Some abundant representatives of the Tanypodinae (*Procladius choreus* (Meigen); 925m^{-2}, W12), Chironomini (*Polypedilum 'nubeculosum'* sp. 2; 6925m^{-2}, W12) and Tanytarsini (*Cladotanytarsus vanderwulpi* (Edwards); 65m^{-2}, W12) were also restricted to the lower catchment (W5 - W13) (Fig. 2).

The value of the Shannon-Weiner index, calculated from total pooled data (H_T), in the Wye catchment varied from 4.32 (W1) to 5.43 (W13) but showed no general pattern of distribution in the catchment (Table 1). Recalculation of these indices including the Chironomidae as a single taxon (H_C) considerably reduced the numerical value of the index, which ranged from 3.07 (W12) to 4.36 (W7). The values of H_T and H_C were not significantly correlated ($r = 0.403$, $P > 0.05$).

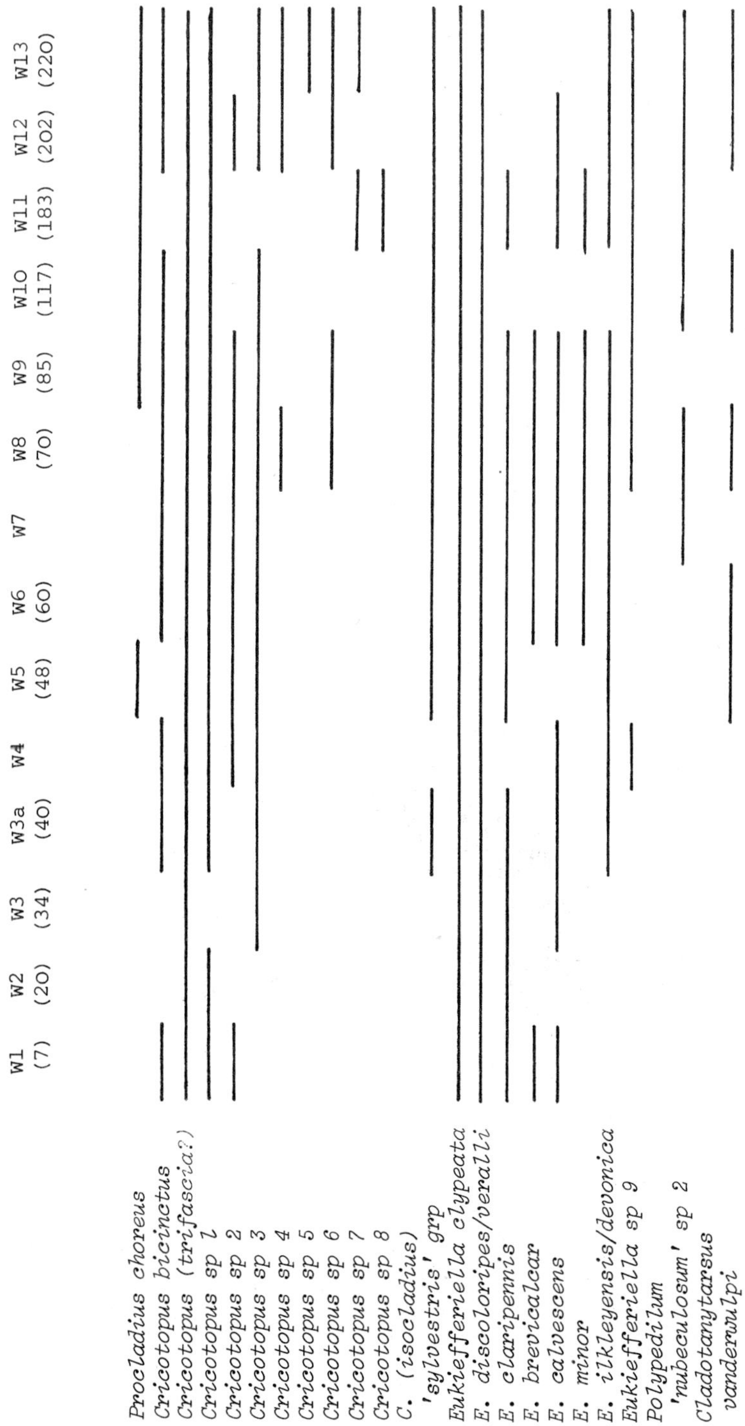

W1 (7) W2 (20) W3 (34) W3a (40) W4 W5 (48) W6 (60) W7 W8 (70) W9 (85) W10 (117) W11 (183) W12 (202) W13 (220)

Procladius choreus
Cricotopus bicinctus
Cricotopus (trifascia?)
Cricotopus sp 1
Cricotopus sp 2
Cricotopus sp 3
Cricotopus sp 4
Cricotopus sp 5
Cricotopus sp 6
Cricotopus sp 7
Cricotopus sp 8
C. (isocladius) 'sylvestris' grp
Eukiefferiella clypeata
E. discoloripes/veralli
E. claripennis
E. brevicalcar
E. calvescens
E. minor
E. ilkleyensis/devonica
Eukiefferiella sp 9
Polypedilum 'nubeculosum' sp 2
Cladotanytarsus vanderwulpi

Fig. 2. The spatial distribution of selected chironomid taxa. Distance (km) of R. Wye sites from source in parentheses.

TABLE 1. Calculated Values of H_T and H_C from Pooled (1976-1977) Data in the Wye Catchment.

Site	H_T	H_C	Site	H_T	H_C
W1	4.32	4.01	W7	5.02	4.36
W2	4.76	4.35	W8	5.02	4.29
W3	4.42	3.99	W9	5.12	4.35
W3a	4.74	4.08	W10	5.13	4.22
W4	4.78	3.51	W11	4.77	4.21
W5	4.73	4.15	W12	4.49	3.07
W6	4.49	3.81	W13	5.43	4.16

Average linkage clustering of Jaccard similarity coefficients (I), calculated using all taxa (including the Chironomidae) from pooled collections in 1976 and 1977, indicated that sites in the Wye catchment can be conveniently divided into major groups at I > 0.4, W1 - W5 and W7 - W13. The latter grouping was subdivided at I > 0.5 into two associations, W7 - W9 and W10 - W13 (Fig. 3a). Further sub-

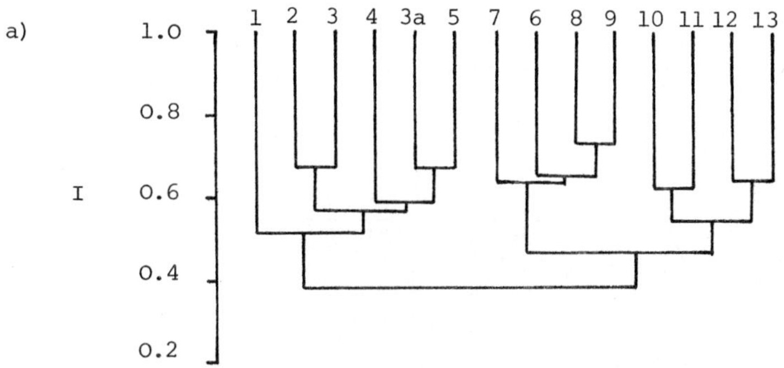

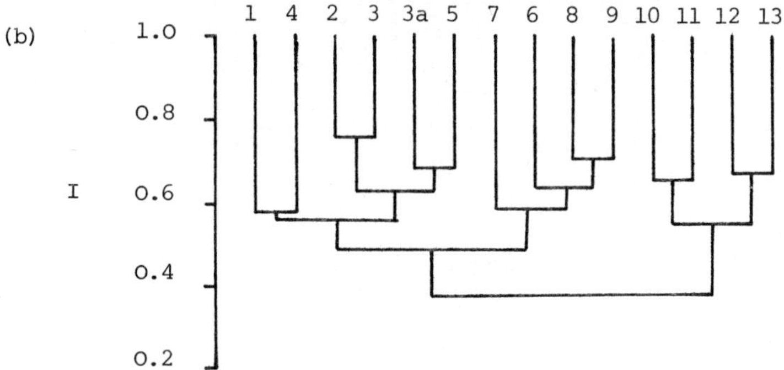

Fig. 3. Average linkage site clustering of the Jaccard index (I), Wye catchment 1976-1977, using a) all taxa and b) including chironomids as a single taxon.

division of W1 - W5 excludes W1, the most upstream site in the catchment, and W4, the impounded River Elan, clusters with sites W2 - W5 (Fig. 3a). Consideration of clusters derived from data in which the chironomids are treated as one taxon indicates a generally similar distribution but the two major groups at I > 0.4 are W1 - W9 and W10 - W13 (Fig. 3b). Further subdivision of W1 - W5 in this analysis, however, results in W4 clustering closely with W1 rather than nearby main river sites.

Analysis of the Spearman rank correlation coefficients between sites using masked data (generally taxa which were recorded at fewer than five sites or at densities less than $50m^{-2}$ were excluded to avoid excessive numbers of mutual absences) from pooled collections indicated two major site clusters, W1 - W9 and W10 - W13 at r_s > 0.3 (Fig. 4a). At higher values of r_s it was possible to separate further site groups e.g. W1-W4; W2-W5; W6-W9; W10-W13 (Fig. 4a). When the same

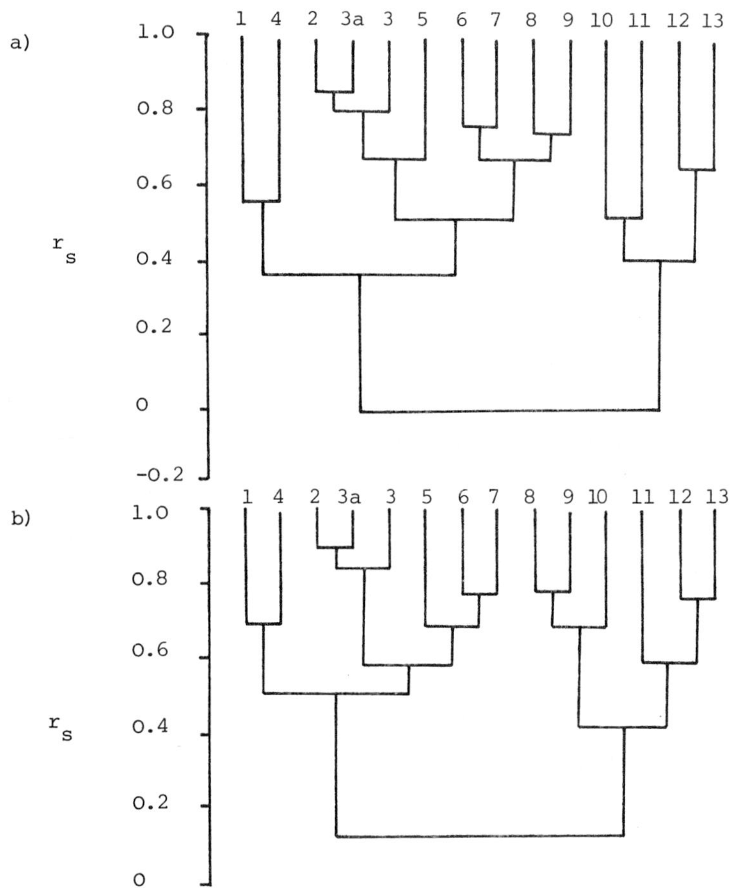

Fig. 4. Average linkage clustering of the Spearman correlation coefficient (r_s), Wye catchment 1976-1977, using a) all taxa and b) including chironomids as a single taxon.

analysis is undertaken using the Chironomidae as a single taxon the major division at $r_s > 0.3$ is retained but sites W8 and W9 are associated with sites lower in the catchment (Fig. 4b). At higher values there were further differences in site clusters (Fig. 4).

DISCUSSION

Results from the present study demonstrate the rapid and substantial qualitative and quantitative changes in the invertebrate and chironomid fauna of the Wye, with peaks during May to September, and the importance of the chironomids. These data generally support the reports of other workers (Maitland, 1964; Learner and co-workers, 1971). However, Hynes (1970) concluded that when insects, particularly Diptera, do not form a major component of the fauna peak densities of invertebrates occur in spring and autumn with a period of low density during mid-summer. Such seasonal variability is likely to be a critical problem in selecting an optimal sampling strategy in surveillance studies but few objective analyses of sampling strategy have been undertaken in support of the wide variation in the number and timing of collections (Morgan and Egglishaw, 1965; Learner and co-workers, 1971; Armitage, MacHale and Crisp, 1974). Unpublished analysis of data from the present study of sites in the upper Wye catchment indicate that most taxa, and hence the most information, are likely to be recorded from two surveys by a combination of two summer collections: such a sampling programme is likely to be appropriate for rivers in which summer species, like chironomids, form a large proportion of the fauna. The penalty of undertaking summer surveys, when rapid changes in invertebrate communities occur, is the possible temporal variation of summary statistics (Hughes, 1978; Murphy, 1978) which may lead to misinterpretation of spatial relationships.

Data from the present study indicated that some chironomids had a restricted distribution in the River Wye (see Fig. 2) and some workers, e.g. Wilson and Bright(1973), have suggested that the Chironomidae may provide a sensitive method of classifying freshwater habitats. A comprehensive assessment of such proposals has not been attempted although the distribution of chironomids has been related to sources of pollution (e.g. Learner and co-workers, 1971).

Several workers (Edwards, Hughes and Read, 1975; Hellawell, 1978; Hughes, 1978) have investigated the effects of using different levels (e.g. genera, family) of identification for the calculation of summary statistics and concluded that, although the numerical value may change considerably, the general spatial pattern was not greatly affected. Data derived from different levels of identification have been widely used to calculate summary indices (Balloch, Davies and Jones, 1976) but the effects of neglecting the specific identification of important invertebrate groups (e.g. the Chironomidae) have rarely been investigated. Results from the present study indicate that the change in overall pattern of such indices was generally small. It is clear that the interpretation of the spatial distribution of invertebrate community summary statistics is not substantially influenced by the inclusion of a considerable number of chironomid species as a single taxon and it seems likely that the specific identification of the Chironomidae for routine monitoring purposes may not be essential. This conclusion is supported by unpublished analyses of data collected from the River Ystwyth, a river polluted by heavy metals, and from the River Cynon, which receives considerable quantities of organic material and suspended solids (Learner and co-workers, 1971).

Nevertheless, some differences in the summary statistics computed in the present study were of particular significance. For example, differences in the classification of W4, the impounded River Elan, were apparent in the Jaccard analysis (see Fig. 3) and these resulted from the similarity between the chironomid fauna at W4 and nearby main river sites but an impoverishment of the remaining fauna at this impounded site (Brooker and Morris, 1980). Using all data, major spatial divisions derived from Jaccard and Spearman analyses divided the catchment into W1-W5 and W6-W13, coinciding with a major change in the chemistry of the river (Brooker and Morris, 1980), but when chironomids were included as a single taxon this major division occurred lower in the catchment. Furthermore, when biological studies are undertaken for purposes other than assessing water quality, and particularly when an appraisal for conservation purposes is required, the description of the chironomid fauna, generally diverse and abundant, is most important.

ACKNOWLEDGEMENTS

This work formed part of a contract sponsored by the Welsh Water Authority and supported by funds from the Craig Goch Joint Committee and Central Water Planning Unit. The authors wish to thank the Llysdinam Trust and Dr. I.F.Grant. Professor R.W.Edwards read and suggested alterations to the manuscript.

REFERENCES

Armitage, P.D., A.M. MacHale and D.C.Crisp (1974). A survey of stream invertebrates in the Cow Green basin (upper Teesdale) before inundation. *Freshwat. Biol.* 4, 369-398.

Balloch, D., C.E.Davies and F.H.Jones (1976). Biological assessment of water quality in three British rivers: the North Exe (Scotland), the Ivel (England) and the Taf (Wales). *Wat. Poll. Cont.* 75, 92-114.

Brooker, M.P. and D.L.Morris (1980). A survey of the macroinvertebrate riffle fauna of the River Wye. *Freshwat. Biol.* 10.

Brooker, M.P., D.L.Morris and C.J.Wilson (1978). Plant-flow relationships in the River Wye catchment. *Proc. EWRS 5th Symposium on Aquatic Weeds*, 63-70.

Edwards, R.W., B.D.Hughes and M.W.Read (1975). Biological survey in detection and assessment of pollution. M.J.Chadwick and G.T.Goodman (Eds). *The Ecology of Resource Degradation and Renewal*, 139-156. Blackwell, Oxford.

Hellawell, J.M. (1978). *Biological Surveillance of Rivers.* Water Research Centre. 332pp.

Hughes, B.D. (1978). The influence of factors other than pollution on the value of Shannon's diversity index for benthic macroinvertebrates in streams. *Wat. Res.* 12, 359-364.

Hynes, H.B.N. (1970). *The Ecology of Running Waters.* Liverpool University Press. 555pp.

Learner, M.A., R. Williams, M. Harcup and B.D.Hughes (1971). A survey of the macro-fauna of the River Cynon, a polluted tributary of the River Taff (South Wales). *Freshwat. Biol.* 1, 339-367.

Lindegaard-Petersen, C. (1972). The Chironomid fauna of a lowland stream in Denmark compared with other European streams. *Verh. Internat. Verein. Limnol.* 18, 726-729.

Maitland, P.S. (1964). Quantitative studies on the invertebrate fauna of sandy and stony substrates in the River Endick, Scotland. *Proc. Roy. Soc. Edinburgh.* 68, (B), 277-301.

Morgan, N.C. and H.J.Egglishaw (1965). A survey of the bottom fauna of streams in the Scottish Highlands. Part 1. Composition of the fauna. *Hydrobiologia* 25, 181-211.

Murphy, P.M. (1978). The temporal variability in biotic indices. *Environ. Poll.* 17, 227-236.

Wilson, R.W. and P.L.Bright (1973). The use of chironomid pupal exuviae for characterising streams. *Freshwat. Biol.* 3, 283-302.

A Contribution to the Knowledge of Chironomids in Italy, including Cluster Analysis of Presence-Absence Data and Factor Analysis with Per Cent Composition of Species in a Stream

B. Rossaro* and U. Ferrarese**

*Department of Zoology, University of Milan, Italy
**Museum of Natural History, Verona, Italy

ABSTRACT

Chironomids have been collected in different streams of Italy. Samples of larvae and pupal exuviae collected during different months and in various stations of a stream in northern Italy have been the starting point of a cluster and principal components analysis aiming to establish similarities among different stations within a determined yearly range, using pertaining information supplied by Chironomids taxonomical determinations.

KEYWORDS

Chironomids, larvae, pupal exuviae, biological survey of pollution,cluster analysis, principal component analysis.

INTRODUCTION

A list of species known so far to be present in Italy is being prepared.At present, 8 species of Diamesinae and 57 of Orthocladiinae have been determined (Rossaro, 1977, 1978, 1979a, 1979b, 1979c) while, up to this moment, Chironominae and Tanypodinae are less known. The research has chiefly concerned the running waters of northern Italy, while no sufficient information is available for central and southern Italy. The Lambro stream is a very polluted water-stream of Lombardy (Vendegna, 1968). The object of this research was to establish if presence-absence of Chironomids species, per cent composition both of larvae and pupal exuviae allowed to cluster different stations and months in a fashion congruent with hydrological, chemical and biological data reported in the literature (Vendegna, 1968; Vendegna and Marchetti, 1973). Different methods of clustering are proposed and results are compared.

METHODS

Larvae have been collected with a Surber sampler (Hynes, 1970), pupal exuviae with a Brundin net (Brundin, 1966) in 18 stations (Vendegna, 1968) during the following months: III 76, VI 76, IX 76, II 77, XI 77, XII 77, I 78, III 78. Stations with even numbers have been sampled one day and stations with odd numbers the next day. The first 7 stations have a rather uniform stony bottom; there is an increasing discharge proceeding from the first station to the other ones downstream.Pollution strongly affects station 4, owing to inlet of domestic sewage from a nearby village upstream. In station 5 there is a partial restoration owing to some sources, feeding waters into this stretch. Pollution is heavy again in station 6 and increases at the lower stations. Station 8 represents a different situation as it receives waters from the Pusiano lake (Vendegna 1968), which may be producing effects also in station 9. Only the first 9 stations have been included in our analyses. The muddy bottom and strong pollution in stations from 10 to 18 favoured a peculiar fauna composition, showing normally the presence of Chironomus gr. thummi only (Rossaro 1979a); for this reason these stations have been excluded.

Input data have been tabulated in matrices showing the different species (or genera) as columns and stations of the various months as rows. Separate matrices summarized data of larvae and pupal exuviae. 24 taxa have been selected through the analysis with larvae and 40 taxa with pupae.

Input matrices contained taxa presence-absence data codified as 1 and 0: this has been the starting point of single linkage cluster analysis. Otherwise, input matrices contained percent composition of taxa of one station in a single month. In this case a principal components analysis has been carried out after arsin square root transformation of percentages for normalization. Data have been processed at the UNIVAC 1100/80 computer installation of the University of Milan. Programs have been obtained from Davies (1971). The single linkage cluster analysis program has been modified, so that 6 different similarity indexes could be the starting point of the analysis. These indexes have been discussed by Blanc and co-workers (1976) and are identified as follows : Dice, Jaccard, Sokal and Sneath, Kulczynski-1, Ochiai, Kulczynski-2. For reasons discussed by Blanc and co-workers (1976), the Sokal-Sneath and Kulczynski-2 indexes seemed to be the best choice for processing our data; the former is to be preferred when there is a higher fauna homogeneity, as it happens in our case where the stations are rather similar, often only a few kilometers far from one another, the latter is less affected by drawbacks due to the different number of species presented by the specimens collection; in fact, each single month may supply a different number of species, according to various factors such as seasons, discharge conditions, etc.

The principal component analysis has been carried out starting from dispersion matrix of species.

RESULTS

Dendrograms resulting from single linkage cluster analysis show that figures obtained using different indexes well agree with one another in the order of clustering, while the similarity level in cluster formation may be rather different; as expected, amalgamation of the same sampling points is reached at lower similarity level with the Sokal and Sneath index rather than with Kulczynski-2;for instance,a cluster of 6 sampling points (II 77, stations 2-3-5-6 and IX 76, stations 3-4) is made at 0.49 similarity level with Sokal and Sneath index and at 0.83 with Kulczynski-2 index. The clustering process is rather different whether larvae or pupal exuviae are used; larvae seem to give better results than pupal exuviae, but in both cases presence-absence data lend too much weight to rare species, whose presence or absence in samples may be subject to chance.

In Fig. 1 it may be seen the dendrogram of the cluster analysis of larvae carried out on the basis of Sokal and Sneath index: only stations clustering at a similarity level greater than 0.3 are reported. Stations may be arranged in the dendrogram better than the months; only february 77 and partly june 76 meet in a single cluster; often different stations and months are clustered together.

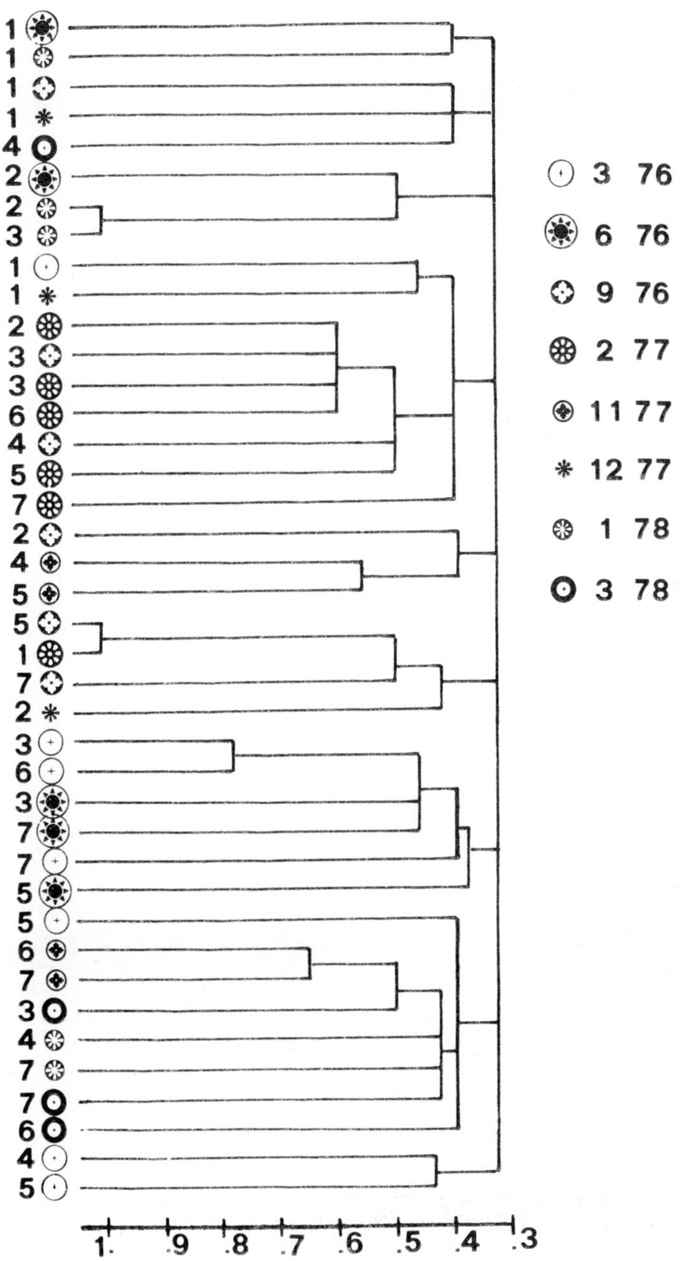

Fig. 1. Dendrogram of the cluster analysis of larvae starting from Sokal and Sneath index. Numbers on the left are sampling stations; similarity levels are on the bottom.

Principal components analysis results of larvae are shown in Table 1, where a factor pattern is reported showing latent vectors (factor loadings) and latent roots of the first five principal components. All together, the first 5 principal components account for 64.77 percent of total variation in analysis of larvae and for 53.78 percent in analysis of pupal exuviae.

TABLE I - Results of Principal Components Analysis with Larvae

	I	II	III	IV	V
Latent roots	.177	.151	.133	.118	.091
Percentage Variances	17.052	14.599	12.860	11.406	8.837
Latent vectors (factor loadings)					
Pseudodiamesa	-.002	.007	.002	.011	-.002
D. aberrata	-.040	-.009	.035	-.021	.026
Diamesa sp. A	-.745	-.010	.152	-.159	-.091
Diamesa sp. B	.001	.000	.000	.000	.000
P. olivacea	.005	.043	-.061	.038	-.102
B. modesta	.032	.076	.090	-.037	.087
Hydrobaenus	-.021	.004	.003	-.016	-.005
Eukiefferiella	.187	.468	.383	-.099	.646
S. semivirens	.037	-.047	.003	.048	-.003
P. nudipennis	.007	-.006	.001	.008	.003
Euorthocladius	-.210	-.333	-.195	.400	.395
Orthocladius s. str.	-.303	-.057	.104	-.062	-.162
P. rufiventris	.172	-.212	-.284	.501	.141
C. bicintus	.235	-.122	-.572	-.642	.030
C. trifascia	-.016	-.008	.007	.012	.016
I. sylvestris	.013	-.018	.019	.003	-.018
Rheocricotopus	.407	-.444	.566	-.002	-.335
Psectrocladius	.049	-.016	.029	-.023	-.053
P. stylatus	-.010	.019	.005	.002	.028
Metriocnemus	.038	-.013	-.001	-.035	-.017
Corynoneurini	.017	-.028	-.001	.060	.055
Pentaneurini	.099	.615	-.195	.348	-.483
Tanytarsini	.038	.135	.022	-.066	-.007
Chironomini	.059	-.026	.012	-.027	-.002

As it may be seen in Table 1, the first principal component has Diamesa (D.bertrami, according to rearings) and in a lesser degree Orthocladius s. str. and Euorthocladius with high negative factor loadings, while Rheocricotopus and Cricotopus bicinctus have high positive factor loadings.The second principal component has Pentaneurini (Conchapelopia) and Eukiefferiella with high positive and Rheocricotopus with high negative factor loadings. In the third principal components there is a contrast between Reocricotopus and C. bicinctus, while in the fourth Paratrichocladius rufiventris is opposed to C.bicinctus.

Stations of different months have been plotted according to their value in principal component axes (factor scores); in Fig. 2 the first and second principal components from analysis of larvae are plotted; only the results of 3 months are given. It is possible to see that all stations of february 1977 are plotted together, while stations 1-2-3 in january 1978 are plotted far from station 5 and still

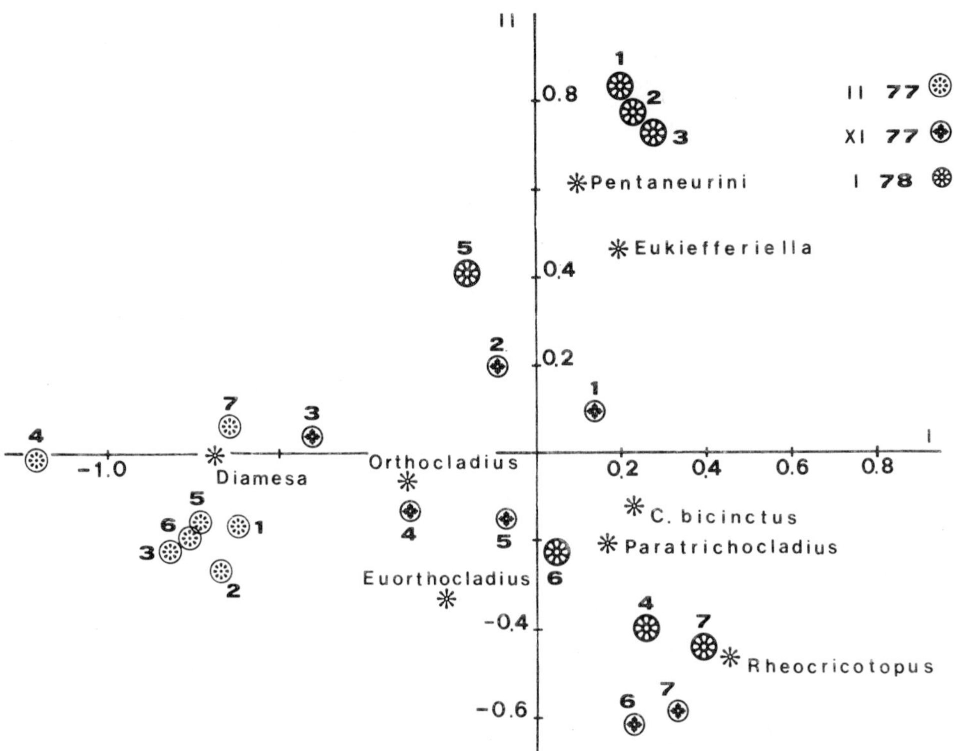

Fig. 2. Ordination of sampling stations (numbers 1,2...7 in heavy type) of 3 months, with the 1st and 2nd principal components.

farther from stations 4-6-7. Stations of november 1977 seem to be in an intermediate situation. In general, it is possible to note that in some months there is a rather uniform distribution of fauna in different stations; this may be explained with the conditions of high discharges in these cases; during february 1977, for instance, there had been high waters in the Lambro stream; on the other hand, in january 1978, samples have been collected during the low waters period (high waters appeared only at the end of this month); in these cases stations show a fairly different fauna composition.

The analysis of pupal exuviae has been carried out because pupae allow a better taxonomy, and counts of species are easier. On the other hand there is the danger that pupal exuviae coming from larvae living in a certain station might be collected in lower stations and the risk is greater during the periods of higher discharge. In the analysis of pupal exuviae Diamesa bertrami and Rheocricotopus dispar have again high factor loadings of opposite sign in the 3rd principal component, while in the 1st the contrast of factor loadings arises between D.bertrami and P. rufiventris; in the 2nd D.bertrami and P.rufiventris are opposed to R. dispar and Micropsectra sp.

DISCUSSION

The object of this work is an effort to use determinations of species of Chironomids to classify stations of a certain waterstream, showing differences with respect to hydrology and to pollution degree.

Our results are certainly affected by sampling technique: for instance, percent composition of species may be different according to the various days and it may happen that rare species will be collected or not by the Surber net only by chance. Taxonomical determinations to genus on larvae include different species only in one genus; for example, many Eukiefferiella species have been determined but all counted together. Most larvae have been determined as E.calvescens. but in lower numbers are also present E. fittkaui, E.minor, E.lobifera, E.claripennis. Despite these limits our results on principal components analysis with larvae seem to show that it is possible to discriminate among stations because some species, such as P.rufiventris, R. dispar and C.bicinctus, are more abundant in polluted stations, while Diamesa and Eukiefferiella species dominate in other situations.

Multivariate methods seem to be very useful in summarizing results, but an effort is required for a better taxonomy knowledge and more detailed information in autoecology of species.

REFERENCES

Blanc, F., P. Chardy, A. Laurac, and J. P. Reys (1976). Choix des métriques qualitatives en analyse d'inertie. Implications en écologie marine bentique. Marine biology, 35, 49-67.

Brundin, L. (1966). Transantartic relationships and their significance, evidenced by Chironomid midges. With a monograph of the subfamilies Podominae, Aphroteniinae and the austral Heptagyiae. K. Svenska Vetensk. Akad. Handl., 11, 1-472.

Davies, R. G. (1971). Computer programming in quantitative biology. Academic Press, New York, pp. 1-492.

Hynes, H. B. N. (1970). The Ecology of Running Waters. Liverpool Univ. Press. Liverpool., pp. 236-255.

Rossaro, B. (1977). Note sulle Orthocladiinae italiane con segnalazione di specie nuove per la nostra fauna. Boll. Soc. entom. ital., 109, 117-126.

Rossaro, B. (1978). Contributo alla conoscenza dei generi Orthocladius, Parorthocladius e Synorthocladius. Rassegna delle specie catturate sinora in Italia. Boll. Soc. entom. ital., 110, 181-188.

Rossaro, B. (1979a). Elenco faunistico e dati preliminari sull'ecologia dei Chironomidi di un fiume inquinato: il Lambro. Atti Soc. ital. Sci. nat. Museo civ. Stor. nat. Milano, Accepted for pubblication.

Rossaro, B. (1979b). Contributo alla conoscenza delle Orthocladiinae e Diamesinae italiane. Seconda nota. Memorie Museo Civ. St. nat. Verona. Accepted for publication.

Rossaro, B. (1979c). Composizione tessonomica e fenologia delle Orthocladiinae (Dipt. Chironomidae) nel Po a Caorso (Piacenza), determinate mediante analisi delle exuvie delle pupe. Riv. di Idrob. (Italy). Accepted for publication.

Vendegna, V. (1968). Studi sull'inquinamento delle acque italiane. 1. Carico zoologico ed evoluzione dell'inquinamento del fiume Lambro (Lombardia). Riv. di Idrob. (Italy), 7, 135-191.

Vendegna, V., and R.Marchetti (1973). 1. Il riequilibrio ecologico del bacino del fiume Lambro. Ecologia (Italy), 12, 20-27.

Classifying Rivers using Chironomid Pupal Exuviae

R. S. Wilson

Dept. of Zoology, University of Bristol, Bristol, England

ABSTRACT

The Chironomidae, one of the most important aquatic insect families, are easily sampled by collecting their floating pupal exuviae. This technique permits the family to be used in the biological classification of lakes and rivers. This paper describes work carried out on English rivers using qualitative collections of chironomid pupal exuviae to erect practical classifications of rivers both for management and water quality surveillance purposes.

KEYWORDS

Chironomidae; biological classification of rivers; pollution assessment; water quality surveillance; river management.

INTRODUCTION

Thienemann (1910) first published an account of the collection of chironomid pupal exuviae as a simple method of determining the species living in a water-body. Since then many researchers have adopted the method as an adjunct to distributional or taxonomic studies (e.g. Fittkau, 1962). Brundin (1966) used the method in his great work on the transantarctic relationships of animals, as did Lehmann (1971) on the Fulda to supplement detailed larval studies. In the U.S.A., Coffman (1973) has studied the phenology of chironomids in Linesville Creek by making extensive exuvial collections, and has even attempted quantitative work which has recently been followed up by Wartinbee (1976). For lakes, one may mention the classic studies of the Grosser Plöner See by Humphries (1938), and of Bodensee by Reiss (1968).

There is therefore a good precedent for the collection of pupal exuviae as a technique for evaluating the chironomid population of a river or lake, and is one which often reveals species which rarely occur in larval collections. This is due presumably to the difficulty of making representative larval collections from all available habitats.

It became apparent to the author some years ago that the ease of collection and identification of chironomid pupal exuviae, and its efficiency at obtaining a comprehensive list of species present, could make the technique useful in the classification of waters, both from an ecological and a water quality standpoint (Wilson and Bright, 1973). Moreover, it was applicable to both lakes and rivers, and could be developed for use in any country of the world. The award of a contract from the Water Data Unit of the Department of the Environment has allowed the technique to be tested extensively on rivers in England and Wales over the last four years, and this paper will give a short account of some of the work and its results.

RIVER CLASSIFICATION AND THE CHIRONOMIDAE

The biological classification of rivers is important both for fisheries management and for the monitoring and control of pollution. Biological changes occur normally in a river in response to natural changes in its physical and chemical conditions, and a knowledge of such natural variation must be built up to support water quality assessment and pollution monitoring. Abnormal biology often results from organic enrichment or industrial pollution, and rivers may be classified to show how far they have been changed by man's activities away from the established norm.

While biologists firmly believe that there is great and intrinsic value in biological monitoring and classification, they are by no means unanimous in choosing which taxa to use for the purpose. Most groups of aquatic animals and plants have had their protagonists. Till now, however, the chironomids have not been seriously considered, probably because of the difficulties of handling the larvae, yet they possess many characteristics which make the group almost ideal for such work. In particular they are abundant in deep muddy rivers which are notoriously difficult to study in comparison with shallower rivers with riffles.

The Chironomidae are one of the most common and abundant freshwater insect groups, and have in Great Britain at least 448 species (Cranston, 1975; Pinder, 1978), which is more than all the Ephemeroptera, Plecoptera and Trichoptera put together. If one may accept the theory that each species has its own particular niche, and its own tolerances to water and substrate conditions, then the Chironomidae has great potential for supplying potential indicator species. Chironomids are widely distributed from mountain tops to lowlands; and inhabit all types of substrate in rivers, from the surfaces of rocks, stones and macrophytes, to burrowing in mud, silt and plant material. Some are predatory and live freely in the water.

A very wide distribution of chironomids is ensured by the flying adult stage, and by the photopositive, migratory second larval instar. Moreover, chironomid larvae of all instars occur regularly in the river drift. It may thus be assumed that each particular habitat will contain its appropriate chironomid species, and that each type or section of river will support its own characteristic chironomid community.

Their ecology is not simple, however, as many larvae can adapt to different foodstuffs and substrates under special conditions, and it would be an oversimplification if one assumed that the presence or absence of a single species could be relied on to delimit certain river conditions. Far more useful are "indicator communities" which reflect more truly the river's ecological state. The large number of chironomid species and individuals that occur in suitable samples permits the community approach to be adopted even within this single taxon. Theoretically, of course, all taxa should be included in a study to make it truly integrative and reliable, but in practice some restriction of effort is necessary. This often takes the form of gross neglect of the Chironomidae themselves, or of grouping them under crude colour categories - a confusing and scientifically unjustifiable procedure.

The practical use of Chironomidae in river classification has been limited by the difficulties of identification of the larvae, many of which are difficult to recognise especially in the early instars, and are tedious to handle in large numbers. Flying adults are also not suitable for distributional studies as it is impossible to tell from which water body they derive, even though they may be trapped readily. Emergence trapping is of limited application, and relies on the maintenance of bulky and vulnerable apparatus over an extended time period.

With pupal exuviae, however, the situation is very different: they may easily be trapped, they obviously derive from the river being sampled, and they have no means of avoiding capture. Moreover, they show striking and obvious morphological characters which are of great value in identification, and are in many cases species-specific. Exuviae are, within limits, of a standard size and can easily be handled on slides or in wet collections.

Certain problems are inherent in the compilation of a comprehensive species list from exuvial collections. Firstly, different species may have restricted emergence periods both seasonally and diurnally. Secondly, it is not easy to be certain from what part of a river particular exuviae are derived, as they may drift in the surface water or be moved by the wind, for some distance downstream before lodging against an obstruction or in an eddy. Thirdly, the exuviae float for only a limited period of time, and are subject to fungal and bacterial attack which finally destroys them.

Much of the work carried out by the author and his associates at Bristol has concentrated on evaluating these difficulties, and the following points have been established. Exuviae float for up to two days buoyed up by gas trapped in the tracheae and elsewhere, and do not suffer fungal destruction until after they have sunk. They break up after about a week in the summer, and after about two weeks in the winter. The distance they float downstream is determined by many factors, including the strength and direction of the wind, the speed and turbulence of the current, the sinuosity of the river and the occurrence of suitable obstructions such as weedbeds. Evidence has been gained from studies of floating particles and from sequential samples of exuviae taken at close intervals down a river stretch, that in large rivers such as the lower Severn or Bristol Avon, exuviae travel for no more than a kilometre before being caught up on the bank. In smaller rivers like the River Chew of about five to ten metres across, they travel for five hundred metres at the most, while in very small streams and brooks the distance is even less. Detailed studies have not yet been made of tidal rivers.

Phenological studies of emergence have shown that many riverine species emerge almost continuously throughout the summer, although they often show one or more peak emergence periods (Wilson, 1977). It is therefore possible to construct a reasonably comprehensive species list for a site from a single summer sample, provided enough material is examined, say at least five hundred exuviae. Better results will of course be obtained from the examination of several samples taken at different times of year.

ANALYSIS OF EXUVIAL SAMPLES

Sample analysis can be either quantitative, semi-quantitative or purely qualitative. Attempts at making exuvial samples quantitative have met with little success, as it is necessary to trap all the exuviae coming down the stream over a significant length of time, normally twenty-four hours, and repeat this many times during the year. A surface boom as used by Coffman (1973) does not stop material from being sucked underneath and so lost, while a complete stop-net across a river becomes clogged very quickly, and rapidly becomes impossible to maintain. The technique may, however, be used satisfactorily within small delimited areas as Wartinbee (1976) has shown.

Semi-quantitative work may be carried out by taking regular samples weekly or monthly over an extended period, normally a year. From these samples the relative abundances of the different species may be calculated as percentages, and these will relate directly to the relative abundance of larval species on the river bed. Another way in which the relative percentages of exuvial species may prove useful is in comparing two or more samples taken at closely-spaced intervals down the river on the same day. Such samples may be useful in comparing the effects of sewage discharges on various rivers, as is shown by McGill, Wilson and Brake (1979).

Much easier to attain, and of great flexibility in application, is the purely qualitative sample which results in the compilation of a detailed species list for each site. Such lists can be analysed for diversity with respect to the numbers of exuviae examined; for similarity between sites or between whole rivers; and for community structure relating to certain ecological or pollutional conditions. Although better work is possible when two or more samples are taken at a site at different times of year, it has proved possible to evaluate the ecological conditions in a stretch of river using only a single sample taken between early June and the middle of September.

RIVER CLASSIFICATION USING EXUVIAE

For river management it is necessary to evaluate and compare both whole rivers and sections of rivers. It has been said that each river is an individual and that there are so many variables that no proper comparison is possible. This rather negative approach may be valid if one considers all the detailed flow patterns, sediment variations and other individualistic traits. On the other hand, each river is made up of the same basic features: shallow riffles and deep pools, rhithron and potamon; rock, pebbles, gravel, sand, silt and mud substrates; aquatic algae and macrophytes; although their detailed distribution varies almost infinitely both in time and space.

Running water is a very unstable environment in the short term, and the quantity of mud and silt at any point will constantly change through floods and erosion. The actual course of a river may be altered in a single spate. On the other hand, the quality of substrate will not be altered, and it can with justice be argued that under such conditions, qualitative samples will prove more characteristic of the biological nature of a river than will quantitative samples. Thus a species list of the chironomid community from a particular stretch of river, obtained by virtue of the comprehensive technique of exuvial sampling, will provide a "fingerprint" by which that stretch may be characterised. It is then possible to compare river sections and even whole rivers, and, through a knowledge of individual species' ecology and tolerances, to describe the actual biological conditions that exist in the river. A stable and effective biological classification of rivers may thus be set up, independent from the influence of mere quantity.

The qualitative approach is therefore suitable both for long-term base-line studies as well as for pollutional assessment, and is easily carried out using chironomid pupal exuviae which can provide comparable samples throughout the length of a river, at least down to the tidal zone. The species found may be grouped into categories to suit the effect being studied, such as rhithral/potamal, pollution tolerant/intolerant or hard/soft substrate preferences. In some cases several of these categories may be combined to differentiate say pollutional effects in the mud from those in the water itself. This flexibility of approach allows the method to be tailored to suit individual circumstances and requirements.

SELECTED EXAMPLES

To illustrate the value of the qualitative approach to river classification using chironomid pupal exuviae, certain selected examples will now be given. Firstly, one may compare one river with another by calculating Sørensen's coefficient of similarity S by using the formula S = 2C/A+B (Sørensen, 1948), where A and B are the total species in samples A and B, and C is the number of species common to both samples, and converting to percentage similarity if necessary. A number of rivers may be related in this way by building up a matrix of similarities, and then performing cluster analysis and constructing a dendrogram. Figure 1 is a dendrogram constructed in this way for a number of British rivers using species lists derived from the whole length of the river. It can be seen that the rivers fall into two basic groups: those with a fast, turbulent flow, for example the Duddon (Cumbria), Usk (South Wales) and Exe (Devon); and those with less turbulent flow, for example the Thames (Southern England), Avon (Avon) and Bure (East Anglia).

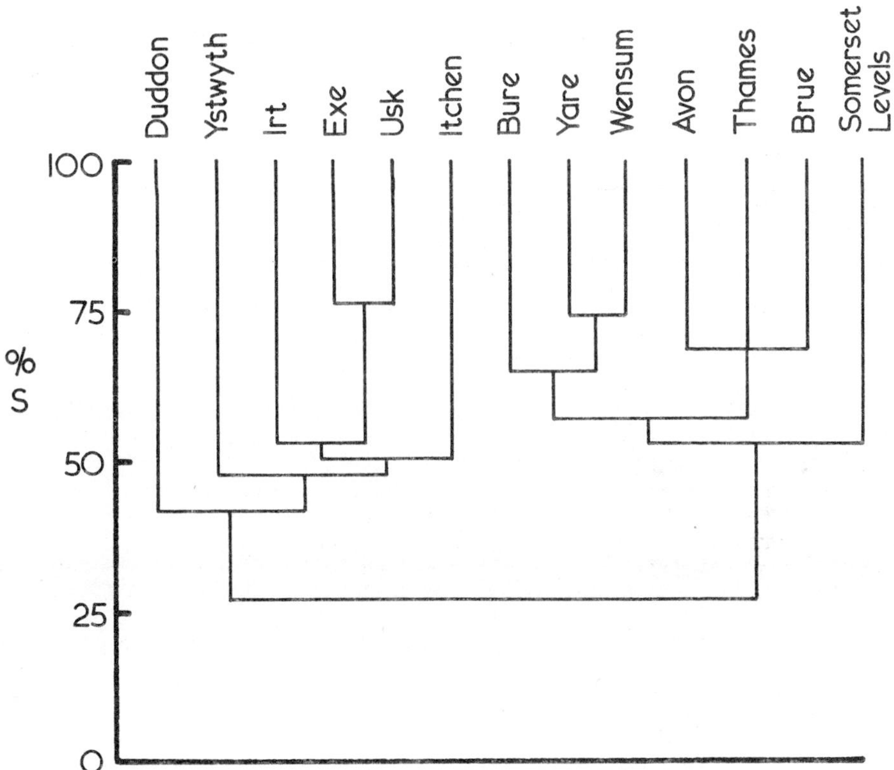

Fig. 1. Similarity dendrogram for selected British rivers.

Secondly, in order to make an absolute standard for relating and classifying rivers, it is convenient to divide the chironomids taxonomically into categories that approach a rhithral/potamal grouping as follows:

Rhithral groups: Pentaneurini, Diamesinae, Orthocladiinae, Chironomini connectentes

Potamal groups: Tanypodini, Macropelopiini, Prodiamesinae, Chironomini genuini, Tanytarsini

By calculating the percentage of rhithral types, the rivers in Fig. 1 may be arranged in series (Table 1). Any river may be classified according to this scheme.

TABLE 1 Percentage of Rhithral Species in various Rivers

Percentage	River
80 - 89	Duddon
70 - 79	Exe, Irt, Itchen, Usk and Ystwyth
60 - 69	Avon, Brue
50 - 59	Thames
40 - 49	Bure, Somerset Levels, Wensum, Yare

Finally, by grouping the chironomids into pollution "tolerant" and "intolerant" one may calculate the percentage of intolerant species in a sample, and plot this as a graph for a series of samples taken down the length of a river. It is important to recognise that this very crude categorisation is amenable to future refinement as our ecological knowledge of the different genera and species improves. In the present analysis the term "tolerant" refers not only to physiological tolerance, but also to behavioural tolerance, for instance where a species is able to live in the surface film and so avoid the effects of low oxygen in the water itself. Figure 2 shows graphs of selected rivers plotted to show the percentage intolerant species at sequential stations along their lengths. Low values indicate serious pollution, and a subsequent rise in value, recovery downstream. The Willow Brook is seriously polluted at its source in the Corby steelworks, while the River Churnet receives industrial and sewage effluents from the town of Leek.

In contrast, the River Duddon is a fast mountain stream in the Lake District, the Usk a much larger river rising in the mountains of South Wales and joining the Severn at Newport, and the Thames, the second longest river in Britain which rises in the Cotswolds and flows across Southern England to London. Neither the Duddon nor the Usk are seriously polluted, while the 500 km stretch of Thames studied (from its source down to Teddington Lock) reveals a very steady level of values of about 50% intolerant species. It is to be expected that a deeper river should naturally contain species more tolerant of low oxygen than those to be found in a turbulent mountain stream such as the Duddon, and so the results do not indicate any serious pollution of the Thames above London.

ACKNOWLEDGEMENTS

Much of the work reported here was carried out with the aid of a contract from the Water Data Unit of the Department of the Environment, and is included with their kind permission. I should also like to thank sincerely Mr J.D. McGill, Mrs Alison Griffies and Miss Lena Clarke, for their help in conducting the research and preparing the manuscript, also Mr P. Langton for valuable assistance in the identification of the exuviae.

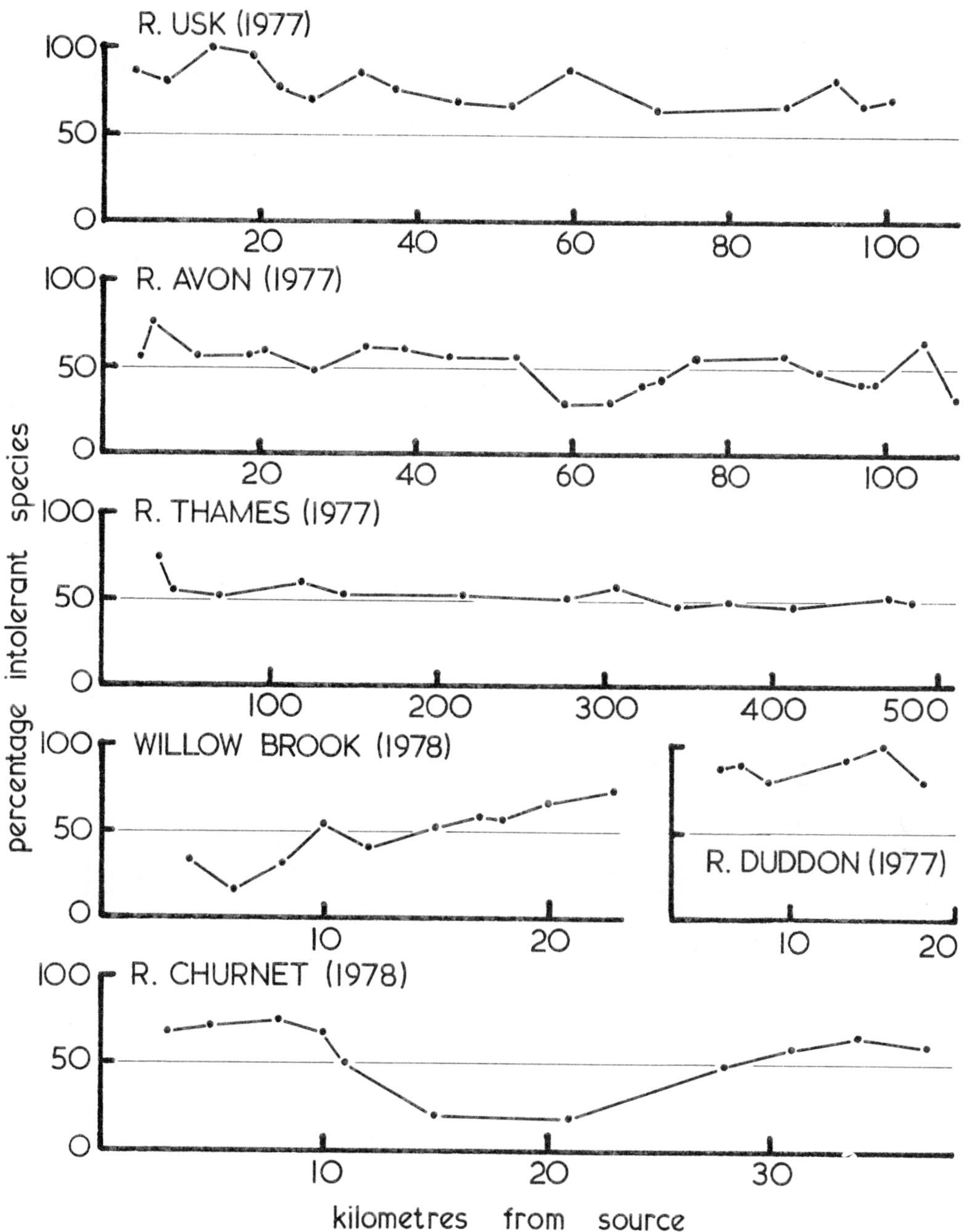

Fig. 2. Graphs of the percentage intolerant chironomid species taken along the lengths of selected rivers.

REFERENCES

Brundin, L. (1966). Transantarctic relationships and their significance as evidenced by chironomid midges. Kungl. Svenska Vetenskapacad. Handl., 11, 1-472.

Coffman, W. P. (1973). Energy flow in a woodland stream ecosystem. II. The taxonomic composition and phenology of the Chironomidae as determined by the collection of pupal exuviae. Arch. Hydrobiol., 71, 281-322.

Cranston, P. S. (1975). Chironomidae. In G.S. Kloet and W.D. Hincks, A Check List of British Insects. 2nd Edition, R. ent. Soc. London.

Fittkau, E.J. (1962). Die Tanypodinae. Akademie Verlag, Berlin.

Humphries, C. F. (1938). The chironomid fauna of the Grosser Plöner See, the relative density of its members and their emergence period. Arch. Hydrobiol., 33, 538-584.

Lehmann, J. (1971). Die Chironomiden der Fulda. Arch. Hydrobiol., Suppl. 37, 466-555.

McGill, J. D., R. S. Wilson, and A. M. Brake (1979). The use of chironomid pupal exuviae in the surveillance of sewage pollution within a drainage system. Water Res., in press.

Pinder, L. C. V. (1978). A key to the adult males of British Chironomidae. Freshwater Biological Assn., Scient. Publs. No. 37.

Reiss, F. (1968). Okologische und systematische Untersuchungen an Chironomiden (Diptera) des Bodensees. Arch. Hydrobiol., 64, 176-323.

Sørensen, T. (1948). A method of establishing groups of equal amplitude in plant sociology based on similarity of species content and its application to analyses of the vegetation on Danish commons. Biol. Skr., 5, 1-34.

Thienemann, A. (1910). Das Sammeln von Puppenhäuten der Chironomiden. Eine bitte um Mitarbeit. Arch. Hydrobiol., 6, 213-214.

Wartinbee, D. C. (1976). Quantitative determination of chironomid emergence from enclosed channels in a small lotic system. Am. Midl. Nat., 95, 479-485.

Wilson, R. S. (1977). Chironomid pupal exuviae in the River Chew. Freshwat. Biol., 7, 9-17.

Wilson, R. S. and P. L. Bright (1973). The use of chironomid pupal exuviae for characterizing streams. Freshwat. Biol., 3, 283-302.

Methods of Summarizing Survey Data from Lakes, illustrated by Reference to Lough Neagh, Northern Ireland

C. E. Carter

Limnology Laboratory, New University of Ulster, Traad Point, Drumenagh, Magherafelt, Co. Derry, N. Ireland

ABSTRACT

Data on chironomid abundance in areas of differing water quality in Lough Neagh are analysed by the methods of indicator species, Benthic Quality Index, Index of Diversity and Cluster Analysis. All give some indication of water quality but the Index of Diversity is found to be the most useful in reflecting differences in water quality between sites.

KEYWORDS

Chironomidae; Lough Neagh; benthic quality index; index of diversity; cluster analysis; water quality.

INTRODUCTION

With the increasing interest in the use of the benthic fauna as an indicator of water quality in rivers and lakes (Bryce and others, 1978; Hellawell, 1978; Wiederholm, in press), it is becoming important to find ways of presenting data on benthic fauna so that they are easily intelligible to the water manager or engineer. This paper explores the usefulness of several methods of data analysis in summarizing data on chironomid abundance in a lake, with this end in mind. The data used are from sites in different areas of Lough Neagh, Northern Ireland, a eutrophic lake of area 367 km^2 and mean depth 8 m. They are analysed to determine whether known differences in water quality between the sites are both reflected by the chironomid fauna and sensibly summarized by any of the methods used. An annual cycle is summarized for one site to show differences in the results due to the life cycles of the Chironomidae.

METHODS

Quantitative samples of Chironomidae were obtained with a corer, methods of processing and identification of samples are in Carter (1978). Chemical analysis of water were by standard methods (Golterman, 1969). The methods of data analysis were as follows:

<u>Benthic Quality Index (BQl)</u>. This is derived from Widerholm (in press). BQl = $\Sigma n_i k_a / N$ where $k_a = K_i - 1 + c_i$ and n_i = number of individuals in ith indicator.

species, N = total number of individuals in all indicator species, c_i = proportion of samples containing i^{th} indicator species (range 0-1), k_i = constant for i^{th} indicator species. Indicator species present in Lough Neagh were Chironomus plumosus (k_i = 1) and C. anthracinus (k_i = 2).

Index of Diversity ($\bar{d}$). This was used by Wilhm (1970) for rivers and streams.

$$\bar{d} = - \sum_{1}^{s} (n_i/N) \log_2 (n_i/N)$$ where n_i = number of individuals per taxon, N = total number of individuals, s = number of taxa. The taxon used here was the genus in a stream, values of 0-1 are considered indicative of pollution, 3-4 of clean water (Wilhm, 1970).

Cluster Analysis. This used a standard computer program - CLUSTAN (Wishart, 1969), with squared Euclidean Distance to construct the similarity matrix on standardized scores, and Ward's Method (Error Sum of Squares) to form the clusters.

RESULTS AND DISCUSSION

The data on species composition and abundance of the chironomid fauna at the sites sampled are shown in Table 1.

TABLE 1. Density of Chironomidae at sampling sites (No. m^{-2})

	JANUARY												MARCH											
	2	3	4	5	6	7	8	9	11	13	14	30	3	5	6	8	9	11	12	14	30	40	50	60
C. plumosus	673	842	589	337	168		84		505	842	912		168	337			84			168	37			
C. cingulatus					84		84		926	210	631				1347	1178		1347	84	253				
C. anthracinus				168			1094	926			701	635					589			505	442	663	939	221
Glyptotendipes							253	421	505	4209	842			84	926	253	253	1010	104	1263				
Endochironomus							421	673	84	421	281		421	505	253		589	84					55	
Stictochironomus																84	168	84	337					
Cryptochironomus "defectus"									84	210	491			84	253	168	84	84	168	589	221	55		
Polypedilum					84			337	2357	2525	491	83		253	253		337	1178	168	1263	111			
Dicrotendipes																		168						
Cryptochironomus																			84					
Tanytarsini											140	331			84	84	253			337	221	166	110	
Psectrocladius													84											
Procladius	3451	926	1263	8669	2188	2273	3956	6228	4125	8628	5261	3370	6986	13216	5219	84	6650	5724		6651	3204	2486	2099	55
Pentaneura															253				84					

14 groups (species and genera) were found, none present at all the sites, although Procladius was at all but one. The most abundant was also Procladius, numbers of the other groups varying quite widely between sites. Of the sites sampled in January, higher numbered sites generally have a greater number of groups present, sites 2-7 and 30 $\leqslant$ 4 groups and 8-14 $\geqslant$ 5. In March, however, this did not appear, there being $\geqslant$ 4 groups at all sites except 60. This helps to illustrate the difficulty of interpreting this type of data. From all the groups present it is possible to pick out indicator species, in the sense of Brundin (1958), and show presence or absence (Table 2).

TABLE 2. Presence and Absence of Indicator Species

	2	3	4	5	6	7	8	9	11	13	14	30
C. plumosus	+	+	+	+	+		+		+	+	+	
C. anthracinus				+			+	+			+	+
Tanytarsus											+	+

C. plumosus was the most common species, present at 9 of the 12 sites, *C. anthracinus* was at 5 sites and *Tanytarsus* only at 14 and 30. One might conclude from this that site 7 was extremely eutrophic (no indicator organisms), sites 2, 3, 4, 6, 11 and 13 eutrophic, and then becoming less so 5 and 8, 14 and finally 30. This method does simplify the data and provide some discrimination between sites, but there are still a lot in one category and a lot of potentially useful information has been ignored if this is the only summary method used.

Benthic Quality Index for the sites (Table 3) ranged from zero to two.

TABLE 3. Benthic Quality Index

Site No.	January	March
2	0.8	
3	1.0	0.2
4	0.8	
5	0.7	0.8
6	0.4	0
7	0	
8	1.9	0
9	2.0	2.0
11	0.8	0
13	1.0	
14	1.2	1.4
30	1.8	1.4
40		2.0
50		1.9
60		1.3

In January, sites 2-7 had values $\leqslant$ 1, while, except for 11, the other sites were $\geqslant$ 1. In March it was fairly similar with 8 as well as 11 exceptional. Plotting BQl against total phosphate/depth of site, as done by Wiederholm (in press) for some Swedish lakes, shows no very clear relationship (Fig. 1), although the range of values is obviously small.

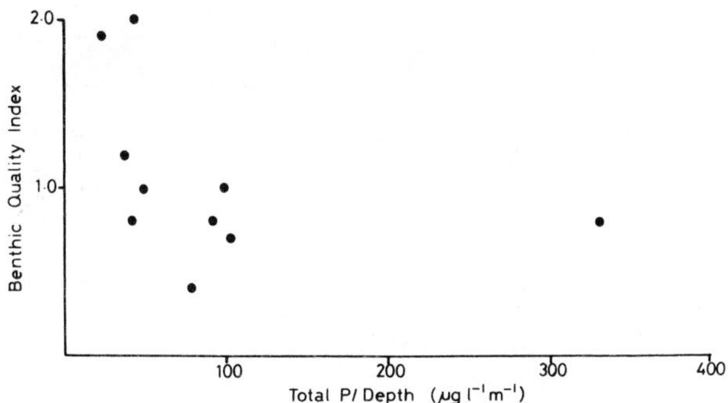

Fig. 1. Benthic quality index in relation to total phosphate/depth.

One difference to note between this and Wiederholm's similar figure is that he used mean total P and this figure was not available for these sites so the concentration on the sampling date was used. This being a January figure will be higher than annual mean. So, some separation of sites is given by the BQl but the degree of resolution is not very great.

The Index of Diversity (Table 4), calculated at the genus level, reveals greater differences between sites, although the range of values in the lake is smaller than that reported by Wilhm (1970) for streams.

TABLE 4. Index of Diversity

Site No.	January	March
2	0.64	
3	0.99	0.54
4	0.90	
5	0.31	0.60
6	0.67	1.40
7	0.00	
8	1.33	1.91
9	1.37	1.54
11	1.82	1.83
13	1.86	
14	1.94	1.84
30	1.09	1.24
40		1.10
50		1.19
60		0.72

In January sites 2-7 gave values less than 1, with all other sites greater. In March sites 3, 5 and 60 were under one and the others above. This difference in January also corresponded to one in total P/depth ratio, with those sites of $\bar{d} < 1$ having a ratio > 80, and those with a higher $\bar{d}$ a ratio < 60 (Fig. 2).

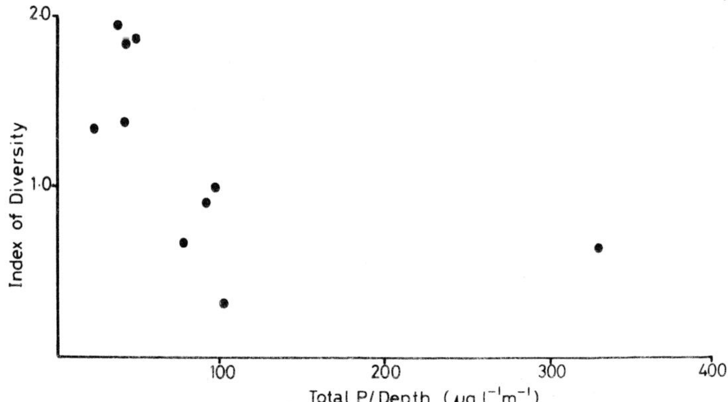

Fig. 2. Index of diversity in relation to total phosphate/depth.

Cluster analysis was performed on data from the two sampling dates both separately and together.

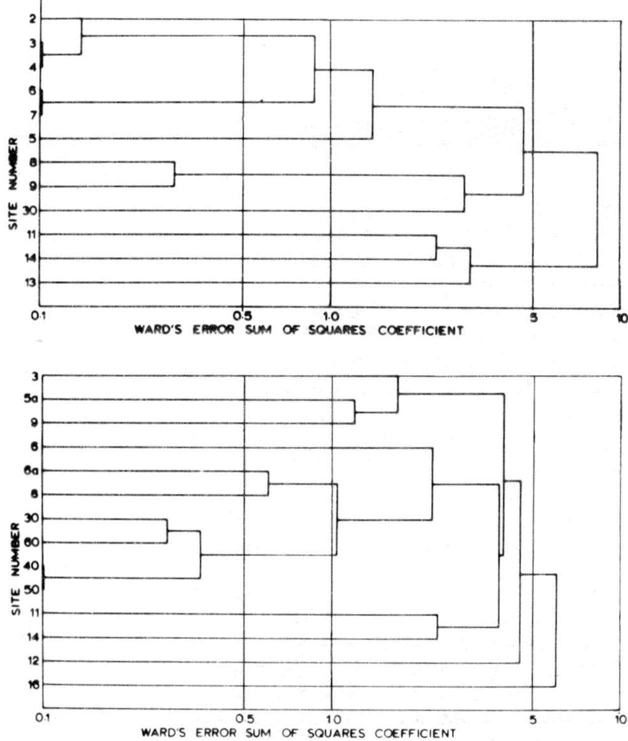

Fig. 3. Cluster analysis dendrogram. Top-January. Bottom-March.

In January (Fig. 3, top), the first groups were sites 2, 3 and 4, 6 and 7, and 8 and 9. Less close groupings were formed by 2, 3, 4, 6, 7 and 5, 8, 9 and 30, and 11, 14 and 13. In March (Fig. 3, bottom), the groupings were less close, except for 30, 60, 40 and 50. Other groups were composed of 5a and 9, 6, 6a, 8, 30, 60, 40 and 50, and 11 and 14. 12 and 16 were not incorporated into any groups until a late stage of the analysis. When the two dates were taken together (Fig. 4), many of the sites that had been sampled twice clustered closely, 30, 5, 9 and 14, although some were widely separated, 3, 6 and 11. Once again the low number sites tended to be more closely associated with each other and then with 30-60. 11, 13, 14 and 6M formed another group and 12M and 16M were again anomalous.

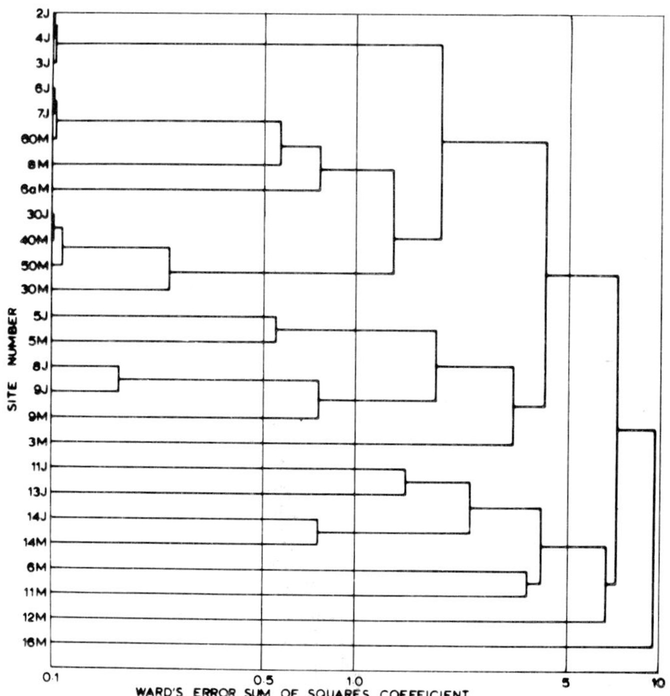

Fig. 4. Cluster analysis dendrogram for all sites.

To illustrate the variation in some of these indices caused by the seasonal cycles of numbers and occurrence of chironomids, the benthic quality index and index of diversity were calculated for one site (30) for samples taken throughout a year (Fig. 5).

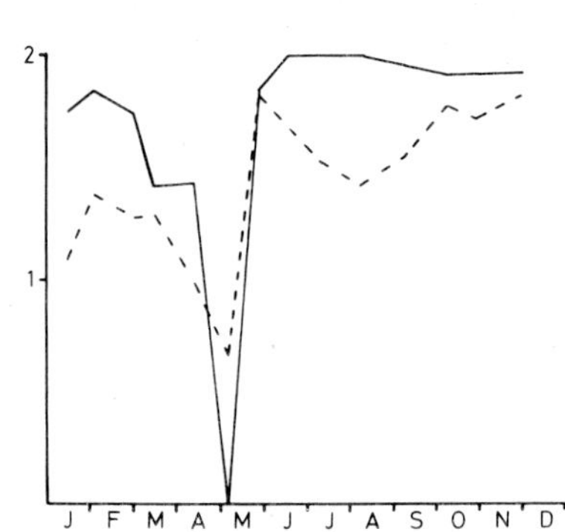

Fig. 5. Seasonal variation in Benthic Quality Index and Index of Diversity.

The benthic quality index showed the greater range of variation, being based on only a few species and therefore very susceptible to fluctuations in one of these, but was less variable for most of the year when occurrence of the indicator species was fairly steady. The index of diversity reflected its greater number of components in having a smaller range but more small variations. Both illustrated the importance of avoiding peak periods of emergence for water quality studies and the necessity therefore for some basic knowledge of life cycles for this type of work.

To summarize the four analyses (Table 5), the indicator species gave five groups with site 7 most eutrophic and site 30 least. Cluster analysis of all sites gave three main groups (at level of coefficient < 3) with principally low number sites and 30-60 together, 5, 8 and 9 and 11, 13 and 14. It, of course, gives no indication of the reasons for these groupings. The numbers for BQl and $\underline{d}$ are arranged in ascending order of value i.e. from most eutrophic (or polluted) to least. Site 7 gave the lowest value in each case and lower number sites generally gave lower values, followed by 30-60 and then the rest.

TABLE 5. Summary of Groups and Rankings given by Analyses

Method	
Indicator Species (groups)	7/2,3,4,6,11,13/5,8/14/30
Cluster Analysis (groups)	2J,4J,3J,6J,7J,60M,8M,6a M,30J,40M,50M,30M/5J,5M, 8J,9J,9M/11J,13J,14J,14M/3M/6M/11M/12M/16M
Benthic Quality Index (increasing value)	7J,6M,8M,11M,3M,6J,5J,2J,4J,5M,11J,3J,13J,14J, 60M,14M,30M,30J,8J,50M,9J,9M,40M
Index of Diversity (increasing value)	7J,5J,3M,5M,2J,6J,60M,4J,3J,30J,40M,50M,30M, 8J,9J,6M,11J,11M,14M,13J,8M,14J

Finally, the map of Lough Neagh (Fig. 6) shows the positions of these sites.

Fig. 6. Map of Lough Neagh (● indicates sampling sites).

Sites 2-16 were all at depths of 2-4m. Kinnego Bay, in the southeast corner of the lake, receives sewage effluent and site 7 was closest to the input. Total phosphate levels in Kinnego Bay in January were between 220-740 μg P/l. The Closet and Derryadd Bay both have reasonable water quality, although Derryadd Bay is now receiving treated sewage effluent and is being watched for possible deterioration. Total phosphate levels in the Closet and Derryadd Bay were 90-180 µg P/l. Sites 30-60 were in the open lake at increasing depths (8m, 12m, 15m, 25m). Thus they represent areas subject to an increasing probability of oxygen depletion and 60 (25m) was lower in both BQl and $\bar{d}$ than the other sites.

So, both the methods based on indicator species reveal something of these relationships, simple indicator species rather crudely. The benthic quality index is also rather variable and does not provide a particularly fine discrimination, in part because it does not utilize all the information available from this type of survey. It also does not give a clear distinction when plotted against phosphate levels at the sites. However, it is obviously of use when greater differences are being observed (Wiederholm, in press) and also because it does not require the identification of all species present in a sample. Cluster analysis provides valuable information on similarities between sites but none on any underlying causes for this. Its greatest use might be in showing differences when one site is being repeatedly sampled for long-term monitoring of water quality. The index of diversity appears to be the best indicator of water quality in the circumstances investigated here, where differences between sites are small but, nonetheless, important. It distinguishes the Kinnego Bay and deep water sites from the others, the remaining open water sites have intermediate values and The Closet and Derryadd Bay the highest. It is less affected by life cycles than the BQl, although these are still factors to be considered, as found by Hughes (1978), and it utilizes all the information available from a quantitative survey of chironomids. The lower the taxonomic level at which it can be calculated the more informative it is likely to be i.e. species level might have provided better discrimination than the genus level used here. It would be interesting to see whether the levels of total phosphate in lakes which Wiederholm (in press) found reflected by the BQl, are also reflected by differences in $\bar{d}$, evidence from the limited range of values in Lough Neagh is that this would be so.

REFERENCES

Bryce, D., I. M. Caffoor, C. R. Dale and A. F. Jarrett (1978). Macro-invertebrates and the Bioassay of Water Quality: A Report based on a Survey of the River Lee. Science Faculty of North East London Polytechnic Occasional Paper.

Brundin, L. (1958). The bottom faunistical lake type system and its application to the southern hemisphere. Moreover a theory of glacial erosion as a factor of productivity in lakes and oceans. Verh. internat. ver. Limnol., 13, 288-297.

Carter, C.E. (1978). The fauna of the muddy sediments of Lough Neagh, with particular reference to eutrophication. Freshwat. Biol. 8, 547-559.

Golterman, H. L. (1969). Methods for the Chemical Analysis of Fresh Waters. IBP Handbook No. 18. Blackwell Scientific Publications, Oxford.

Hellawell, J. M. (1978). Biological Surveillance of Rivers. Water Research Centre, England.

Hughes, B. D. (1978). The influence of factors other than population on the value of Shannon's Diversity Index for benthic macro-invertebrates in streams. Wat. Res., 12, 359-364.

Wiederholm, T. (in press). Chironomids as indicators of water quality in Swedish lakes. Acta. Univ. Carol. Biol.

Wilhm, J. L. (1970). Range of diversity index in benthic macroinvertebrate populations. J. Wat. Pollut. Control Fed., 42, R221-224.

Wishart, D. (1969). Fortran II programs for eight methods of cluster analysis (CLUSTAN 1). Computer Contribution No. 39, Kansas State Geological Survey.

Bathymetric Distribution of Chironomidae (Diptera) in the Oligotrophic Lake Thingvallavatn, Iceland[1]

C. Lindegaard

Freshwater Biological Laboratory, University of Copenhagen, Denmark

ABSTRACT

Macrozoobenthos of the oligotrophic Lake Thingvallavatn (84 km^2, 114 m deep), Iceland, was sampled along a number of transects from 0.4 m to a maximum of 75 m. Forty taxa were recorded, with 21 belonging to the Chironomidae.

A bathymetric distribution was described for the 13 most abundant chironomid species. *Eukiefferiella minor, Orthocladius oblidens, Euorthocladius frigidus* and *Thienemanniella* sp. cfr. *morosa* made up a surf zone community, whereas *Pseudodiamesa nivosa, Heterotrissocladius grimshawi, Pogonocladius consobrinus, Psectrocladius edwardsi, Corynoneura* sp. and *Tanytarsus gracilentus* occurred in the more calm water from 4-10 m. *Cricotopus sylvestris* and *C. tibialis* dominated within the transition between these two communities. Beyond 10 m in depth the Orthocladiinae were gradually replaced by *Chironomus islandicus,* which penetrated with a few individuals to the Tubificidae dominated profundal zone.

This distribution pattern was explained mainly by wave action, substrate type and available food.

KEYWORDS

Bathymetric distribution; macrozoobenthos; Chironomidae; Lake Thingvallavatn.

INTRODUCTION

The Thingvallavatn project, started in 1975, focuses on the function and dynamics of a deep subarctic lake ecosystem. Within this project I had the responsibility for determining the abundance, population dynamics, and production of zoobenthos. After a pilot investigation in 1975 it became obvious that zoobenthos of the littoral zone made up a very important part of the ecosystem. In spite of the difficulty in sampling this zone, we made efforts to include this habitat in our study. This paper

[1]Publication No. 340 from Freshwater Biological Laboratory, University of Copenhagen, 51 Helsingørsgade, DK-3400 Hillerød, Denmark.

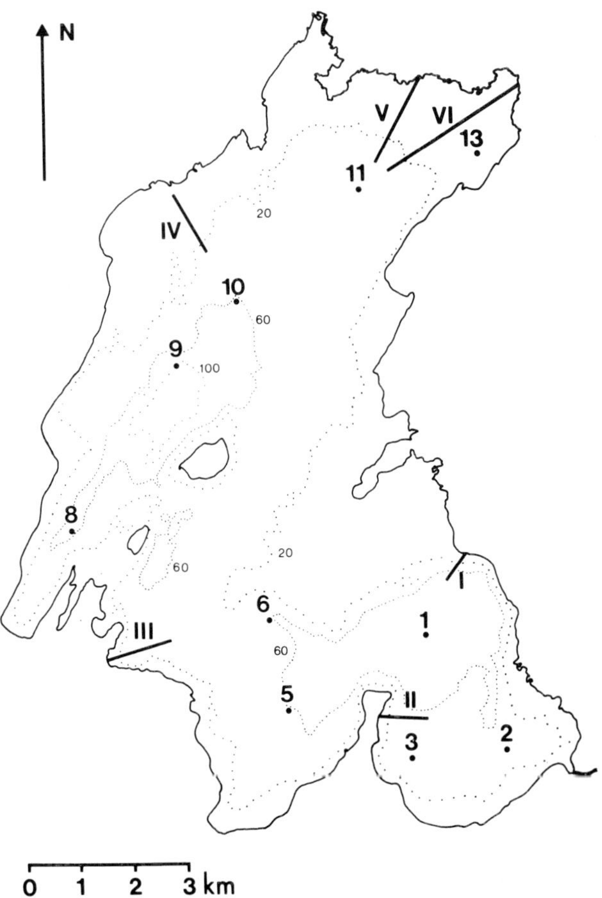

Fig. 1. Lake Thingvallavatn showing the 6 transects, and the 11 profundal stations. The dotted lines show the 20, 60 and 100 m contours.

presents the bathymetric distribution of the dominating Chironomidae in Lake Thingvallavatn.

Description of Lake Thingvallavatn

Lake Thingvallavatn (64° 10' N, 21° 15' E, 101 m a.s.l.) is located in southeast Iceland, within an area of postglacial volcanism. It has an area of 84 km^2, and it is the largest lake in Iceland. The maximum depth is 114 m, with a mean depth of 34 m. The littoral zone extends to approximately 20 m (Fig. 1), and makes up about 38% of the lake area. The surrounding bedrock is porous, and the large inflow is mostly subterranean. It has a retention time about 300 days. The outlet, the river Sog, is used by a set of power plants, which causes the lake level to fluctuate about 0.5 m. Due to the large volume, temperatures in summer reach only 10-11°C in surface waters and 6-7°C below 25 m. Thus, no real thermocline exists though a separation of the photic and aphotic zone during July and August occurs. In winter, ice cover is complete by January, and remains until April. Conductivity is low

(55 μS cm^{-1}). Transparency is 12-15 m in summer and the gross production of phytoplankton is 75-80 g C m^{-2} yr^{-1}. The production of benthic algae, epiphytes and macrophytes is not yet known, but a large variety (> 120 species) of epi- and periphytes is found in the photic zone. A large population (0.4 ind. m^{-2}) of the pelagic form of arctic char (*Salvelinus alpinus* L.) was recorded in 1975 by Nunnallee and Kristjánsson (1978).

The zonation of substrate from shore to profundal varies within the lake, depending on the different developments of slopes. However, the following description summarizes a general pattern (cfr. Fig. 2). From shore to about 6-10 m the substrate consists of varying sizes volcanic rock and boulders. A rather steep slope, coupled with wave action, prevents sedimentation of mud and sand in this zone. In the upper metre the stones are covered by green algae, mainly *Ulothrix tenuissima* Kütz. and *U. zonata* Kütz. From 1-2 m bluegreen algae and diatoms dominate. *Cladophora glomerata* (L.) and *C. aegagrophila* (L.) show maxima from 2-6 m. From 6-10 m to about 20-25 m, the slope is less steep and sedimentation of sand and organic matter provides growth conditions for *Nitella opaca* Ag. From 20-25 m to the profundal mud flats at approximately 70 m a very steep slope of bare rock was found. This is refered to as the bare rock zone (Fig. 2). The profundal mud consisting of a very fine diatomite begins at different depths according to morphometry of the lake basins.

Methods

A number of transects and profundal sampling stations was established (Fig. 1).The transects began at shoreline and extended to 20-25 m, where (at most transects) the steep drop-off zone led to the profundal (Fig. 2). SCUBA divers collected stones at a number of stations along the transects; especially in the boulder zone (0-10 m), where conventional methods could not be used. In the *Nitella* belt samples were taken by tubes (269 cm^2). The steep, bare rock zone could not be sampled (Fig. 2). The profundal stations were sampled by Ekman dredge (250 cm^2).

As the stones were of volcanic origin, the stone surface was covered by numerous

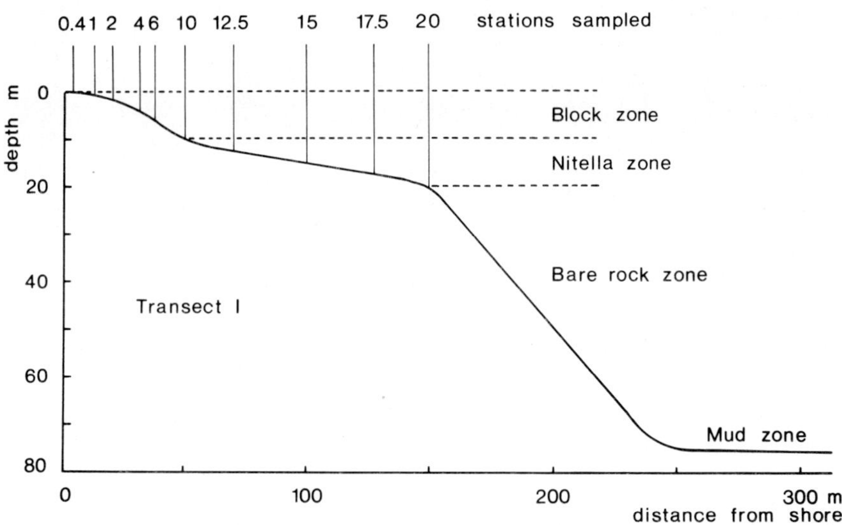

Fig. 2. Depth profile of transect I showing the 10 stations sampled in 1977.

TABLE 1 Mean Numbers of the Species found at 10 Stations along Transect I, and at Profundal Station 1 during 1977 in Lake Thingvallavatn

	no. m^{-2}	%
Coelenterata		
Hydra sp. cfr. *attenuata* Pallas	53	0.4
Turbellaria		
Rhabdocoela	2	<0.1
Nematoda	34	0.3
Oligochaeta		
Chaetogaster diaphanus (Gruith.)	301	2.4
Nais spp.	623	4.9
Uncinais uncinata (Ørsted)	8	0.1
Peloscolex ferox (Eisen)	130	1.0
Tubifex tubifex (Müller)	1,474	11.6
Enchytraeidae	2,241	17.6
Stylodrilus heringianus Clap.	7	0.1
Lumbriculus variegatus (Müller)	5	<0.1
Eiseniella tetraedra (Savigny)	15	0.1
Hirudinea		
Glossiphonia complanata (L.)	12	0.1
Trichoptera		
Apatania zonella (Zett.)	7	0.1
Limnephilus spp.	2	<0.1
Chironomidae		
Macropelopia nebulosa (Meig.)	3	<0.1
Procladius islandicus (Goetgh.)	1	<0.1
Arctopelopia griseipennis (Wulp)	9	0.1
Diamesa sp.	2	<0.1
Pseudodiamesa nivosa (Goetgh.)	36	0.3
Heterotrissocladius grimshawi Edw.	110	0.9
Eukiefferiella minor (Edw.)	511	4.0
Rheocricotopus effusus (Walker)	21	0.2
Orthocladius oblidens (Walker)	822	6.5
Pogonocladius consobrinus (Holmgren)	466	3.7
Euorthocladius frigidus (Zett.)	215	1.7
Cricotopus sylvestris (Fab.) } *Cricotopus tibialis* (Meig.) }	1,023	8.0
Psectrocladius edwardsi Brundin	388	3.0
Corynoneura sp.	70	0.6
Thienemanniella sp. cfr. *morosa* (Edw.)	38	0.3
Chironomus islandicus Kieffer	322	2.5
Paracladopelma laminata Kieffer	2	<0.1
Micropsectra atrofasciata Kieffer } *Micropsectra lindrothi* Goetgh. }	3	<0.1
Tanytarsus gracilentus (Holmgren)	15	0.1
Empedidae		
Atalanta stagnalis (Haliday)	8	0.1
Acarina		
Oribatidae	1,805	14.2
Sperchon glandulosa Koenike	95	0.7
Mollusca		
Radix peregra Müller	1,816	14.3
Pisidium spp.	32	0.3
Total	12,727	100.2

small pits, and this combined with a more or less thick algae growth made it very difficult to sort out the animals. Therefore, to ensure a high sorting out percent the following procedure was used. First the stone was brushed carefully in water 3 successive times until no more animals were seen. Then the stone was placed in a weak solution of formalin for 30 minutes. This caused animals, especially Enchytraeidae, to emerge from the deepest holes. All samples were preserved in 4% formalin. Sieves with mesh size of 100 µm were used in order to retain 1st instar chironomid larvae. The number of animals found was converted to no. m^{-2} of lake area; thus, the estimated no. m^{-2} actually lived on a larger stone area. Five Ekman samples were taken at each profundal station and on each date. Due to the large sorting work only two samples from each transect station were processed.

Samples considered here are from 1976-77, where profundal stations were sampled 3 and 4 times, respectively, from May to September, and transects were sampled 26 July 1976 and 5 times from May to September 1977. Additional samples were taken 8 times from May to December 1976 at 0.4 m in the transects. Data presented here are primarily from transect I and profundal station 1.

FAUNAL COMPOSITION AND BATHYMETRIC DISTRIBUTION

Approximately 40 taxa of invertebrates were collected from the benthos of Lake Thingvallavatn. The estimated average abundance for all depths along transect I, and profundal station 1 is given in Table 1. Oligochaeta and Chironomidae were the numerically dominating groups making up 70% of the total fauna. However, the Mollusca, *Radix peregra,* is (due to its large biomass) presumably the most important producer, though it made up only 14% of the total number.

The chironomid community was composed of 21 species dominated by Orthocladiinae (13 species and 3,700 ind. m^{-2}), whereas Chironominae (5 species and 350 ind. m^{-2}), and Tanypodinae (3 species and 13 ind. m^{-2}) were less important. Their location along the transect in 1977 is shown in Figs. 3-4. The following section summarizes the occurrence of each species including some notes from the 1976 data.

The three Tanypodinae species were found from 4-10 m, but they were so rare that this distribution may not be accurate.

Diamesa sp. was in 1977 found in very small numbers, whereas in 1976 (transect I) its maximum density in the surf zone was 2,600 m^{-2}.

Pseudodiamesa nivosa was found from 4-10 m in 1977, whereas it showed a vertical distribution of 7-30 m on stone samples taken in 1976 (transect V).

Heterotrissocladius grimshawi occurred from 1-75 m, but with a distinct maximum from 4-10 m. It was common on stone-, vegetation- and mud substrate. Its maximum density was about 500 m^{-2} in 6 m depth.

Eukiefferiella minor is a typical surf zone dweller found in large numbers at 0.4 m; in 1977 it had an average density of 4,300 m^{-2} at this depth. The maximum density found was 50,000 m^{-2} in July 1976. A few individuals were found at 10 m.

Rheocricotopus effusus is also a surf zone species, but with an average density of only 200 m^{-2}.

Orthocladius oblidens occurred in the upper 10 m primarily on stones, and with a maximum in the surf zone. In 1977 it was fairly abundant, when it made up 6.5% of the total fauna.

Pogonocladius consobrinus occurred down to 15 m with a maximum from 2-10 m. It was mainly found in the stone samples.

Euorthocladius frigidus is primarily a surf zone species, but penetrates as far as to 15 m. Its maximum density in July 1977 was about 3,000 m^{-2}; in July 1976 20,000 m^{-2} were recovered.

The larvae of *Cricotopus sylvestris* and *C. tibialis* were not separated, but according to the density of pupae *C. tibialis* made up about 90% of the *Cricotopus* population. They were abundant (8% of the total fauna) occurring down to 20 m, with maximum numbers between 2-6 m. Obviously they preferred the stone substrate.

Psectrocladius edwardsi had the same distribution as the 2 *Cricotopus* species, with a maximum from 4-10 m. It was also taken in the upper part of the *Nitella* zone.

Corynoneura sp. occurred down to about 20 m, with maximum numbers from 4-6 m. It was absent from the surf zone, where it was replaced by *Thienemanniella* sp. cfr. *morosa*. *Thienemanniella* was not as abundant in 1977 as in 1976 (1,400 m^{-2} vs 20,000 m^{-2} in July at 0.4 m depth).

Chironomus islandicus was found from 10-75 m, but was most abundant in the *Nitella* zone from 10-20 m, with an apparent maximum from 10-15 m. The larval tubes were found both in the *Nitella* vegetation and in the bottom mud.

Paracladopelma laminata was found at transect I at 10 m depth, but at other locations it penetrated to 30 m. It was found in small numbers, and restricted to the mud substrate.

Micropsectra larvae were found in the upper 10 m, but in so few numbers that the vertical distribution is uncertain.

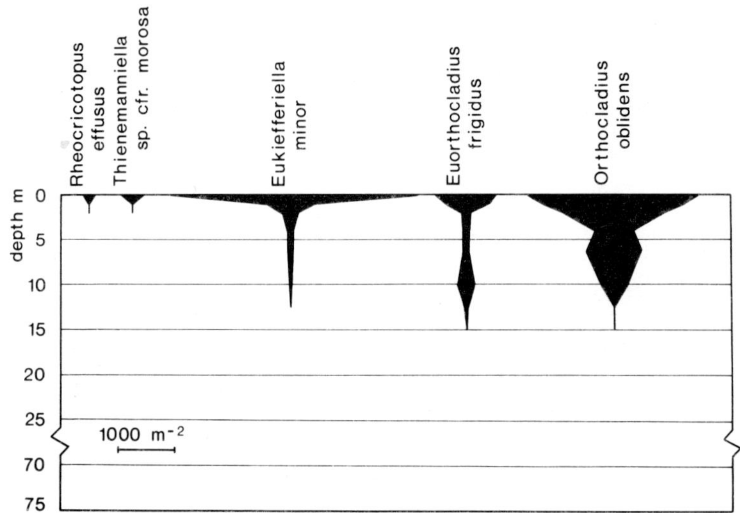

Fig. 3. Bathymetric distribution along transect I in 1977 of the chironomids primarily associated with the surf zone.

Tanytarsus gracilentus occurred down to 20 m, apparently with a maximum at 10 m. It was not abundant making up only 0.1% of the total fauna.

DISCUSSION

The chironomid fauna in Lake Thingvallavatn may be divided into three faunistic communities. A surf zone community composed of *Diamesa* sp., *Eukiefferiella minor*, *Rheocricotopus effusus*, *Thienemanniella* sp. cfr. *morosa*, and with *Euorthocladius frigidus* and *Orthocladius oblidens* also abundant in the upper metre (Fig. 3). These species are also common menbers of lotic communities, and their habitat in Lake Thingvallavatn is characterized by water movement caused by wave action. A second community composed of *Pseudodiamesa nivosa*, *Heterotrissocladius grimshawi*, *Pogonocladius consobrinus*, *Psectrocladius edwardsi*, *Corynoneura* sp., and *Tanytarsus gracilentus* occurred in the deeper water from 4-10 m, which was not as turbulent (Fig. 4). *Cricotopus* spp. was abundant in the transition between these two communities (2-4 m, Fig. 4).

At 10 m there was a transition zone, physically characterized by a shift from the rock substrate to a *Nitella* zone which had a muddy bottom. The transition zone had a mixed community (Fig. 4), but below 10 m most Orthocladiinae species (with the exception of *Psectrocladius edwardsi* and *Heterotrissocladius grimshawi*) were absent. *Chironomus islandicus* was dominant in the *Nitella* zone, with some Tubificidae also present. The Tubificidae became the dominant group in the profundal zone (below 70 m).

The distribution of chironomids below the surf zone is reasonably clear; however, the factors causing the patterns are not clear. Most Orthocladiinae seem to be limited to the depths which had stone substrate, although the lower limit of their distribution is difficult to determine. There was no oxygen deficit with depth. It

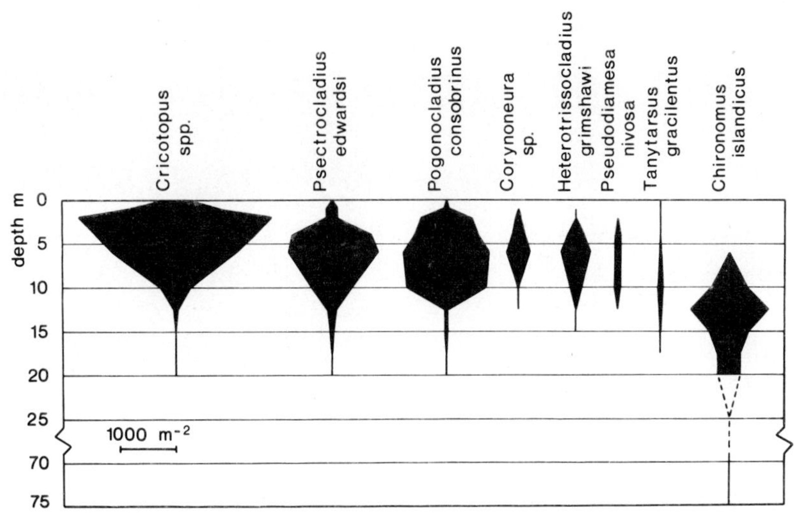

Fig. 4. Bathymetric distribution along transect I in 1977 of the chironomids not associated with the surf zone.

is possible that food availability in the form of peri- and epiphyton changed between 10 and 20 metres. Another potential factor could be the differential predation by fish over the different substrates that could affect the community composition.

Tubificidae were the only benthic invertebrate found in the profundal. Sedimentation of low energy organic matter at deeper depths in Lake Thingvallavatn could explain the absence of other taxa. Tubificidae can live on low energy food (cfr. Jónasson, 1978; Jónasson and Lindegaard, 1979). However, at the present time no exact information on the energy content of the different food items in Lake Thingvallavatn are available.

ACKNOWLEDGEMENTS

I am greatly indebted to the Icelandic parliament, Althingi, the direction of the power plant Landsvirkjun, the Icelandic Science Foundation, and the Nordic Council for Ecology for defraying the cost of the project. Thanks are due to my colleagues S. Snorrason B. Sc. and Ú. Antonsson B. Sc. for valuable help in sampling of material, and to M. C. Whiteside Ph. D., who critically reviewed the manuscript.

REFERENCES

Jónasson, P.M. (1978). Zoobenthos of lakes. *Verh. Internat. Verein. Limnol.*, 20, 13-37.

Jónasson, P.M., and C. Lindegaard (1979). Zoobenthos and its contribution to the metabolism of shallow lakes. *Arch. Hydrobiol. Beih. Ergebn. Limnol.* (in press).

Nunnallee, E.P., and J. Kristjánsson (1978). Hydroacoustic assessment of the Lake Thingvallavatn and Lake Skorradalsvatn fish populations. *J. Agr. Res. Icel.* 10,2, 141-155.

The Chironomidae (Diptera) in Two Polyhumic Reservoirs in Western Finland

L. Paasivirta and E. Koskenniemi

Department of Biology, University of Jyväskylä, Finland

ABSTRACT

Composition and distribution of chironomid and other benthic fauna was studied at two adjacent 15 years old polyhumic reservoirs in western Finland by taking benthic and emergence samples. The littoral (0.5 m) coarse debris habitats, previously coniferous forest, had considerably less chironomid larvae (6-7 types, maximally 800 individuals or 0.1 g, AFDW/m^2) than the mossgrown habitats, previously peatland (9-10 types, maximally 4000 individuals or 3.4 g/m^2). The *Chironomus* larvae which were dominant at the moss sites were almost lacking at the coarse debris sites. *Zalutschia zalutschicola* Lipina and *Tanytarsus* larvae were found only at the deepest areas at 6 m. Altogether 17 species emerged from the shallow (1 m) moss habitats which were dried and frozen in late winter. *Ablabesmyia phatta* (Eggert), *Psectrocladius edwardsi* Brund., *P. psilopterus* K., *Chironomus cf. longistylus* Goetgh., *Ch. macani* Freeman and *Limnochironomus lobiger* K. were considered as characteristic species for such habitats. The three first-mentioned species seemed to be sensitive to a complete oxygen deficiency prevailing for three months in winter in one of the two reservoirs.

KEYWORDS

Chironomidae; polyhumic reservoirs; coarse debris; water mosses; freezing; drying; emergence.

INTRODUCTION

Several reservoirs have been constructed for the purposes of flood control and production of hydro power in western and northern Finland during recent decades. These reservoirs, situated mainly on previous peatland and coniferous forest, have rather acid and humic water poor in nutrients and have a severe oxygen deficit when covered with ice (Vogt, 1978). Since the reservoirs are shallow vast bottom areas will be dried and/or frozen in late winter, when the water level reaches its annual minimum. Composition of the benthic fauna is quite different from that in the natural lakes owing to the severe environmental conditions and peculiar bottom habitats. Benthic communities tend to be less diverse and more unstable than in the natural lakes. Knowledge on the chironomid fauna in Fennoscandian reservoirs is so far very restricted (Wiederholm, Danell and Sjöberg,

1977). We have collected chironomid larvae and adults at two reservoirs in western Finland in 1975 and 1976 as a part of the faunistic-ecological research on chironomids carried out in Finland.

DESCRIPTION OF THE RESERVOIRS

The reservoirs, Lake Vissavesi (63°30'N, 23°50'E, maximally 370 ha) and Lake Venetjärvi (63°30'N, 24°15'E, maximally 1600 ha), have been constructed in 1964-65 in order to prevent spring floods in the valley of the river Perhonjoki. The volume of the reservoirs is lowest in late winter (April) and highest in early summer (June). Water level is kept nearly constant until the next winter. Annual variation of the water level was about 2 m at Lake Vissavesi and 3 m at Lake Venetjärvi. Both reservoirs have a mean depth of 2 m, maximum depth of 6 m and maximum thickness of ice 0.7 m. Ice covers the reservoirs from November to May. The water of both reservoirs is characterized by a shortage of oxygen in late winter, moderate acidity and brown humus colour (Table 1). The water in Lake Vissavesi was deoxygenized already in February but not until April in Lake Venetjärvi.

TABLE 1 Some Physico-Chemical Data of the Reservoirs in late winter and summer 1976. Measurements made by the local authorities of the National Board of Waters in Finland.

Reservoir	Vissavesi				Venetjärvi			
Date	8.IV		2.VIII		8.IV		2.VIII	
Depth, m	1	5	1	5	1	5	1	5
Oxygen saturation, %	0	0	56	30	0	0	78	77
pH	5.0	5.0	5.4	5.3	5.3	5.5	5.8	5.8
Colour, mg Pt/l	420	470	290	330	450	530	130	130
Conductivity, $\varkappa_{25}$ µS/cm	46	50	33	35	56	79	27	24
Total nitrogen, mg/l	1.33	1.19	1.12	0.85	1.48	1.64	0.52	0.59
Total phosphorus, µg/l	33	86	68	87	86	93	27	24

Organic matter on the bottom of the reservoirs, previously peatland and coniferous forest (c.1:1), was still only slightly decomposed. Previous forest areas were covered by coarse plant debris and spatially water mosses. Previous bog areas were covered by water mosses (mainly *Drepanocladus* spp.) down to a depth of 2 m. The deepest areas are situated at the sites of previous bog lakes, where the bottom substrate is soft brown mud ("dy"). One of the two deepest sites at Lake Venetjärvi is, however, situated on previous peatland, where the bottom is covered by decomposed *Sphagnum*. The littoral benthos sampling sites were frozen solid and the emergence sampling sites dried and frozen in late winter.

METHODS

The littoral benthic samples were taken at a depth of 0.5 m with a plastic box (sampling area of 236 cm^2) which was pressed tightly on the bottom. Surface layer of the sample area and the water inside the box was sieved through a 0.4 mm mesh and the animals were picked as alive from a white dish in the laboratory. One box sample was taken at each station on each occasion (Tables 2 and 3). The deepest sites at a depth of 6 m were sampled only once in August with an Ekman grab covering 300 cm^2. Three replicates at two stations were taken at both reservoirs. Sieving and picking was performed as with the littoral samples. The biomasses were obtained by using specific length-weight relationships or mean individual weight values. The biomasses are reported as ash-free dry-weights (AFDW).

The chironomids emerging from moss-grown sites, previously peatland, at a depth of 1 m were sampled with submerged funnel traps covering 0.5 m^2. Two traps were used at both reservoirs (Table 4). Since the emergence had began about one week before the sampling the numbers are somewhat underestimated and it was not reasonable to calculate the sex ratios for most of the species.

RESULTS AND COMMENTS

The density of the chironomid larvae was considerably lower at the coarse debris sites than at the moss sites in the littoral of both reservoirs (Tables 2 and 3). The density was lowest in June since majority of the chironomids has already emerged before the larval sampling. Mean individual weight of the larvae was lowest in July when most larvae were young. *Endochironomus* and *Chironomus thummi* -type larvae were dominant at the moss sites in Lake Vissavesi and *Chironomus plumosus*- and *thummi*-type larvae in Lake Venetjärvi. Notably *Chironomus* larvae were almost lacking at the coarse debris sites of both reservoirs.

TABLE 2 Mean Densities (individuals/m^2) of the Larval Chironomids at the coarse debris (CD) and moss-grown (M) sites and at the muddy sites of the deepest areas of Lake Vissavesi in 1975.

Date	11.VI		22.VII		28.VIII		17.VIII
Depth, m	0.5		0.5		0.5		6
Bottom type	CD	M	CD	M	CD	M	Mud
Number of stations	4	4	4	6	4	6	2
Ablabesmyia	-	-	21	7	-	-	-
Procladius	-	-	11	7	74	7	11
Psectrocladius	-	21	-	7	-	-	11
Zalutschia zalutschicola	-	-	-	-	-	-	111
Chironomus plumosus-type	43	-	21	685	-	184	144
Ch. thummi-type	-	159	-	982	-	1096	189
Cryptochironomus	-	-	-	-	-	14	-
Endochironomus	21	-	687	1138	64	1484	-
Glyptotendipes	-	11	21	162	11	177	-
Limnochironomus lobiger	-	-	-	-	-	35	-
Phaenopsectra (Lenzia)	-	-	11	-	-	-	-
Tanytarsus	-	-	-	-	-	-	50
Total	64	191	763	2988	149	2997	516
S.E.	50	107	475	1753	54	1043	41
Total mg/m^2, AFDW	50	210	140	1730	70	3420	210
Chir./whole zoobenthos,							
density, %	5	13	24	72	8	84	77
biomass, %	6	24	9	69	7	87	81

The chironomids were highly dominant at the moss sites in July and August. The other dominant benthic animals at the littoral habitats of both reservoirs were *Lumbriculus variegatus* (Müller) and *Asellus aquaticus* (L.), at the coarse debris sites of Lake Venetjärvi in August, however, *Erpobdella octoculata* (L.) and *Cyrnus* larvae.

The dominant chironomid larvae at the muddy sites of the deepest areas of Lake Vissavesi in late August were *Chironomus thummi*-type, *Ch. plumosus*-type and *Zalutschia zalutschicola* Lipina and in Lake Venetjärvi *Ch. thummi*-type and *Procladius* (Tables 2 and 3). Notably *Endochironomus* and *Glyptotendipes* larvae were found only at the peatty site and *Zalutschia zalutschicola* larvae only at the muddy sites of the deepest areas. At an English bog lake *Chironomus lugubris* Zett. occurred only at the zone of more decomposed fine peat and *Glyptotendipes paripes* Edw. only at the zone of less decomposed coarse peat (McLachlan and McLachlan, 1975).

TABLE 3 Mean Densities (individuals/m^2) of the Larval Chironomids at the coarse debris (CD) and moss-grown (M) sites and at the muddy and peatty sites of the deepest areas of Lake Venetjärvi in 1975.

Date	12.VI		24.VII		30.VIII		17.VIII	
Depth, m	0.5		0.5		0.5		6	6
Bottom type	CD	M	CD	M	CD	M	Mud	Peat
Number of stations	3	5	3	9	3	9	1	1
Ablabesmyia	14	34	28	5	-	188	11	22
Procladius	28	-	14	5	-	5	278	156
Psectrocladius	-	-	-	14	-	14	-	-
Zalutschia zalutschicola	-	-	-	-	-	-	11	-
Chironomus plumosus-type	-	9	-	1098	-	2059	11	11
Ch. thummi-type	-	882	-	1074	-	1687	278	744
Demicryptochironomus	-	-	-	-	-	-	-	11
Endochironomus	-	9	127	254	14	99	-	89
Glyptotendipes	-	-	-	5	14	33	-	356
Limnochironomus lobiger	-	-	-	-	-	52	-	-
Microtendipes	-	-	28	5	155	-	11	200
Parachironomus	-	-	-	-	-	-	-	22
Paratendipes	-	9	-	-	-	-	-	-
Phaenopsectra (Lenzia)	14	-	-	-	-	-	-	-
Stenochironomus	14	-	-	-	14	-	-	-
Tanytarsus	-	-	-	-	-	-	44	100
Total	72	943	197	2460	211	4123	644	1711
S.E.	37	536	157	957	130	943	161	882
Total mg/m^2,AFDW	10	940	20	1250	80	3220	200	550
Chir./whole zoobenthos,								
density, %	7	62	48	88	47	85	54	73
biomass, %	2	65	5	80	22	83	56	73

The other dominant benthic animals at deepest areas were *Chaoborus* larvae and Tubificidae in Lake Vissavesi and *Pisidium casertanum* Poli at the muddy site and *Asellus aquaticus* at the peatty site in Lake Venetjärvi.

Chironomus cf. longistylus Goetgh. was highly dominant in the emergence numbers in Lake Vissavesi, but *Ablabesmyia phatta* (Eggert) and *Psectrocladius* species were more abundant in Lake Venetjärvi, where there was better oxygen supply during winter (Table 4). The total emergence numbers were only c. 10% of the larval density at the moss sites in both reservoirs. However, drying and freezing of the trapping areas in late winter was not able to kill all the larvae. In a Swedish reservoir the bottom drying in winter was immediately covered with ice, which served as insulation causing only 30% mortality for chironomid larvae during an exposure of three months (Grimås, 1961).

During the 10 first days of June 87% of the chironomids had emerged at Lake Vissavesi and 56% at Lake Venetjärvi. A similar pronounced emergence peak was observed at about the same time at a northern Swedish man-made lake (Wiederholm, Danell and Sjöberg, 1977). *Psectrocladius edwardsi*, *Chironomus cf. longistylus*, *Ch. macani*, *Ch. pilicornis* and *Glyptotendipes paripes* were also living in the Swedish lake, which had a depth of only 0.3-0.5 m and the bottom covered with decomposed sedges. According to the existing data, characteristic species for shallow moss-grown habitats frozen in winter seem to be *Ablabesmyia phatta*, *Psectrocladius edwardsi*,

P. psilopterus, *Chironomus cf. longistylus*, *Ch. macani* and *Limnochironomus lobiger*. The three first-mentioned species were, however, rare in Lake Vissavesi, which had a severe oxygen deficit already in February in the whole water column.

TABLE 4 Percentage Composition of Chironomid Emergence from the moss-grown littoral (1 m) habitats of the two reservoirs in 1976. The periods are: 1=1.-4.VI, 2=4.-10.VI, 3=10.-17.VI, 4=17.-21.VI, 5=21.-30.VI, 6=12.-15.VII and 7=17.30.VIII.

Species	Vissavesi		Venetjärvi	
	%	period	%	period
Ablabesmyia monilis (L.)	-		2	5-7
A. phatta (Eggert)	2	3-5	39	1-4,6
Psectrocladius edwardsi Brund.	-		19	5
P. psilopterus K.	1	1,7	19	1-7
Chironomus cf. longistylus Goetgh.	75	1-3	14	1-2
Ch. macani Freeman	1	3,5	2	2,4-5
Ch. pilicornis (Fabr.)	+	1	-	
Cryptochironomus supplicans (Meig.)	1	5	-	
C. sp.	1	2	-	
Endochironomus impar (Walk.)	1	2-3	1	1-2
E. cf. albipennis (Meig.)	3	1-3	-	
Glyptotendipes spp.[x]	8	1-3	-	
Limnochironomus lobiger K.	7	1-3	4	1-4
Parachironomus digitalis (Edw.)	-		+	4
Paratanytarsus sp.	-		+	3
Total individuals/m^2	353		447	
Number of species	13		10	

[x] According to the identified males, most abundant was *G. pallens* (Meig.), but some specimens of *G. gripekoveni* K. and *G. paripes* (Edw.) were also present.

Our *Chironomus cf. longistylus* has a dark brown thorax and abdomen, the wing length (from arculus to the wing tip) 3.8-4.6 mm, AR 3.8-4.0, LR 1.37-1.44, BR c.2, am-setae 6-15 without fields and hypopygium according to Pinder (1978). The hypopygium also resembles *Ch. riihimäkiensis* Wülker which has a shorter wing (3.4-3.9 mm), lower AR (3.5-3.7) and higher LR (1.43-1.58)(Wülker, 1973). These differences may, however, be due to the different water temperatures during pupal stage (Paasivirta, 1972).

Our *Chironomus (Chaetolabis) macani* has an identical AR, LR and hypopygium with the Swedish specimens (Wiederholm, 1979), but its thorax is green-light brown with black scutal stripes, wing length is higher (4.8-5.0 vs. 3.9-4.3 mm) and there is no visible tarsal beard. *Chironomus pilicornis* (body entirely black, wing length 4.7-5.0, AR 5.6, LR 1.0, BR c. 7 and only 1 am-seta) and *Glyptotendipes* species were identified according to Pinder (1978).

Our *Endochironomus cf. albipennis* has a black thorax and green abdomen thus resembling *E. lepidus* (Meig.) and *E. stackelbergi* Goetgh., front tibiae are pale greenish but the last three segments of tarsus darkened, LR is 1.1 and there is a moderate tarsal beard (BR c. 4) as with *E. albipennis* (Kalugina, 1961), AR is 3.0 and wing length 4.5 mm. The pupal exuvia is of the *albipennis*-type (Kalugina, 1961). Our specimens and *E. stackelbergi* may be a dark colour form of *E. albipennis*, but *E. lepidus* which has brown or black front tibiae and no tarsal beard is obviously a true species.

REFERENCES

Grimås, U. (1961). The bottom fauna of natural and impounded lakes in northern Sweden (Ankarvattnet and Blåsjön). Inst. Freshwater Res. Drottningholm, Rep. 42, 183-237.

Kalugina, N. S. (1961). Sistematika i razvitie komarov Endochironomus albipennis Mg., E. tendens F. i E. impar Walk. Entomol. Obozrenie, 40, 900-919 (In Russian).

McLachlan, A. J., and S. M. McLachlan (1975). The physical environment and bottom fauna of a bog lake. Arch. Hydrobiol., 76, 198-217.

Paasivirta, L. (1972). Taxonomy, ecology and swarming behaviour of Tanytarsus gracilentus Holmgr.(Diptera, Chironomidae) in Valassaaret, Gulf of Bothnia, Finland. Ann. Zool.Fennici, 9, 255-264.

Pinder, L. C. V. (1978). A key to adult males of British Chironomidae. Freshwater Biol. Assoc., Scien. Publ., 37, 1-169.

Vogt, H. (1978). An ecological and environmental survey of the humic man-made lakes in Finland. Aqua Fennica, 8, 12-24.

Wiederholm, T. (1979). Morphology of Chironomus macani Freeman (Diptera:Chironomidae) with notes on the taxonomic status of the subg. Chaetolabis Town. Entomol. Scand., Suppl. 10 (in print).

Wiederholm, T., K. Danell, and K. Sjöberg (1977). Emergence of chironomids from a small man-made lake in northern Sweden. Norw. J. Entomol., 24, 99-105.

Wülker, W. (1973). Revision der Gattung Chironomus Meig. III. Europäische Arten des thummi-Komplexes. Arch. Hydrobiol., 72, 356-374.

Benthic Populations Dynamics in Artificial Samplers in a Spanish Reservoir

Narcis Prat

Dept. Ecologia, Fac. Biologia, Universidad de Barcelona, Gran Via, 585, Barcelona, Spain

ABSTRACT

This paper deals with the benthic fauna that develop on submerged artificial substrates in a reservoir in southwestern Spain over a time period of one year. A spectacular growth of the fauna in the first few months was followed by a decrease in the number of individuals and at same time an increase in the number of species. This led to a more equal distribution of the number of individuals per species. The least number of individuals ocurred in summer coinciding with a higher percentage of cyanophytes in the phytoplankton.

KEYWORDS

Benthos; population dynamics; Chironomidae; reservoir; artificial substrates.

INTRODUCTION

Recent studies have been made of the colonization and dynamics of the benthos of reservoirs; both dredges (Mac Lachlan, 1971; Paterson and Fernando, 1970; Kryzanek, 1977) and artificial substrates (Armitage, 1977) have been used. On Spain we have recently began to study the benthos of reservoirs (Prat, 1979). This work has produced a typology based on the composition of the benthos (Prat, 1978).

The present paper will contribute to a better understanding of the benthic fauna of Spanish reservoirs. Further, with the use of artificial substrates, a better understanding of the initial phases of the colonization of the reservoirs will be avalaible. The study was made in the reservoir of Arrocampo, in the province of Cáceres (Spain), in the river of same name which flows into the Tajo in the reservoir of Torrejón (Fig. 1). The reservoir has a maximum volume of 33 Hm^3 and a maximum area of 7 Km^2. The maximum depth is 20 m.

MATERIALS AND METHODS

Plastic buckets (21'5 x 21'5 x 15 cm) filled with mud to a depth of 5 cm. were placed on the bottom at stations 2 and 6 (Fig. 1) in February 1978. The first station had a depth of 2 m and the second a depth of 20 m. Replicate buckets were withdrawn in April, June, August and October of the same year and in February of 1979. When withdrawn the mud was filtered through a net of 250 microns and the residue was preserved in 10% formalin. The samples were examined in the laboratory under a binocular dissecting microscope at 12 x.

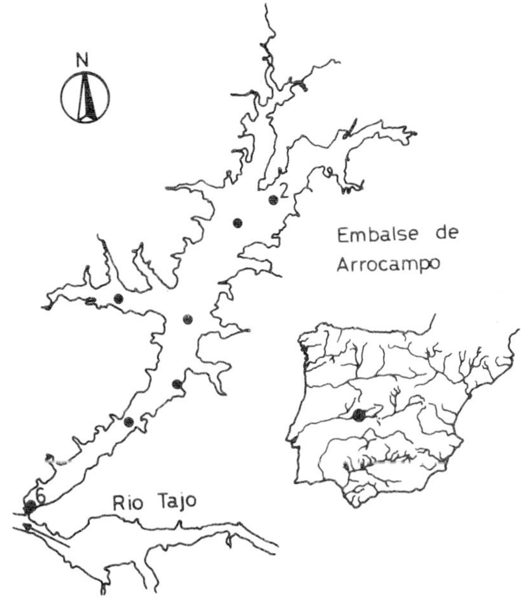

Fig. 1. Location of the Arrocampo reservoir and the sampling stations.

RESULTS

Anoxia during all the summer and part of spring and autumn at station 6 prevented the devolopment of many species. Only a few individuals of Chironomus and ocasionally large numbers of Chaoborus ocurred in these samples. At station 2 the prevailing conditions were more suitable and the results are better. Because of this only data from station 2 will be reported. In any case, the data should be interpreted with caution since at the moment when the buckets were withdrawn some of the surface material could escape and with it some components of the benthic fauna may have been lost.

Physical and Chemical Characteristics near the Sediment of Station 2.

Station 2 is located in the tail of the reservoir. The water is shallow and during the sampling period no important changes of depth are ocurred. It received important flows of water irregularly, principally in winter. At the same time that benthic samples were taken, samples of water close to sediment were taken to study the variation of some physical and chemical parameters.

The conductivity of the water close to sediment was not high in absolute values. It increased in summer and low values occurred in winter due to the dilution caused by inflows from the basin (Fig. 2). Oxygen was always abundant; a slight decline was seen in December due to a large quantity of suspended material (Fig. 2). Temperature fluctuated widely, reaching values of 26 ºC in summer (Fig. 2).

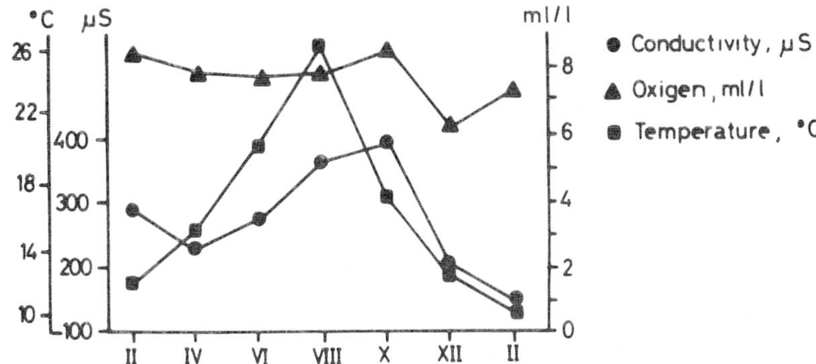

Fig. 2. Conductivity, Oxygen and temperature near the bottom at the sampling station 2.

Chlorophyll, Primary Production and Phytoplankton Composition.

Arrocampo is a very eutrophic reservoir. Although there are no data on chlorephyll or primary production at station 2, the data from station 6 show that the reservoir is very eutrophic. On August values of 181 mg Chl. m^{-2} and 156 mg C m^{-2} h^{-1} were measured. Minimum values were seen in February 1979 (21'8 mg Chl. m^{-2} and 12'8 mg C m^{-2} h^{-1}).

The composition of the plankton changed radically during the year (Fig. 3). In April and June chlorophytes dominated. In August the cyanophytes comprised over 95% of the cells. In October the chlorophytes and others groups increased due to the mixing in of river water. In December and February it was imposible to count the number of cells due to the quantity of inorganic material brought in by the rivers. In other sampling stations at this time of year, chlorophytes and diatoms dominated. The large increase of the total biomass in summer was largely composed by cyanophytes and therefore are little used by benthic organisms.

Composition and Density of the Benthic Community.

The benthic community that develop in the buckets contained at least 34 species of several taxonomic groups, most of them insects and specially of the groups Trichoptera and Chironomidae. The oligochaeta were represented by the Tubificidae. Between the worms, in addition to Tubificidae, some leeches (Glossiphonia sp.) and the turbellarian Dugesia tigrina (which occasionally was very abundant) were present. Ostracods (Isocypris sp.,Cypridopsis sp.) were very abundant in certain periods. Occasionally a few hidracarids and moluscs (Physa sp.) were found.

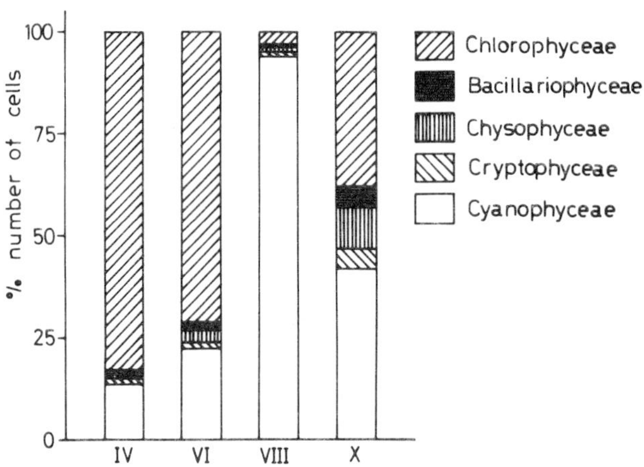

Fig. 3. Variation of the percentage composition of phytoplankton with time at sampling station 2.

The greatest diversity occurred in the insects with presence of species of the groups Odonata (Coenagrion coeruscelens), Ephemeroptera (Caenis sp.), Hemiptera (Micronecta sp.), Trichoptera (Cyrnus trimaculatus, Ecnomus tenellus and Psychomyia pusilla) and Diptera (Ceratopogonidae, Chaoborus and Chironomidae). Of these only the Cyrnus larvae and the larvae of some genera of Chironomidae (Polypedilum, Endochironomus, Glyptotendipes, Procladius and Microchironomus) were very abundant at certain season.

The total number of individuals varied with time, fluctuating between 2.260 ind. per square meter in August and 10.679 ind. per square meter in April (Fig. 4). The maxima occurred in the first two months of colonization and the number decreased to the minimum in August. In October the number was up again but it never reaches values as high as those of the precedent April. In February 1979 number was virtually equal to that the preceding 4 months (Fig. 4).

This quantitative change was accompanied by an important qualitative shift of the component species. At the beginning the Chironomidae comprised over 95% of the species. In June the Diptera decreased, principally due to the appearance of Cyrnus and some ostracods. In August there were even more species, and other organisms, principally tubificids, began to proliferate and continued to increase in subsequent months at the expense of the Chironomidae which number remains stationary.

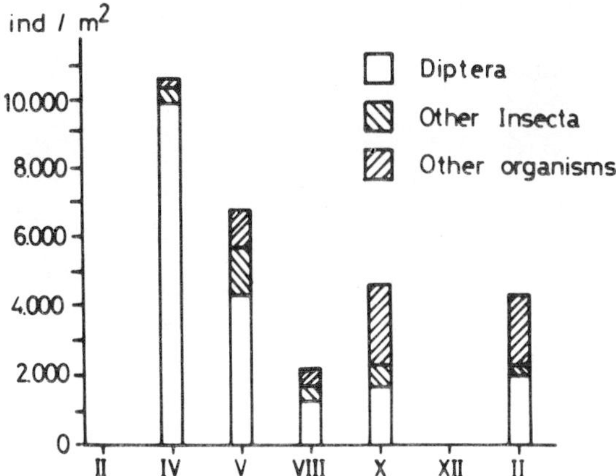

Fig. 4. Individuals per square meter in the artificial samplers.

Substitution of some species by others.

The relative shifts of the different groups are related to the substitution of some species by others. One group seem to be colonizing species. These are mostly chironomids of the genera Polypedilum, Endochironomus and Glyptotendipes. They were very abundant in April and June, but very reduced in numbers in later months (Fig. 5). Other species were more abundant in June (Fig. 6) in the intermediate phases of colonization and later decreased in importance. These are principally carnivorous species (Cyrnus, Procladius) which fed on the great quantity of organisms previously present. Finally other species arrived later, but appeared to be better adapted to the environment and continued to increase in importance (Fig. 7). The tubificids and Microchironomus, which is predator on the tubificids, are characteristic of this group.

The community changed species, but never totally lost those which previously existed and therefore the total number of species increased with time (Fig. 8). This increase in the number of species is parallel to a more balanced distribution of the different species and thus the diversity increased with time (Fig. 8).

DISCUSSION

On spite of difficulties in assesing sampling errors, I believe that seasonal sampling shows the organization processes of the benthic community starting at the moment when a new environment is avalaible for colonization (in this case a bucket in the reservoir) up until the moment of a principle of stabilization. It also shows the processes which influence sucession with time. In the beginning there is a phase of expansion into a empty ecological space by species which disperse rapidly (mainly chironomids, Fig. 5). These few species develop a large number of animals and because of this the diversity is low (Fig. 8).

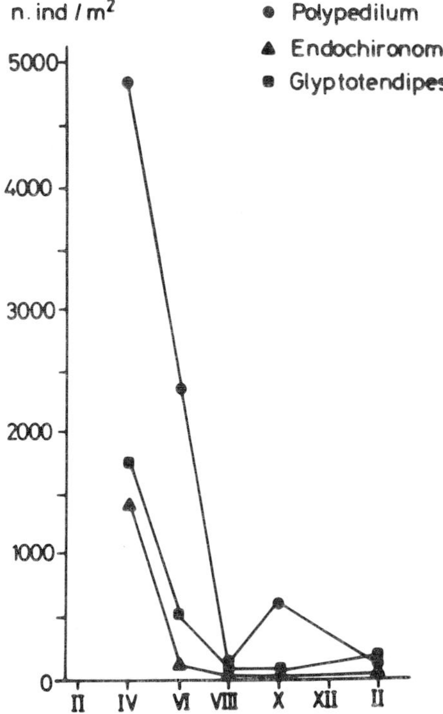

Fig. 5. Species characterstic of the first phase of colonization.

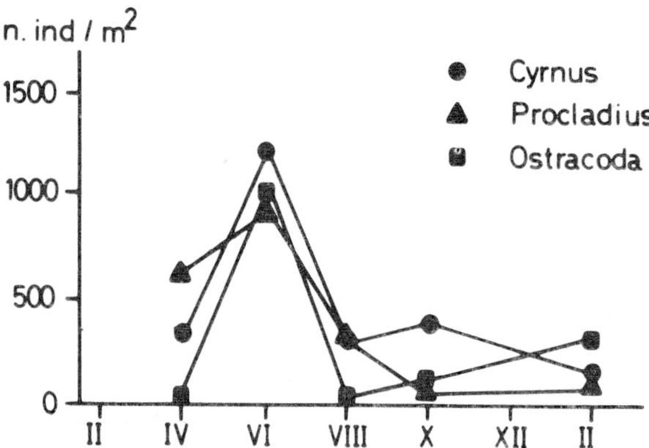

Fig. 6. Species more abundants in the second phase of colonization.

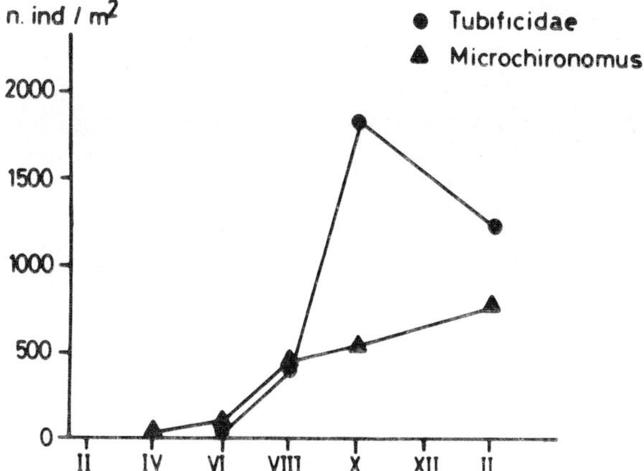

Fig. 7. Species which increased with time.

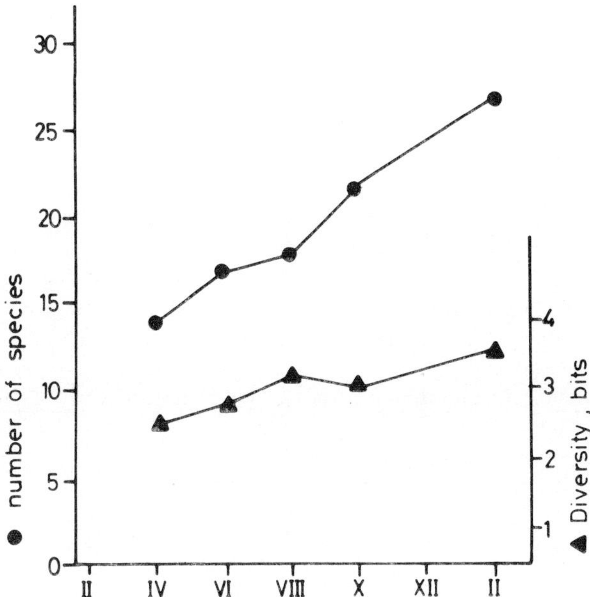

Fig. 8. Number of species and diversity in the artificial samplers of station 2.

As the community becomes more structurated, the number of species increases and the preponderance of the few species declines. Consequently, the diversity increases (Fig. 8). This a basic process which can be observed in all ecological sucession (Margalef, 1974).

Superimposed on this process there is a change in the quantity and quality of the food which arrives at the bottom. In spite of being more abundant, the summer plankton is composed of cyanophytes which float and are largely inedible by benthic organisms. The August results the worst month for the subsistence and growth of benthos due to the inavaibility of food and the high temperature (Figs. 2 and 3). In October the mixing waters and the better temperature change the algal composition; the cyanophytes decrease while other algae increase and this causes more benthic organisms to be present but with different composition from similar periods earlier in the year.

ACNOWLEDGEMENTS

I would like to express my thanks to Dr. R. Margalef, in whose laboratory this work was done and who make critical remarks on the manuscript. M. Alonso, I. Gozalvo, A. Lavall and M.A. Puig helped in different parts of the sampling programm. A.M. Domingo made the drawings. Data on phytoplankton are based on J.M. Vilaseca studies. LIMNOS S.A. financed the study. I am very indebted to Dr. E. Fee who has translated the manuscript into English.

REFERENCES

Armitage, P.D. (1977). Development of the macro-invertebrate fauna of Cow-Green reservoir (Upper Teesdale) in the first five years of its existence. Freshwat. Biol., 7, 441-454

Kryzanek, E. (1977). Bottom macrofauna of the dam reservoir at Goczalzowice in the years 1970-1975. Acta Hydrobiol., 19, 51-67.

Mac Lachlan, A.J. and S.M. Mac Lachlan (1971). Benthic fauna and sediments in the newly created lake Kariba (Central Africa). Ecology, 52, 800-809.

Margalef, R (1974). Ecologia. Omega. Barcelona

Paterson, C.G. and Fernando, C.H. (1970). Benthic fauna colonization of a new reservoir with particular reference to the Chironomidae. J. Fish. Res. Bd. Canada, 27, 213-232.

Prat, N. (1978). Benthos typology of Spanish reservoirs. Verh. Internat. Verein. Limnol., 20, 1647-1651

Prat, N. (1979). Quironomidos de los embalses españoles (1ª parte) (Diptera). Graellsia, 33, 37-96.

The Benthos of Lake Huddingsvatn, Norway, after Five Years of Mining Activity

K. Aagaard* and B. Sivertsen**

*Tromsö Museum, N-9000 Tromsö, Norway
**Sogn og Fjordane Distriktshöyskole, N-5801 Sogndal, Norway

ABSTRACT

Mining activity with deposition of finegrained rock wastes containing copper- and zinc pyrites has been going on since 1972 in Lake Huddingswatn. The bottom of the inner basin, where the depositions take place, is covered by a layer of variable thickness, from a few millimetres in the littoral zone to several metres in the profundal zone. The bottom fauna has been greatly reduced in the inner basin. All groups except Oligochaeta and Chironomidae have been almost completely eliminated. Many of the chironomids have also disappeared, the remaining species/genera are mostly carnivorous. The oligochaetes seem to be remarkably little affected, qualitatively as well as quantitatively, by the disturbance of the environment.

KEYWORDS

Bottom fauna; pollution; mining activity; Chironomidae; Oligochaeta.

INTRODUCTION

Lake Huddingsvatn (64°52'N, 13°48'E) is situated within the subarctic region in the northeastern part of the county Nord-Tröndelag, Norway. The lake is divided into two basins separated by a series of islets with shallow sounds, 1-2 m deep (Fig. 1). The area of the two basins together is 7 km^2. Average depth in the inner basin is 9 m, maximum depth is 22 m. The lake is moderately oligotrophic, with average pH-value of about 7, specific conductivity 30-50 µS/cm, and total phosphorus concentration 4-10 µg P/l. Extensive data on geology, hydrography, bottom conditions, vegetation and fauna up to 1968 are given by Sivertsen (1973).

Mining activity was started close to the lake in 1972. This involves discharging of large amounts of tailings, consisting of finegrained rock with ca. 0.2 % copper and zinc (mainly as pyrites) into the inner basin. The tailings were supposed to settle in the deepest parts, but after a few years small amounts of tailings were found on the bottom all over the inner basin. In shallow water (0-1 m depth) the thickness of the layer is only a few millimetres, but increases gradually with increasing depth. At 10 m it is between 5 cm and half a meter, depending on the distance from the discharge orifice. There are also considerable amounts of almost colloidal suspension of tailings in the water; the transparency

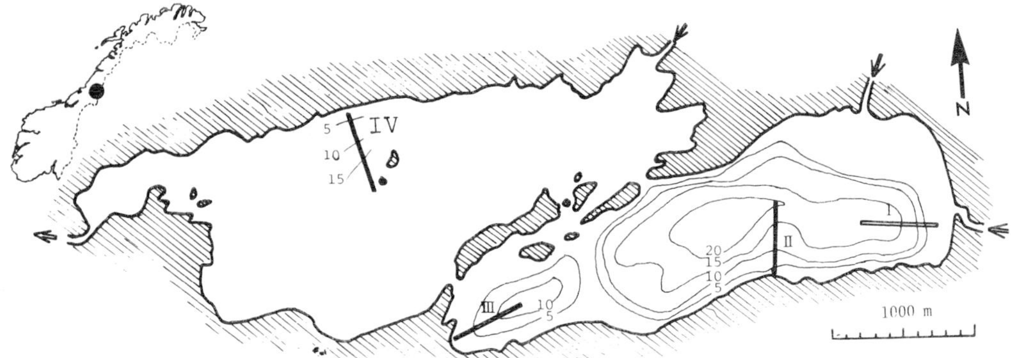

Fig. 1. Location of lake Huddingsvatn, bathygraphical map of the eastern basin and the sampling transects (No I-IV).

was reduced from 9-10 m in 1968 to 4-5 m in 1977.

The aim of this paper is to report the main changes in the bottom fauna after the first 2-5 years of mining activity. The fishery-biological aspects has been dealt with in technical reports in Norwegian (i.a. Sivertsen 1978). The investigations were carried out during the first half of July in 1974, 1976 and 1977.

METHODS

The bottom samples in 1968 and in 1974, 1976 and 1977 were taken with a van Veen grab (Schwoerbel 1970) covering an area of 200 cm^2. This makes all the samples comparable, and with the very moderate amounts of natural sediments in this lake, the van Veen grab should be quite suitable for this project. Five grabs were taken at each sampling depth. The material was sifted through a screen with 0.5 mm mesh width.

The authors are fully aware of the limitation of these techniques for the estimation of the total numbers of benthic animals. The meiofauna are not considered at all, and the numerical estimates are very approximate. However, the trends shown by the results given here are so clear that we find the results worth presenting.

RESULTS

The results from the three transects investigated in the inner basin are given in Figs 2, 3 and 4. (In 1974, only two transects were investigated.) In addition, one control transect (No VI in Sivertsen 1973, here No IV) in the outer basin was sampled all the three years, and the results are given in Fig. 5.

Before the mining activity started, the bottom fauna was generally as it is in an moderately oligotrophic lake, i.e. with Chironomidae and Oligochaeta as the most numerous groups, but also considerable densities of Bivalvia (Sphaeriidae), Gastropoda, Hirudinea, Crustacea, Plecoptera, Ephemeroptera, and Trichoptera. Among the crustaceans *Gammarus lacustris* was dominant, this species accounted for about 15 % of the total macrobenthos biomass.

Transect I was before the mining activity dominated by the chironomid genus *Stictochironomus* which occured in great numbers (ca. 800 ind./m^2) at 5-10 m depth.

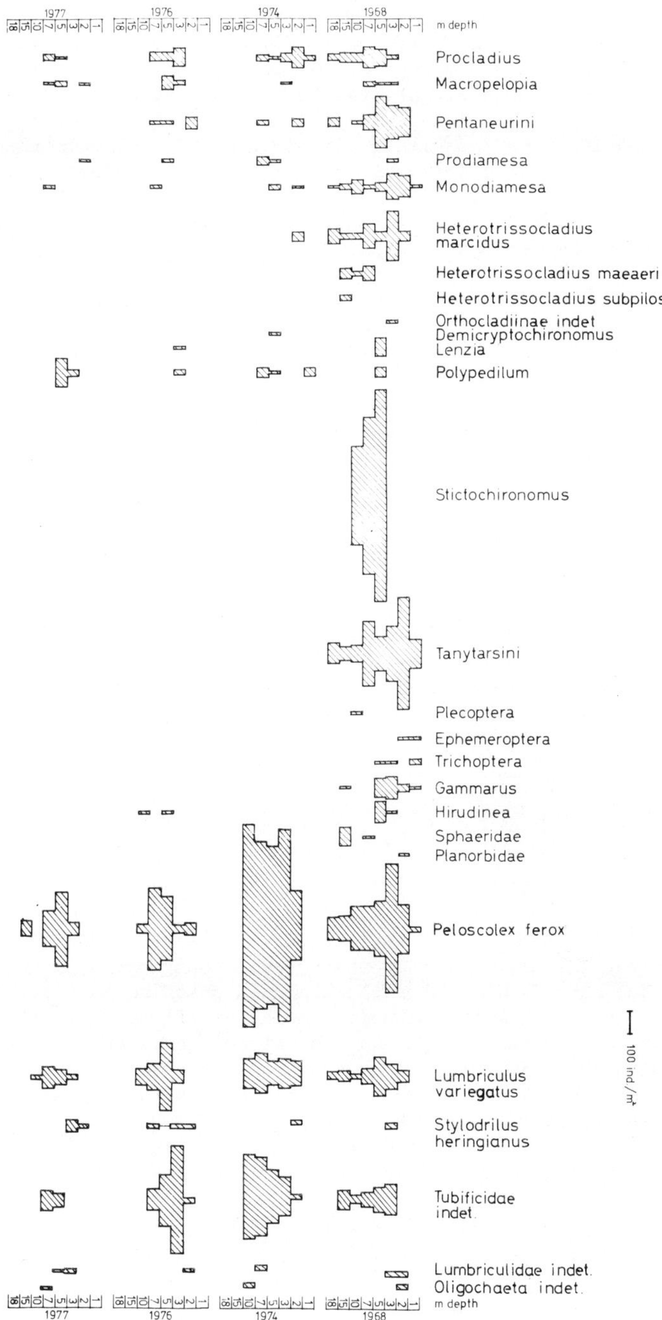

Fig. 2. Depth distribution of the macrobenthos at Transect I in Lake Huddingsvatn in 1968, 1974, 1976 and 1977.

Besides *Stictochironomus*, Tanytarsini and the oligochaete *Peloscolex ferox* were numerous in 1968. The chironomids indicated weak mesotrophic character of the transect, caused by two rivers emptying into the lake near this transect and depositing a zone of decaying organic material including leaves of *Salix* and *Betula*.

At transects II and III, the fauna in 1968 indicated more oligotrophic conditions. Here the bottom fauna was less affected by streams and therefore more typical for the lake as such. Important groups here were the chironomids *Heterotrissocladius*, *Heterotanytarsus*, *Procladius*, Pentaneurini and Tanytarsini, the oligochaetes *Peloscolex ferox* and *Lumbriculus variegatus*, and *Gammarus lacustris*.

The effect of the mine tailings was obvious in the 1974 samples from the inner basin. Most of the fauna was strongly reduced, both in number of species and in density. Such groups as *Gammarus lacustris*, Sphaeriidae, Gastropoda, Hirudinea, Trichoptera, Ephemeroptera and Plecoptera had almost completely disappeared in the samples from 1974 and have scarcely been recorded later. Oligochaeta is the group that has been least affected by the mine tailings. At all transects all the most numerous species found in 1974 were still present in 1977, and the densities are also much of the same order as before. Most of the specimens collected give a clear impression of the change in the environment: they are grey in colour, both in gut content and on the body wall. This is especially conspicuous with *Peloscolex ferox*, whose papillary epidermis are completely covered with a thin layer ooze from the mine tailings.

In addition to the Oligochaeta, Chironomidae was the only group recorded in any numbers in the inner basin during the period 1974-1977. *Procladius* is reduced at all transects, but still exists as a population in the lake. Some other genera also survive, but most of them considerably reduced in numbers.

Comparing the results from the years 1974, 1976 and 1977, no significant changes could be noted during these years, except for a temporary increase in numbers of *P. ferox* at transect I in 1974.

DISCUSSION

The reason for the disappearance of the detritivore larvae at all transects seem quite obvious, since the deposition of the sterile rock wastes in most areas of the inner basin far exceeds the natural sedimentation of organic detritus. It is therefore remarkable that the oligochaetes, being distinctly detritivore, manage so well. In addition to the reduced availability of nourishment, one might expect that the extremely finegrained ooze from the mine tailings would retard the gas diffusion both through the bottom substrate and through the worms' skin. Evidently this can hardly be any problem, since *P. ferox* and *S. heringianus* - both occurring about as frequent as before - are known to be two of the most sensitive oligochaete species as to oxygen demands (Brinkhurst 1964, Milbrink 1972).

Procladius seems to survive better than most of the other chironomids, this is probably due to their ability to move freely at the top of the sediments and their carnivore habits. This behaviour is shared by the Pentaneurini, which, however, is strongly reduced in number. The genus *Lenzia* is remarkable resistent at transects II and III. This genus is known to live on, or mining in, water plants and in sand. It is possible that minor amounts of detritus washed out from the streams can give nutrition for the larvae of *Lenzia*. The few specimens of *Isoëtes lacustris* present at 2-4 m depth may also be the explanation for the survival of this genus. Other genera which seem to survive at transect I are *Monodiamesa* and *Prodiamesa*, both predatory, and *Polypedilum*. *Polypedilum* is surely able to exist in detritus washed out by the river. At transect II, the genus *Paracladopelma* is found in all the

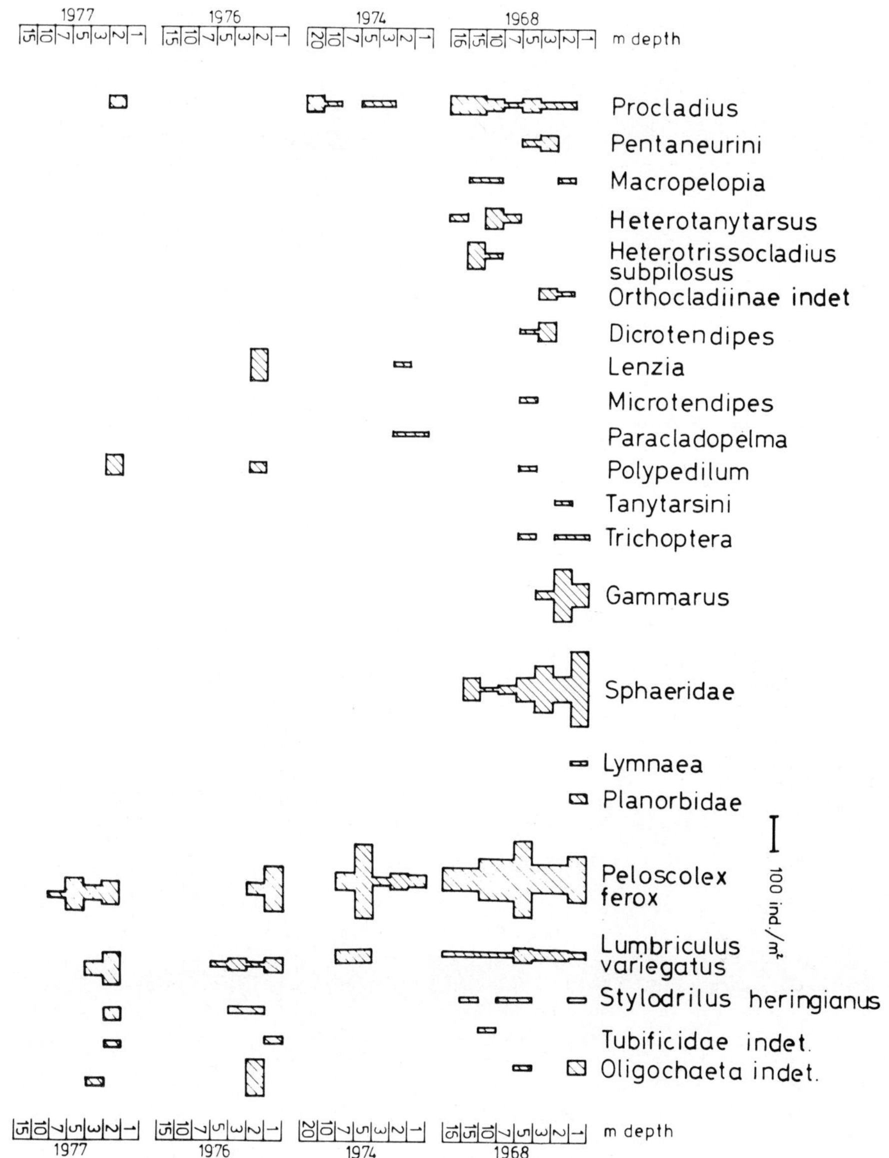

Fig. 3. Depth distribution of the macrobenthos at Transect II in Lake Huddingsvatn in 1968, 1974, 1976 and 1977.

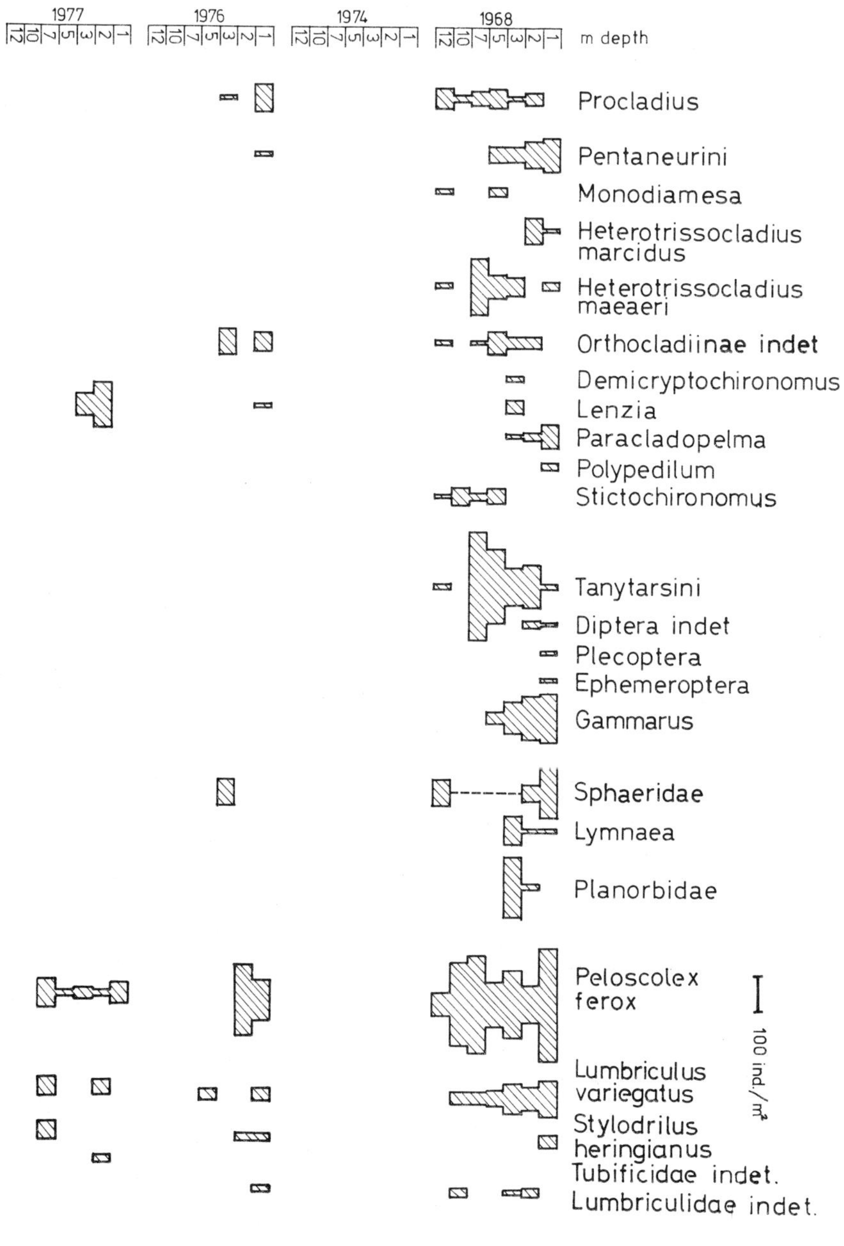

Fig. 4. Depth distribution of the macrobenthos at Transect III in Lake Huddingsvatn in 1968, 1976 and 1977.

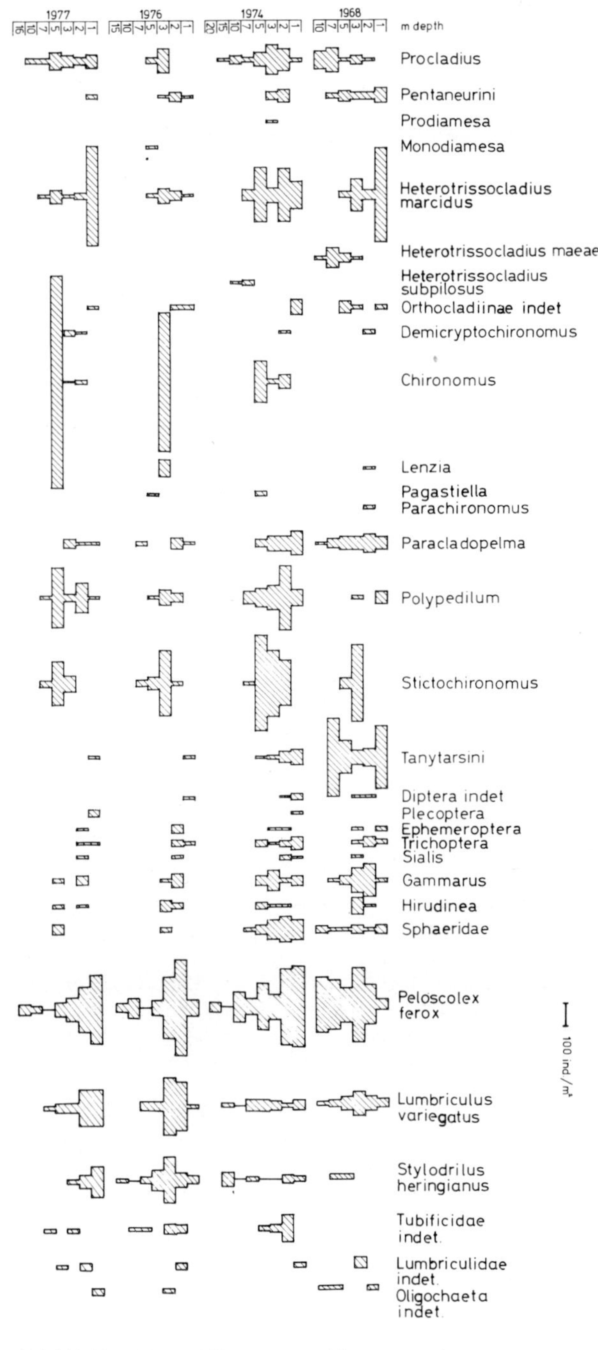

Fig. 5. Depth distribution of the macrobenthos at Transect IV in Lake Huddingsvatn in 1968, 1974, 1976 and 1977.

three sampling years 1974-1977. At transect III, some larvae of an unidentified Orthocladiinae still existed in 1976, but were not recorded in 1977.

As shown by i.a. Shiozawa and Barnes (1977) the first instar of chironomid larvae live nearly exclusively in the upper 5 cm of the sediment. A new colonization of the mining sediment by chironomids is impossible as long as this deposition continues. This means that the inner basin is, with the exception of a few chironomids and the Oligochaeta, a dead basin with respect to benthic macrofauna.

The control sampling transect IV in the outer basin shows no significant changes during the period 1968-1977, neither in species composition nor in numbers of each of the groups, which might be supposed to be caused by the mine tailings. An increase in the number of *Chironomus* sp. and a parallel decrease of *Heterotrissocladius maeaeri*, *H. subpilosus* and the Tanytarsini is probably due to an eutrophication effect from a small brook draining cultivated areas.

A very thin layer of mine tailings was observed in 1976 and 1977 in the sound between the basins and in the inner parts of the outer basin. The future of the benthos community in the outer basin is questionable if no regulation of the water exchange between the two basins is undertaken, or the sedimentation process in the inner basin gives better results.

ACKNOWLEDGEMENT

The authors would like to express their gratitude to the Royal Norwegian Society of Sciences and Letters, the Museum, where this work was carried out under the management of Professor E. Sivertsen.

REFERENCES

Brinkhurst, R.O. (1964). Observations on the biology of lake-dwelling Tubificidae. *Arch. Hydrobiol.*, *60*, 385-418.

Milbrink, G. (1972). Communities of Oligochaeta as indicators of water pollution in Swedish lakes. *Acta Univ. Upsal.*, *221*, 1-14.

Schwoerbel, J. (1970). *Methods of Hydrobiology (Freshwater Biology).* London. 200 pp.

Shiozawa, D.K. and J.R. Barnes (1977). The microdistribution and population trends of larval *Tanypus stellatus* Coquilett and *Chironomus frommeri* Atchley and Martin (Diptera: Chironomidae) in Utah Lake, Utah. *Ecology*, *58*, 610-618.

Sivertsen, B. (1973). The bottom fauna of Lake Huddingsvatn, based on quantitative sampling. *Norw. J. Zool.*, *21*, 305-321.

Sivertsen, B. (1978). Fiskeribiologiske undersökelser i Huddingsvatn, Röyrvik, 1974-1977. *K. norske Vidensk. Selsk. Mus. Rapport Zool. Ser.*, *1978-8*, 1-25.

Pasqua Lake, Southeastern Saskatchewan: a Preliminary Assessment of Trophic Status and Contamination Based on the Chironomidae (Diptera)

W. F. Warwick

National Water Research Institute, 501 University Crescent, Winnipeg, Manitoba R3T 2N6, Canada

ABSTRACT

The chironomid fauna was examined in two basins of Pasqua Lake, southeastern Saskatchewan, to assess the degree of eutrophication and the possible impact of contaminants. The western basin yielded (n=354) 12 taxa with a mean larval density of 8,673 ind.m^{-2}. *Chironomus* spp. made up 79.4% of the larvae and 2.26% of the larvae were deformed. The degree of trophy was assessed ν or eutrophic. The eastern basin yielded (n=32) five taxa with a mean larval density of 182 ind.m^{-2}. *Paratendipes* sp. predominated and 3.13% of the larvae were deformed. Although the community did not fit traditional trophic classification indices, the basin was tentatively assessed ξ or strongly eutrophic. The effects of contaminants are suspected of modifying the response of the chironomid communities to trophic parameters in the eastern basin.

KEYWORDS

Chironomidae; deformities; eutrophication; contamination.

INTRODUCTION

The demands for water in the semi-arid regions of southern Saskatchewan for recreational, agricultural, urban and industrial purposes have placed a premium on the water resources of the Qu'Appelle River basin (Fig. 1). In recent years growing concern has been voiced that domestic and industrial effluents from the main cities in the basin, Regina and Moose Jaw, and materials from other sources have degraded the water resources of the downstream lakes, including Pasqua Lake.

Pasqua Lake (50° 47.1' N Lat., 104° 00' W Long.) is located in a glacial spillway cut about 14,000 B.C. by the drainage of glacial Lake Regina into glacial Lake Agassiz. (The origin of the lake is discussed by Christiansen and colleagues (1977) and the physiography of the area is described in detail by Atton and Johnson (1962) and Hammer (1971).) Pasqua Lake is the largest river lake in the modern Qu'Appelle River system with a length of 15.9 km and a maximum width of 1.9 km (Atton and Johnson, 1962). Although its maximum depth is 15.5 m, more than 58% of the lake is less than 2.5 m deep. The mean depth is 5.9 m. The surface area of the lake is

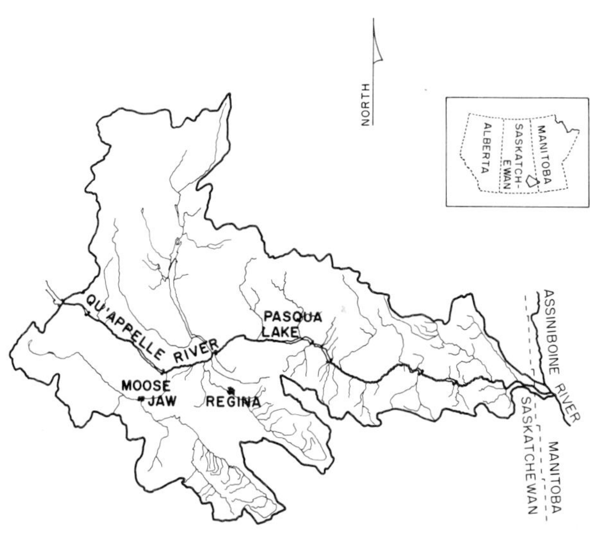

Fig. 1. The Qu'Appelle River drainage basin.

20.2 km^2 and its volume is 120.9 $m^3 \times 10^6$ (Allan and Kenney, 1977). Pasqua Lake does not stratify consistently; any tendency to stratify is usually short-lived or prevented by almost constant winds (Hammer, 1971).

Pasqua Lake is divided into four distinct basins by the intrusion of alluvial fans from inflowing streams (Fig. 2). Basins 1 and 2 are shallow areas (maximum depth 2.5 m) characterized by extensive beds of rooted aquatic vegetation. The two basins probably act as efficient sinks for coarser suspended sediments brought into the lake by the Qu'Appelle River (Warwick, 1979). The third basin, referred to here as the western basin, is a deep-water basin (maximum depth 13.2 m) in which the finer suspended sediment fractions are deposited. The effect of the dissipation of hydraulic energy caused by the Bernoulli effect of the Leader's Point constriction on the accumulation of fine sediments is apparent in the fan-like contours of the basin's bottom. A fourth basin, the eastern basin, is also a deep-water basin (maximum depth 15.5 m), but here accumulating sediments are primarily autochthonous in origin.

The Qu'Appelle River lakes derive rich supplies of nutrients from the glacial drift on which the basin is situated. The natural phosphorus loading to Pasqua Lake from the dark brown and black soil zones of the basin, estimated by Cross (1978) at 2.2 $g.m^{-2}.yr^{-1}$, have been increased by the introduction of sewage effluent from Regina (population 149,593) and Moose Jaw (population 32,581) via Wascana and Moose Jaw Creeks (Warwick, 1967; Peters, 1973). Wastes from several smaller towns and numerous animal feed lots along the tributaries of the Qu'Appelle River also contribute to nutrient loadings. Runoff from agricultural lands throughout the large

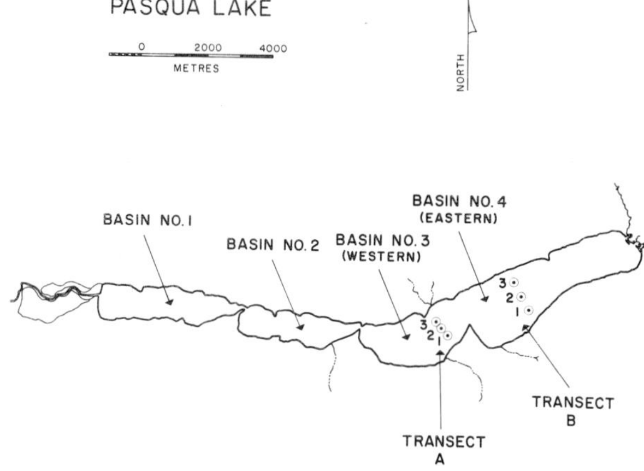

Fig. 2. Pasqua Lake: physiography and macroinvertebrate sampling sites.

drainage basin (17,508 km^2) is a third major source of nutrients. The current input of phosphorus from urban and agricultural sources was estimated respectively at 2.3 and 2.2 $g.m^{-2}.yr^{-1}$ (Allan, 1979). Compared to the external phosphorus loading of 6.5 $g.m^{-2}.yr^{-1}$, Cross (1978) estimated an internal loading of 3.2 $g.m^{-2}.yr^{-1}$ for the lake. Seven year means for total phosphorus, total nitrogen and chlorophyll-a of 647±372 (n=369), 2,994±1,976 (n=370) and 25.5±33.8 (n=162) $mg.m^{-3}$ respectively reflect the high nutrient loadings to Pasqua Lake (Allan and Roy, 1979).

Dense algal blooms have been cited as evidence that eutrophication has reached undesirable levels (Hammer, 1973) and the recent closure of Pasqua Lake to commercial fishing because of high mercury levels in fish tissues suggests contaminants have also become a problem. Management programs featuring extensive reclamation and/or rehabilitation measures have been implemented to arrest or reverse these undesirable trends.

The purpose of the present study was to define the status of Pasqua Lake in terms of eutrophication and contamination processes and to establish a baseline against which the effectiveness of these remedial measures could be gauged at a future date.

METHODS

Benthic samples were collected in triplicate with a 232.3 cm^2 unweighted Ekman-type grab (Burton and Flannagan, 1973) fitted with an automatic closing device (Burton, 1974) at each of three sampling sites along transect lines across each deep-water basin (Fig. 2). Samples were sieved on site through 200 μ mesh nets and preserved in 10% formalin. All samples were sorted under stereomicroscopes, generally at 25X.

Chironomid larvae were mounted according to Saether (1969). Rather than leaving the head capsules fully flexed, however, they were flattened by exerting gradually increasing pressure accompanied by gentle rotation to the coverslip covering the head capsule. This motion spreads the mouthparts and prevents them from obscuring other diagnostic features. Flattening makes aberrant mouthparts more readily recognizable and measurements more accurately made. Mentum width here replaces the measurement of head capsule width used in the literature.

RESULTS

Chironomid larvae were ca. 48 times more abundant in the western basin than in the eastern basin of Pasqua Lake (Table 1). Compared to an average population of 8,673

TABLE 1 Numbers of Chironomidae Specimens (larvae per grab) in the Western (Transect A) and Eastern (Transect B) Basins of Pasqua Lake, May 1976

Transect Line	Transect Site	Site Depth (m)	Site Replicate a	b	c	Average Site Population	Average Transect Population
A	1	12.5	361	214	338	304.3	
	2	11.8	212	274	245	243.7	201.4
	3	12.3	101	35	33	56.3	
B	1	16.1	1	3	3	2.3	
	2	14.4	1	8	5	4.7	
	3	14.3	9	2	6	5.7	4.2

larvae.m^{-2} for Transect A, an average of only 182 larvae.m^{-2} was found on Transect B. The reason for the consistently poorer fauna at Site 3 on Transect A is not known at this time.

Twelve taxa were identified among the larvae from Transect A compared to only five taxa from Transect B (Table 2). *Chironomus* spp. and *Procladius* spp. were the dominant members of the Transect A communities, providing 79.4 and 13.3 per cent respectively of the total fauna. In the Transect B communities *Chironomus* spp. were displaced by *Paratendipes* sp. as the most numerous members of the chironomid community. These two taxa made up 20.6 and 61.8 per cent respectively of the total fauna from Transect B.

Community comparisons indicate that the similarity between the chironomid communities of the two basins was low. Coefficient of community (C.C.) and percentage similarity of community (P.S.C.) values were 0.454 and 28.45% respectively. Since, according to Southwood (1966), the former index overvalues the rarer species while the latter overvalues the more dominant, the intermediate estimate of low similarity in which C.C. values range between 0.25 and 0.40 and P.S.C. values range between 35 and 50% was adopted from Warwick's (1978) scales to describe the relationship between the communities of the two basins.

Seven deformed specimens of *Chironomus* and one of *Procladius* were found among the larvae from Transect A (P-A-1-a) while a single deformed specimen of *Chironomus* was found among the larvae from Transect B (P-B-3-b). The deformed larvae formed 2.26 and 3.13 per cent respectively of the fauna examined from the western and eastern basins.

TABLE 2 Composition of the Chironomidae from the Western and Eastern Basins of Pasqua Lake, May 1976

Taxa	Percentage Composition Western Basin	Eastern Basin
Tanypodinae		
Procladius spp.	13.3	5.9
Tanypus sp.	0.6	---
Orthocladiinae		
Psectrocladius sp.	0.3	---
Cricotopus (*Isocladius*) spp.	0.8	8.8
unidentified	0.3	---
Chironominae		
Chironomus spp.	79.4	20.6
Cryptotendipes sp.	2.3	---
Polypedilum sp.	1.4	---
Paratendipes sp.	0.3	61.8
Cladopelma sp.	0.6	---
Cryptochrionomus sp.	0.3	---
Tanytarsini sp.	0.6	2.9

NOTE: Population estimates for Transect A based on single sample P-A-1-a; estimates for Transect B based on full transect results (n=9).

All deformed larvae had aberrant mouthparts, but the degree of deformation differed among specimens. The more obvious were in the mentum or ligula, but deformations were also apparent in other mouthparts. Deformations in the mentum of *Chironomus* ranged from mild asymmetry, like differing numbers of lateral teeth on either side of the mentum (Fig. $3B_1$) or overlapping of the outer lateral teeth, to more severe cases where the median tripartite tooth of the mentum was replaced by numerous, haphazardly arranged, smaller overlapping teeth (Fig. $3C_1$). In the more extreme case, the only other evidence of deformation appeared in the mildly deformed teeth on the mandible (Fig. $3C_2$). In contrast, the mandibles and especially the premandibles and epipharyngeal pectin of the specimen figured with only differing numbers of lateral teeth were more strongly deformed (Fig. 3B). The head capsules of the deformed specimens were not heavily pigmented and comparison of head capsule and body wall measurements with those of normal specimens revealed little or no thickening.

DISCUSSION

Levels of Trophy

Historically, lake classification theory has been based on the response of the chironomid community to the availability of dissolved oxygen in the bottom waters of stably stratified lakes where the degree of trophy determines the hypolimnetic oxygen deficit. Because Pasqua Lake does not achieve stable stratification, the use of lake classification theory to determine the trophic level of Pasqua Lake, may be questionable. Shallow prairie lakes, including Pasqua Lake, which are characterized by high solar energy inputs, high nutrient loadings, significant internal nutrient regeneration and high levels of productivity, are subject to long periods (5-7 months) of ice and snow cover during which respiration and decomposition processes predominate and oxygen depletion is often severe (Barica, 1979). The length

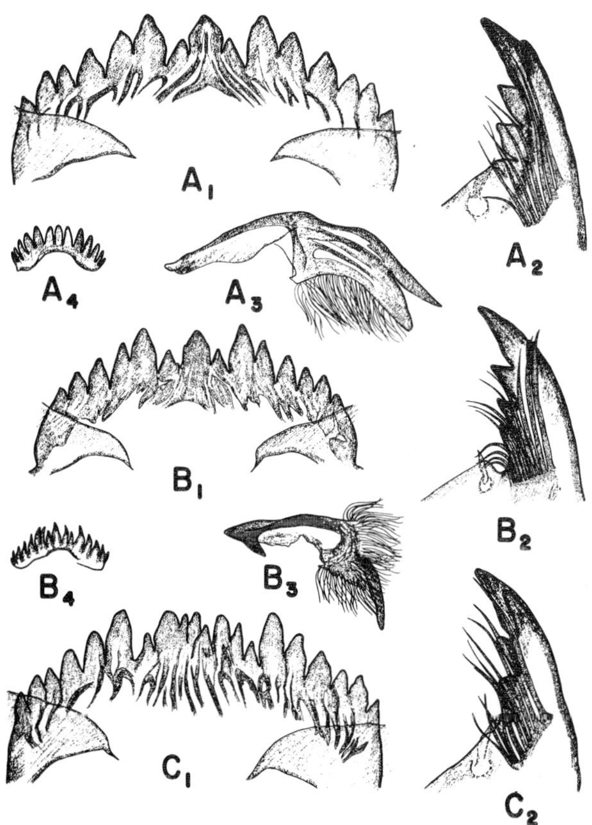

Fig. 3. Comparison of mouthparts of normal (A) and deformed larvae larvae (B and C) of *Chironomus*. 1, mentum; 2, apex of mandibles; 3, premandibles; 4, epipharyngeal pectin.

of the period during which oxygen levels become critical is often equivalent to, or greater than, the same period in stably stratified lakes. The unimodal oxygenated-deoxygenated annual cycle of prairie lakes may thus be equated to the classical bi-modal cycle where the periods of re-oxygenation occur at spring and fall overturn. Since the resistance of the different chironomid species used in water quality assessments depends on the length of the anoxic period (Nagell and Landahl, 1978), which can be long in prairie lakes, the lake classification theory should be applic-able to Pasqua Lake.

Under the revised lake classification system of Saether (1979) and Warwick (1979)*, the western basin of Pasqua Lake is assessed ν or eutrophic (TIN 13) on the basis of Saether's couplet "only *Chironomus* spp. and the subfamily Tanypodinae present". The presence of two, and possibly three, species of *Chironomus* among specimens reared from the western basin preclude a more eutrophic assessment. Although ten other minor taxa were also enumerated from the western basin (Table 2), only one - *Cryptotendipes* sp. - challenges the two per cent cut-off guideline implicit in the use of the trophic key (O. A. Saether: pers. comm.). If the guideline was strictly adhered to, the western basin would be assessed μ or moderately eutrophic (TIN 12). Because the margin between the abundance of *Cryptotendipes* sp. (2.26%) and the guideline is so small and because it comprises the only departure from the rule, the more eutrophic assessment (TIN 13) is more reasonable.

The deeper eastern basin is assessed ξ or strongly eutrophic (TIN 14) in spite of the fact that Saether's couplet "only *Chironomus plumosus* type and Tanypodinae present" could not be strictly adhered to. This assessment is based primarily on the reduction in the numbers of taxa from 12 in the western basin to 5 in the eastern basin, and the anaerobic conditions that persist throughout the winter months in the eastern basin. In late winter 1979, dissolved oxygen concentrations in the waters immediately overlying the sediment surface in the western basin ranged from 2.3 to 3.4 $mg.l^{-1}$ (Warwick, 1979). No measurable oxygen could be detected in the eastern basin. In low spring runoff years, these conditions persist well into the early summer months in the eastern basin (Allan and Roy, 1979). Saether's two per cent guideline was not applicable because the specimens from Transect B were more or less evenly distributed among the five surviving taxa.

Members of the Orthocladiinae and Tanytarsini formed small but consistent components of the Pasqua Lake fauna. However, they are excluded from use in Saether's trophic key by the two per cent guideline. Possibly as the parameters for more eutrophic lakes become better known, these groups will add to the key's usefulness in defining trophic states.

The relatively high proportion (61.8%) of the total fauna provided by *Paratendipes* sp. was partly a function of the absence of significant numbers of any other genus. In real terms, however, the genus was three times more abundant in the eastern basin than in the western basin. The difference in distribution could be related to the different sediment types in the two basins. A small genus, *Paratendipes* may be more capable of exploiting coarser organic sediments in the eastern basin than the more highly mineralized sediments in the western basin (Brundin, 1951).

Levels of Contamination

Hamilton and Saether (1971) and Hare and Carter (1976) presented circumstantial evidence that industrial and/or agricultural contaminants rather than pollution from domestic wastes are the cause of deformities among larval chironomids. Hamilton and Saether (1971) also presented preliminary experimental evidence to support the correlation between contaminants and deformities: larvae of *Chironomus tentans* Fabr. exposed to 10 $\mu g.l^{-1}$ concentrations of DDE developed thickened body walls similar to those found in Lake Erie and the Okanagan lakes of British Columbia. Their attempts to reproduce larvae with deformed mouthparts may have been unsuccessful because the sandy substrate on which the larvae were reared

---

*NOTE: Under the revised lake classification system, the three primary trophic categories are subdivided into 15 finer gradations, six of which apply to oligotrophy, three to mesotrophy and six to eutrophy. Each gradation is identified according to standardized terminology and evaluated semi-quantitatively by a Trophic Index Number (TIN). For eutrophic lakes the Trophic Index Numbers range from TIN 10 for slightly eutrophic lakes to TIN 15 for ultra-eutrophic lakes.

caused a high degree of wearing to the teeth and mandibles of larvae which may have obscured the effects of the other chemical agents tested. An absolute relationship between contaminants and deformities has not yet been established. Nevertheless Hamilton and Saether (1971) suggested that any discernible biological effects of pollutants on individual organisms might usefully extend the traditional use of ecological analysis of benthic communities to define the impact of man's activities on aquatic environments.

The incidence of deformities in Pasqua Lake was 2.33% of the total fauna. The most comparable figure (Table 3), in that it is not referable to an immediate point

TABLE 3 Comparison of the Incidence of Deformities among Larval Chironomid Communities from Selected Locations

Location		Total No. of Larvae Examined	Total No. of Deformed Larvae	Incidence of Deformities (%)	Authority
Pasqua Lake	Eastern Basin	32	1	3.13	
	Western Basin	354	8	2.26	
	Overall	386	9	2.33	
Bay of Quinte, Lake Ontario	1972	201	4	1.99	Warwick (1978)
	ca. 1951	282.5*	3	1.06	
	ca. 1087	1110.0*	1	0.09	
	ca. 238 B.C.	1133.0*	1	0.09	
Skaha Lake	Average	278	4	1.43	
	1969	32	3	9.38	Saether (1970)
	1971	246	1	0.41	Saether & McLean (1972)
Okanagan Lake	1969	671	5	0.75	Saether (1970)
Lake Erie	Western Basin	>753	3	<0.40	Brinkhurst, Hamilton & Herrington (1968);
	Overall	>1700	3	<0.18	Hamilton & Saether (1971)
Parry Sound,† Lake Huron	Overall	569	34	5.98	
	Parry Sound	455	1	0.22	
	Parry Sound Harbor	114	33	28.95	Hare & Carter (1976)

*Note: Rated totals.

†Note: Estimated values.

source of contamination, is the incidence of deformities found in live larvae collected from the Bay of Quinte, Lake Ontario, in 1972 (Warwick, 1978). Levels of deformities in natural chironomid populations were determined at this site by examining fossil chironomid remains in sections of sediment cores known to pre-date the arrival of European colonists in the area. The incidence of deformities in the 1972 fauna (1.99%) was approx. 22 times greater than that (0.09%) in the pre-European sediments. Of perhaps greater significance, the incidence in deformities began in the immediate post-war period when industrial activity in the area was expanding rapidly and organochlorines and other pesticides were coming into widespread use.

The results from Skaha Lake, British Columbia, may also be comparable if the 1969 and 1971 survey date are combined. In 1969, Saether (1970) found single specimens of deformed larvae from three genera at a site near the mouth of the Okanagan River. (Note that the typographical error in Saether, 1970: Table 6 indicating 19 deformed larvae of C. *semireductus* type is repeated in Hare and Carter, 1976.) Saether and McLean (1972) resampled the lake in 1971 and although the number of samples was increased three fold, found only one additional deformed larvae of a Genus near *Polypedilum* near the center of the lake. The results of the combined surveys provide an areal estimate of the incidence of deformed chironomids in Skaha Lake (1.43%) somewhat less than that (2.33%) in Pasqua Lake. The deformed larvae from the 1969 survey, however, came from near the mouth of the Okanagan River which receives wastes directly from the city of Penticton, B.C., only 5 km upstream from Skaha Lake. If the 1969 data is deleted because it is referable to a point source of contamination, the estimate of the incidence of deformed chironomid larvae in Skaha Lake (0.41%) is much less than in Pasqua Lake.

The incidence of deformities from the remaining examples in Table 3 are not directly comparable to those in Pasqua Lake because they are all referable to local point-sources of contamination. The five deformed larvae from Okanagan Lake, B.C. (Saether, 1970), came from localized areas polluted by wastes discharged from the communities of Kelowna, Westbank and Vernon. The three deformed larvae from Lake Erie (Brinkhurst, Hamilton and Herrington, 1968) came from a restricted area in the southwest corner of the western basin. Because of the localized distribution, Hamilton and Saether (1971) hypothesized that contaminants from the industrial complex in and around Toledo, Ohio, were the cause of deformities in the Lake Erie chironomid fauna. A considerable number of deformed chironomid larvae were found in and adjacent to Parry Sound Harbor, Lake Huron (Hare and Carter, 1976). The city of Parry Sound, Ontario, was easily identified as the source of contamination because of the restricted physiography of Parry Sound. Similarly, a high proportion (25-37%) of the *Chironomus* larvae collected from a canal in Berlin, West Germany, polluted by waste water and heated effluents were deformed (T. Köhn, these proceedings). Industrial contaminants were identified as the cause of the deformities because the deformed larvae came from two isolated areas of the canal receiving industrial wastes. Although not directly comparable to the situation in the open lake, these site specific correlations support a cause and effect relationship between contaminants and deformities in chironomid larvae.

The deformities found in the Pasqua Lake chironomids are morphologically similar to those shown by Hare and Carter (1976) and T. Köhn (these proceedings). If Hamilton and Saether's (1971) hypothesis that different types of deformities are referable to different types of contamination is correct, this similarity suggests that these deformities are due to contaminants of industrial origin. Hare and Carter (1976) ruled out agricultural contaminants and domestic wastes as the agents causing deformities in the chironomids of Parry Sound Harbor because little or no agricultural chemicals are used in the area and no deformed larvae were found in areas of the Sound polluted solely by organic wastes. Hamilton and Saether (1971) similarly discounted domestic wastes as a causative agent because no deformed larvae were found near domestic sewage outlets in Okanagan Lake, B.C. T. Köhn (these proceedings) attributed the deformities in larvae from a canal in Berlin, West Germany, to industrial effluents and referred in particular to the presence of heavy metals. Abnormal thickening occurred in the head capsule and body walls of the larvae exposed to DDE (Hamilton and Saether, 1971). The absence of such thickening in the deformed larvae from Pasqua Lake may indicate that the contaminants effecting the morphological deformities are not agricultural in origin. Although unusually high concentrations of arsenic, lead, cobalt, cyanide, and mercury have been monitored periodically in the Qu'Appelle River immediately above Pasqua Lake (W. D. Gummer:

pers. comm.), the presence of aldrin, lindane, α-BHC, 2,4-D, 2,4-DP and 2,4,5-T in the river waters (Gummer, 1979) make it difficult, however, to rule out the involvement of agricultural contaminants.

Interrelationship Between Contaminants and Trophic Indices

The population parameters describing the chironomid communities of the eastern basin of Pasqua Lake do not follow the trends established in response to increasing trophic levels in the Bay of Quinte (Warwick, 1978) and the western basin of Pasqua Lake (Table 4). The fact that the incidence of deformed larvae was greater in the

TABLE 4 Comparison of the Chironomidae Community Parameters for the Western and Eastern Basins of Pasqua Lake with those from the Historical Development of Eutrophic Conditions of the Bay of Quinte, Lake Ontario

Parameter	Bay of Quinte 424 A.D. (114.5 cm)	Bay of Quinte 1972 A.D. (surface)	Pasqua Lake Western Basin	Pasqua Lake Eastern Basin
Trophic State	ε or weakly oligotrophic	μ or moderately eutrophic	ν or eutrophic	ξ or strongly eutrophic
Trophic Index Number	5	12	13	14
Total *Chironomus* spp. (%)	6.1	61.7	79.4	20.6
Deformed *Chironomus* spp. (%)	---	2.4	2.5	14.3
Total *Procladius* spp. (%)	7.9	23.9	13.3	5.9
Deformed *Procladius* spp. (%)	0.8	8.1	2.1	---
Number of Taxa (5)	100	18	12	5
Mean no. of ind. (N)	---	67.0	201.4	4.2
Diversity ('H(S)')	5.2	3.3	1.1	1.6
Equitability ('ε')	0.3	0.8	2.7	2.4

eastern basin (3.13%) than in the western basin (2.26%) suggests that these discrepancies are due to the presence of contaminants. In the eastern basin, *Chironomus* spp. makes up only 20.6% of the total fauna and 14.3% of these are deformed. If the inhibiting effects of anaerobic conditions were solely responsible for species shifts, *Chironomus* spp. probably would make up a greater proportion of the total fauna of the eastern basin (>80%) than it does in the western basin. In the Bay of Quinte and the western basin of Pasqua Lake, only 2.4 and 2.5% respectively of the *Chironomus* fauna were deformed. The factors responsible for the 6 fold increase in the incidence of deformities in *Chironomus* spp. undoubtedly were also responsible for the 4 fold reduction in their abundance in the eastern basin.

These same factors were probably also responsible for the 48 fold reduction in the mean numbers of larvae between the western and eastern basins of Pasqua Lake. If trophic parameters alone were operative, the size of their respective communities would probably be roughly similar in terms of numbers and biomass. Although less tangible, the reduction in the numbers of taxa expected because of the increasingly severe conditions in the eastern basin appears greater than might be expected from trophic changes alone.

The carnivorous species of *Procladius* probably declined in abundance as much through the elimination of its prey species as through the direct effects of contaminants.

Oligochaetes were absent in the eastern basin and present only in limited numbers in the western basin of Pasqua Lake. Brinkhurst (1966) attributed the absence of oligochaetes or even a marked reduction in their abundance to the presence of toxic compounds. The *Procladius* community probably was reduced indirectly by contaminants through elimination of the oligochaetes and the reduction in the abundance of chironomid larvae because both are primary food sources for the genus (Roback, 1969). The direct effect of contaminants on the genus *Procladius* probably was similar to that on *Chironomus*. Although too few *Procladius* larvae were found in the eastern basin to provide more definitive information, the correlation between the incidence of deformities in *Chironomus* and *Procladius* in the Bay of Quinte (2.4: 2.1) and the western basin of Pasqua Lake (2.5: 2.1) suggests that the two genera are probably more or less equally affected by contaminants.

The changes imposed on the composition and structure of the eastern basin chironomid communities were documented by the retroversion in the species diversity and equitability indices. Although the indices do not link the changes with contaminants, they clearly indicate that a new factor influencing the chironomid community has become operative.

The disharmony created by the presence of contaminants appears to have accentuated the differences in oxygen availability, morphometry and other factors regulating the benthic communities in the two basins to the extent that Saether's (1979) trophic key is not directly applicable and the degree of eutrophy may have been overestimated in the eastern basin. If the assessment of the trophic state in the eastern basin is indeed too high, then the effects of contaminants throughout the lake are even greater. Although the incidence of deformed chironomid larvae in Pasqua Lake is not as high as in areas near point sources of contamination, it is higher than in other comparable sites where the effects of contaminants have been dispersed areally throughout the entire lake. Although it is difficult to determine from the limited data available the extent of the problem, contamination in the lake is probably considerable. The presence of deformed larvae is evidence that contaminants are involved in the degradation of Pasqua Lake and their effect on the fauna raises the question of the ability of the lake to absorb the effects of further contamination without risk.

ACKNOWLEDGEMENTS

I thank Drs. J. H. Mundie and R. J. Allan for their constructive reviews of the manuscript and Drs. R. E. Hecky and D. M. Rosenberg and Mr. J. F. Flannagan for their comments and suggestions. Mrs. D. Hoeppner typed the manuscript. The work was carried out as part of the continuing commitment of the Inland Waters Directorate to research in the lakes of the Qu'Appelle Valley.

REFERENCES

Allan, R. J. (1979). Control of blue-green algal blooms in the Fishing Lakes of Saskatchewan: A position paper documenting progress, deficiencies and future considerations as of July, 1979. Can. Dept. Envir., Inl. Waters Direct., Nat. Water Res. Inst. Tech. Rep. W.N.R.-PR-79-3, 1-30.

Allan, R. J., and B. C. Kenney (1977). Rehabilitation of eutrophic Prairie lakes in Canada. Verh. int. Verein. theor. angew. Limnol., 20, 214-224.

Allan, R. J., and J. D. H. Williams (1978). Trophic status related to sediment chemistry of Canadian prairie lakes. J. Environ. Qual., 7, 99-106.

Allan, R. J., and M. Roy (1979). Lake water nutrient chemistry and chlorophyll-a in the Fishing Lakes, Crooked and Round Lakes, Qu'Appelle River Basin, June 1977 to June 1978. Can. Dep. Envir., Inl. Waters Direct., Sci. Ser. 112, 1-33.

Atton, F. M., and R. P. Johnson (1962). Report on limnology and fisheries of six lakes of the lower Qu'Appelle Valley in southern Saskatchewan. Saskatchewan Fisheries Lab., Saskatoon. 1-123.

Barica, J. (1979). Some biological characteristics of plains aquatic ecosystems and their effect on water quality. In Proceedings of the Plains Aquatic Research Conference. Univ. Regina Wat. Stud. Inst., Regina, Saskatchewan, in press.

Brinkhurst, R. O. (1966). Detection and assessment of water pollution using oligochaete worms. Wat. Sewage Wks., 113, 398-401.

Brinkhurst, R. O., A. L. Hamilton, and H. B. Herrington (1968). Components of the bottom fauna of the St. Lawrence, Great Lakes. Univ. Toronto, Great Lakes Inst., Rep. PR 33, 1-50.

Brundin, L. (1951). The relation of O_2- microstratification at the mud surface to the ecology of the profundal bottom fauna. Rep. Inst. Freshwat. Res. Drottningholm, 32, 32-42.

Burton, W. (1974). A semiautomatic release gear for grabs and corers. J. Fish. Res. Bd Can., 31, 1244-1246.

Burton, W., and J. F. Flannagan (1973). An improved Ekman-type grab. J. Fish. Res. Bd Can., 30, 287-290.

Christiansen, E. A., D. F. Acton, R. J. Long, W. A. Meneley, and E. K. Saver (1977). Fort Qu'Appelle Geolog. Interpretive Report No. 2. Modern Press, Saskatoon, Saskatchewan.

Cross, P. M. (1978). The application of nutrient loading-productivity models to the Qu'Appelle Valley lakes of Saskatchewan. Can. Dep. Envir., Inl. Waters Direct., Nat. Water Res. Inst. Tech. Rep. W.N.R.-PR-78-1, 1-136.

Gummer, W. D. (1979). Pesticide monitoring in the prairies of western Canada. Can. Dep. Envir., Inl. Waters Direct., Wat. Qual. Interp. Rep. 4, 1-14.

Hamilton, A. L., and O. A. Saether (1971). The occurence of characteristic deformities in the chironomid larvae of several Canadian lakes. Can. Ent., 103, 363-368.

Hammer, U. T. (1971). Limnological studies of the lakes and stremas of the upper Qu'Appelle River System, Saskatchewan, Canada. I. Chemical and physical aspects of the lakes and drainage system. Hydrobiologia, 37, 473-507.

Hammer, U. T. (1973). Eutrophication and its alleviation in the upper Qu'Appelle River System, Saskatchewan. In Proceedings of the Symposium on Lakes of Western Canada, Univ. Alberta Press, Edmonton, pp 352-369.

Hare, L., and J. C. H. Carter (1976). The distribution of Chironomus (s.s.)? cucini (salinarius group) larvae (Diptera): Chironomidae) in Parry Sound, Georgian Bay, with particular reference to structural deformities. Can. J. Zool., 54, 2129-2134.

Nagell, B., and C.-C. Landahl (1978). Resistance to anoxia of Chironomus plumosus and Chironomus anthracinus (Diptera) larvae. Holarct. Ecol., 1, 333-336.

Peters, R. H. (1973). Nutrient balances for the evaluation of nutrient sources in water quality management. Wat. Resour. Bull., 9, 49-53.

Roback, S. S. (1969). Notes on the food of Tanypodinae larvae. Entomol. News, 80, 13-19.

Saether, O. A. (1969). Some nearctic Podonominae, Diamesinae and Orthocladiinae (Diptera: Chironomidae). Bull. Fish. Res. Bd Can. No. 170, 1-154.

Saether, O. A. (1970). A survey of the bottom fauna in lakes of the Okanagan Valley, British Columbia. Can. Fish. Mar. Serv. Tech. Rep., 196, 1-29.

Saether, O. A. (1979). Chironomid communities as water quality indicators. Holarct. Ecol., 2, in press.

Saether, O. A., and M. P. McLean (1972). A survey of the bottom fauna in Wood, Kalamalka and Skaha Lakes in the Okanagan Valley, British Columbia. Fish. Res. Bd Can. Tech. Rep. 342, 1-27.

Southwood, T. R. E. (1966). Ecological methods with particular reference to the study of insect populations. Methuen and Co. Ltd., London.

Warwick, W. F. (1967). Some chemical and biological aspects of water pollution in a portion of the upper Qu'Appelle River System. M.Sc. Thesis. Univ. Saskatchewan, Saskatoon.

Warwick, W. F. (1978). Man and the Bay of Quinte, Lake Ontario: 2800 years of cultural influence, with special reference to the Chironomidae (Diptera), sedimentation and eutrophication. Ph.D. Thesis, Univ. Manitoba, Winnipeg.

Warwick, W. F. (1979). The effects of 2800 years of cultural development on the Chironomidae (Diptera) fauna of the Bay of Quinte, Lake Ontario. Can. Ent., 111, in press.

Warwick, W. F. (1979). Palaeolimnology of Pasqua Lake: Preliminary report on benthic fauna responses to the sediment-water environment and long core collection during February-March, 1979. Can. Dep. Envir., Inl. Waters Direct., Nat. Water Res. Inst. Tech. Rep. W.N.R.-PR-79-4, 1-113.

Vorstudien zur Bedeutung der Sediment-bewohnenden Zuckmücken im Stoffhaushalt des Balatonsees (Ungarn)

Gy. Dévai

Dept. of Zool. and Anthr., L. Kossuth Univ., Debrecen, Hungary

ABSTRACT

The significance of the sediment dwelling chironomids in the nutrient budget of Lake Balaton (Hungary)
This paper is intended to give a summary of the findings of the first examinations which aimed at analysing the role and importance of the chironomids in the matter circulation and energy flow in Lake Balaton through the examination of the characteristics of the distribution in space and time of the sediment dwelling chironomids. The examinations carried out in 1978 in the Basin of Keszthely, the most endangered part from the viewpoint of water quality, led to conclusion that chironomids can substantially contribute to the elimination of the two key factors of eutrophication, namely P- and N-compounds and also the organic matter in the water and the sediment.

KEYWORDS

Sediment dwelling chironomids; Lake Balaton, Hungary; water quality; eutrophication; organic C-, N- and P-budget.

EINFÜHRUNG

Die modernen hydrobiologischen Forschungen bezeugen mit großer Beweiskraft, daß die Bodenablagerungen eine wesentliche und vielseitige Rolle im Leben der Flachgewässer und so auch in dem des Balatonsees spielen. Von den vielen möglichen Faktoren ist die Dynamik des biogenen Stoff- und Energiehaushalts des Sediments - oder wie Ohle (1956, 1958) es kurz und treffend nennt: seine Bioaktivität - von hervorragender Bedeutung. Die Bioaktivität hängt in erster Linie von der Stoffwechseltätigkeit der Lebewesen, d.h. vom komplexen System der von ihnen als Biokatalysatoren regulierten Stoff- und Energieumsetzungsprozesse ab (Dévai et al., 1976, 1977).

Zum überwiegenden Teil beruhen auf diesen Prozessen die natürliche Reinigung ("Selbstreinigung") der Gewässer und letztendlich auch alle Verfahren zur biologischen Reinigung von Abwässern. Die Lebewesen nutzen nämlich nur einen Teil der aufgenommenen Nährstoffe zum Aufbau ihres Körpers, den anderen Teil verbrauchen sie während ihrer Lebensvorgänge (z.B. "verbrennen" sie bei der Atmung die großmolekularen, zusammengesetzten organischen Stoffe, die makroenergetische chemische Bindungen enthalten, indem sie alle in einfachere Verbindungen mit geringem Molekulargewicht und mit weniger chemischer Energie zerlegen).

Dieser Gedankengang läßt eindeutig darauf schließen, daß bei der biologischen Reinigung von Gewässern die heterotrophen Lebewesen besonderes Interesse verdienen. Unter den heterotrophen Organismen haben dann wieder die "amphibischen" Insektengruppen, deren Imagines das Wasser verlassen, eine besondere Bedeutung, denn sie nutzen die im Wasser und im Sediment vorhandenen Stoffe nicht nur zu ihrer Lebenstätigkeit, sondern entfernen diese beim Schlüpfen aus dem Wasserkörper. Dies ist besonders beim Phosphor von entscheidender Bedeutung, denn von den Bausteinen der organischen Verbindungen können C, O, H, N und S auch auf andere Weise aus dem Wasserraum gelangen (z.B. in der Form von CO_2, CH_4, NH_3 oder H_2S können sie gasförmig entweichen), wobei die Belastung des Wasserraums durch organische Stoffe gesenkt wird. Beim Phosphor ist uns ein solcher wesentlicher Vorgang aber nicht bekannt (die Phosphin-Bindung tritt in natürlichen Gewässern nur ausnahmsweise und massenanteilig nicht bedeutend auf), so daß beim Schutz gegen die Eutrophierung dieser "Phosphor-output", welcher beim Schlüpfen der Insekten - und hier in erster Linie bei den in zumeist riesiger Individuenzahl und jährlich in mehreren Generationen vorkommenden Zuckmücken - von besonders großer Bedeutung sein kann.

In erster Linie leiteten uns diese Gesichtspunkte, als wir die Forschungsarbeiten zur Bedeutung der Zuckmückenfauna im Sediment des Balatons aufnahmen.

MATERIAL

Wir begannen unsere Untersuchungen im Jahre 1978 im südwestlichen Teil des Balatons, im Keszthelyer-Becken, das durch die Verschlechterung der Wasserqualität - im Zusammenhang mit der raschen Eutrophierung - am meisten gefährdet ist.

Im Verlaufe unserer Untersuchungen studierten wir einerseits den Gehalt an organischem Material und an organischem Kohlenstoff der Sedimentproben aus dem Keszthelyer-Becken, bzw. die Individuenzahl der Zuckmückenlarven und ihre Verteilung nach der Körperlänge. Im weiteren maßen wir das Naß- und Trockengewicht der Larven, die zum Formenkreis der Chironomus s.l. gehören sowie deren Gehalt an organischem Kohlenstoff, Stickstoff und Phosphor. Unsere Ergebnisse zeigen wir auf der Grundlage einer Analyse von Proben, die z.Z. der ersten großen Frühlingsschwärme (zwischen dem 2. und 5. Mai) gemacht wurden (vgl. Tab. 1).

ERGEBNISSE

Der Gehalt an organischem Material und an organischem Kohlenstoff in der oberen, 20 cm dicken Sedimentschicht des Keszthelyer-Beckens ist von mittlerer Höhe, die im Jahre 1978 genommenen 40 Proben betragen im Durchschnitt 2,97 % org. Mat., bzw. 1,72 % org. C. Die Werte der beiden Komponenten sind in der nörlichen Hälfte und in der Mitte des

Beckens um einiges höher als im Bereich der südlichen und westlichen Uferregion. Diese Ergebnisse stimmen sehr gut mit den Angaben von Frankó und Ponyi (1975) aus dem Jahre 1971 überein. Daß einige Werte niedriger sind, kann wahrscheinlich durch den höheren Gehalt an organischem Material in der von ihnen untersuchten oberen 5 cm dicken Sedimentschicht erklärt werden. Aufgrund der obigen Angaben können nahezu 15 kg organisches Material auf einer Fläche von 1 m^2 in der durchschnittlich 20 cm dicken, von Zuckmückenlarven bevölkerten Sedimentschicht gefunden werden.

TABELLE 1
Die wichtigsten Gewichts- und Inhaltsstoffangaben der zu dem Formenkreis Chironomus s.l. gehörenden sedimentbewohnenden Zuckmücken im Keszthelyer-Becken des Balatonsees, in der ersten großen Schlüpfperiode (4. und 5. Mai 1978)

Komponenten	Einheit	Larven[1]	Männchen[2]	Weibchen[2]
Naßgewicht	mg/Ind.	47,75	7,07	15,92
Trockengewicht	mg/Ind.	7,73	1,95	4,67
	%[+]	16,19	27,60	29,32
Glührückstand	mg/Ind.	0,70	0,10	0,22
	%[++]	9,00	4,87	4,61
Glühverlust	mg/Ind.	7,03	1,85	4,45
	%[++]	91,00	95,13	95,39
Org. Kohlenstoff-	C mg/Ind.	3,87	1,02	2,45
-Gehalt	%[++]	50,06	52,31	52,46
Stickstoff-	N mg/Ind.	0,599	0,210	0,503
-Gehalt	%[++]	7,75	10,77	10,77
Phosphor-	P mg/Ind.	0,061	0,019	0,043
-Gehalt	%[++]	0,79	0,97	0,92

[1] = Keszthelyer-Becken, K/1 Probeentnahmestelle (in der Mitte des Beckens) - 4. Mai 1978

[2] = Vonyarcvashegy, I/1 Probeentnahmestelle (in der Mitte des nördlichen Uferrandes) - 5. Mai 1978

[+] = in bezug auf das Naßgewicht

[++] = in bezug auf das Trockengewicht

Die Anzahl an Zuckmückenlarven lag im mittleren Bereich in der ersten großen Schlüpfperiode im Jahre 1978: am 2. Mai fanden wir durchschnittlich 1725 Ind.m^{-2} im Keszthelyer-Becken. Einen Großteil der Larven - insgesamt 50 bis 80 % - bildete der Formenkreis der großleibigen <u>Chironomus</u> s.l., deren Maße und Gewichte um ein Vielfaches das der im Sediment gefundenen anderen Chironominae- und Tanypodinae-Larven übertrifft. Daher konzentrierten wir unsere Aufmerksamkeit hauptsächlich auf das Studium dieser Gruppe. Im folgenden berichten wir über unsere Ergebnisse bei der Untersuchung dieser Tiere.

Das Naßgewicht der verpuppungsreifen Larven, die durchschnittlich 22,4 cm lang waren, betrug zumeist zwischen 45-50 mg. Das Trockengewicht bei Larven war ca. 15 % vom Naßgewicht. Der Glühverlust, der annähernd dem organischen Materialgehalt entspricht, betrug etwa 91 % des Trockengewichts. Das Verhältnis des Gehaltes an organischem Kohlenstoff zu Stickstoff und zu Phosphor beträgt durchschnittlich etwa 50,1:7,8:0,8 (in % des Trockengewichts).

Aufgrund der Angaben in g m^{-2} erscheint die Menge an organischem Material, organischem Kohlenstoff, Stickstoff und Phosphor im Körper der Larven als beträchtlich, wirklich beachtenswert wird sie aber umgerechnet auf das gesamte Gebiet des Keszthelyer-Beckens, denn die nahezu 220 t organischer Materie entsprechen insgesamt 110 t organischem Kohlenstoff, 20 t Stickstoff und 2 t Phosphor. Es stimmt aber auch, daß der Gehalt an organischer Substanz im Körper der Zuckmückenlarven verschwindend gering ist gegenüber der Menge an organischen Stoffen im Sediment (im Durchschnitt insgesamt 5,65 g m^{-2}, das sind nur 0,04 % der im Sediment befindlichen organischen Stoffe). Wie aus den obigen Angaben zu ersehen ist, ist der Anteil der Larven nach ihrem Körpergewicht im Sediment nicht relevant, ihre Tätigkeit aber, d.h. die Menge des Sediments, das von den Larven durchwühlt wird, ist dagegen sehr viel bedeutender. Nach Untersuchungen von Entz (1964, 1965) und Oláh (1976), und aufgrund eigener Erfahrungen sind dies 0,5-1,5 g m^{-2} täglich bei einer Individuendichte von 800 Ind.m^{-2}. Da der größte Teil hiervon organisches Material (z.B. Detritus) ist, verarbeiten die Larven jährlich etwa 2-3 % des organischen Materials der oberen 20 cm dicken Sedimentschicht. Hierbei bereiten sie einen Teil dieser organischen Stoffe für die bakteriologische Zersetzung auf, andererseits nutzen sie ihn bei der Selbsterhaltung und beim eigenen Wachstum. Mit dieser Tätigkeit haben sie einen bedeutenden Anteil an der Senkung der Belastung durch organisches Material im Sediment. Auf diese Rolle der Zuckmückenlarven, die in der oberen Schicht des Sediments eine aktive Tätigkeit des Schlammumwälzens vollführen, hat auch Entz (1964) schon früher einmal hingewiesen.

Trotz des beträchtlichen Gewichtsunterschiedes zwischen den Larven und Imagines, verkörpern die geschlüpften Tiere noch immer eine große Menge an organischem Material. Sie entfernen aus dem Wasserkörper rund 50 % der in den Larven enthaltenen Materie. Diese Menge beträgt umgesetzt auf das gesamte Gebiet des Keszthelyer-Beckens - bei einem Absinken der Individuenzahl während des Auftauchens der Puppen und während der Umwandlung um 10 % und bei einem Verhältnis der schwereren Weibchen zu den Männchen von 1:1 - ca. 90 t organisches Material, 50 t organisch gebundener Kohlenstoff, 10 t Stickstoff und 1 t Phosphor. Dieser "output" ist auch dann noch von Bedeutung, wenn wir in Betracht ziehen, daß durch die ins Wasser abgelegten Eier und durch die Imagines, die auf das Wasser fallen, eine gewisse, heute leider zahlenmäßig noch nicht abzuschätzende Menge an organischen Stoffen in den Wasserkörper zurückgelangt.

Die obigen Angaben sind offensichtlich nur ausreichend für eine grobe Schätzung der Rolle des Stoff- und Energiehaushalts bei sedimentbewohnenden Zuckmücken. Die Untersuchungen weisen aber auf alle Fälle darauf hin, wie notwendig ihre Fortsetzung und Präzisierung ist. Außerdem geben sie die Gelegenheit, die folgenden Schlußfolgerungen zu formulieren.

1) In Zukunft wäre es wichtig, den heterotrophen Organismen bei der Analyse der Prozesse im Stoff- und Energiehaushalt der Gewässer viel mehr Beachtung zu schenken, hierunter hauptsächlich den aus den Gewässern schlüpfenden und massenhaft vorkommenden Insektengruppen, damit wir ihre wahre Bedeutung im Leben der Gewässer so schnell wie möglich aufdecken können und in Erkenntnis dessen ihre Tätigkeit lenken und nützen können.

2) Die Angaben aus den grundlegenden Arbeiten sowie eigene Untersuchungsergebnisse beweisen eindeutig, daß die Vorgänge, die eine natürliche Reinigung der Gewässer zur Folge haben, noch gründlicher und genauer als bisher analysiert werden müssen. Die sich in dieser "selbstregulierenden Fähigkeit" verbergenden Möglichkeiten müssen bei der Lösung unserer Aufgaben in der Wasserwirtschaft noch viel intensiver eingesetzt werden. Hierzu ist aber eine Steigerung der Wirksamkeit der biologischen Wasseranalysen von unbedingter Notwendigkeit.

DANKSAGUNG

Die in dieser Arbeit vorgestellten Untersuchungen wurden mit der Unterstützung des Unterrichtsministeriums und der Ungarischen Akademie der Wissenschaften, im Rahmen der Arbeitsgruppe, die unter der Leitung von Dr. F. Máté die physikalisch-chemischen und biologischen Eigenschaften der Sedimente im Balaton untersucht, durchgeführt. Für diese Unterstützungen meinen verbindlichen Dank! Den Mitarbeitern unserer Arbeitsgruppe, Dr. I. Dévai, Dr. A. Kovács, A. Bagyó, I. Molnár, Zs. Enyedi und A. Petró bin ich für die Hilfe bei den Probenahmen, Analysen und Berechnungen dankbar. Ich danke Herrn Dr. F. Reiss und Herrn Dr. E.G. Burmeister (Zoologische Sammlung des Bayerischen Staates, München) sehr herzlich für die kritische Durchsicht des Manuskripts.

LITERATURVERZEICHNIS

Dévai, Gy., Gy. Kollár and G. Öllös (1976). Acta Biol. Debrecina, 13, 163-191.
Dévai, Gy., I. Dévai, I. Wittner and E. Bondár (1977). Acta Biol. Debrecina, 14, 9-20.
Entz, B. (1964). Annal. Biol. Tihany, 31, 165-175.
Entz, B. (1965). Annal. Biol. Tihany, 32, 129-139.
Frankó, A. and J.E. Ponyi (1975). Annal. Biol. Tihany, 42, 157-163.
Ohle, W. (1956). Limnol. Oceanogr., 1, 139-149.
Ohle, W. (1958). Verh. Internat. Verein. Limnol., 13, 196-211.
Oláh, J. (1976). Annal. Biol. Tihany, 43, 83-92.

The Distribution of Chironomid Communities and Controlling Sediment Parameters in L. Derravaragh, Ireland

M. L. McGarrigle

Zoology Department, University College, Dublin, Ireland

ABSTRACT

The chironomid communities in Clinton's Bay L. Derravaragh, Co. Westmeath, Ireland, are described. Sediment parameters: Organic content, particle size composition and pigment content were measured and related to faunal communities. Species groupings defined by recurrent group analysis corresponded to chironomid communities defined by their response to sediment characteristics.

KEYWORDS

Sediment/fauna relationships; sedimentary pigments; organic content; particle size; recurrent groups.

INTRODUCTION

The ecology of chironomid larvae has been treated almost exclusively in relation to the characteristics of the overlying water column. Very little quantitative work has been done on larval/sediment relationships (Maitland, 1979). This paper describes the chironomid communities in Clinton's Bay L. Derravaragh and examines some of the interrelationships between key taxa and sediment characteristics. Sediment particle size, organic content, and pigment derivatives in the surficial sediments were measured and related to chironomid distribution patterns by means of correlation coefficients.

AREA OF INVESTIGATION

The location and physico-chemical features of L. Derravaragh are shown in Table 1.

TABLE 1 Characteristics of L. Derravaragh.

Location	Co. Westmeath, O.S. N.42 67
Altitude	63m a.s.l.
Length, Area	9.5km, 1120ha.
Max. Depth	23m.
Geology	Carboniferous limestone, glacial moraines.
Conductivity	310-415µS
pH	8.1
Chlorophyll a	1-20µg/1

The lake is subject to a certain amount of agricultural runoff and is moderately eutrophic.

MATERIALS AND METHODS

The study concentrated on Clinton's Bay (Fig. 1). Twenty-six sampling stations were chosen on a stratified random basis in order to give equal representation to all sediment types between 2m and 23m. Two Ekman grabs were taken at each site. The sediment was sieved through a 250μ mesh and preserved in 4% formalin. The samples were handsorted and the chironomids identified and counted. Corresponding surficial sediment samples were taken from the undisturbed sediment surface, while still in the Ekman grab. The sediment was frozen and later analysed for particle size, pigment derivatives and organic content (L.O.I.). The samples were taken on the 22/23 February 1977.

Particle size determinations were made according to the method of Galehouse (1971). Organic matter was not oxidised before analysis, however. Eight size fractions were measured (Table 3).

The equivalent of one gram (approx.) dry weight, of wet sediment, was extracted in a known volume of 90% acetone for 12 hours, in the dark, at 4°C after vigorous mixing. The extract was read at 480nm for total carotenoid pigments and at 665nm for chlorophyll derivatives. The results are expressed as units per gram dry weight and as units per gram organic weight. One unit is defined as being equivalent to an absorbance of 1 in a 10cm cell when dissolved in 100ml of solvent (Sanger and Gorham, 1972). Pigment ratio is defined as O.D. at 665nm divided by O.D. at 480nm.

The organic content of the sediment was estimated as loss on ignition at 480°C for 6 hours. Control experiments showed only fractional losses due to the presence of carbonates.

RESULTS

Chironomid Communities

Twenty-one larval taxa were found. The most important of these were: *Procladius*, *Heterotanytarsus apicalis* K., *Chironomus anthracinus* Zett., *C. plumosus* L., *Cryptochironomus*, *Microtendipes*, *Polypedilum*, *Cladotanytarsus*, and *Tanytarsus*. Other taxa were found in smaller numbers (Table 3.). Positive identification to species level was not possible in the majority of cases. However, reared larval material indicates that virtually all of the *C. anthracinus*-type larvae found are *C. anthracinus* Zett. Similarly, *C. plumosus* has been positively identified also. Two species of *Procladius* have been identified from reared larval material: *P. signatus* Zett. from shallow regions and *P. barbatus* Br. from the deeper zones.

The distribution data for the 21 recorded larval taxa was subjected to a recurrent group analysis in order to delimit species groupings. This analysis provides an objective method for defining recurrent species groupings (Fager, 1957). Members of a group show a statistically significant affinity for all other members of the group ($p < 0.05$). Associate members of a group show significant affinity for some members of that group but no other group. Following preliminary analyses taking all samples together the

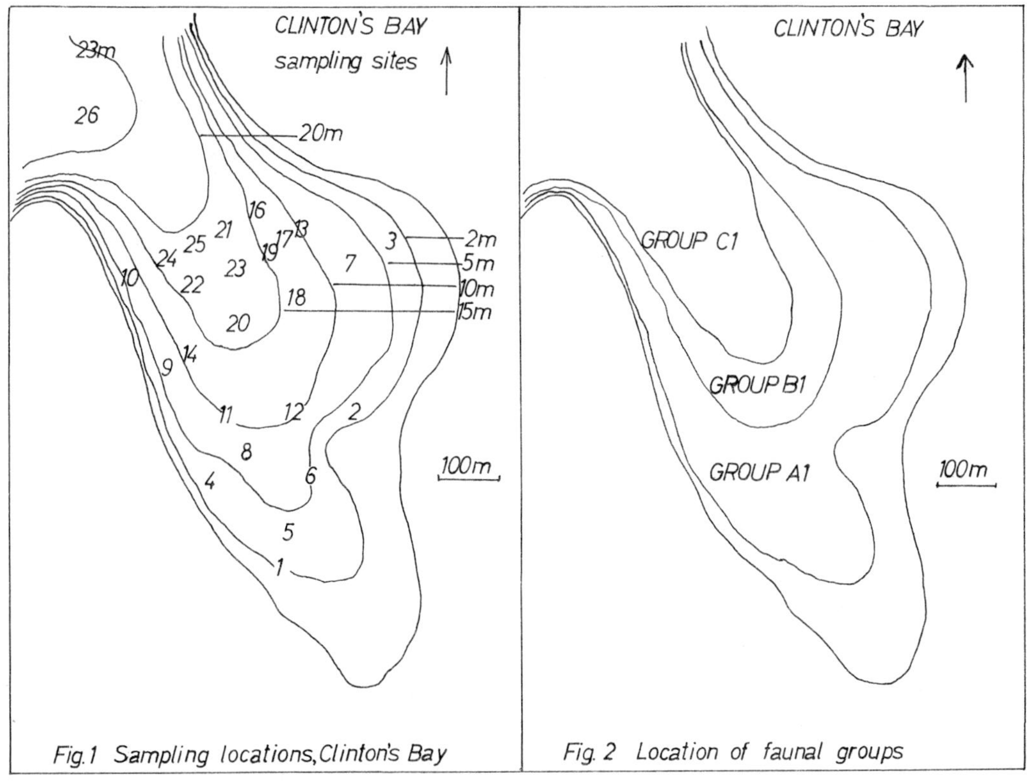

Fig.1 Sampling locations, Clinton's Bay

Fig. 2 Location of faunal groups

sample stations were divided into three sets: 2-10m, 11-14m and 14-23m. These yielded recurrent groups which had minimal overlap and maximum homogeneity between samples. (Station numbers are shown on the bathymetric map of Clinton's Bay. (Fig. 1).)

The recurrent groups are shown in Table 2 with taxa listed in order of dominance.

TABLE 2 Recurrent Groups in Clinton's Bay (Feb 1977)

Sample Set A Nos. 1-12 (2-10m)		Sample Set B Nos.13-18 (11-14m)		Sample Set C Nos.1-26 (19-26)	
GROUP A1		GROUP B1		GROUP C1	
Rank	Taxon	Rank	Taxon	Rank	Taxon
1	*Procladius cf signatus*	1	*Chironomus anthracinus* / *Tanytarsus*	1	*Chironomus anthracinus*
2	*Tanytarsus*	2	*Procladius cf signatus* and *P. barbatus*	2	*Procladius cf barbatus*
3	*Microtendipes*	3	*Chironomus plumosus*	3	*Chironomus plumosus*
4	*Polypedilum*	4	*Polypedilum*		
5	*Cladotanytarsus*		Associate Member		
	Associate Members	5	*Microtendipes*		
6	*Cryptochironomus*				
7	*Heterotanytarsus apicalis*				

This sequence was calculated by ranking the species within each sample and summing the rankings for each sample set. The ranking orders were tested for statistical significance using the coefficient of concordance, W, and testing with Snedecor's F test (Fager, 1957). All the rankings are significant at least at the 5% level. The recurrent groups thus defined are shown on the map of Clinton's Bay (Fig. 2).

Fauna/Sediment Relationships

Sediment particle size, organic content and surficial sediment pigments were chosen, a priori, as parameters likely to be of importance to a predominantly tube-building, detritivorous, benthic community. Sedimentary pigments were chosen in order to qualify the relationships between fauna and sedimentary organic matter. It is not possible to differentiate between the more refractory allochthonous organic matter and the autochthonous matter produced within the lake by ignition or oxidative techniques. Pigment quantities and ratios in the sediment can go some way toward differentiating between these ecologically distinct categories of organic matter.

Sediment particle size distribution with depth is illustrated in Fig. 3. Pigment data and organic content are shown in Fig. 4. Faunal data were transformed using Log(n+1) and correlated with the 17 environmental parameters indicated in Table 3. A 17 x 21 correlation matrix resulted. Of the 357 correlations obtained 61 were significant at the 5% level of probability. The significant correlations are shown in Table 4. Positive and negative correlations are indicated by 1 and -1 respectively. Rows correspond to environmental parameters and columns to chironomid taxa, with labels as shown in Table 3.

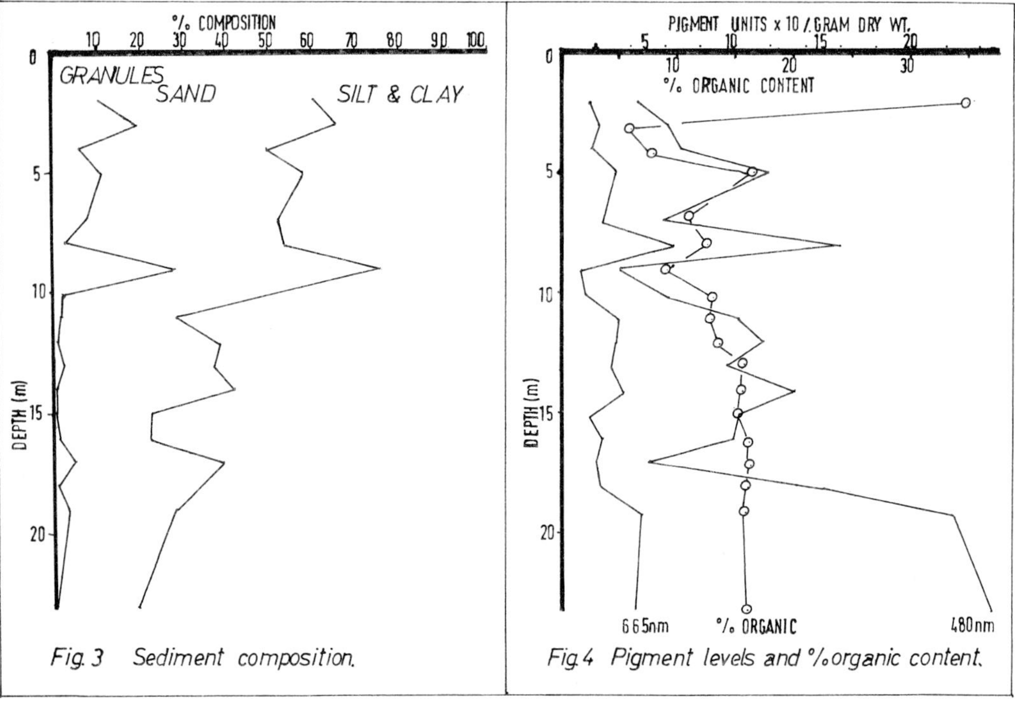

Fig. 3 Sediment composition.

Fig. 4 Pigment levels and % organic content.

TABLE 3 Chironomid Taxa and Environmental Parameters Measured.

No.	Parameter/Taxon	No.	Parameter/Taxon
1	% organic matter	20	*Pentaneurini*
2	Depth	21	*Monodiamesa*
3	Pigment Ratio	22	*Cricotopus*
4	Units 665nm/g dry wt.	23	*H. apicalis*
5	Units 480nm/g dry wt.	24	*Psectrocladius*
6	Units 665nm/g org wt.	25	*C. anthracinus*
7	Units 480nm/g org wt.	26	*C. plumosus*
8	Particles < 2mm	27	*Cryptochironomus*
9	" 250µ-2mm	28	*Cryptocladopelma*
10	" 62.5-250µ	29	*Demicryptochironomus*
11	" 31.2-62.5µ	30	*Dicrotendipes*
12	" 15.6-31.2µ	31	*Endochironomus*
13	" 7.8-15.6µ	32	*Microtendipes*
14	" 3.9-7.8µ	33	*Parachironomus*
15	" < 3.9µ	34	*Paralauterborniella nigrohalteralis*
16	" < 62.5µ		
17	Mean particle diameter(ϕ)	35	*Polypedilum*
18	*Apsectrotanypus*	36	*Cladotanytarsus*
19	*Procladius*	37	*Stempellina*
		38	*Tanytarsus*

TABLE 4 Correlation Matrix for Fauna/Sediment Data Showing Significant Values ($p < 0.05$)

	18	19	20	21	22	23	24	25	26	27	28	29	30	31	32	33	34	35	36	37	38
1	0	-1	-1	0	0	-1	0	0	0	0	0	0	0	0	0	0	0	0	0	0	0
2	0	0	-1	0	0	-1	0	1	1	-1	0	0	0	0	-1	0	0	-1	-1	0	0
3	0	0	0	0	0	1	0	-1	0	0	0	0	0	0	0	0	0	1	0	0	1
4	0	0	0	0	0	0	0	1	0	0	0	0	0	0	0	0	0	0	0	0	0
5	0	0	0	0	0	0	0	1	0	0	0	0	0	0	0	0	0	-1	-1	0	0
6	0	0	0	0	0	0	0	0	0	0	0	0	0	0	0	0	0	0	0	0	0
7	0	0	0	0	0	0	0	0	0	0	0	0	0	0	0	0	0	-1	-1	0	-1
8	0	0	1	0	0	0	0	-1	-1	0	0	1	0	1	1	0	0	0	0	0	0
9	0	0	0	0	0	0	0	0	0	0	1	0	0	0	0	0	0	0	0	0	0
10	1	0	0	0	0	1	-1	0	0	0	0	1	0	0	0	0	0	0	0	0	0
11	0	0	0	1	0	1	0	0	0	0	0	0	0	0	0	0	0	0	0	0	0
12	-1	0	0	0	0	0	-1	1	0	0	0	-1	0	0	-1	0	0	0	-1	0	0
13	0	0	0	0	0	-1	1	1	0	0	0	0	0	0	0	0	0	-1	0	0	0
14	0	0	0	0	0	0	1	1	0	0	0	0	0	0	0	0	0	0	0	0	0
15	0	0	0	0	0	0	1	1	0	0	0	0	0	0	0	0	0	0	0	0	0
16	-1	0	0	0	0	0	1	1	1	0	0	-1	0	0	0	0	0	0	0	0	0
17	-1	0	0	0	0	0	1	1	1	0	0	-1	0	0	-1	0	0	-1	-1	0	0

In order to help decide on the ecological significance of these correlations the interactions between the various sediment parameters were first explored, particularly those between organic matter and pigment levels.

It has been shown that the pigment ratios of sediments depend on the origin of the pigments (Sanger and Gorham, 1972; Murray and Douglas, 1976). In the deep water sediments of eutrophic lakes where phytoplankton remains dominate the organic content of the sediment this ratio is low (0.1-0.3). In oligotrophic lakes where allochthonous organic matter is more important the ratio is higher (0.3-1.0)

(Murray and co-workers, unpublished). The relationship between organic matter and pigment levels in L. Derravaragh is shown in Table 5. Three depth zones were chosen in order to highlight the changing nature of organic matter with increase in depth.

TABLE 5 Correlations Between Sedimentary Pigment Values and Organic Matter

Pigment Category	% Organic Matter (L.O.I.)		
	2m-7m	7-23m	2-23m
Units 665nm/g dry wt.	0.777*	0.216	0.068
Units 480nm/g dry wt.	0.856**	0.456*	0.155
Units 665nm/g org wt.	-0.776*	0.086	-0.445*
Units 480nm/g org wt.	-0.605	0.369	-0.140
Pigment Ratio	0.265	-0.457*	-0.263

*: $P < 0.05$; **: $P < 0.01$

It seems reasonable to conclude from these figures that the nature of organic matter changes from shallow to deep-water sediments. Chlorophyll derivatives do not appear to increase significantly with increasing organic matter in sediments below 7m depth whereas carotenoids show a significant correlation with organic matter. This contrast is also reflected in the pigment ratio correlations, which change from a positive (non-significant) value to a significant negative value below 7m. The negative correlation between pigment levels expressed per gram organic matter in the shallow zone indicates an influx of refractory, pigment-poor organic material into the littoral and sublittoral regions of the lake. This is especially so in a small number of samples containing "bog oak". It is also readily

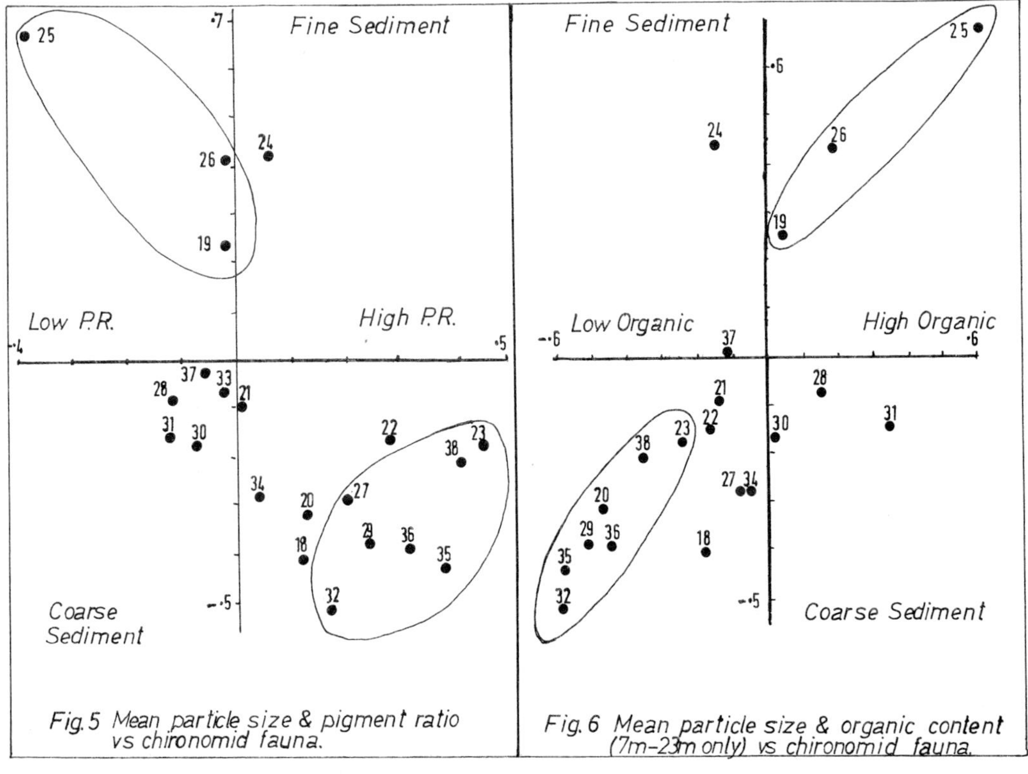

Fig. 5 Mean particle size & pigment ratio vs chironomid fauna.

Fig. 6 Mean particle size & organic content (7m-23m only) vs chironomid fauna.

apparent when sieved samples are being sorted that there is a decreasing amount of organic matter originating from macrophytes in deeper samples.

In order to display and interpret the fauna/sediment relationships in Clinton's Bay the correlation coefficients obtained were graphed on two dimensional axes, taking two environmental parameters at a time. This technique yields ecologically meaningful results and allows for ease of interpretation. It is particularly suited to the present study where the sediment parameters fell naturally into two categories - particle size and organic parameters.

Figure 5 illustrates the response of the chironomid taxa to mean particle size (Ø units) and pigment ratio of the sediment. The position of each taxon is fixed by its correlation coefficients with these parameters. The taxa are identified by numbers corresponding to those in Table 3. The most striking feature of this diagram is the marked similarity of the two groups ringed to Group A1 and C1 defined by recurrent group analysis (Table 2). The bottom right-hand group contains 6 of the 7 species in Group A1. This group, therefore appears to favour coarse sediments and organic matter characterised by a high pigment ratio. The top left-hand group in Fig. 5 comprising *C. anthracinus*, *C. plumosus* and *Procladius* corresponds exactly to Group C1 of Table 2. Both *Chironomus* species show significant correlation with mean Ø diameter. *C. anthracinus* also shows a clear correlation with pigment ratio.

A similar result is obtained when species are plotted against particle size and organic content (greater than 7m depth only), (Fig. 6). *Demicryptochironomus* and *Pentaneurini* show similarity to the members of Group A1. The fine sediment group corresponding to Group C1 again appears uniquely in the top right hand quadrant. Chironomid taxa were plotted against a number of different combinations of sediment parameters but little variation in the groupings resulted. No group corresponding to Group B1 of Table 2 emerged, indicating that this is probably a transition group produced by overlapping of shallow and deep water communities, rather than an ecologically distinct community.

DISCUSSION

A large number of environmental variables control the distribution of larval chironomids. Study of sediment types appears to be an efficient means of studying the joint impact of these variables. The benthic fauna experience the effects of water quality, depth etc., via the sediments in or on which they live. The sediments at a given location will reflect the interactions of water nutrient levels, seston formation, light penetration, wind and wave action, distance from the shore and many other factors. Analysis of particle size and the nature of organic matter in the sediment should therefore give an integrated view of a large number of these factors as they effect a detritivorous, tube-building community.

There are dangers however in drawing conclusions about causative relations between sediment and fauna from correlations such as those presented here. In particular, biotic factors such as competition and predation have not been considered. Such factors are probably important in the case of the predatory *Procladius*. Nevertheless it seems plausible that each group in Fig. 5 and 6 represents a group of ecologically similar animals controlled principally by particle size and texture of sediment and by sediment food quality.

The data presented here should prove of value in suggesting experiental work aimed at verifying causal links between fauna and sediment types. In particular it suggests further work aimed at clarifying the nature and nutritional value of organic matter in different zones of lakes. The use of pigment measurements in respect of the former appears to be an area worthy of further research. Extraction and measurement techniques are straightforward and results seem ecologically meaningful. Further refinement and quantification of pigment/organic matter relationships should prove worthwhile. Similarly, improved knowledge of particle size preferences of chironomid species should improve the value of chironomids as environmental indicators.

The value of chironomid larvae as indicators may also be enhanced by comparison of the results of this study with those of similar studies from other lake systems. It should be possible to gain valuable insight into causal relationships and species tolerance latitudes by such inter-lake comparisons.

ACKNOWLEDGEMENTS

This study was undertaken while the author was in receipt of a grant from the Department of Fisheries, Forestry and Wildlife. I wish to thank Dr. D.A. Murray for his helpful advice and for valuable criticisms of the manuscript. I also wish to thank Mr. J. Greene who assisted with field work on two particularly cold February days.

REFERENCES

Fager, E.W. (1957). Determination and analysis of recurrent groups. Ecology, 38, 586-595.

Galehouse, J.S. (1971). In R.E. Carver (Ed.), Procedures in Sedimentary Petrology. Wiley-Interscience.

Maitland, P.S. (1979). The distribution of zoobenthos and sediments in Loch Leven, Kinross, Scotland. Arch. Hydrobiol., 85, 98-125.

Murray, D.A. and D.J. Douglas (1976). Some sedimentary pigment determinations in a 1.0metre core from L. Ennell - a eutrophic lake in the Irish Midlands. In S. Horie (Ed.), Paleolimnology of Lake Biwa and the Japanese Pleistocene, Vol. 4., pp.703-714.

Sanger, J.E. and E. Gorham (1972). Stratigraphy of fossil pigments as a guide to the postglacial history of Kirchner Marsh, Minnesota. Limnol. Oceanogr., 17, 840-854.

Response of Chironomid Fauna after Autumn Overturn in a Eutrophic Lake

I. Neubert and C. Frank

Institut für Tierphysiologie und Angewandte Zoologie der Freien Universität Berlin, Haderslebener Straße 9, 1000 Berlin 41, Federal Republic of Germany

ABSTRACT

The abundance of Chironomus plumosus (32 %), Endochironomus intextus (42 %), Glyptotendipes paripes (12 %), and Polypedilum nubeculosum (12 %) was investigated from August until December 1978. Depending on O_2-content a migration of C. plumosus into depth was observed. C. plumosus represents the largest part of the biomass with an average of 73 %, E. intextus (24 %), G. paripes (7 %), and P. nubeculosum (4 %). The total biomass increases from 0.02 g dry wt./m^2 at the end of August to 1.6 g dry wt./m^2 at the beginning of December. The production of C. plumosus amounts to 0.81 g dry wt./m^2 for the sampling period. The autumn overturn affects only C. plumosus larvae.

KEYWORDS

Abundance, autumn overturn, oxygen accumulation, migration, availability of food, increase of biomass, production of C. plumosus.

INTRODUCTION

Phytoplankton as a primary producer is the most important energy source for secondary production. Growth and production of chironomids which consume these primary producers were discovered mainly during the spring maximum of phytoplankton and directly after autumn overturn (Jonasson and Kristiansen 1967, Jonasson 1972). This study will describe the effects of autumn overturn on the chironomid population with reference to abundance, possible migration, and biomass. This investigation is part of an ecological study of suburban water, a project of the Technical and the Free University Berlin (Heiligenseeproject).

DESCRIPTION OF STUDY AREA

The Heiligensee (HS), situated in NW of West-Berlin, has a surface area of 32 ha, maximum depth of 9.5 m and a water volume of 1.7×10^6

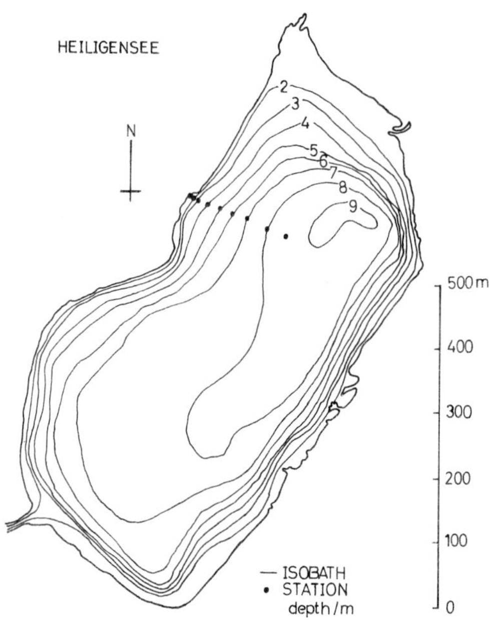

Fig. 1. Bathymetric chart of Heiligensee.

m^3. The altitude is 31.5 m a.s.l., the shore line measures 2.3 km (Fig. 1). The lake is a kettle lake originating from the last glacial and is connected with the Havel by a 12 m wide and 2.5 m deep channel in the South-West. In HS the littoral amounts to 33 %, the transition zone with empty shells (mussel zone) to 8 %, and in 4 m depth the profundal (59 %) begins (Franke 1978). The results up to now show a stagnation phase between mid-May and mid-September with a disappearance of oxygen in hypolimnion characterising the lake as intensively eutrophic (personal communications HS-projectgroup).

MATERIAL AND METHODS

Bottom samples were taken weekly from the end of August to the beginning of December 1978 with an Ekman-Birge-grab. Due to a defect in the grab on 14.11.78 the data from 5 m depth and deeper are underrepresented. Sampling stations are shown in Fig. 1. Down to 5 m depth four samples per meter were taken, after that only two. The samples were pooled, washed through 2 sieves (mesh size 1 mm and 0.3 mm), and preserved in 4 % Formalin. The chemical and physical factors and sedimentation data were determined according to the Deutsche Einheitsverfahren zur Wasser-, Abwasser und Schlammuntersuchung (1975), Chlorophyll a according to Strickland and Parsons (1968).
The identification of larvae was conducted after Bryce and Hobart (1972), Lenz (1962), and Mason (1973). The nomenclature conforms to that of the Limnofauna Europaea (Illies 1967). The larvae were dried for 2 hours at 60 °C and kept over $CaCl_2$ for 16 hours, the biomass was determined with an accuracy of 0.1 µg with an automatic electrobalance. Production of <u>C. plumosus</u> was calculated by the cohort

method (Edmondson and Winberg 1971), the age of instars was determined employing a length/weight-relation.

RESULTS

Physical and Chemical Characterization

The thermocline terminates in the middle of September; at that time the O_2-saturation at 8.5 m depth is less than 50 %. The complete circulation has occurred between 27.9.and 4.10.78. Until the beginning of December the temperature declines to 3.7 °C, the O_2-content rises to 81 % saturation in water layers adjacent to the sediment.
After an increase of phytoplankton at the end of August the chlorophyll content decreases with the beginning of overturn from 227 µg/l in mid-September to 35 µg/l at the beginning of November, and remains constant until the end of the investigation period. Compared with chlorophyll a the sedimentation shows a 14 days lag. After a maximum of 652 g/m²/day at the end of September the sedimentation decreases steadily until the beginning of December and then reaches a constant level of 28 g/m²/day (Fig. 2).

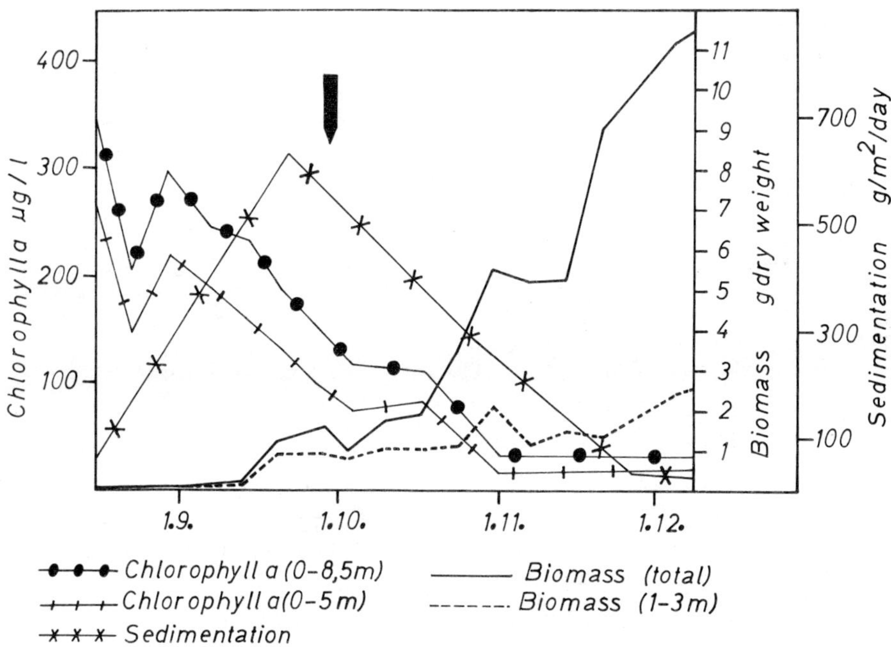

Fig. 2. Seasonal variation in chlorophyll a, sedimentation, and biomass in Heiligensee. Black arrow indicates date of autumn overturn.

Benthosfauna

The following species were identified: Ablabesmyia monilis (L.), Heterotanytarsus apicalis (K.), Procladius choreus (Mg.), Procladius spec., Tanypus spec., Chironomus plumosus (L.), Cryptochironomus defectus (K.), Cryptochironomus spec., Einfeldia pectoralis (K.), Endochironomus impar (Walk.), Endochironomus intextus (Walk.), Glyptotendipes paripes (Edw.), Limnochironomus spec., Microtendipes chloris (Mg.), Polypedilum nubeculosum (Mg.), Pseudochironomus spec., Sergentia coracina (Zett.), Stictochironomus spec., Tanytarsus spec., Micropsectra praecox (Mg.).
The dominant chironomid species are Endochironomus intextus with an average of 42 %, Chironomus plumosus with 32 %, Glyptotendipes paripes with 12 % and Polypedilum nubeculosum with 12 % (Fig. 3).

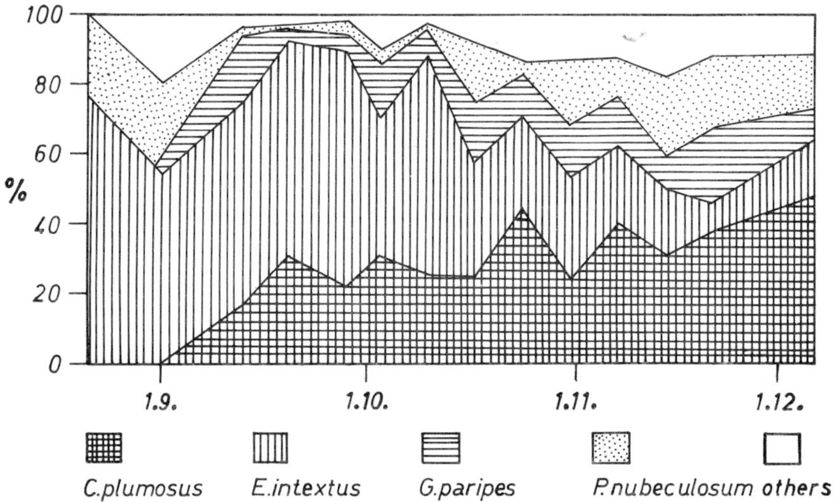

Fig. 3. Distribution of total abundance on chironomids in Heiligensee.

Development of Abundance

E. intextus has its abundance maximum of 1673 nos/m² in September and till mid-October. The distribution of the larvae is limited to 1 - 3 m depth and always above the 50 % O_2-saturation curve (Fig. 4). The distribution of G. paripes was found to be similar. The larvae preferably live at 1 - 3 m depth, partly also at 4 m depth (Fig. 5). The abundance maximum amounts to 225 nos/m². P. nubeculosum shows a clear increase from the end of October up to an average of 388 nos/m² with a maximum distribution at 1 - 2 m depth, and a second maximum at 4 m, thus avoiding the mussel zone (Fig. 5). At the beginning of December numerous larvae were found at 5 m depth, too. Their distribution still lies above the 50 % O_2-saturation curve. Because of the metamorphosis cycle of C. plumosus larvae of the 2nd and 3rd instars were found again only from September onwards and the abundance maximum increases to 881 nos/m² at 4 m

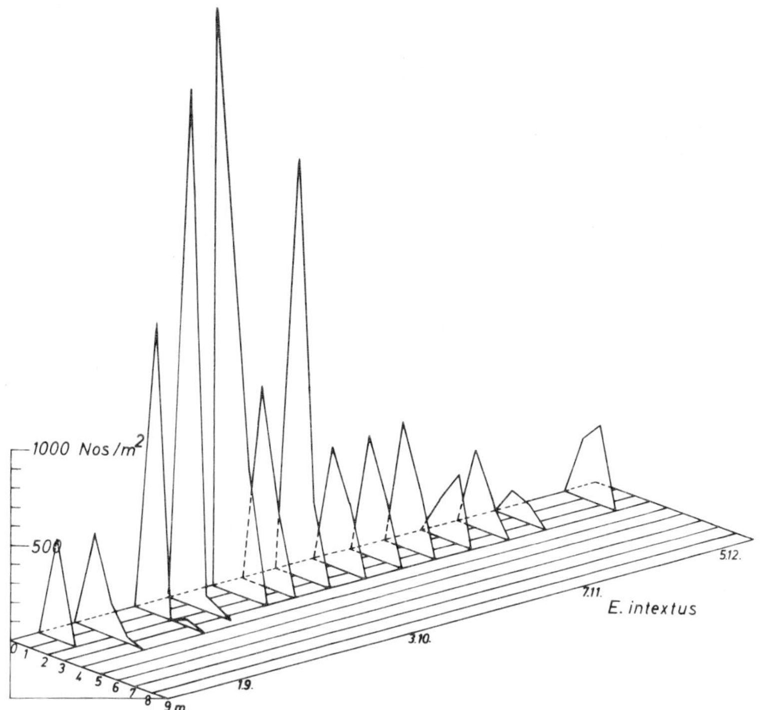

Fig. 4. Numbers of Endochironomus intextus in Heiligensee.

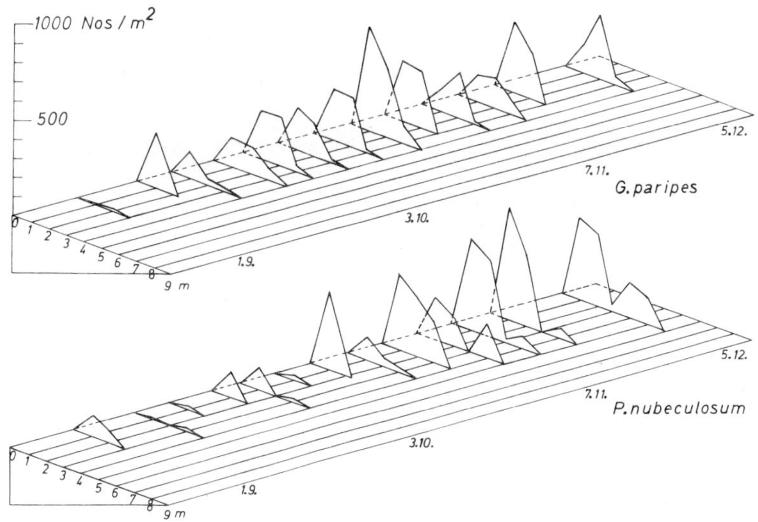

Fig. 5. Numbers of Glyptotendipes paripes and Polypedilum nubeculosum in Heiligensee.

depth. The larvae migrate in accordance with the 50 % O_2-saturation curve into the lower layers of the benthal. The oxygen saturation seems to determine the distribution of the 2nd and 3rd instars whereas the 4th instar migrates also into deeper layers with lower O_2-content. Until December the larvae spread out over the whole benthal with a maximum at 3-6 m depth (Fig. 6). At the end of the sampling period almost all larvae have reached the 4th stage.

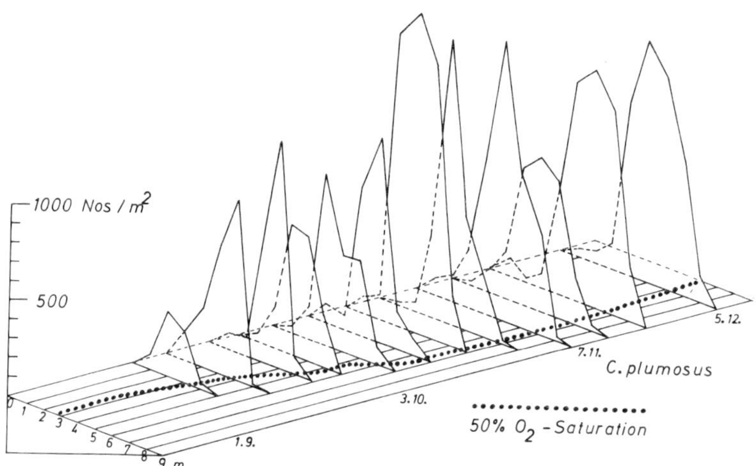

Fig. 6. Numbers of Chironomus plumosus in Heiligensee. Dotted line indicates 50 % oxygen saturation.

Biomass and Production

The average biomass of the four dominant species amounts to 0.76 g dry wt/m² for the investigation period. C. plumosus has the largest share with an average of 73 %, 86 % is reached at the end of November. The biomass of C. plumosus increases from 0.06 g dry wt/m² in mid-September to a maximum of 1.56 g dry wt/m² and decreases to 1.04 g dry wt/m² in December. The highest biomass is reached at 5-7 m depth (on average 1.3 g dry wt/m²). The 4th instar has an average weight of 2.4 mg dry wt at the beginning of December. The biomass of the other species amounts to an average of about 35 %, E. intextus having the largest share with an average of 24 % (0.16 g dry wt/m²). G. paripes and P. nubeculosum contribute to the total biomass 7 % (0.084 g dry wt/m²) and 4 % (0.087 g dry wt/m²), respectively. During the investigation period the production of C. plumosus amounts to an average of 0.82 g dry wt/m² with a production rate of 8.46 mg/m²/day. The P/B-coefficient is calculated to be 1.43.

DISCUSSION

The overturn causes an oxygen accumulation in the hypolimnion and an even spreading of dissolved nutrients. The change in the O_2-content in water layers adjacent to the sediment of the profundal has the greatest effects on the chironomids of HS. The species E. intextus,

G. paripes, and P. nubeculosum prove to be littoral forms showing no migration in relation to a shift of the 50 % O_2-saturation curve. Only C. plumosus reacts to improved oxygen conditions in the deeper layer by migrating to these areas. When comparing these results with the development of biomass and the availability of food measured by chlorophyll a and sedimentation (Fig. 2), the following can be said: The sedimentation of the late summer phytoplankton maximum noticeable by the decrease of chlorphyll a, and the sedimentation rate, leads to an accumulation below the thermocline and is inaccessible to the zoobenthos because of lack of oxygen at these depths. Due to the improved oxygen conditions after the circulation period these food resources are used by C. plumosus larvae, which is reflected by the increase of biomass and abundance of the 4th instar at the depths. The late summer phytoplankton maximum contains up to 80 % diatoms (personal communication Peter Maerker) which according to Kajak and Warda (1968) are preferably consumed as food, explaining the rapid biomass increase of C. plumosus. Down to about 4 °C the consumption activity of the larvae is barely influenced by falling temperatures, the biomass increases until the beginning of December and shows only slower increases at temperatures around 4 °C. Charles and others (1974) observed the same phenomenon for C. anthracinus. In Jonassons study (1978), too, there was no substantial biomass increase at high oxygen saturation during the winter months. This means that temperature, like day length, are important factors determing the activity of the larvae (Fischer 1974 , Moore 1979).

In the littoral there is no accumulation of food because of "short circuit nutrient cycle". Therefore, less food is available to the species. Thus, they reach only a low biomass (Fig. 2). The numbers of the older instars increased towards the end of the investigation period. No relationship could be observed between the abundance development of the individual species and the autumn overturn. The overturn is of importance mainly for sublittoral and profundal species such as C. plumosus because, new food resources are available to them after oxygen accumulation in the profundal. The development of the littoral forms is barely influenced by the circulation period and its effects.

The above described consumption of new food resources also manifests itself in increased production of C. plumosus. Assuming that 1/4 to 1/3 of the annual production takes place in autumn, at least 2-3 g dry wt/m²/year are estimated for C. plumosus . According to Aagard (1978) the Heiligensee can be classified as mesotrophic in productivity.

ACKNOWLEDGEMENT

The authors would like to take this opportunity to express their thanks to Mr. Michael Kretzschmar for supporting this work in providing the data of sedimentation rates and to the members of the projectgroup who took the chemical and physical measurements.

REFERENCES

Aagard, K. (1978). The chironomids of Lake Målsjøen. A phenological, diversity, and production study. Norw. J. Ent., 25, 21-37.

Bryce, D., and A. Hobart (1972). The biology and identification of the larvae of the chironomidae. Entomologist's Gazette, 23, 175-258.

Charles, W. N., K. East, D. Brown, M.C. Gray, and T.D. Murray (1974). The production of larval chironomidae in the mud at Loch Leven, Kinross. Proc. R. Soc. Edinb. (B), 74, 241-258.
Deutsche Einheitsverfahren zur Wasser-, Abwasser- und Schlammuntersuchung (1975). 3. Aufl. Verlag Chemie, Weinheim.
Edmondson, W.T., and G.G. Winberg (1971). A manual on methods for the assessment of secondary productivity in freshwaters. I.B.P. Handbook 17, 258 pp.
Fischer, J. (1974). Experimentelle Beiträge zur Ökologie von Chironomus (Diptera). I. Dormanz bei Chironomus nuditarsis und Ch. plumosus. Oecologia, 16, 73-96.
Franke, C. (1978). Autökologische Untersuchungen über die Larven von Chaoborus flavicans Meigen (Nematocera) unter besonderer Berücksichtigung rhythmischer Phänomene. Dissertation Berlin.
Illies, J. (1967). Limnofauna Europaea. Gustav Fischer Verlag, Weinheim.
Jonasson, P. M. (1972). Ecology and production of the profundal benthos in relation to phytoplankton in Lake Esrom. Oikos (Suppl.), 14, 1-148.
Jonasson, P. M. (1978). Zoobenthos of lakes. Verh. Intern. Verein. Limnol.,20, 13-37.
Jonasson, P. M. and J. Kristiansen (1967). Primary and secondary production in Lake Esrom. Growth of Chironomus anthracinus in relation to seasonal cycles and dissolved oxygen. Int. Rev. Ges. Hydrobiol., 52, 163-217.
Kajak, Z., and J. Warda (1968). Feeding of benthic non-predatory chironomidae in lakes. Ann. Zool. Fenn., 5, 57-64.
Lenz, F. (1962). Die Metamorphose der Tendipedidae. In E. Lindner (Ed.), Die Fliegen der palaearktischen Region. 13c. Schweizerbarth'sche Verlagsbuchhandlung, Stuttgart.
Mason, W. T. jr. (1973). An introduction to the identification of chironomid larvae. Analytical Control Laboratory, National Environmental Research Center, US Environmental Protection Agency, Cincinnati, Ohio.
Moore, J. W. (1979). Some factors influencing the distribution, seasonal abundance and feeding of subarctic Chironomidae (Diptera). Arch. Hydrobiol., 85, 302-325.
Strickland, J. D. H., and T. R. Parsons (1968). A practical handbook of seawater analysis. Bull. Fisch. Res. Bd. Canada, 167, 1-311.

Emergence of Chironomids from Rostherne Mere, England

Catriona M. Tait Bowman

Department of Biology, University of Salford, Salford, England

ABSTRACT

The abundance of emerging chironomid adults from Rostherne Mere, a eutrophic lowland lake, was investigated by means of a Monks Wood light trap during the 1979 spring passage of migrant swifts, swallows and martins.

KEYWORDS

Chironomidae; Rostherne Mere; aerial feeding migrant birds.

INTRODUCTION

Rostherne Mere is a National Nature Reserve which has been well-known for its bird life, particularily the wildfowl, since the beginning of this century. The mere, lying in a deep glacial drift hollow is 48 hectares in area and 30 m deep and is therefore the largest and deepest of the north Cheshire meres. The Cheshire meres are part of the North West Midland meres and mosses formed during the period of the last glacial retreat.

Around most of the perimeter of the mere, the ground slopes steeply therefore there is little shallow water, a factor which severely restricts the feeding habitat for ducks and waders. The littoral zone is sandy and barren with a narrow fringe of reeds.

The deeper waters of the mere are deoxygenated for most of the year due to the deposition of faeces by the large winter gull roosts and duck floats. This phenomenon was reported by Brinkhurst and Walsh (1967) as being an instance of guanotrophy.

The purpose of this research, which is still in its infancy, is to investigate why migrant birds such as swallows (*Hirundo rustica*), swifts (*Apus apus*), house martins (*Delichon urbica*) and sand martins (*Riparia riparia*) tend to flock and feed over a nearby mere - Tatton Mere - instead of Rostherne Mere when they first arrive during the spring migration passage. Rostherne Mere is secluded and protected from casual visitors but Tatton Mere is a popular site for day-trippers and sailing enthusiasts.

After consideration of the various factors which might affect the spring distribution of these migrant birds, the availability of food seemed to be the most worthy of investigation. Swifts, swallows and martins are all insectivorous aerial feeders and can be seen skimming over the water surface in search of their prey at dawn and dusk.

Records kept for many years at Rostherne Mere show that the first migrants are expected at the end of April and therefore insect trapping began in mid-April before the first sightings had been reported.

METHODS

A Monks Wood battery operated light trap designed originally to capture medically important insects was used to sample the aerial insect fauna. The trap was operated once a week from mid-April 1979 for 12 hr overnight from dusk to dawn. The advantage of this trap is that the larger insects such as moths and beetles are excluded by a wire mesh screen. The insects are attracted to the ultra-violet light and are sucked down into the collecting bag by a small motor driven fan.

The insects were extracted from the collecting bag with a pooter and preserved in 70% alcohol before identification. Only the data relating to the Family Chironomidae will be reported in this paper. Following the advice in Pinder (1978), individual specimens were dissected and mounted on a microscope slide and identified using Pinder's (1978) key to the adult male Chironomidae. Species lists were compiled for each week's catch of chironomids.

Ekman grab samples were taken from the narrow sublittoral zone and sorted for chironomid larvae.

Water temperature and oxygen content were recorded monthly using a Mackereth temperature and oxygen metre. Water samples were taken occasionally for pH and conductivity analysis.

Meteorological data for Manchester Airport (5 miles to the east of Rostherne Mere) were obtained from the Meteorological Office at Bracknell, Berkshire. The data included daily minimum and maximum air temperatures, daily wind speeds, daily rainfall and daily hours of sunshine.

RESULTS

On the night of April 15th 1979 when the Monks Wood light trap was first operated, the minimum air temperature was 5.3°C and the surface water temperature was 8°C. No migrant birds had been sighted from the Observatory at Rostherne Mere. The catch was extremely poor as regards both species number and abundance of individuals but two species caught that night were to feature strongly in almost every catch in the succeeding weeks. These were *Polypedilum nubeculosum* Mg. and *Orthocladius glabripennis* Goet. Other species caught were *Prodiamesa olivacea* Mg., *Eukiefferiella calvescens* Edw. and *Heleniella ornaticollis* Edw. but numbers were very low.

The first sighting of migrant birds at Rostherne Mere was reported on April 23rd 1979 when 20 swallows and 5 sand martins were seen feeding low over the mere. House martins were sighted the following day. The weather was becoming colder and on the night of April 25th when the water temperature was still 8°C, the minimum overnight temperature was 4.3°C. The light trap catch was poor although *Polypedilum nubeculosum* and *Orthocladius glabripennis* still featured strongly. The emergence period of *Procladius choreus* Mg. had obviously begun as this species was also caught in the trap that night and was to appear in every succeeding catch.

The numbers of swallows and house martins increased steadily until by the end of

April over 100 swallows, 20 house martins and 15 sand martins were sighted. Swifts were not sighted at Rostherne Mere until early May when house martins had reached the peak of their spring passage population. Swallows reached peak population number in mid-May and swifts were most abundant towards the end of May. Thereafter the sightings of all 4 species became fewer and reached a plateau, so that at any time during June and July at least 20 swallows, house martins and swifts could be seen indulging in aerial acrobatics over the mere. Sand martins disappeared from the mere during June and July. Harrison and Rogers (1977) report that this species leaves the mere entirely during its breeding season.

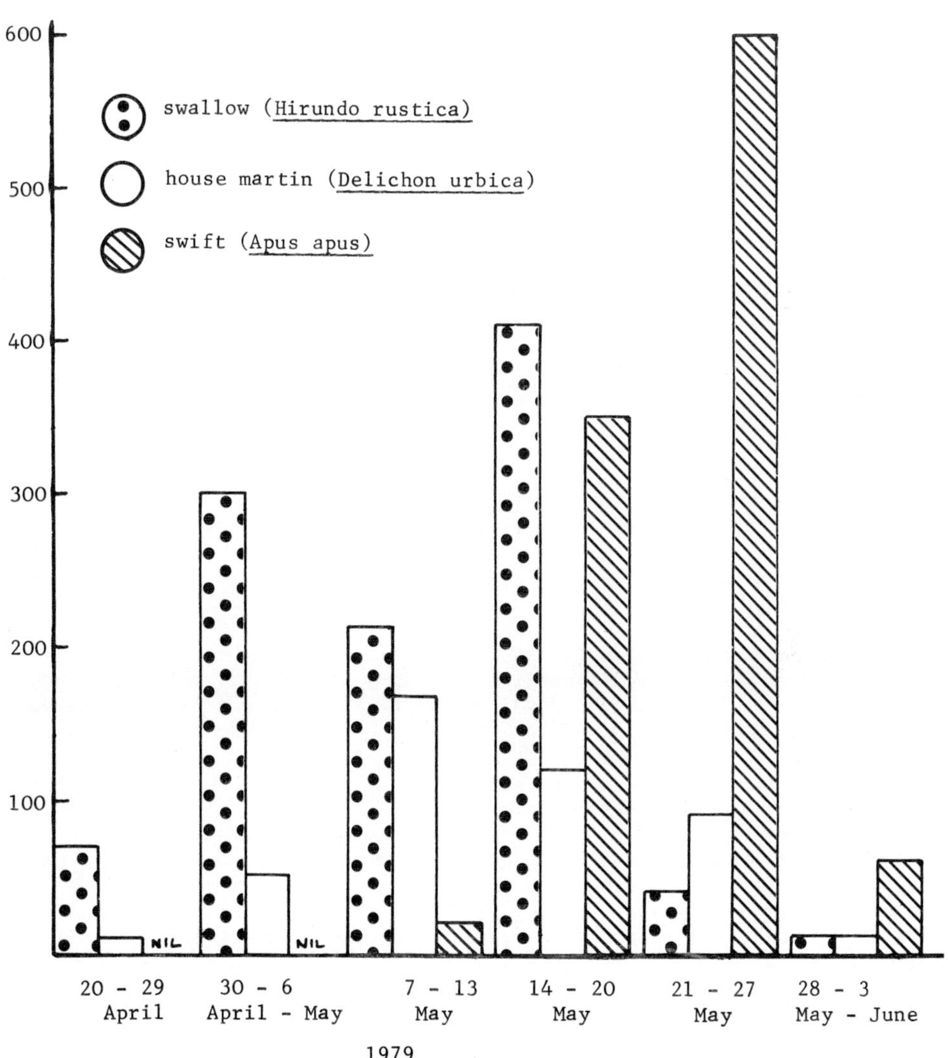

Fig. 1. Numbers of sightings of migrant birds during the 1979 spring passage.

During the peak population periods for swallows and house martins (Fig. 1) the weather was very cold. The overnight minimum temperature on May 3rd 1979 fell to -1.5°C and the catch was the lowest recorded, although *Orthocladius glabripennis* was still abundant. The only other species caught were a few *Tanytarsus heusdensis* Goet. and *Microtendipes nitidus* Mg.

Swifts reached peak population numbers (Fig. 1) at the end of May when the weather was improving. The minimum overnight temperature on May 29th was 8.8°C and the water temperature had risen to 12.3°C. This increase in water temperature is significant as low water temperatures have an inhibiting effect on pupal development and emergence of adult chironomids. The light trap catches improved and apart from *Polypedilum nubeculosum*, *Orthocladius glabripennis* and *Procladius choreus*, 3 other species caught that night were to become important components of later catches. These were *Chironomus longistylus* Goet., *Camptochironomus tentans* Fab. and *Cladotanytarsus atridorsum* Kieff. Other genera such as *Endochironomus* and *Glyptotendipes* were insignificant in number. The species which constituted the greatest biomass in this and every later catch was *Cricotopus sylvestris* Fab. but apart from a few males, all of the hundreds of individuals caught were female.

The spring passage of migrants ceased by the beginning of June and only the breeding colonies of swifts, swallows and martins remained. Harrison and Rogers (1977) state that these 3 species nest locally in the surrounding villages and farms.

The pattern of chironomid emergence which had established itself at the end of May was still evident but many new species were added to the list. By mid-June, 14 species of Chironominae, 9 species of Orthocladiinae and 3 Tanypodinae were identified. *Cricotopus sylvestris*, *Chironomus longistylus* and *Procladius choreus* were still important in terms of biomass as were *Orthocladius consobrinus* Holm., *Ablabesmyia longistyla* Fitt., *Stictochironomus pictulus* Mg., *Krenopelopia binotata* Wied., *Micropsectra atrofasciata* Kieff. and 3 *Cladotanytarsus* species.

The lake temperature in mid-June was 17.2°C at the surface and 7.5°C at 30 m. Conductivity levels were generally greater than 500 µmho/cm and the surface water was alkaline.

DISCUSSION

Rostherne Mere is a warm monomictic eutrophic lake with low hypolimnetic oxygen levels in summer. From this description, it might be expected that the substratum of the mere would be a rich muddy ooze capable of supporting a large tubiculous chironomid population as was found for 3 similar meres in Shropshire by Tait Bowman (1976).

However, due to the unique morphometry of the mere, the littoral zone is narrow and has a bare sandy substratum, colonised principally by opportunistic Corixidae. The mere bottom shelves steeply to 30 m and this profundal zone has been described by Brinkhurst and Walsh (1967) as "lifeless" due to continuous anaerobic conditions caused by faecal deposition by large roosts of gulls and ducks. The zone which is capable of supporting an invertebrate fauna is therefore necessarily narrow. The extent of this zone is to be investigated in future studies. Ekman grab samples from this area revealed a low larval *Chironomus* population (less than 100 larvae/m^2).

The chironomid assemblage in Rostherne Mere differs from the Shropshire meres assemblage described by Tait Bowman (1976) in one important respect. The chironomid populations of the meres studied by Tait Bowman were dominated by the large *Chironomus* species, principally *Chironomus anthracinus* Zett. and *Chironomus plumosus* L. whereas at Rostherne Mere the dominant species are *Orthocladius glabripennis*,

Polypedilum nubeculosum, *Cricotopus sylvestris*, *Procladius choreus* and *Cladotanytarsus* species.

The average body size of the Rostherne adult chironomid assemblage is lower than the Shropshire meres assemblage. Using wing lengths as easily obtainable data from keys such as Coe (1950) and Pinder (1978), it has been found that the average wing length of the dominant Shropshire mere *Chironomus* species is 6.5 mm, but the average wing length for the dominant Rostherne Mere species is 4.3 mm.

Waugh (1979) believes that the incorporation of insect prey into the diet of migrant birds on the basis of size is an important selection mechanism in aerial feeding. He states that swallows, swifts, sand martins and house martins select the largest prey available when feeding. These birds must consume at least their own body weight in food per day.

The relevance of this information is that the chironomid fauna at Tatton Mere (to which these birds tend to flock in early spring) is dominated by *Chironomus anthracinus* and *Chironomus plumosus* (Dr. C. Goldspink; pers. comm.) which enter their spring emergence period in April when the first migrants arrive in Britain.

It is tentatively suggested therefore that the migrant birds such as swifts, swallows and martins tend to flock and feed over Tatton Mere in preference to Rostherne Mere in early spring because of the greater availability of large insect prey.

ACKNOWLEDGEMENT

The author would like to express her gratitude to the warden at Rostherne Mere, Tom Wall, for his friendly assistance and to Bob Bowman for gallantly carrying the light trap battery. Warm thanks are also due to Miss Doreen Tinker for typing the manuscript.

REFERENCES

Brinkhurst, R.O., and B. Walsh (1967). Rostherne Mere, England, a further instance of guanotrophy. *J. Fish. Res. Bd. Canada*, *24*, 1299 - 1313.

Coe, R.L. (1950). Family Chironomidae. *Handbk. Ident. Br. Insects*, *9* (2), 121 - 206.

Harrison, R. and D.A.Rogers (1977). *The Birds of Rostherne Mere*. Nature Conservancy Council.

Pinder, L.C.V. (1978). *A key to adult males of British Chironomidae (Diptera) the non-biting midges*. *Scient. Publs. Freshwat. Biol. Ass.* No. 37.

Tait Bowman, C.M. (1976). Factors affecting the distribution and abundance of chironomids in 3 Shropshire Meres, with special reference to the larval tracheal system. Unpubl. Ph.D. thesis. University of Keele.

Waugh, D.R. (1979). The diet of sand martins during the breeding season. *Bird Study*, *26* (2), 123 - 128.

Sampling Chironomid Emergence Using Submerged Funnel Traps in a New Northern Canadian Reservoir, Southern Indian Lake, Manitoba

D. M. Rosenberg, A. P. Wiens and B. Bilyj

Freshwater Institute, Department of Fisheries and Oceans, 501 University Crescent, Winnipeg R3T 2N6, Canada

ABSTRACT

We examined sampling characteristics of submerged funnel traps which were used to study emergence of Chironomidae in a large boreal riverine reservoir. Clay, bedrock and marsh shorelines were sampled at 1.0, 2.0, 3.5 and 4.5 m depths with 4 replicate traps at each depth. No. m^{-2} emerging from the three shorelines were similar but differences among depths were significant. The most common species emerging offshore (3.5 and 4.5 m) differed from those emerging inshore (1.0 and 2.0 m). Species emerging from all three shorelines were similar offshore. Inshore, clay and bedrock shorelines were similar but differed from the marsh shoreline. A $\pm$ 30% precision of the mean no. m^{-2} emerging was obtained for most of the depths and shorelines using 12 and 16 traps respectively. Single traps collected $\frac{1}{2}$ the number of species collected by 16 traps. All of the most abundant species were caught in 2-4 traps. A minimum of 4 traps were required to interpret emergence patterns of species with one emergence peak; 16 for species with two emergence peaks. Discontinuous trapping (48 hr wk^{-1}) gave similar results to continuous trapping (168 hr wk^{-1}). Our studies suggest that an optimal sampling strategy would be to trap discontinuously and use high numbers of traps.

KEYWORDS

Chironomidae; sampling (biological); submerged funnel traps; reservoirs (water); trapping time; shorelines; depths; replicates; precision.

Production and Emergence of Chironomids in a Wet Gravel Pit

G. Titmus and Ruth M. Badcock

Dept. of Biological Sciences, University of Keele, Keele, Staffs. ST5 5BG, England

ABSTRACT

Chironomid production and emergence were monitored in a wet gravel pit in Buckinghamshire, England, during 1978. Production estimates for three stations ranged from 45 to 70 kg $ha^{-1}yr^{-1}$; these are comparable with results from oligotrophic lakes but *Chironomus* spp. accounted for over 70% of the chironomid production at each station. The emergence period was more extended than in previous years and showed a clear series of peaks as different species emerged. Production : standing crop estimates ranged between 4 to 6:1 for univoltine species. Production : emergence ratios were mainly within the range 2 to 3:1, indicating that a very large proportion (30-50%) of the annual production is exported from the lake. The importance of emerging chironomids for mallard ducklings is considered.

KEYWORDS

Chironomids; gravel pits; production; emergence; export of production; duckling feeding.

INTRODUCTION

Recently the trend towards the analysis of communities or single species in terms of their production has been more prevalent and this has lead to a greater understanding of the inter-relationships within a habitat. However, for aquatic insects one component of the production, namely the emergence, is usually not studied in any detail and although larval production and standing crop data are presented, the fate of the elaborated tissue is usually ignored. For animals other than insects this material is recycled within the ecosystem but insect emergence may result in a net export from the habitat.

The aim of this paper is to present production and emergence estimates for the four larval genera which were abundant in the benthos of the lake studied and to discuss the data, especially with reference to inter-relationships in the functioning of the ecosystem.

STUDY SITE AND METHODS

The pit chosen was one of a series of quarries along the River Ouse at Great

Linford in North Buckinghamshire. This pit was one of the oldest in the site being c. 39 years old. It is fringed on one side by a lagoon area which is slightly more recent. The pit and associated lagoon area together form a separate wildfowl reserve set aside for the study of gravel pit ecology (Titmus, 1979). Three stations were chosen within this reserve. The two stations in the lagoon area were in water c. 2m deep with little macrophyte growth on the bottom. The third station, in the main lake was in slightly deeper water (2.5-3m); no macrophytes grew on the bottom mud there.

Larvae were collected with an Ekman grab. Five replicate samples were taken from each station at fortnightly intervals from 4th April until 2nd October 1978. The samples were immediately sieved (mesh size 0.38mm) to remove the fine mineral sediment, sorted and then preserved in Carnoy's fluid. Larvae were identified using a manuscript key by Mr. P. S. Cranston (British Museum). Additional larvae of the common species were collected, killed and measurements of body length and dry weight taken to determine the coefficients of the length-weight relationship:-

$$W = a.L^b \qquad (1)$$

where W = dry weight (μg) and L = body length in mm, whilst a and b are coefficients the values of which were determined empirically. These data were then used to convert the length-frequency data, obtained from measurements of the preserved samples, into biomass and production estimates. Production was calculated by Hamilton's method (1969). Only larvae > 6mm were used in the calculations since any less than this length were not quantitatively retained within the sieve.

Adult emergence was monitored by the use of surface traps (Mundie, 1971) which were operated from 28th April until 23rd August 1978. The traps were emptied twice weekly, giving a maximum trapping period of four days between servicing. The estimates of emergence biomass were calculated from the number of adults trapped, using the dry weight data given by Potter and Learner (1974). Weights for imagines of *Polypedilum nubeculosum* (Meigen) and *Tanypus* spp were assumed to be the same as that of *Procladius choreus* (Meigen) on the basis that the body weights of the largest final instar larvae were similar.

RESULTS

The relationship between length and biomass for the common species is given in Table 1. In all except *Procladius* the value of the exponent was close to three. This is in contrast to results presented by other workers. Johnson and Brinkhurst (1971) found this parameter to be highly variable within the genus *Chironomus*. However, this variability was probably an artefact introduced by the small number of animals taken from a restricted range of body lengths with all regressions based on less than ten individuals. Similarly Mackey (1977) presented some data with the exponent markedly less than two in a number of instances. Many of these were again based on less than 20 specimens. In addition he stored his material in formalin for a few days before measuring, this is known to cause a marked loss in dry weight with the magnitude dependent upon the length of time between preservation and weighing (Dermott and Paterson, 1974).

The importance of obtaining reliable estimates of these length-weight relationships is often overlooked. However, they form a significant part of the raw data and, if erroneous, can severely bias the estimates of biomass and production.

Length-frequency histograms were constructed for each larval genus for individual sampling sites on each occasion. There was no obvious growth pattern which was sufficiently distinct to allow loss summation methods to be applied and the data from each sampling were therefore combined for each station and Hamilton's method

TABLE 1 Length-weight regression parameters for some chironomid genera

Genus	a*	b*	N*	length range	R*
Chironomus	0.55	2.91	51	4.5 - 24.0	.95
Polypedilum	0.38	3.22	33	4.0 - 10.5	.96
Procladius	3.30	2.25	29	4.0 - 12.0	.91
Tanypus	0.84	2.84	47	4.0 - 14.0	.94

*Coefficients a and b are those in equation 1, N is the number of data pairs and R the correlation coefficient.

applied. Larval abundance and biomass were fairly constant throughout the sampling period; the estimates of standing crop and production for individual species at the three stations are given in Table 2.

The pattern of adult emergence during 1978 was essentially similar at all three stations and the combined data were used to construct Fig. 1. The first emergence peak in early June was due to large numbers of *Procladius choreus*, *Tanypus punctipennis* (Meigen) and *Cricotopus sylvestris* (Fabricius). The second peak in mid-July was a combination of *Endochironomus albipennis* (Meigen) and *P. choreus*. The following peak in late July was of *Glyptotendipes glaucus* (Meigen) and *P. choreus*. The last peak was of *T. punctipennis* and *T. vilipennis* (Kieffer). The estimates of biomass for emerging chironomids during the whole period are given in Table 2.

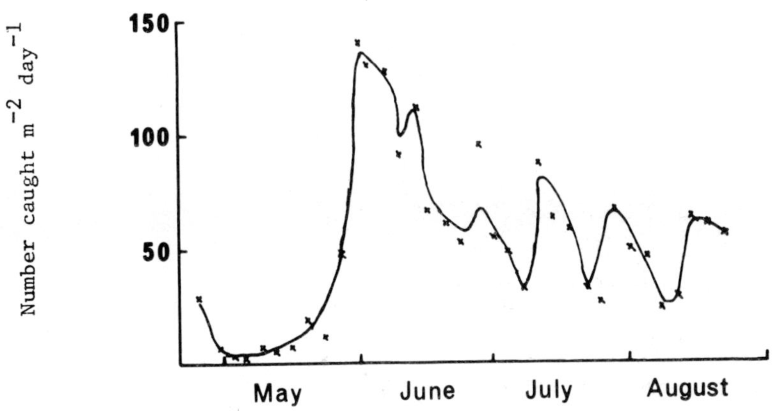

Fig. 1. Adult emergence during 1978, the points are a mean value of all three stations.

The restriction of sampling to just seven months of the year would not be expected to influence the production estimates strongly since the period studied was that in which most growth takes place. From previous work it had been found that there was little increase in body length during the period November-March. It is also to be noted that Hamilton's method is based on a loss-summation technique where summation is between successive length classes rather than over a time interval and Hamilton (1969) has shown that the introduction (or omission) of a period when the animals do not increase in length does not influence the production estimates provided negative losses are included.

TABLE 2 Production, standing crop and emergence estimates

Genus	Station	Annual Production (P) (kg $ha^{-1}yr^{-1}$)	Standing Crop (B) (kg ha^{-1})	Emergence (E) (kg ha^{-1})	P:B*	P:E*
Chironomus	1	50.10	8.77	7.14	5.7	7.0
	2	31.30	5.38	13.72	5.8	2.3
	3	42.92	7.28	17.44	5.9	2.5
Polypedilum	1	1.85	0.79	0.68	2.4	2.7
	2	2.37	0.93	1.00	2.5	2.4
Procladius	1	8.82	2.07	3.04	4.3	2.9
	2	6.14	1.40	4.72	4.4	1.3
	3	5.24	1.21	9.36	4.3	0.6
Tanypus	1	11.98	2.45	4.24	4.9	2.8
	2	9.35	1.89	7.88	4.9	1.2
	3	7.17	2.93	2.12	2.4	3.4

*The ratios P:B and P:E are calculated from the first three columns of data in this table.

The other factors which would have been expected to bias the production estimate is the omission of small larvae from the calculations. Previous studies have shown that such errors are fairly small. Kimerle and Anderson (1971) calculated that production due to first instar larvae of *Glyptotendipes barbipes* (Staeger) was only 5% of the total. Similarly Maitland and others (1972) reported that the loss of *Stictochironomus* through a 0.5 mm sieve accounted for only 3% of the annual production. It is therefore considered that the production estimates are both reasonably close to the actual production and comparable to those produced by workers in other ecosystems.

DISCUSSION

The total range of production, based on the three stations for the larval genera of chironomids abundant at the pit studied was 45 to 70 kg $ha^{-1}yr^{-1}$ which is considerably lower than results in literature for established lowland lakes but comparable to that from oligotrophic lakes. Potter and Learner (1974) reported an annual production of 210 kg $ha^{-1}yr^{-1}$ in Eglwys Nunydd and this is similar to values from other eutrophic lakes: 160 kg $ha^{-1}yr^{-1}$ was reported by Jonasson (1972) for the profundal of Lake Esrom; Maitland and Hudspith (1974) found a range from 150-420 kg $ha^{-1}yr^{-1}$ in the sandy littoral zone of Loch Levan and Charles and co-workers (1974) gave an estimate of 335 kg $ha^{-1}yr^{-1}$ for the mud area of the same lake.

The production of *Chironomus spp* accounted for 70% of the total at each station. The absolute production of this genus was similar to that at Eglwys Nunydd but these other species had higher levels of production than was seen at Linford.

The production estimates are important in indicating the major pathways through which energy flows occur in the chironomid communities. Thus, whilst *Chironomus spp* larvae were not as abundant as certain other species, because they are large, they accounted for most of the larval production within the habitat. Their *per capita* functional role is thus more important than that of other smaller species present at the same stations. Whilst the production of detritivorous *Chironomus spp* was low in comparison with certain other lakes, it is nevertheless the nutrient-poor detritus, which is the major food resource within the lake.

The production of the other abundant genera, *Polypedilum*, *Procladius*, and *Tanypus*, was much lower than that of *Chironomus* but similar to that reported by Laville (1971) for species inhabiting an oligotrophic lake in the Pyrenees.

The emergence season of imagines in 1978 was more extended than that reported for 1975/76 (Titmus, 1979). However, the pattern was one of a succession of peaks, each predominantly due to one or several species. Thus, whilst adults were present for a longer period, the actual emergence, after the initial maximum in early June, was highly variable.

The relationship between production and standing crop has been widely calculated and indeed used to calculate production in some cases. This ratio is known as the turnover ratio. Empirically derived values have indicated that the constancy of this ratio is sufficient to enable fairly accurate production estimates to be calculated from standing crop data. A more recent concept, proposed by Spier and Anderson (1974), is the use of a production to emergence ratio (P:E). They found that this was fairly constant for simuliid populations in streams where it ranged from 4 to 5:1. They also provided some data for chironomid populations where the P:E estimates ranged from 2.3 to 9.6:1. This variability may be due, in part, to the range of trap types used in the studies from which they extracted the data.

The production:standing crop ratios (P:B) calculated here fell into two distinct categories; the ratios for *Polypedilum nubeculosum* and for *Tanypus spp* at station 3 were all c. 2.5. All other values were > 4. The first group contained species where the larvae were only present for a short period during the year and only completed one generation. P:B ratios of similar magnitude for univoltine species were found by Potter and Learner (1974), who also found a ratio of c. 5 for bivoltine species which comes into the second category here.

The P:E ratio was less constant, ranging from 0.6-7.0, however, most values were between 2-3. This is again similar to the data of Potter and Learner (1974: using a figure of 8 to convert submerged trap catch to surface trap catch) which also cover a wide range (0.6-14), although most fall within the range 2-6. The higher variability of Potter and Learner's study may be due to the use of submerged traps which are more selective in species caught. The proposal of Illies (1971), that emergence is a constant proportion of production and so could be used to calculate production, is supported by our data where most values were between 2-3. However, the value of 0.6 obtained in the present study is indicative of trapping error since adult emergence cannot exceed larval production over the whole lake. Furthermore, the range of P:E ratios for the same species at different stations indicates that the ratio is partly a function of trap site.

The overall conclusion one may draw from this ratio is that, if the traps are c. 100% efficient (as indeed has been shown by McCauley (1976) for small surface emergence traps), then between 30 to 50% of the annual production is exported from the lake. This estimate is supported by a similar computation by Jonasson (1972) who reported that c. 50% of the annual production of *C. anthracinus* Zeterstedt emerged from lake Esrom and Potter and Learner (1974), who estimated emergence as c. 30% of production.

This high level of export will have obvious implications in the functioning of the ecosystem in that the benthic production is split into two categories

i) that consumed within the lake

ii) that lost to other ecosystems

In management terms, the use of crude production estimates to calculate stocking level for fish should be modified to take this inevitable export into account. However, certain fish may be able to take a higher proportion of the production so the exact level of the P:E ratio may vary. For example, in the lake studied, the only abundant fish was the bream (*Albramus albramus*) which is a benthic feeder; predation of ascending pupae in the water column and at the surface by fish such as trout would undoubtedly raise the P:E ratio.

The implications of the low P:E ratio are that the high biomass leaving the lake is available for consumption by other predators. Some such as duckling chicks feed on emerging flies on the water surface and indeed rely heavily upon this food source (Street, 1977). Chura (1961) has shown that chironomids normally constitute c. 60% of the diet of 0-6 day old mallard and that their chironomid food is made up entirely of imagines and pupae both of which are caught at the water's surface. In the absence of enough emerging chironomids mallard chicks may die since the ducklings rely upon these insects to provide a diet of suitable quality to ensure growth; a low-protein vegetarian diet alone is not adequate (Street, 1978). So production of chironomids is available in approximately equal amounts to predators within the water body and to animals, such as ducks, living on or near the lake.

The high level of export of production indicates that the lake ecosystem is not as closed as was once thought, acting solely as an energy and mineral sink. Its functional relationship with other adjacent ecosystems, with exchanges occurring at different trophic levels, deserves further investigation.

ACKNOWLEDGEMENT

The authors thank Mr. M. Street and the Game Conservancy for facilities at Great Linford and also for help with field work; they are grateful to the National Federation of Anglers and the University of Keele for financial assistance with travel costs and to the University of Keele for the research studentship supporting G.T.

REFERENCES

Charles, W. N., and others (1974). Production studies of the larvae of four species of Chironomidae in the mud at Loch Levan in Scotland in 1970-71. *Ent. Tidskr.*, 95, suppl. 34-41.

Chura, N. J. (1961). Food availability and preferences of juvenile mallard. *Trans. 26th N. Amer. Wildl. Conf.*, 2, 121-134.

Dermott, R. M., and C. G. Patterson (1974). Determining dry weight and percentage dry matter of chironomid larvae. *Can. J. Zool.*, 52, 1234-1250.

Hamilton, A. L. (1969). On estimating annual production. *Limnol. Oceanogr.*, 14, 771-782.

Illies, J. (1971). Emergenz 1969 im Breitenbach. *Arch Hydrobiol.* 69, 14-59.

Johnson, M. G., and R. O. Brinkhurst (1971). Production of benthic macro-invertebrates in the Bay of Quinte and Lake Ontario. *J. Fish. Res. Bd., Canada*, 28, 1699-1714.

Jonasson, P. M. (1972). Ecology and production of the profundal benthos in relation to phytoplankton in Lake Esrom. *Oikos Suppl.*, 14, 1-148.

Kimerle, R. A., and N. H. Anderson (1971). Production and bioenergetic role of the midge *Glyptotendipes barbipes* (Staeger) in a waste stabilisation lagoon. *Limnol. Oceanogr.*, 16, 646-659.

Laville, H. (1975). Recherches sur les Chironomides (Diptera) lacustres du Massil de Neouvielle (Hautes-Pyrenees). *Annls. Limnol.*, 7, 335-414.

McCauley, V. J. E. (1976). Efficiency of a trap for catching and retaining insects emerging from standing water. *Oikos*, 27, 339-348.

Mackey, A. P. (1977). Growth and development of larval Chironomidae. *Oikos*, 28, 270-275.

Maitland, P. S., and others (1972). Preliminary research on the production of Chironomidae in Loch Levan, Scotland. *Proc. IBP-UNESCO Symposium, Kazimierz Dolny, Poland*, 795-812.

Maitland, P. S., and P. M. C. Hudspith (1974). The zoobenthos of Loch Levan, Kinross, and estimates of its production in the sandy littoral area in 1970 and 1971. *Proc. R. Soc. Edinb.*, 74, 219-239.

Mundie, J. H. (1971). Techniques for emerging aquatic insects. In W. T. Edmonson and G. G. Winberg (Eds.), *A manual for the assessment of secondary productivity in fresh waters* Blackwell Pubs., London. pp. 80-93.

Potter, D. W. B., and M. A. Learner (1974). A study of the benthic macroinvertebrates of a shallow eutrophic reservoir in South Wales with emphasis on the Chironomidae (Diptera); their life histories and production. *Arch. Hydrobiol.*, 74, 186-226.

Spier, J. A., and N. H. Anderson (1974). Use of emergence data for estimating annual productivity of aquatic insects. *Limnol. Oceanogr.*, 19, 154-156.

Street, M. S. (1977). The food of Mallard ducklings (*Anas platyrhynchos* L.) in a wet gravel quarry, and its relation to duckling survival. *Wildfowl*, 28, 113-125.

Street, M. S. (1978). The role of insects in the diet of Mallard ducklings - an experimental approach. *Wildfowl*, 29, 93-100.

Titmus, G. (1979). The emergence of midges (Diptera: Chironomidae) from a wet gravel pit. *Freshw. Biol.*, 9, 165-179.

Emergence Phenologies of Some Arctic Alaskan Chironomidae

Malcolm G. Butler

Division of Biological Sciences, University of Michigan, Ann Arbor, Michigan, U.S.A.

ABSTRACT

Adult chironomids emerging from tundra ponds near Barrow, Alaska (72°N) were trapped quantitatively through three complete seasons. All major species showed highly synchronous emergence patterns, and protandry was observed in most cases. Each species occupied a consistent position within the overall emergence season. Species specific timing may act as a reproductive isolating mechanism for congeneric species, and may reflect other biotic interactions within this community.

KEYWORDS

Chironomidae; emergence phenologies; tundra ponds; Alaska; synchrony; protandry; reproductive isolation.

INTRODUCTION

Adult emergence timing is an important aspect of aquatic insect life-histories, especially for chironomids and other taxa with short-lived adults. Physical and biotic selective pressures may act upon emergence phenologies to maximize mating success and provide optimal timing for oviposition.

In this study I consider chironomid emergence from several ponds on the coastal tundra of arctic Alaska near Barrow (72°N). Temporal patterns observed over three years are described for 18 abundant species, and provide data on two aspects of emergence phenologies: *synchrony* of individuals within populations, and *seasonal timing* of different species. I compare these results to those from two other arctic study sites, Hazen Camp ponds at 82°N (Danks and Oliver 1972, Oliver 1968) and Char Lake at 75°N (Welch 1973,1976), and suggest some biotic and physical selective pressures which may contribute to these patterns.

The ponds studied occur in low-centered ice wedge polygons and are similar to thousands of such habitats along the Beaufort Sea coast. These ponds were the site of the U.S. I.B.P. Tundra Biome aquatic studies, and their limnology is described in Stanley (1976) and Hobbie (in press). Ponds used for this study are roughly 30 m square and do not exceed 35 cm depth. They are frozen solid about 9 months of the year, and are thoroughly wind-mixed throughout the summer. Emergent *Carex aquatilis* stands extend into the ponds from all edges, but more than half of the total pond area is open water over a fine black peat sediment. Further details of chironomid biology in these ponds will be found in Butler (1979). All species studied had multi-year life cycles (2-7 years) with a single cohort emerging each summer. There is considerable variation in species composition between ponds, but marked year-to-year changes and the close proximity of ponds suggest that the regional tundra pond community is the basis for long term biological interactions.

METHODS

In 1976 and 1977, circular 0.05 m^2 emergence traps made of clear polycarbonate plastic were used in three ponds. These traps rested on the sediment surface, and were lifted from the water on a 0.5mm mesh screen, retaining pupal exuviae and pupae which had failed to emerge as well as adults. No temperature or dissolved oxygen differences were detected between the inside and outside of the traps, even on the warmest days. Three traps were maintained continuously in the emergent *Carex* and three in the open water of Ponds E, J, and G in 1976, and were emptied every second day. In 1977 the emergent *Carex* in Ponds E and J, and the open water in Ponds E and G were sampled with three traps, while the open water of Pond J contained nine traps. All traps in Pond J were emptied daily in 1977, and those in Ponds E and G every second day. Emergence collections from Ponds E and J during 1975 were discontinuous, and these data are referred to only qualitatively here.

Daily maximum and minimum temperatures at the sediment surface were recorded to the nearest 0.5°C in four ponds (E,J,G, and D) through the 1977 emergence season.

Pupae of five species were reared in the laboratory at 10°C under constant fluorescent lighting. Each species was collected from a single pond prior to the start of its emergence. Rearing beakers were checked every 6 hr to record the number of each sex emerging within that time period.

RESULTS

The day on which a species' emergence exceeded 50% of the season's total is referred to as its EM_{50}. *Trichotanypus alaskensis* is the first abundant species to emerge in the region every year, and *Tanytarsus inaequalis* is the last. When both species emerge from all ponds, as in 1976, the length of the season between their EM_{50}s varies little (Table 1). Year-to-year differences in emergence season length occur, especially when either of these species is absent, but the bulk of the emergence occurs within 3-4 weeks.

TABLE 1 Length of Emergence Seasons in 1975-1977

	Pond	Earliest sp.	Date of EM_{50}	Latest sp.	Date of EM_{50}	Length of Season (Days)
1975	E	*T. alaskensis*	7-vii	*C. pilicornis*	22-vii	16
	J	"	7-vii	*T. inaequalis*	3-viii	28
1976	E	"	1-vii	"	19-vii	19
	J	"	3-vii	"	20-vii	18
	G	"	6-vii	"	23-vii	18
1977	E	"	23-vi	*C. pilicornis*	6-vii	14
	J	"	23-vi	*T. inaequalis*	16-vii	24
	G	*T. gregarius*-gr. sp.2	30-vi	"	16-vii	17

Synchrony

Temporal distributions of the ten most abundant species in Pond J during 1977 are shown in Fig. 1. All species are quite synchronous, and each occupies only a fraction of the total 37 day season. There are two apparent exceptions. Chironomids keying to *Chironomus pilicornis* emerged in two discrete periods in most ponds all three years. The average dates of EM_{50} for these two groups differed by 9-10 days each year. Adult life spans are probably less than one week, and with highly synchronous emergence, the two populations are effectively reproductively isolated. Slight differences suggest that they may actually be two sibling species. Emergence of the last species, *T. inaequalis,* shows slight bimodality and a similar pattern ocurred in Pond J in 1976. In both years the abdomens of over 90% of the later individuals were filled with large parasitic nematodes. I observed this infestation in other ponds with large populations of *T. inaequalis,* and it always resulted in a greatly protracted emergence period.

Protandry

Many of the histograms in Fig. 1 suggest a tendency for male emergence to peak earlier than female emergence. Table 2 lists the EM_{50} for both males and females of these species based on daily trapping in Pond J in 1977.

TABLE 2 EM_{50}s for Males and Females

Species	Field Data* ♂	Field Data* ♀	Lab Data* ♂	Lab Data* ♀
Trichotanypus alaskensis	2 (20)	2 (17)	18 (47)	36 (45)
Procladius prolongatus	4 (7)	4 (15)	42 (34)	60 (33)
P. vesus	6 (43)	6 (37)		
Derotanypus alaskensis	-	-	42 (28)	108 (37)
Tanytarsus gregarius-gr.sp. 2	3 (64)	4 (69)		
T. inaequalis	2 (19)	4 (41)		
Paratanytarsus penicillatus	5(200)	6(235)	24 (73)	30 (71)
Constempellina sp.	3 (31)	3 (43)		
Cladotanytarsus sp.	1 (7)	2 (19)		
Chironomus pilicornis-late	3 (36)	4 (27)	24 (15)	24 (9)
Cricotopus tibialis	2 (14)	4 (5)		

*Field data in days, lab data in hours, total numbers collected in parentheses.

In 6 of 10 cases the male EM_{50} preceeded the female by 1-2 days. Table 2 also shows the results from laboratory rearing of pupae. In 4 out of 5 species male emergence peaked during an earlier interval than female. Protandry which could not be detected for *T. alaskensis* or *P. prolongatus* from field data was evident in the laboratory rearings.

Timing of Emergence Periods

Species tend to emerge in the same general sequence each year in all ponds. The actual dates of emergence vary markedly from year to year, and to a lesser degree from pond to pond. Danks and Oliver (1972) and Welch (1973) concluded that temperatures during prepupal and pupal development determine emergence timing in arctic pond and lake chironomids. Annual variation in emergence at Barrow suggests that the thermal environment determines timing in these ponds as well. Ponds thawed in late June in 1975, in mid-June in 1976, and early in June in 1977. *T. alaskensis* emerged latest in 1975 and earliest in 1977 (Table 1), and set the pattern for year-to-year differences in the other species. Variation in emergence timing between

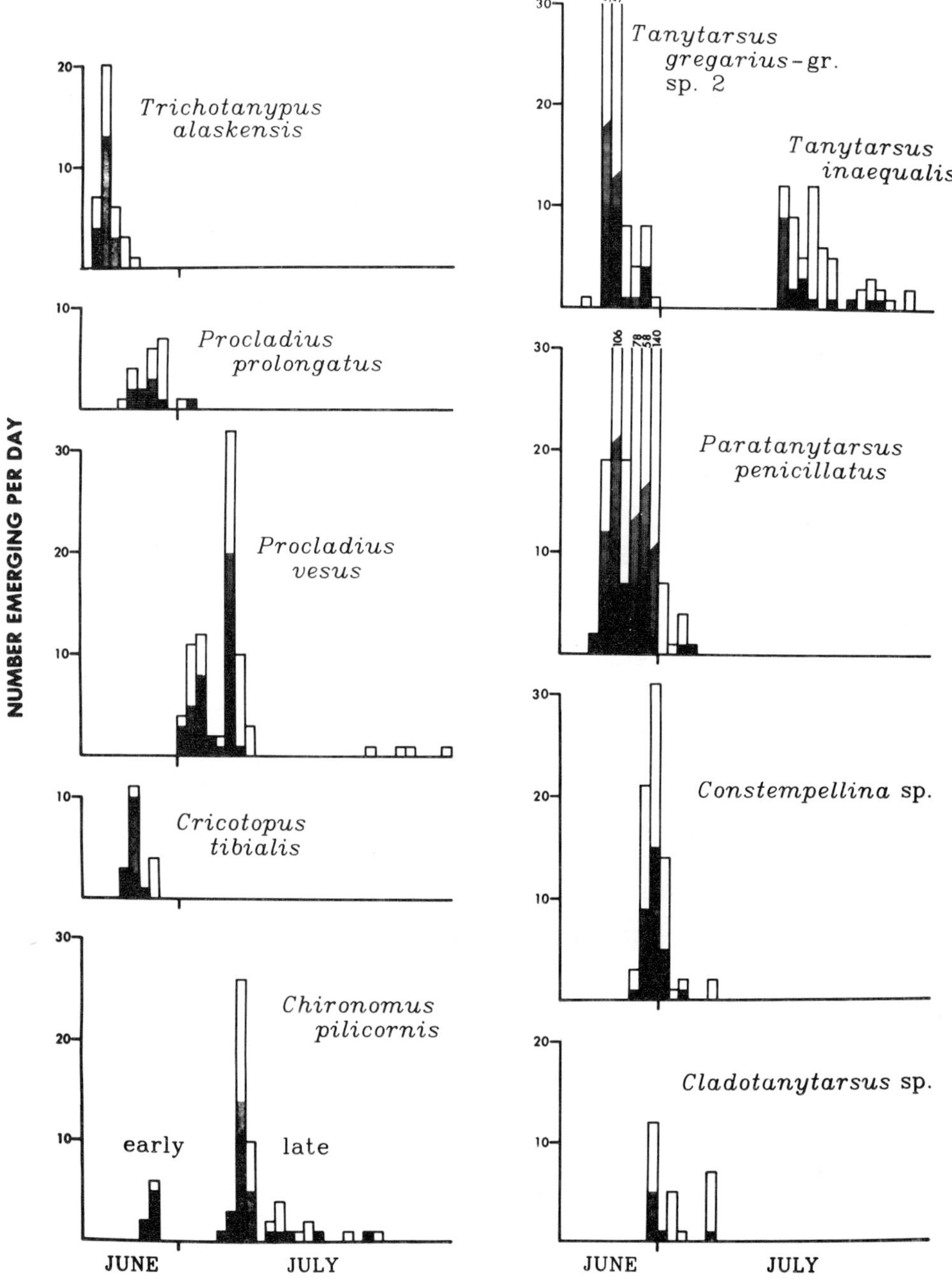

Fig. 1. Emergence of 11 species from Pond J, 1977. Shading indicates proportion males.

ponds can also be attributed to rates of thaw, but not to temperature differences once the ice is gone. Pond G is about 5cm deeper than Ponds E or J and more ice must melt before larvae are released from the frozen sediments. Emergence of most species in Pond G began and peaked several days later than in Ponds E and J all three years. Once the ice has melted and the dark sediments are exposed the ponds can warm over 10° during one sunny day, but may lose as much heat at night when the sun is low. Figure 2 shows the course of maximum and minimum daily temperatures in Pond J about 2 weeks after the 1977 thaw through the end of the emergence season. Temperatures in three other ponds did not deviate more than 1°C from these values, and no consistent differences existed between ponds. Oliver (1968) suggested relationships between seasonally increasing pond temperatures and emergence timing for Hazen Camp chironomids. The diel fluctuations in Barrow pond temperatures preclude such a relationship, and emergence timing appears to be controlled by the accumulation of a species-specific heat sum.

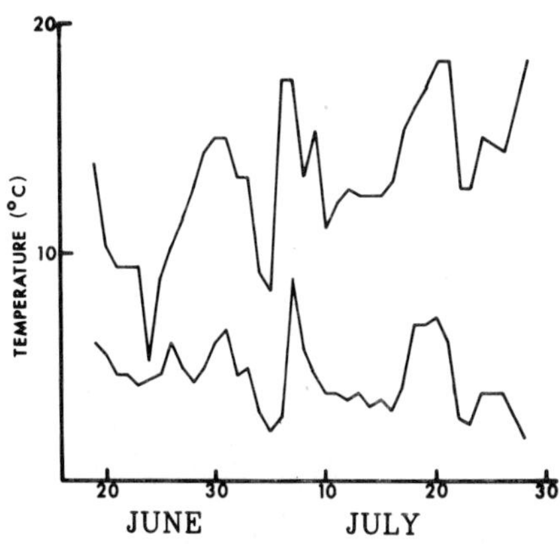

Fig. 2. Maximum and minimum temperatures in Pond J 1977.

In Table 3 the 18 most abundant species are ranked according to their position within the emergence season. To correct for year and pond variance, I standardized the emergence date of each population to the EM_{50} for *T. alaskensis*. Average positions of EM_{50} for the species are indicated, based on up to 6 estimates for each. Although many species' emergences peak at about the same time, there is a consistent sequence of species appearing in each pond. Seven species from Pond G are clustered around day 9. This may result from the late thaw of this pond in 1976. *T. alaskensis* larvae are found among the emergent sedges and can pupate and develop as soon as moats form. When the ice finally leaves Pond G and the remaining species are released from the frozen sediments, water temperatures in all ponds are higher due to warmer air and greater insolation later in the season. Pond G populations then develop under warmer conditions. Different heat-sum thresholds may be obscured in samples taken at 2-day intervals, if development is faster than occurred in the earlier melting ponds.

DISCUSSION

Synchronous emergence appears to be characteristic of arctic chironomids. Data given by Oliver (1968) shows that five Hazen Camp pond species reach EM_{75} in 7 days, the maximum value obtained in this study. Welch (1973) also reports "highly synchronized" emergence for Char Lake chironomids, although his data indicate EM_{75} values ranging from 10-30 days. Physiological mechanisms for synchronization in the arctic must be especially effective, for cohorts may have several years to diverge in growth and development (Oliver 1968, Welch 1976). Danks and Oliver (1972) have

TABLE 3 Day of 50% Emergence for 18 Species from Ponds E, J, and G in 1976 and 1977

SPECIES	-2	-1	0	1	2	3	4	5	6	7	8	9	10	11	12	13	14	15	16	17	18	19	20	21	22	23	24
	DAY OF SEASON*																										
Derotanypus aclines	_J_		* EJ		_E_																						
Trichotanypus alaskensis				E * J _EJG_																							
Cricotopus tibialis						_J_	* _E_J	E																			
Tanytarsus gregarius-gr. sp. 2					_E_	_J_	* EJG				_G_																
Chironomus pilicornis- early						_J_	EG	*	J			_G_															
Procladius prolongatus						_J_	G	* _E_E	J			_G_															
Paratanytarsus penicillatus							_JG_	_E_	* EJ			_G_															
Derotanypus alaskensis							E	_E_		* J	_J_	_G_															
Stictochironomus sp.								_J_	E	* J_E_		_G_															
Constempellina sp.							G		_E_	*	E_J_J	_G_															
Psectrocladius psilopterus-gr. spp.							E	_E_			*	_G_	J			_J_											
Cladotanytarsus sp.									G				J	*		E_J_	_G_										
Procladius vesus													EG		* _EJ_		J										
Dicrotendipes lobiger													J	_E_	* _J_		E										
Cricotopus nr. _perniger_																_E_		* _J_	E								
Chironomus pilicornis- late																	EGJ	* _EJG_									
Cricotopus sp. 3																					_J_	* _E_					
Tanytarsus inaequalis																					_JG_	_E_	E	* G			J

* letters in _italics_ are ponds in 1976, others 1977; * indicates mean for each species.

suggested that high arctic pond species are largely "absolute spring species" in which a final winter diapause synchronizes development of mature prepupal larvae, and emergence follows without further feeding or growth. Char Lake chironomids lack a winter diapause (Welch 1976) and are less synchronous than pond species. Not all Barrow species use this mechanism. *T. inaequalis* molts to the fourth instar after the thaw of its second year, and larvae must feed and grow during the summer in which they will emerge. Emergence is just as synchronous for this species as for earlier emergers, many of which are absolute spring species. There is a continuum of life history types in the Barrow community and this is reflected in the continuous sequence of emergence times. Protandry probably occurs in all these species, and the slight timing differences reflect differing selection on males and females. Emergence synchrony may result from natural selection for species as well as sexes to emerge at very precise times.

Barrow is unique among these three arctic sites in that species' emergence periods are staggered within ponds, and the pond environments are uniform enough to prevent broad seasonal overlap of species. At Hazen Camp, emergence of species may vary between ponds by weeks, and adults may be present in the area most of the summer (Danks and Oliver 1972). The Barrow chironomid community has much higher species richness (at least 18 abundant pond species), as well as many congeneric species. Distinct emergence times may serve as reproductive isolating mechanisms for many closely related species. The differences in average EM_{50} for 6 congeneric pairs range from 7 to 17 days, enough to prevent extensive co-occurence of the short-lived adults. The mating behavior of many Barrow species suggests another possible source of selection for life histories with divergent emergence times. Wind is a dominant feature of the exposed coastal tundra and this limits aerial swarming to the larger species. Many smaller species swarm and mate on the pond surface. Such "pelagic swarming" has been observed by Lindeberg (1974) on a Lapland lake, and is common in arctic Alaska (personal observation, S. Mozley personal communication). Males skate on the pond surface seeking mates, and are frequently observed grasping conspecific males and even members of other subfamilies. Time spent interacting with inappropriate individuals may decrease the chance of successful mating for both sexes. When the sequence of surface-swarming species (*T. alaskensis*, all Tanytarsini, *C. nr. perniger*) is considered alone, EM_{50} are separated by 3.2, 1.5, 1.5, 3.4, 4.1, and 5.1 days. Poole and Rathcke (1979), in a discussion of flowering phenologies, have warned against interpreting such patterns as resulting from natural selection acting to minimize competition unless a statistically uniform timing distribution can be shown. This might not be expected if other selective pressures act on emergence timing. The total emergence season at Barrow is restricted to the first half of the summer, and Myers and Pitelka (1979) have attributed this to variability in air temperature in late July and August. The degree of segregation required by two species will vary with their taxonomic relationship and behavioral similarities. There may be an equilibrium between selection for optimal weather conditions and maximal avoidance of potential biotic interference. I have observed many of the Barrow species at Prudhoe Bay (350 km east of Barrow) where they appear to show the same general sequence of emergence. Danks and Oliver (1972) suggest that the Canadian high arctic chironomid community consists of southern species with life-histories preadapted to arctic conditions. The coastal plain of northern Alaska was not glaciated, and its rich chironomid community may be highly adapted not only to the physical environment but to its own biotic environment as well.

ACKNOWLEDGEMENTS

This research was funded by the U.S. Energy Research and Development Administration. I am indebted to J. Hobbie and S. Mozley for support and encouragement. S. Roback identified the Tanypodinae, and K. Keljo assisted with the emergence collections.

REFERENCES

Butler, M. G. (1979). Population ecology of some arctic Alaskan Chironomidae. Ph.D. thesis, Univ. Michigan.

Danks, H. V., and D. R. Oliver (1972). Seasonal emergence of some high arctic Chironomidae (Diptera). *Can. Ent.*, 104, 661-686.

Hobbie, J. E. (Ed.) (In press). *Limnology of Tundra Ponds at Barrow, Alaska*. Dowden, Hutchinson, and Ross.

Lindeberg, B. (1974). Parthenogenetic and normal populations of *Abiskomyia virgo*. *Ent. Tidskr.*, 95, 157-161.

Myers, J. P., and F. A. Pitelka. (1979). Variations in summer temperature patterns near Barrow, Alaska: analysis and ecological interpretation. *Arct. Alp. Res.*, 11, 131-144.

Oliver, D. R. (1968). Adaptations of Arctic Cironomidae. *Ann. Zool. Fenn.*, 5, 111-118.

Poole, R. W., and B. J. Rathcke (1979). Regularity, randomness, and aggregation in flowering plant phenologies. *Science*, 203, 470-471.

Welch, H. E. (1973). Emergence of Chironomidae (Diptera) from Char Lake, Resolute, Northwest Territories. *Can. J. Zool.*, 51, 1113-1123.

Welch, H. E. (1976). Ecology of Chironomidae (Diptera) in a polar lake. *J. Fish. Res. Board Can.*, 33, 227-247.

Stanley, D. W. (1976). Productivity of epipelic algae in tundra ponds and a lake near Barrow, Alaska. *Ecology*, 57, 1015-1024.

Aestivating Chironomid Larvae Associated with Vernal Pools

Gail Grodhaus

Vector Biology and Control Section, California Department of Health Services, 2151 Berkeley Way, Berkeley, California 94704, U.S.A.

ABSTRACT

In northern California, vernal pools exist for 3-6 months during the winter and spring. Dry soil taken from 3 vernal pool sites in the summer or autumn was found to contain aestivating chironomid larvae in cocoons. Specimens, including some that were reared to the adult stage, were identified as *Hydrobaenus pilipes* (Malloch), *Hydrobaenus* sp., *Paratanytarsus* sp., *Calopsectra* sp., *Tribelos atrum* (Townes), *Tribelos* sp., *Phaenopsectra pilicellata* Grodhaus, and *Wirthiella* sp. Aestivating larvae were 2nd instars in some species and 2nd and 3rd instars in others. Observations of the larvae at various stages of life indicate that at least some of the species are in an obligatory diapause while they aestivate.

KEY WORDS

Hydrobaenus; *Paratanytarsus*; *Calopsectra*; *Tribelos*; *Phaenopsectra*; *Wirthiella* drought resistance; diapause; cocoons.

INTRODUCTION

This study was an outcome of a survey of vernal pool sites in northern California, which revealed 3 localities where larval Chironomidae could be extracted from soil during the dry season. I shall present a summary of observations of 8 species encountered at these sites. The paper will be concerned mainly with the ability of the species to withstand drying of the habitat, the type of dormancy exhibited by the larvae, and the role of the cocoons that they construct. It will be shown, apparently for the first time, that drought resistance and diapause occur in the same species of chironomids.

Studies of drought-resistant chironomids from other parts of the world have dealt with the amount of water lost by the larvae and their metabolism during the dry state (Hinton, 1960; Jones, 1975). Diapause was not mentioned as part of the life history of these species.

Previous work with diapause in the Chironomidae is mainly concerned with overwintering of species that inhabit permanent water. Summer diapause or aestivation has been mentioned a few times (Hudson, 1971; Mozley, 1970; Saether, 1976) but not in connection with drought resistance.

A preliminary report of drought resistance in 2 of the vernal pool species (Grodhaus, 1976) mentioned cocoons briefly. There are additional references to cocoons or cocoon-like structures among species that survive drought (Danks, 1971; Danks and Jones, 1978; Edward, 1968), but these authors also treat the subject briefly.

COLLECTION SITES

Specimens were collected from vernal pool sites at 3 locations: Murphy Well, Siskiyou County (elevation 1502 m); Redding, Shasta Co. (elevation 170 m); Sears Point, Sonoma Co. (sea level). The source of water is rain and snow at Murphy Well and rain at the other locations. The pools form during the winter and ordinarily last for 3-6 months. During periods of exceptional drought, the sites may remain dry for several years at a time. The pools, of which several exist at each location, cover ca 50 to 200 m^2 and reach ca 0.5 m in depth. The previously inundated land supports an abundance of annual grasses and usually a sparse to moderate growth of *Eleocharis* or *Juncus*. During summer and autumn, the soil becomes very hard and shows no visible moisture.

METHODS AND MATERIALS

Samples were usually taken with a shovel. Dry or wet soil was taken to a depth of 20 cm. Most of the samples were collected during the dry season. No method was devised to remove larvae from dry soil without first wetting it. The simplest method of processing dry material was to put it into a pan of water and wait to see if larvae would appear (the "macroscopic method"). Cocoons would be missed by this method. To extract larvae in cocoons, soil in quantities of 100 cc or less was mixed with water; washed through a series of sieves, mesh sizes 18, 35, and 60 (U.S. Standard system); and examined under a dissecting microscope (the "microscopic method"). The search was done quickly so as to minimize the chances of larvae becoming activated and leaving their cocoons. Many objects, including chironomid cocoons, tend to float while they are becoming hydrated, so a floatation-separation technique would not have been useful.

Larvae extracted from soil were isolated in dishes of water to determine if they were alive. A larva was considered to be alive if it emerged actively from the cocoon, or if it moved within 48 hrs after being freed by opening the cocoon with forceps. Larvae were categorized as fully active if they crawled or swam, or as semiactive if they demonstrated movements of lesser coordination, such as simple contractions of parts of the body. Larvae that did not move within 48 hrs invariably had begun to decay by that time, indicating that they had been dead or injured when the cocoons were openened.

Specimens were also collected during the wet season and extracted from mud in a manner similar to that described above. Some larvae of *Hydrobaenus* sp., *T. atrum*, and *Wirthiella* sp. were obtained from eggs deposited by field-collected females.

Larvae kept for rearing or observation were maintained individually, in vials, or in groups, in pans. They were fed a mixture of chopped *Eleocharis* and Tetramin tropical fish food.

Simple experiments were performed on semiactive larvae or larvae that seemed not to be developing. They were put into a refrigerator for 6-8 weeks to determine if their activity state would be altered. While in the refrigerator, the specimens were in the dark and exposed to a temperature range of 1.0-4.0 °C.

Active larvae or those in cocoons were tested for their ability to recover from artificial drought. These specimens were put into vials or dishes along with a small amount of substrate and left to dry.

RESULTS

For all 8 species I was able to extract living larvae from samples taken during the dry season and to associate the species with their cocoons. Except for *Paratanytarsus* sp. and *Calopsectra* sp., examples of adults of each species were reared from dry-soil collections. Early instar larvae that were not reared were identified by comparing them with exuviae of reared ones. I attempted to minimize identification errors by replicating rearing experiments throughout the study. Several of the species constructed cocoons in the laboratory, which helped to confirm the observations of cocoons extracted from dry soil.

The information presented below was compiled from many individual observations and from the literature. Observations were fragmentary for some species, due to the scarcity of specimens. Table 1 is a summary of the results of the examination of the cocoons extracted by the microscopic method. It cannot be ruled out that additional instars and other activity characteristics will be recorded in the future. Information on the survival of laboratory-dried larvae, presented under the individual species, was included only if specimens lived longer than a few days under the experimental conditions.

TABLE 1 Stage of Development and Activity State of Aestivating Chironomidae Removed from Cocoons*

Species	Larval instar		Activity state**	
	2nd	3rd	Semiactive	Active
Hydrobaenus pilipes	+		+	+
Hydrobaenus sp.	+		+	+
Paratanytarsus sp.	+	+		+
Calopsectra sp.	+?	+?		+
Tribelos atrum	+	+		+
Tribelos sp.	+	+		+
Phaenopsectra pilicellata	+	+	+	+
Wirthiella sp.	+	+		+

*From observation of larvae collected when the habitat was dry, but subsequently immersed in water and treated for various periods in the refrigerator.

**Active--able to swim or crawl. Semiactive--made simple contraction of parts of the body.

Hydrobaenus pilipes (Malloch)

According to Saether (1976) this species has a Holarctic distribution and is associated with winter and spring pools and other habitats. The seasonal occurrence of H. pilipes was studied in Europe by Mozley (1970), who suggested that this species (under the synonym Trissocladius grandis) might aestivate as eggs or larvae. Hudson (1971), who studied a North American population, found that 2nd instars did indeed aestivate.

Identification of this species in the present study was based on adults reared from soil samples collected at Murphy Well. H. pilipes has not been reported from any other locality in California.

Cocoons of this species (Fig. 1) are occupied by 2nd instars folded into a tight "S". Undoubtedly, the "canopy-like" structures described by Hudson (1971) are what are called cocoons in the present paper. They are spheroidal, with debris adhering to the surface but apparently without soil particles incorporated into the cocoon wall. The wall is rather transparent. The color of the greyish yellow larva is imparted to the structure.

Two samples of soil yielded active larvae that proceeded to complete their metamorphosis. One of these was a sample collected in the winter and moist from a recent rain. The other sample consisted of dry soil from an autumn collection, which had been immersed in water and chilled in the refrigerator. I was unable to duplicate these results with dry soil collected on other occasions. Many larvae were extracted from unrefrigerated soil samples. These larvae remained in their cocoons for many days after immersion, and when they were taken from the cocoons they demonstrated only feeble contractions of the body. Such semiactive larvae could be induced into full activity by treatment in the refrigerator while inside or out of their cocoons. In most cases, however, chilling did not stimulate larvae to exit on their own even if they had regained the capability of normal mobility.

Collections made in the wet season yielded larvae that were already in cocoons before the pools had become dry. Such larvae were kept in water in the laboratory for more than a year, during which they remained alive but did not exit from their cocoons. Hudson (1971) found that larvae hatched from eggs in the laboratory underwent a diapause as 2nd instars. He noted that the diapause terminated when the temperature was reduced from 23 °C to 3 °C and the day length was reduced from 15.5 hr to 10.5 hr.

Cocoons from the pools at Murphy Well were placed, with ca 5 mm of substrate, in petri dishes and allowed to dry. The encased larvae were found to be alive when the material was flooded with water after a year of storage in the laboratory. These larvae were in the semiactive state.

Hydrobaenus sp.

Specimens of this apparently undescribed species have been reared from soil collected at Sears Point. Larvae extracted from dry soil were 2nd instars in cocoons resembling those of H. pilipes. Specimens from early summer collections were found to be semiactive when removed from cocoons. Larvae from eggs that hatched in the laboratory reached the 2nd instar and proceeded to build cocoons.

Paratanytarsus sp.

Dry soil taken from Murphy Well at the end of the dry season yielded 2 Paratanytarsus

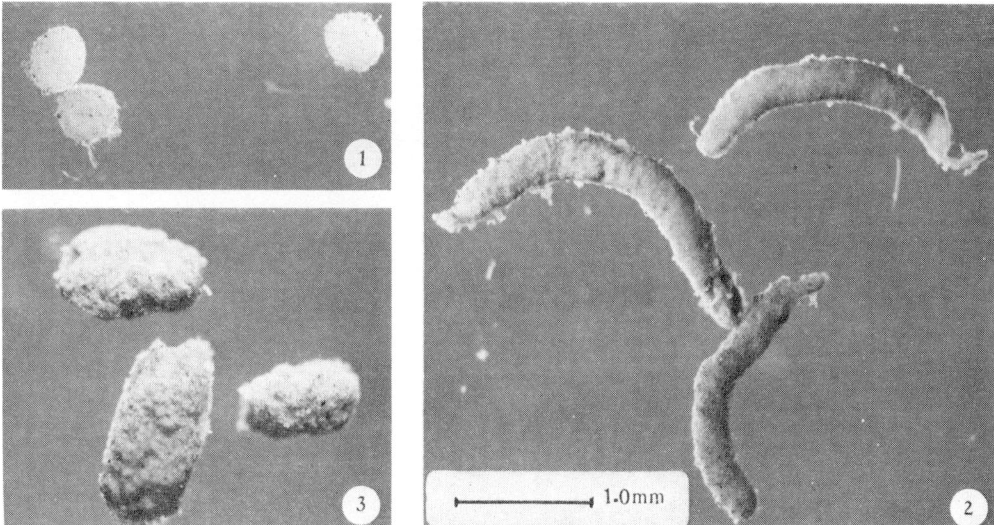

Figs. 1-3. Cocoons of aestivating Chironomidae. 1, Hydrobaenus pilipes; 2, Tribelos atrum; 3, Phaenopsectra pilicellata. Magnification is the same in each figure.

larvae. One of these, a 3rd instar when detected by the macroscopic method, developed as far as the pupal stage. The other specimen, a second instar apparently of the same species, did not molt. This specimen was in a cylindrical cocoon when it was found.

Calopsectra sp.

Several cocoons of Calopsectra sp. were extracted from a sample collected after a long dry period at Redding. The identification was based on specimens believed to be 2nd and 3rd instars. They each occupied an unbent, cylindrical cocoon which was strongly reinforced with soil particles. Larvae removed from cocoons shortly after wetting appeared to be fully active. The few individuals that emerged from their cocoons without assistance had been chilled for several weeks. All of the larvae died before pupation.

Tribelos atrum (Townes)

The unidentified species mentioned earlier (Grodhaus, 1976) has subsequently been determined to be T. atrum. Larvae were collected many times at Redding and Murphy Well and, less frequently, at Sears Point. This species is rather widely distributed in the U.S.A. but its natural history has received little attention. The preliminary report (Grodhaus, 1976) did not include anything about the cocoons of T. atrum. At that time, only one type of cocoon had been detected. Those cocoons were later identified as belonging to Phaenopsectra pilicellata.

Cocoons of T. atrum were occupied by 2nd instars and occasionally by 3rd instars. As shown in Fig. 2, the cocoons are cylindrical and somewhat sinuate. They have soil particles incorporated into their structure and are opaque. Many larvae from the dry-season collections left their cocoons within a few hours or days after immersion. Larvae of this species always appeared fully active when assisted from their cocoons, yet many of them did not exit on their own until many days after wetting.

Specimens that were reared from eggs suspended their development in the 2nd and, rarely, the 3rd stadia. This was accompanied by cocoon formation. The dormancy could be terminated by chilling. A drought period was not essential for the larvae to complete their metamorphosis.

Second instars within cocoons survived 28 days of drought under experimental conditions. In the field, the species survived a prolonged drought; a living larva was taken approximately 32 months after the last standing water. In stored soil, larvae survived for more than 4 years. Additional observations of this species are to be published elsewhere.

Tribelos sp.

This species has been reared to the adult stage from larvae extracted on several occasions from dry soil collected at Murphy Well. It appears to be an undescribed species. The larvae were associated with cylindrical cocoons as 2nd and 3rd instars. Delays of a few hours were noted between the time of immersion in water and the time that larvae emerged from cocoons. All larvae removed from cocoons were active.

Phaenopsectra pilicellata Grodhaus

This species was described from specimens from Enterprise (Grodhaus, 1976), which is close to the present study area in the vicinity of Redding. It has been encountered only at Enterprise and Redding.

The cocoons of *P. pilicellata* (Fig. 3) are elipsoidal, opaque and reinforced with particles of soil. Cocoons of *P. pilicellata* were extracted from samples taken at various times during the wet and dry seasons. In each sample there were about equal numbers of 2nd and 3rd instars within cocoons. Many of the larvae removed from cocoons were semiactive, making simple contractions of the body only. Semiactive larvae became capable of full mobility after several weeks of chilling in the refrigerator. Some larvae were induced to exit from cocoons by chilling.

Many field-collected larvae constructed cocoons in the laboratory. This was true of larvae that had already been in cocoons, as well as those whose history was unknown. Larvae sometimes made new cocoons without having molted. Experimental drying of larvae, naked or in cocoons, resulted in their death within a few days. However, *P. pilicellata* larvae were found alive after 32 months of drought in the field and after more than 4 years of dry storage. Additional observations of this species will be published elsewhere.

Wirthiella sp.

This species was collected at several localities in northeastern California, but only at Murphy Well was it found aestivating in dry soil. Adult specimens obtained by rearing indicate that the species is undescribed.

Cocoons are elipsoidal, occupied by folded 2nd and 3rd instars. The cocoon walls are somewhat reinforced with soil particles but are not as rigid as those of other species in the present study.

Wirthiella sp. larvae within cocoons were always found to be capable of full mobility as long as they were hydrated, but they did not necessarily leave after wetting alone. Larvae that hatched in the laboratory reached the 2nd or 3rd instar quickly, after which they slowed or suspended their development. Most of them constructed cocoons. Chilling the dormant or slowly developing larvae seemed to cause a renewal of growth. Experimentally dried larvae in cocoons were alive 15 days later.

DISCUSSION

Evidently, all of the chironomids that survive drying of the vernal pools spend the summer as larvae encased in cocoons. The physical protection afforded by the cocoons probably does not keep the larvae from losing moisture. These larvae may be cryptobiotic, but this was not determined by the present study. Survival under field conditions was much better than it was in the laboratory. Only *Hydrobaenus pilipes* withstood experimental drying for more than a few days.

During an exceptional drought, *Tribelos atrum* and *Phaenopsectra pilicellata* remained alive for 32 months. These species also recovered after storage in dry soil for 4 years. Of the drought-resistant chironomids from other regions, only *Polypedilum vanderplanki* Hinton from Africa has been tested for its ability to withstand long periods of storage. According to Hinton (1960), the cryptobiotic larvae of *P. vanderplanki* have been kept alive in dry material for as long as 10 years.

Vernal pool chironomids showed much variation in their readiness to leave their cocoons after immersion in water. This variation is probably partly due to species differences and partly to differences among the specimens. For example, larvae collected at different times of the year would have been exposed to different environmental stimuli. Low temperature is probably a stimulus to larval activity. Semiactive larvae of *H. pilipes* and *P. pilicellata* became fully active as the result of the refrigerator treatment. *T. atrum* and *Wirthiella* sp. larvae, which always appeared to be active within their cocoons, were induced to exit by being placed in the refrigerator. Thus it seems that cold weather, possibly combined with darkness is necessary for aestivating larvae to complete their life cycle.

The work of Hudson (1971) on *H. pilipes*, and my studies of *Hydrobaenus* sp., *T. atrum*, and *Wirthiella* sp. indicate that dormancy occurs in 2nd and 3rd instars while they are being held in the laboratory. Larvae continuously in water do not avoid the dormancy. This indicates that these species have an obligatory diapause.

The drought-resistant chironomids elsewhere, all of which are associated with rockpools, have not as yet been linked to any type of diapause. The life histories of the rockpool species from Nigeria (Hinton, 1951, 1960, 1968; Miller, 1970) and Australia (Edward, 1968; Jones, 1974, 1975) are undoubtedly determined by different environmental stimuli from those affecting the vernal pool species in California.

The postdiapause development of the vernal pool chironomids was given relatively little study. These species do not thrive at room temperatures. On several occasions, *P. pilicellata* larvae were observed to return to dormancy in the laboratory. In nature, however, the postdiapause development is probably uncomplicated. Unpublished collection records indicate that the adults of most of the species listed here are only present during the winter and early spring at low elevations and during the spring in the mountains.

The life history of the vernal pool Chironomidae probably conforms to this pattern: Eggs are deposited in the spring when the pools are in prime condition for aquatic life. The young larvae hatch in a few days, and they grow rapidly for awhile. When they reach the 2nd and 3rd stadia they cease to develop and build cocoons.

Subsequently the pools dry up. The larvae spend the summer and autumn in diapause in the soil. Unseasonal rain at this time does not activate the larvae, because their diapause development is incomplete. Diapause is terminated during cold weather. Larvae are able to leave their cocoons when the pools form from winter rain or snow. After they exit the larvae undergo successive molts, proceeding through 3rd and 4th stadia and the pupal stage to become adults. The adults reproduce and die after a few days, as is typical of the Chironomidae.

REFERENCES

Danks, H. V. (1971). Overwintering of some north temperate and arctic Chironomidae. II. Chironomid biology. Can. Entomol., 103, 1875-1910.

Danks, H. V., and J. W. Jones (1978). Further observations on winter cocoons in Chironomidae (Diptera). Can. Entomol., 110, 667-669.

Edward, D. H. (1968). Chironomidae in temporary freshwaters. Aust. Soc. Limnol. Newsl., 6, 3-5.

Grodhaus, G. (1976). Two species of Phaenopsectra with drought-resistant larvae (Diptera: Chironomidae). J. Kans. Entomol. Soc., 49, 405-418.

Hinton, H. E. (1951). A new chironomid from Africa, the larva of which can be dehydrated without injury. Proc. Zool. Soc. Lond., 121, 371-380.

Hinton, H. E. (1960). Cryptobiosis in the larvae of Polypedilum vanderplanki Hint. (Chironomidae). J. Ins. Physiol., 5, 286-300.

Hinton, H. E. (1968). Reversible suspension of metabolism and the origin of life. Proc. R. Soc., B171, 43-57.

Hudson, P. L. (1971). The Chironomidae (Diptera) of South Dakota. Proc. S. Dakota Acad. Sci., 50, 155-174.

Jones, R. E. (1974). The effects of size-selective predation and environmental variation on the distribution and abundance of a chironomid, Paraborniella tonnoiri Freeman. Aust. J. Zool, 22, 71-89.

Jones, R. E. (1975). Dehydration in an Australian rockpool chironomid larvae, (Paraborniella tonnoiri). Proc. R. Entomol. Soc. Lond., A49, 111-119.

Miller, P. L. (1970). On the occurrence and some characteristics of Cyrtopus fastuosus Bigot (Dipt., Stratiomyidae) and Polypedilum sp. (Dipt., Chironomidae) from temporary habitats in western Nigeria. Entomol. Mon. Mag., 105, 233-238.

Mozley, S. E. (1970). Morphology and ecology of Trissocladius grandis (Kieffer) (Diptera, Chironomidae), a common species in the lakes and rivers of Northern Europe. Arch. Hydrobiol., 67, 433-451.

Saether, O. A. (1976). Revision of Hydrobaenus, Trissocladius, Zalutschia, Paratrissocladius, and some related genera (Diptera: Chironomidae). Bull. Fish. Res. Board Can., 195, 1-287.

Chironomid Larvae and Pupae in the Diet of Brown Trout (*Salmo Trutta*) and Rainbow Trout (*Salmo Gairdneri*) in Rutland Water, Leicestershire

A. E. Brown, R. S. Oldham and A. Warlow

School of Life Sciences, Leicester Polytechnic, Leicester LE1 9BH, England

ABSTRACT

The chironomid component of the diet of trout from a lowland, eutrophic reservoir was studied using 373 stomachs obtained during the fishing season, April to October 1977. A comparison of their diets indicates that brown trout prefer deeper water to rainbow trout. Larval migration and individual species behaviour may considerably influence the degree of predation. In the main, however, free living species were heavily predated whilst the tube dwelling species were not. Pupae were consumed during periods of emergence. Chironomid larvae and pupae occurred frequently in trout stomachs and contributed 20% by weight to the total diet.

KEYWORDS

Chironomidae; trout diet; reservoir.

INTRODUCTION

Rutland Water is a 1,260 ha pump-storage reservoir situated 30 km east of Leicester. There are three main sources of water, the natural catchment and the rivers Nene and Welland. Filling began in February 1975 with the fastest rise occurring from September 1976 to March 1977. The reservoir is highly eutrophic and has a nutrient loading (mean for 1975-1977) of 55 gm/sq. metre Nitrate and 3 gm/sq. metre Phosphate (Harper, 1978). The trout fishery is managed on a "put and take" basis and up to April 1977 had been stocked with 272,740 brown trout and 359,600 rainbow trout.

The feeding habits of trout, especially brown trout, in natural waters have been studied by many workers (see for example Allen, 1938; Frost and Smyly, 1952; Kennedy and Fitzmaurice, 1971; Southern, 1935) but few data are available for new reservoirs or artificially regulated lakes. Trout are essentially carnivorous, feeding on aquatic insects, molluscs and crustaceans but also taking terrestrial food such as insects, earthworms and spiders. These become important during flooding of terrestrial vegetation (Campbell, 1963; Crisp, Mann and McCormack, 1978). Trout may concentrate their feeding on an abundant or transitory food item; as in the consumption of large numbers of chironomid pupae during periods of emergence (Thorpe, 1974; Wilson and co-workers, 1975). In this investigation larvae, pupae and adults of the Chironomidae found in 373 trout stomachs obtained between April and September 1977 were identified to genus and the results compared with those of a benthic survey.

METHODS

Trout stomachs obtained during the first fishing season at Rutland Water were collected approximately fortnightly from boat and bank fishermen. Whole stomachs were preserved in 5% formalin and subsequently slit longitudinally; chironomid larvae and pupae were separated from other food items and stored in 70% alcohol. Larvae and pupae were identified to genus using unpublished keys by Cranston (1977) and Wilson (1978) respectively. Dry weights were determined on preserved material after oven drying at 105 degrees C for 24 hours.

The available food was estimated using twenty grab samples across two transects monthly, employing a modified van Veen grab (Wilson and co-workers, 1971). The transects ran from shore to shore and had an average depth of 3.0m and 5.6m.

RESULTS

A total of 373 stomachs was analysed, 248 rainbow trout (mean length 342mm) and 125 brown trout (mean length 425mm). Twelve genera of larvae were recorded in trout stomachs. _Micropsectra_ and _Tanytarsus_ are grouped together as Tanytarsini due to the difficulty in separating the two taxa. Table 1 shows the composition of larvae in the diet of trout during the seven month sampling period.

TABLE 1 Composition of Chironomid Larvae in the Stomachs of Rainbow and Brown Trout between April and October 1977

(Taxa grouped into subfamilies Tanypodinae, Orthocladiinae and Chironominae)

	Rainbow trout (248 stomachs)			Brown trout (125 stomachs)		
	No.	Mean No. per stomach	% No. per stomach	No.	Mean No. per stomach	% No. per stomach
Procladius	476	1.9	4.0	419	3.4	28.6
Ablabesmyia	6	0.1	0.1	6	0.1	0.4
Cricotopus	525	2.1	4.4	6	0.1	0.4
Orthocladius	12	0.1	0.1	1	0.1	0.1
Psectrocladius	2469	10.0	20.5	182	1.5	12.4
Chironomus	109	0.4	0.9	223	1.8	15.2
Cryptochironomus	288	1.2	2.4	200	1.6	13.7
Endochironomus	7952	32.1	66.0	367	2.9	25.1
Glyptotendipes	95	0.4	0.8	10	0.1	0.7
Polypedilum	73	0.3	0.6	39	0.3	2.7
Tanytarsini	43	0.2	0.4	12	0.1	0.8
Totals	12041	48.6	100	1465	11.7	100

Rainbow trout consumed a larger number of larvae ($\bar{x}$=49) than brown trout ($\bar{x}$=12). Only one of the two Tanypodinae, _Procladius_, was found in stomachs in large numbers. Two of the shallow water Orthocladiinae, _Cricotopus_ and _Psectrocladius_, were consumed in considerably larger numbers by rainbow trout than by brown trout. Of the tube builders, the Chironominae, the major species taken by both fish was _Endochironomus albipennis_, and 76% of the 8,319 recorded were found in rainbow stomachs collected at the end of September. Chironomus was consumed in higher numbers by brown trout than by rainbow trout. Microtendipes was the only genus found as pupae in stomachs but not as larvae. Psilotanypus, Eukiefferiella, Paracladius, Corynoneura, Metriocnemus, Pseudosmittia, Camptochironomus and Parachironomus have all been recorded in small numbers from the reservoir but were not found in stomachs. A total of 6,561 larvae was obtained in benthos samples between May and October 1977 in the proportions shown in Table 2. In order to gain an idea of the proportion of organisms in the diet relative to the proportion measured in the benthos an index of selective feeding, or electivity (Ivlev, 1961) was calculated.

TABLE 2 Electivity Index for Rainbow and Brown Trout relating Occurrence of Chironomid Larvae in the Benthos and in Fish Stomachs from May to October 1977

		Rainbow trout		Brown trout	
	% No in benthos	% No/fish stomach	Electivity	% No/fish stomach	Electivity
Procladius	18.9	3.4	-0.69	29.0	+0.21
Ablabesmyia	0.5	0.1	-0.89	0.4	-0.10
Cricotopus	5.5	3.3	-0.25	0.1	-0.95
Orthocladius	1.7	0.1	-0.92	0.1	-0.92
Psectrocladius	9.6	22.0	+0.39	12.5	+0.13
Chironomus	24.2	0.9	-0.93	15.3	-0.22
Cryptochironomus	2.1	2.4	+0.07	13.2	+0.73
Endochironomus	2.4	67.0	+0.93	25.2	+0.83
Glyptotendipes	0.2	0.1	-0.67	0.7	+0.55
Polypedilum	7.1	0.5	-0.86	2.7	-0.45
Tanytarsini	27.4	0.4	-0.97	0.8	-0.94

Positive electivity, or selection for an organism, is expressed by values from +1 to 0 and negative electivity by values from 0 to -1. Strong positive electivity was shown for Endochironomus (0.93) larvae in rainbow trout. Brown trout showed strong positive electivity for Cryptochironomus (0.73), Endochironomus (0.83) and Glyptotendipes (0.55) larvae.

TABLE 3 Composition of Chironomid Pupae in the Stomachs of Rainbow and Brown Trout between April and October 1977

	Rainbow trout (229 stomachs)			Brown trout (104 stomachs)		
	No.	Mean No. per stomach	% No. per stomach	No.	Mean No. per stomach	% No. per stomach
Procladius	1943	8.5	20.5	481	4.6	8.6
Ablabesmyia	76	0.3	0.8	2	0.1	0.1
Cricotopus	242	1.1	2.6	19	0.2	0.3
Orthocladius	211	0.9	2.2	631	6.1	11.3
Psectrocladius	1954	8.5	20.6	165	1.6	3.0
Chironomus	1568	6.9	16.6	2638	25.4	47.1
Cryptochironomus	11	0.1	0.1	96	0.9	1.7
Endochironomus	999	4.4	10.6	378	3.6	6.8
Glyptotendipes	2	0.1	0.1	1	0.1	0.1
Microtendipes				2	0.1	0.1
Polypedilum	188	0.8	2.0	11	0.1	0.2
Tanytarsini	2278	10.0	24.1	1178	11.3	21.0
Totals	9472	41.4	100	5602	53.9	100

The composition of the pupal diet of trout is shown in Table 3. The mean number of pupae per fish was 48 compared to 36 larvae per fish, and brown trout in particular consumed pupae ($\bar{x}$=54) more heavily than larvae ($\bar{x}$=12). Procladius, Endochironomus and Tanytarsini were prominant in the diets of both species. Rainbow trout preyed more heavily than brown trout on Psectrocladius and brown trout preyed more heavily than rainbow trout on Chironomus and Orthocladius. An electivity index cannot be calculated for mid-water and surface organisms as estimates of their abundance are difficult.

A oneway analysis of variance was used to test for significant differences in the diet between rainbow and brown trout. Significant differences at the 1% level occurred for three larval genera and five pupal genera (Table 4). Psectrocladius and Chironomus pupae showed the most significant differences.

TABLE 4 Analysis of Variance comparing the Occurrence of Larvae and Pupae in Rainbow and Brown Trout Stomachs

	Larvae		Pupae	
	F Value	Significance	F Value	Significance
Procladius	0.631	0.4274	2.466	0.1173
Ablabesmyia	0.401	0.5269		
Cricotopus	8.946	0.0030	7.581	0.0062
Orthocladius	2.244	0.1350	7.132	0.0079
Psectrocladius	8.114	0.0046	15.832	0.0001
Chironomus	4.103	0.0435	12.621	0.00C4
Cryptochironomus	0.321	0.5711	2.682	0.1024
Endochironomus	9.665	0.0020	0.238	0.6263
Glyptotendipes	1.276	0.2594	0.006	0.9373
Microtendipes			14.463	0.0354
Polypedilum	0.007	0.9336	6.789	0.0096
Tanytarsini	0.374	0.5415	0.107	0.7434

The five most abundant genera occurring in stomachs are shown in Fig. 1. Procladius, Chironomus and Tanytarsini pupae occurred in stomachs in larger numbers than larvae over the whole of the sampling period. Psectrocladius larvae and pupae occurred in approximately the same numbers until October when the mean number of pupae in stomachs fell. Endochironomus larvae occurred in larger numbers than pupae throughout the sampling period and reached a maximum of 90/ stomach in September.

Few larvae or pupae of any genus were found in stomachs during April and May.

The monthly mean number of larvae per square metre of benthos is also shown in Fig. 1. All genera show an increase in larval numbers from May to August. Tanytansini and Chironomus larvae occurred in the largest numbers, 1,080 per square metre and 741 per square metre although these were the two groups least predated by trout. Procladius and Chironomus show similar trends of high numbers in the benthos but low numbers in stomachs. Endochironomus and Psectrocladius show the reverse trend of low numbers in the benthos but high numbers in fish stomachs.

A high proportion of fish stomachs sampled contained chironomid larvae and pupae (Fig. 2). Larvae occurred more frequently than pupae in stomachs only in April and October. Chironomid larvae and pupae contributed 17% (based on dry weight) to the diet over the whole of the period, with pupae reaching a maximum of 38% in July (Fig. 3). The remaining composition of the stomach contents consisted of vegetation (29%), earthworms (22%), fish (11%), Lymnaea pereger (7%), Gammarus pulex (4%), Daphnia (2%) and others (8%).

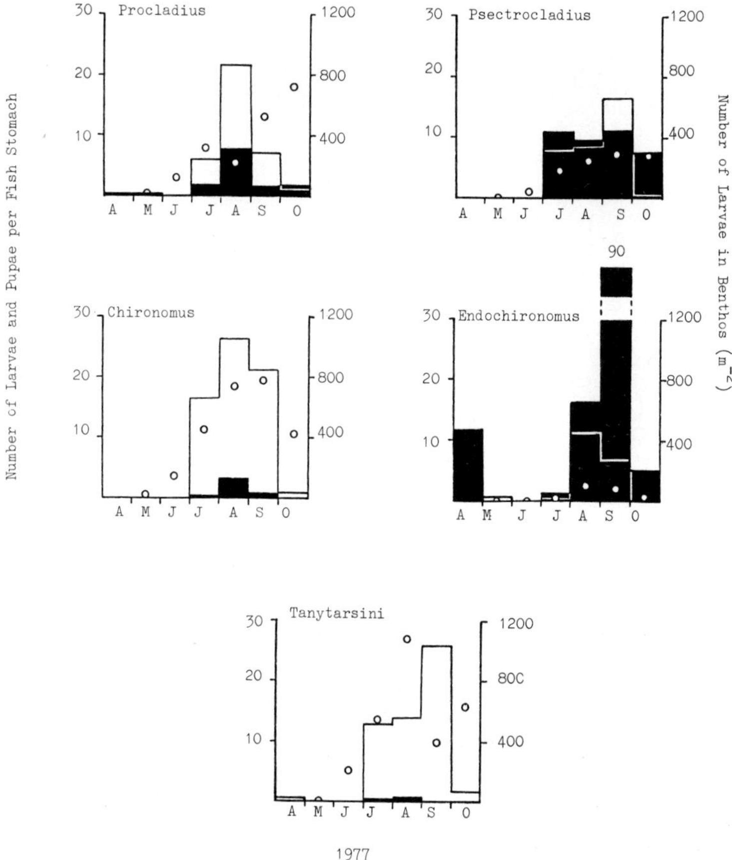

Fig. 1. Monthly changes in the mean number of larvae and pupae in trout stomachs and benthos. Black: larvae in stomachs; white: pupae in stomachs; o number of larvae (per square metre) in benthos. No stomach samples in June.

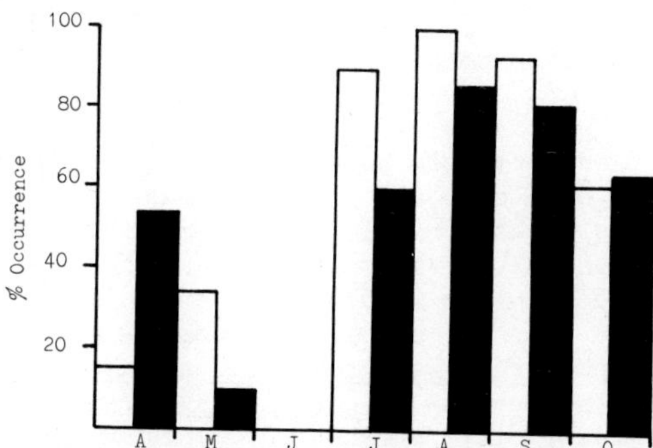

Fig. 2. Percentage occurrence of chironomid larvae and pupae in fish stomachs. Black: larvae; white: pupae.

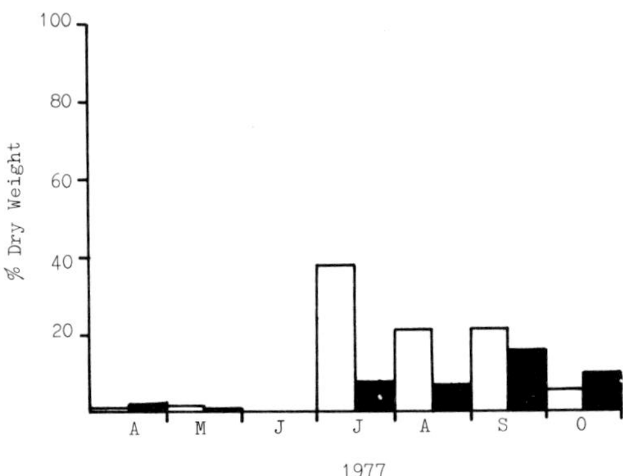

Fig. 3. Chironomid larvae and pupae in fish stomachs expressed as percentage composition by dry weight. Black: larvae; white: pupae.

DISCUSSION

Chironomid larvae appear to be predated according to their accessibility and not according to their numerical abundance. Free living species such as Procladius and the Orthocladiinae are consumed whilst tube dwelling species such as Chironomus and the Tanytarsini are not. Endochironomus albipennis is an exception and was consumed in large numbers. This species has a propensity to leave the tube at the least disturbance and to be one of the first colonisers of new substrates (Kalugina, 1959). Laboratory and field observations by the authors support this view. This behaviour, particularly migrations through the water column, may account for the large numbers in stomachs. Larval migrations of all instars have been shown to occur for a number of species (see for example Davies, 1973). Pedley and Jones (1978) record Endochironomus (species name not recorded) as occurring regularly and abundantly in the benthos of Llyn Dwythwch but not in fish stomachs. Two explanations may account for this conflicting result. Either the conditions required to stimulate larval migrations did not occur at Llyn Dwythwch or a different species, with different behaviour, may have been involved.

Larvae are predated in different proportions by brown and rainbow trout. Rainbow trout consume shallow water species in larger numbers than brown trout and this may reflect a habitat difference, rainbow trout feeding in the shallow margins and brown trout feeding in deep water. This is a popularly held belief amongst the anglers at Rutland Water who catch more brown trout by deep water fishing from boats.

In August all stomachs sampled contained pupae (Fig. 2). This heavy use of chironomid pupae during emergence compared to larvae has been recorded by several authors. Ball (1961) records pupae forming 20% by number of the organisms in 254 brown trout from Llyn Tegid whilst larvae only formed 0.2%. Pedley and Jones (1978) found 24.1% by number of the organisms in 378 brown trout stomachs were pupae whilst only 3.0% were larvae. Significant differences were shown to occur between the two fish species in the number of Psectrocladius and Chironomus pupae consumed. Rainbow trout consumed large numbers of Psectrocladius pupae that were emerging in the shallow margins of the reservoir. Brown trout consumed Chironomus pupae in large numbers and these emerge over the whole area of the reservoir and are the predominant genus in the profundal zone. Few adult chironomids were taken by trout in these lakes or at Rutland Water.

Chironomid larvae are abundant in the benthos and pupae are numerous and accessible during periods of emergence. Together they make a significant contribution to the biomass consumed by fish. This contribution is likely to increase later in the development of the reservoir as the availability of earthworms and vegetation, the other major food items, decreases.

ACKNOWLEDGEMENT

The authors would like to thank the Anglian Water Authority for permission to work on the reservoir, and the Science Research Council and Leicester Polytechnic for financial support and facilities.

REFERENCES

Allen, K.R. (1938). Some observations on the biology of the trout (Salmo trutta) in Windermere. J. Anim. Ecol., 7, 333-349.

Ball, J.N. (1961). On the food of brown trout of Llyn Tegid. Proc. zool. Soc. Lond., 137, 599-622.

Campbell, R.N. (1963). Some effects of impoundment on the environment and growth of brown trout (Salmo trutta) in Lough Garry (Inverness-shire). Sci. Invest. Freshw. Fish Scot., 30, 1-27.

Cranston, P.S. (1977). A provisional key to genus of larvae of the British Chironomidae. Unpublished MS, British Museum (Natural History).

Crisp, D.T., Mann, R.H.K. and McCormack, Jean C. (1978). The effects of impoundment and regulation upon the stomach contents of fish at Cow Green, Upper Teesdale. J. Fish. Biol., 12, 287-301.

Davies, B.R. (1973). Field and laboratory studies on the activity of larval Chironomidae in loch Leven, Kinross. Unpublished, Ph.D. thesis, Paisley College of Technology.

Frost, W.E. and Smyly, W.J.P. (1952). Brown trout of a moorland fish pond. J. Anim. Ecol., 21, 62-86.

Harper, D.M. (1978). Limnology of Rutland Water. Verh. Internat. Verein. Limnol., 29, 1604-1611.

Ivlev, V.S. (1961). Experimental Ecology of the Feeding of Fishes. 302 pp. Yale University Press.

Kalugina, N.S. (1959). Changes in morphology and biology of chironomid larvae in relation to growth (Diptera, Chironomidae). Trudy vseis. girdrobiol. Obshch., 9, 85-107. Transl. from Russian by Fish. Res. Bd. Can. Transl. No. 1160.

Kennedy, M. and Fitzmaurice, P. (1971). Growth and food of brown trout (Salmo trutta (L.) in Irish waters. Proc. R. Ir. Acad., 71B, 270-348.

Pedley, R.B. and Jones, J.W. (1978). The comparative feeding behaviour of brown trout, Salmo trutta L. and Atlantic salmon, Salmo salar L. in Llyn Dwythwch, Wales. J. Fish. Biol., 12, 239-256.

Southern, R. (1935). Reports from the limnological laboratory III. The food and growth of brown trout from Lough Derg and the River Shannon. Proc. R. Ir. Acad., 42B, 87-172.

Thorpe, J.E. (1974). Trout and perch populations at Loch Leven, Kinross. Proc. Roy. Soc. Edinb., B., 74, 297-313.

Wilson, R.S. (1978). A provisional key to exuviae of the British Chironomidae. Unpublished MS, Department of Zoology, University of Bristol.

Wilson, R.S., Maxwell, T.R.A., Mance, G., Sleigh, M.A. and Milne, R.A. (1975). Biological aspects of Chew Valley and Blagdon Lakes, England. Freshwat. Biol., 5, 379-393.

Wilson, R.S., Milne, R.A., Maxwell, T.R.A., Mance, G. and Sleigh, M.A. (1971). The Limnology of Chew and Blagdon Lakes. Interim Report, Department of Zoology, University of Bristol.

Tube Formation and Distribution of *Chironomus Plumosus* L. (Diptera : Chironomidae) in a Eutrophic Woodland Pond

I. D. Hodkinson and K. A. Williams*

Department of Biology, Liverpool Polytechnic, Byrom Street, Liverpool L3 3AF, England
**Present address: Freshwater Biological Association, River Laboratory, East Stoke, Dorset, England*

ABSTRACT

In a shaded eutrophic woodland pond highest numbers of *Chironomus plumosus* larvae were associated with accumulations of allochthonous leaf litter around the pond margin. In contrast, in a comparable unshaded pond, with insignificant litter input, highest larval densities were found at the centre of the pond. Laboratory experiments showed that where the fine substrate is overlaid by leaf accumulations larvae form horizontal feeding tubes on the undersurface of the leaf and do not burrow into the substrate. Where leaves are absent larvae construct J-tubes or U-tubes in the sediment (5 cm). Thus *C.plumosus* larvae are able to override their normal sediment depth requirement in the presence of leaf accumulations. It is suggested that the leaf-tube enables larvae to feed on deposits of high food-quality detritus (faeces) produced during the comminution of leaf material by other animals. High flexibility in its feeding mechanisms allows *C.plumosus* to exploit a broad ecological niche.

KEYWORDS

Chironomus plumosus; pond; tube formation; leaf litter; feeding; population density.

INTRODUCTION

The larvae of *Chironomus plumosus* L. are an ubiquitous element in the fauna of highly eutrophic water bodies (Brinkhurst, 1974) and the life history of the species in ponds is well documented (Smith & Young, 1973). Walshe (1947) showed that larvae of *C.plumosus* form open-ended U-shaped feeding tubes in lentic bottom sediments and recently McLachlan & Cantrell (1976) demonstrated that larvae will in addition form both J-shaped tubes, sealed at the distal end, and open-ended horizontal tubes. The type of tube constructed is related to the depth of sediment, with horizontal tubes formed in shallow sediments around the lake margin and 'J' and U-tubes constructed in the deeper sediments at the centre of the lake. Larvae in U-tubes are largely filter feeders (Walshe, 1951), those in J-tubes are deposit feeders, whereas those in horizontal tubes are capable of both deposit and filter feeding. However the latter are in practice most probably deposit feeders (McLachlan, 1977). Food ingestion rates of filter feeding larvae are higher than those of deposit feeding larvae and the former ingest more small food particles than the latter. McLachlan (1977) concludes that the type of tube formed enables the larvae to exploit efficiently the food available in its immediate environment. Thus larvae in horizontal tubes are able to graze on epipelic diatoms around the lake margin whereas U-tube dwelling larvae can exploit material suspended in the water above the bottom deposits. In his study McLachlan found highest densities of *C.plumosus* larvae in deep water deposits. He suggested that in this situation intraspecific competition for food is reduced if a population contains both deposit (J-tube) and filter (U-tube) feeding forms and that this is a mechanism by which high population densities are sustained.

The above work was carried out in Lady Burn Lough, a new impoundment, in which the newly formed substrate was relatively uniform and homogeneous. The present study demonstrates that McLachlan's conclusions are basically correct but that both substrate quality and seasonal events within an heterogeneous environment can greatly modify the advantage of differing feeding mechanisms and that at least in a woodland pond, a horizontal tube, formed on the underside of a leaf, appears to be the most efficient feeding mechanism, irrespective of substrate depth.

STUDY AREA

This study was carried out on 2 ponds, The Duck Pits and Pond I, in the Croxteth Estate, Liverpool (G.R. SJ 409 941). These two ponds were chosen for an attempt to measure the impact of a large input of allochthonous material on a pond fauna. The experimental pond, the Duck Pits (30 × 20 m, max. depth 2.0 m) was a shaded woodland pond with a high yearly input of allochthonous material, mainly sycamore leaves (*Acer pseudoplatanus* L), around the margin. The control Pond (I) (24 × 16 m, max. depth 3.0 m) was an unshaded pond in open countryside with little input of allochthonous material. Faunistically the two ponds are similar, showing a depauperate fauna typical of eutrophic conditions: only 11 species of benthic macroinvertebrate have been recorded from the Duck Pit and 21 species from Pond I. Chironomid larvae dominate the benthic fauna, constituting 61% and 56% of the bottom fauna of the Duck Pits and Pond I respectively. In the Duck Pits *C.plumosus* makes up 77% of the chironomid fauna and *Chironomus thummi* (Meigen) a further 17%. In Pond I the equivalent proportions are 87 and 7% respectively.

METHODS

Field Studies

To estimate the abundance of *C.plumosus* larvae in different areas of the two ponds substrate samples were taken on a stratified random system using an Ekman-Birge type grab (sample area = 0.0225 m^2). Sampling was carried out during the periods 26 January 1976 - 1 June 1977 in the Duck Pits and 26 January 1976 - 14 January 1977 in Pond I. *Chironomus plumosus* overwinters in both ponds as 2nd, 3rd and 4th instar larvae; during this period there is no recruitment or emergence and population estimates taken at this time form the best basis for comparative studies. Hence sampling was concentrated into the winter-spring periods. All samples were hand sorted for larvae and then subjected to $MgSO_4$ flotation to recover any larvae which may have been missed.

For sampling purposes the Duck Pit was divided into a marginal area, where the particulate substrate was overlaid by unfragmented sycamore leaves and the deeper central area where the fine substrate was exposed. In the marginal area the grab had to be pushed into the substrate to obtain adequate samples. Such a clear cut distinction between edge and centre was not obvious in Pond I and the central area was defined as substrate underlying water deeper than 1.5 m. On each date 10 samples were taken from each sub-area of each pond.

Laboratory Studies on Tube Formation

In practice it is difficult to collect and record with certainty the position of intact larval feeding tubes in the field, particularly in deep water. Thus to investigate tube formation, substrate materials were taken into the laboratory and the tube building response of larvae noted.

Three basic substrate types were used:

1. Flocculent Substrate. The typical substrate of the marginal area of the Duck Pit, lying beneath unfragmented leaves. A flocculent, small particle size substrate largely composed of faecal material (comminuted leaves) but with larger leaf fragments intermixed.

2. Compacted Substrate. The typical substrate of Pond I and the centre of the Duck Pits. A compacted, small particle size sediment with few small leaf fragments.

3. Leaf Substrate. Large unfragmented sycamore leaves.

The tube building response of larvae to 5 different combinations/modifications of these 3 basic substrate types was investigated. All experiments were conducted in 8 cm diameter glass cylinders with the experimental substrate (5 cm deep) overlaid by non-aerated pond water and with the cylinders embedded in sediment within an aquarium. The substrate depth represents the conditions in which larvae might be expected to form both J-tubes and U-tubes. To each cylinder one 4th instar *C.plumosus* larva was added and after a lapse of 24h the type of feeding tube formed was noted. Each treatment was replicated 50 times.

RESULTS

Population Sampling

Figure 1 compares larval densities at margin and centre of each of the 2 ponds throughout the sampling period. Despite large standard errors on the population estimates several conclusions can be drawn. In the Duck pits larval population density was consistently about 4 times higher at the margin than at the centre, whereas in Pond I the reverse was true, larval populations were higher in the centre of the pond than at the margin. The population density at the margin of the Duck Pits was approximately 5 to 10 times higher than at the margin of Pond I whereas populations at the centre of Pond I were marginally greater than at the centre of the Duck Pits.

In addition there were significant differences in the dispersion patterns of the different sub-populations in the two ponds. The variance/mean ratio index of dispersion (I) was calculated for each sub-population and tested for departure from unity using χ^2 at the 95% probability level (Elliot, 1971). For overwintering larvae in the Duck Pits the population at the margin was contagiously distributed whereas that at the centre was randomly distributed. In contrast in Pond I the reverse was true, with populations at the margin being randomly distributed and those at the centre being aggregated.

Tube Formation

In the laboratory experiments 4 different tube types were observed.

1. an open ended horizontal tube, constructed of small particulate detritus, firmly attached to the underside of a leaf.

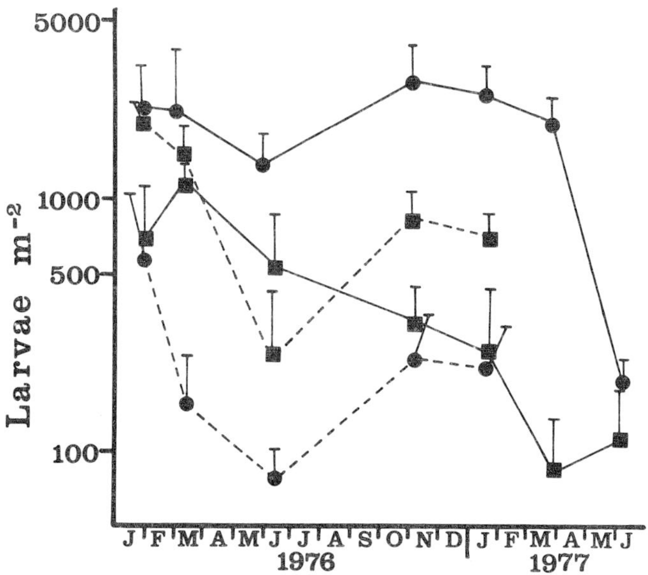

Fig. 1. Larval population densities of *C.plumosus* at the margin and centre of the two Croxteth ponds (note log scale). Solid lines represent Duck Pits, broken lines Pond I. Circles indicate samples from margin, squares indicate centre samples. Error terms are S.E.

2. a typical horizontal tube within the sediment, as described by McLachlan & Cantrell (1976).

3. an open ended horizontal transparent silk tube attached to the underside of a leaf.

4. a typical J or U tube within the sediment, as described by Walshe (1947), Hilsenhoff (1966), and McLachlan & Cantrell (1976).

The types of tube formed in the different experimental substrates are summarised in Table 1. In the absence of overlying leaves, larvae formed predominantly J or U-tubes within both the flocculent and compacted substrates. In the washed leaf treatment larvae were able to construct successfully transparent silk tubes on the underside of leaves. When leaves were placed on the surface of the flocculent or compacted substrates, larvae utilised the sediment particles in tube building but formed horizontal tubes on the underside of leaves and did not burrow into the substrate.

These results indicate that larvae will most probably form tubes of type 1 in marginal areas of the Duck Pit and tubes of type 4 in the centre of the Duck Pit and within Pond I. They confirm casual observations made during the sampling programme.

TABLE 1 Tube Formation by *Chironomus plumosus* in Different Substrates

Substrate	Type of Tube Formed				
	1	2	3	4	inactive/dead
Flocculent (5 cm)	-	1	-	47	2
Compacted (5 cm)	-	3	-	45	2
Washed Leaves	-	-	45	-	5
Flocculent (5 cm) + Leaves	44	2	-	1	3
Compacted (5 cm) + Leaves	45	-	-	1	4

See text for full explanation of substrate and larval tube types.

DISCUSSION

The mean overwintering population densities of *C.plumosus* in the Duck Pits and Pond I of 1993 larvae m^{-2} (biomass 1.38 g m^{-2}) and 862 larvae m^{-2} (0.84 g m^{-2}) are higher than the densities of 200-300 m^{-2} recorded by Palmen & Aho (1966) for the Northern Baltic and by Kajak (1963) in Lake Sniardwy but are comparable with the population densities recorded by Mason (1977) in Alderfen Broad. However larval densities of up to 70,000 m^{-2} have been recorded elsewhere (Thienemann, 1954; Kajak, 1958).

The distribution of *C.plumosus* in two Croxteth ponds differ from the findings of Palmen & Aho (1966) who noted an absence of *C.plumosus* from littoral regions in the Northern Baltic. They suggested that *C.plumosus* is a profundal species "preferring" the more stable conditions found in deeper water. We support McLachlan & Cantrell in suggesting that *C.plumosus* is not an obligate profundal species but can exist in shallow littoral zones where substrate type and food availability permit.

McLachlan & Cantrell (1976) found highest numbers of larvae associated with aggregated distributions of J and U-tubes in deeper water sediments. Results from Pond I tend to support this conclusion. However, in the experimental woodland pond, the Duck Pits, highest larval densities were associated with aggregated distributions of horizontal tubes formed in accumulations of leaf litter around the pond margin. Because tubes are formed on the underside of leaves this would tend to preclude filter feeding and these larvae are most probably deposit feeders. In the absence of leaves at the pond centre, larvae would be able to form U-tubes and filter feed. McLachlan showed that filter feeding larvae feed faster than deposit feeders and in general occur in higher numbers. Why then is the population density highest in the marginal area of the Duck Pits?

Feeding rate is not a measure of food assimilation; one might expect organisms living on a low quality diet to feed more rapidly than those on a high quality diet. *Chironomus* larvae are unable to shred large leaves but they are able to feed on small particulate material made available in the faeces of other leaf shredding organisms (Cummins and others, 1973; Hargrave, 1976). Newly produced faecal material, in the presence of the high levels of nitrogen and phosphorous characteristic of a eutrophic pond, is rapidly colonised by micro-organisms, a readily assimilable source of food (Hynes & Kaushik, 1969; Fleisher & Larsson, 1974; Hodkinson, 1975a, 1975b; Mason & Bryant, 1975). Such high grade food material will only be available to larvae feeding in close association with leaf accumulations.

In contrast a number of factors may act to depress filter feeding populations in the centre of the Duck Pits. Firstly the fine particulate substrate is of a more recalcitrant nature than the faecal material around the pond margin and contains a higher proportion of non-organic particles. Secondly, and perhaps most importantly, the spring bloom of suspended green algae (*Cryptomonas* and *Chlamydomonas* spp) tends to occur early in the year, prior to the resumption of larval feeding. During the summer months the suspended green algae die back rapidly and the bottom of the pond becomes covered in a dense matt of a filamentous green *Spirogyra* sp (Wootton and Durrant, pers.comm.). This will seriously impair the efficiency of filter feeding mechanisms and larvae may be forced to indulge in deposit feeding. In the slightly deeper Pond I growths of filamentous green algae were not observed in the central area and this is reflected in a slightly higher larval population. However, the population densities there are not as high as at the Duck Pit margin.

Odum (1975) suggested that "optimum diversity is a function of the quality and quantity of energy flow. Low diversity may be optimum in ecosystems strongly subsidised by high quality auxiliary energy flows and/or by large nutrient inputs". The Duck Pits represents such a system when compared with Pond I. We suggest therefore that for *C.plumosus* to dominate the energy flow pathways in both systems it must exhibit a high degree of flexibility in its feeding behaviour to cope with the auxiliary energy input (leaves). Our results demonstrate such an adaptation: an horizontal feeding tube, attached to the undersurface of a leaf, which permits the larva to deposit feed on newly comminuted leaf material.

ACKNOWLEDGEMENTS

We thank Merseyside County Museums for permission to work on the Croxteth Estates, Dr. C. Pinder who checked our chironomid identifications and Dr. M. Luxton for his comments on the draft manuscript.

REFERENCES

Brinkhurst, R.O. (1974). *The benthos of lakes*. Macmillan Press, London and Basingstoke.

Cummins, K.W., Petersen, R.C., Howard, F.O., Wuycheck, J.C. and Holt, V.I. (1973). Utilisation of leaf litter by stream detritivores. *Ecology*, 54, 336-345.

Elliot, J.M. (1971). *Statistical analysis of samples of benthic invertebrates*. Freshwater Biological Association Scientific Publication 26, pp.148.

Fleischer, S. and Larsson, K. (1974). Cellulose degradation in different types of limnic environment. *Hydrobiologia*, 44, 523-536.

Hargrave, B.T. (1976). The central role of invertebrate faeces in sediment decomposition. In: J.M. Anderson and A. Macfadyen (Eds.). *The role of terrestrial and aquatic organisms in decomposition processes*. Blackwell Scientific Publications, Oxford. pp.301-321.

Hilsenhoff, W.L. (1966). The biology of *Chironomus plumosus* (Diptera: Chironomidae) in Lake Winnebago, Wisconsin. *Ann.Entomol.Soc.Amer.*, 59, 465-473.

Hodkinson, I.D. (1975a). Dry weight loss and chemical changes in plant litter of terrestrial origin, occurring in a beaver pond ecosystem. *J.Ecol.*, 63, 131-142.

Hodkinson, I.D. (1975b). A community analysis of the benthic insect fauna of an abandoned beaver pond. *J.Anim.Ecol.*, 44, 533-551.

Hynes, H.B.N. and Kaushik, N.K. (1969). The relationship between dissolved nutrient salts and protein production in submerged autumnal leaves. *Verh.Internat.Veirin. Limnol.*, 17, 95-103.

Kajak, Z. (1958). An attempt at interpreting the quantitative dynamics of benthic fauna in a chosen environment in the "Konfederatha" pool adjoining the Vistula. *Ekol.Pol.*, 6, 205-291.

Kajak, Z. (1963). The effect of experimentally induced variations in the abundance of *Tendipes plumosus* L. larvae on intraspecific and interspecific relations. *Ekol.Pol.*, 11, 355-367.

Mason, C.F. (1977). Populations and production of benthic animals in two contrasting shallow lakes in Norfolk. *J.Anim.Ecol.*, 46, 147-172.

Mason, C.F. and Bryant, R.J. (1975). Production, nutrient content and decomposition of *Phragmites communis* Trin. and *Typha angustifolia* L. *J.Ecol.*, 63, 71-95.

McLachlan, A.J. (1977). Some effects of tube shape on the feeding of *Chironomus plumosus* L. (Diptera: Chironomidae). *J.Anim.Ecol.*, 46, 139-146.

McLachlan, A.J. and Cantrell, M.A. (1976). Sediment development and its influence on the distribution and tube structure of *Chironomus plumosus* L. (Chironomidae, Diptera) in a new impoundment. *Freshwat.Biol.*, 6, 437-443.

Odum, E.P. (1975). Diversity as a function of energy flow. In W.H. van Dobben and R.H. Lowe-McConnell (Eds.). *Unifying concepts in ecology*. W. Junk, The Hague. pp.11-14.

Palmen, E. and Aho, L. (1966). Studies on the ecology and phenology of the Chironomidae (Dipt.) of the Northern Baltic, 2 *Camptochironomus* Kieff and *Chironomus* Meig. *Ann.Zool.Fenn.*, 3, 217-244.

Smith, V.G.F. and Young, J.O. (1973). The life histories of some Chironomidae (Diptera) in two ponds on Merseyside, England. *Arch.Hydrobiol.*, 76, 449-474.

Thienemann, A. (1954). *Chironomus* leben Verbreitung und wirtschaftliche Bedeutung der Chironomiden. *Binnengewasser*, 20, 1-834.

Walshe, B.M. (1947). Feeding mechanisms of *Chironomus* larvae. *Nature, Lond.*, 16, 474.

Walshe, B.M. (1951). The feeding habits of certain chironomid larvae (subfamily Tendipedinae). *Proc.Zool.Soc.Lond.*, 121, 63-79.

Role of Invertebrate Predators (Mainly Procladius sp.) in Benthos

Zdzislaw Kajak

Institute of Ecology, Dziekanów Leśny near Warsaw, Poland

ABSTRACT

Benthic invertebrate predators are strongly dependent on the abundance of available prey. They reduce the prey organisms especially intensively, when the latter become overabundant in relation to their food. Paralelly to reducing the abundance of Tubificidae, predators stimulate their production. Due to possibility of surviving on various food, predators are usually present in the environment, being able to start acting immediately and intensively when the prey becomes easily available. The pressure of predators on prey is additionally regulated by the competition between predators.

KEY WORDS

Benthic predators; competition; regulation of benthos abundance; Pelopiinae, Chironomidae, Tubificidae.

INTRODUCTION

The proportion of invertebrate predators in the biomass of macrobenthos usually varies from several to about 20%, although it may be both smaller, and sometimes much bigger - up to almost 100% (Kajak, 1968, Dusoge, 1980). In the littoral and sublittoral of lakes it may reach 40% on the average and 70% periodically; it is decreasing towards deep profundal (Kajak, Dusoge, 1975a, b, 1976, Kajak, Kajak, 1975). This high proportion of predators is impossible from the trophic pyramid point of view. One of the explanations of this high proportion is, that many predators, especially Procladius sp. and other Pelopiinae, feed not only on macrobenthos, (which is often identified with benthos), but mostly on zoo- meiobenthos, and also phyto- microbenthos. Zoo- meiobenthos in some environments composes up to 40-50% of total zoobenthos. Its biomass reaches often more than 10 $g \cdot m^{-2}$, sometimes even 40-50 $g \cdot m^{-2}$. We know nothing about protozoans as possible food for predators. Numbers of protozoans can attain hundreds of thousands $ind. \cdot m^{-2}$ in many situations and as much as 150 milions $ind. \cdot m^{-2}$ in hypertrophic situations (review - Kajak, in press).

RESULTS

The dependence of invertebrate predators on prey abundance is often clear (Fig. 1,2). The biomass of Procladius increases after periods of high prey/predator biomass ratio (Fig. 3).

The proportion of invertebrate predators in the total biomass of macrobenthos is usually higher under bad environmental conditions (low oxygen concentration, scarce food for nonpredatory benthos)

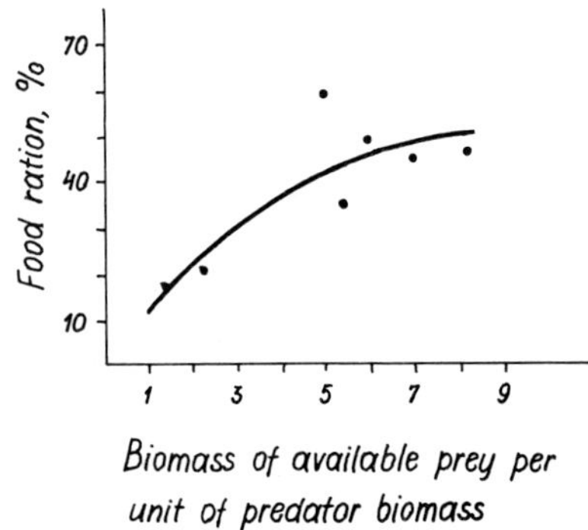

Fig.1. Dependence of the food ration (biomass of food consumed per 24 h. to the biomass of predator) of Procladius choreus on the biomass of available prey. After Dusoge, 1980.

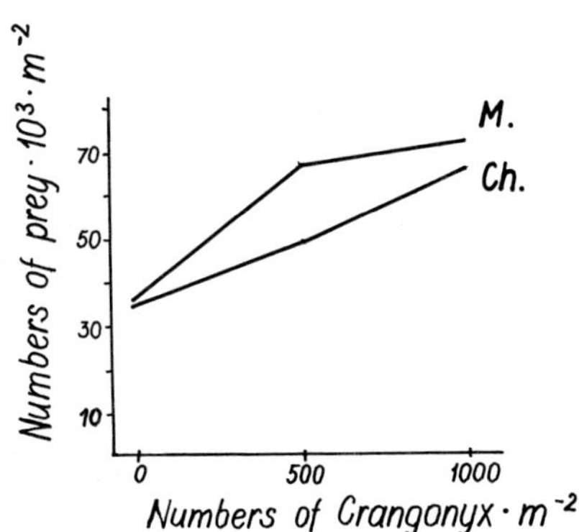

Fig.2. Correlation of the main predator (Crangonyx richmondensis) and prey numbers distribution. Marion Lake. Samples 20 cm^2. Ch - Chironomidae <5mm; M - meiobenthos (Harpacticoida, Rotifera, nauplii Copepoda). After Kajak, Kajak, 1975, modified.

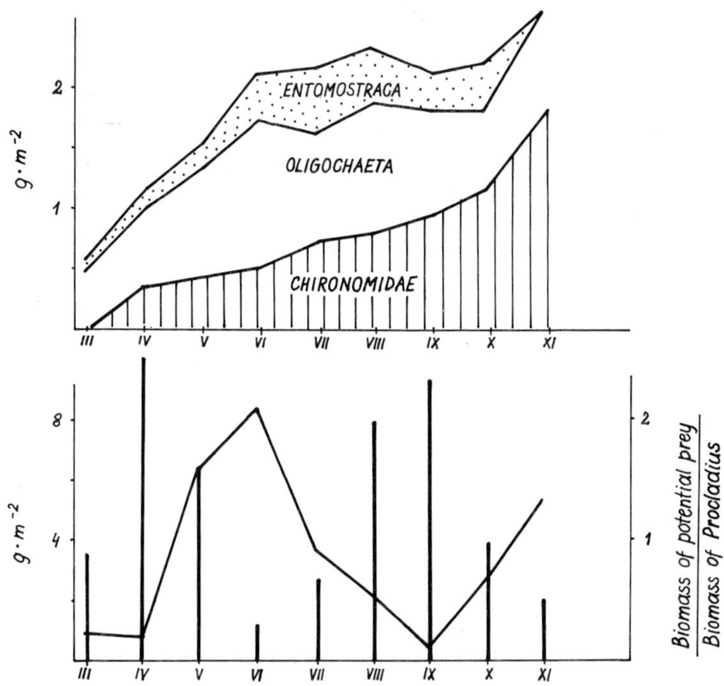

Fig. 3. Increase of the biomass of Procladius after the periods of high biomass of available prey/unit Procladius biomass. No correlation of prey and predator biomass. After Dusoge, 1980, modified.

and lower under good ones. For example usually after addition of food, or intensification of fish culture in fish ponds (mineral fertilization, feeding of fish, mixed fish cultures including planktonophagous fish) the biomass of nonpredatory benthos is higher and the proportion of the predatory benthos is lower (Kajak, 1968a,, 1977; Wasilewski, 1979). This is also shown on Table 1; in control enclosures with very low biomass of phytoplankton the biomass of benthos was lower than outside them (despite the lack of fish pressure in enclosures), because the feeding conditions for benthos deteriorated (Kajak et al. 1975).

This also caused the high proportion of invertebrate predators. Their pressure on nonpredatory benthos was probably stronger than in the open lake, because in enclosures the fish did not disturb the activity of these predators. Better food conditions for benthos in the treatment with planktonophagous silver carp resulted (due to sedimentation of its abundant feaces) in increased benthos biomass and a decreased proportion of predators (Kajak et al. 1975). A similar situation occurred in another experiment (Table 2). The lack of fish pressure resulted in a large increase of non-predatory benthos biomass, probably too high for the poor food conditions.

TABLE 1 Prey-predator relationships in benthos of bond type lake Warniak. 1.5 m depth.

		Low food		High food
		Fish pressure (open lake) -a-	-b-	No fish pressure (enclosures)[x] -c-
Biomass (B) $g \cdot m^{-2}$	total benthos (t.b.)	6.9	4.3	10.2
	non-predatory benthos (N.p.b.)	4.8	3.0	8.6
	predatory[xx] benthos (P.b.)	2.1	1.3	1.6
P.b./t.b.	%	30.4	30.2	15.7
B. of Tubificidae $g \cdot m^{-2}$		2.0	1.4	5.8
B. od nonpredatory Chironomidae		1.8	1.0	2.1

[x] 6 m^2 each, made of plastic foil. 10 weeks exposure.

[xx] Pelopiinae, Heleidae, Hydracarina, Hirudinea, Chaoborus, Trichoptera

a - open lake, near enclosures
b - control enclosures, no fish, scarce phytoplankton, abundant zooplankton, low seston sedimentation due to its consumption by zooplankton
c - enclosures with planktonophagous silver carp; high sedimentation of its feaces, no benthophagous fish.

This made the prey easily accessible for invertebrate predators, enabling their increased biomass and high proportion in the total biomass of the benthos. In the treatment with food added the biomass of nonpredatory benthos also increased several times (although a bit less than in the previous variant; this might be due to better balanced relationships) but the share of predators decreased many times. The importance of prey availability is shown in Table 3; the addition of freshly hatched, easily available Chironomus larvae resulted in their (instead of Crustaceans, mainly consumed before) intensive comsumption by Procladius.

Also in control experimental cylinders, Procladius consumed more chironomid larvae and less Crustacea, obviously due to increased availability of Chironomidae. Often Pelopiinae successfully remove the mass appearance of young, newly hatched larvae of Chironomidae (review - Dusoge, 1980).

TABLE 2 Proportion of benthic invertebrate predators depending on food conditions of fish pressure; lake Warniak, 1.0 m depth. Enclosures 0.2 m^2. Average values for 1 month exposure.

	Fish pressure (open lake)		No fish pressure (enclosures)
	Low food		High food^x
B. of total benthos, $g \cdot m^{-2}$	4.0	18.2	8.6
B. of nonpredatory benthos $g \cdot m^{-2}$	2.1	10.8	8.2
% predators in total benthos biomass	48	41	5

^{x}addition of yeasts

TABLE 3 Dependence of the consumption of Procladius choreus on the availability of prey. Experimental cylinders, 10 cm^2; 10 day exposure. After Kajak, 1968.

		% Procladius with Chironomidae larvae in guts	Crustaceans in guts	Mean number of larvae in 1 gut of Procladius
Open lake		58	86	1
experimental cylincers	control	67	33	1
	addition of freshly hatched larvae	100	11	6.2

The availability of prey for predators depends also on competitive relations in benthos. Increasing the abundance of large Chironomus plumosus larvae caused a deterioration of their feeding. Numbers of invertebrate predators increased, and that of prey-deceased, probably due to worse individual condition, and increased availability of prey to predators in an overcrowded situation (Fig. 4).

Also the stirring of mud by fish (and thus destroying the tubes of benthic organisms) when they feed on benthos, probably increases the availability of prey for invertebrate predators, This can be the cause of the high proportion of invertebrate predators in situations when they are not consumed intensively by fish.

As shown above, the proportion of various components, e.g. Crustacea or Chironomidae in the guts of Pelopiinae, varies; usually there is also various, sometimes sign-

significant, share of benthic algae. This flexibility of feeding, together with the resistance of invertebrate predators to poor oxygen conditions and to food deficiency, is very important for the regulation of benthos abundance. These predators can start immediate and intensive consumption of prey when it becomes possible, e.g. with overcrowding of prey in relation to food conditions.

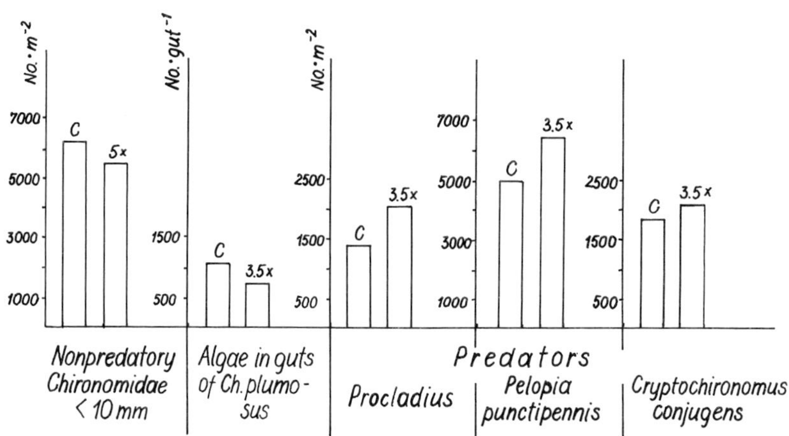

Fig. 4. Influence of artifically increased numbers of grown up (>20 mm) Chironomus plumosus larvae on prey-predator relationships. Benthos from eutrophic, polymictic lake Sniardwy in experimental cylinders. After Kajak, 1968.
C - control. "3.5" - 3.5x increased numbers of Ch. plumosus, as related to control (Ch. plumosus numbers in control- 800 ind.$\cdot m^{-2}$). After Kajak, 1968.

The amount of food consumed daily related to the biomass of the consumer (of Pelopiinae, Heleidae, Crangonyx) measured in close to natural conditions (natural benthic communities and near natural environmental conditions - Kajak, 1966, 1968) varies usually between about 10 and 60% - on the average much less than in artificial laboratory conditions (Kajak, Kajak, 1975; Dusoge, 1979). Inspite of the mentioned possibility of feeding of some predators on algae, an increase of the ratio of animal to plant food and also of Chironomidae to Crustacean speeds up the development of predators (Kajak, 1968a; Hilsenhoff - cit. in Kajak, in press).

The influence of invertebrate predators on Tubificidae is very specific: Procladius usually eats the posterior portion of individual worms decreasing the individual, and often total biomass of Tubificidae (Table 4) but stimulating their production (Table 5) by sometimes as much as 55% (Wiśniewski, 1978). (However very strong predation decreases the numbers of sexually mature individuals Kajak, Wiśniewski, 1966). Usually all this is more pronounced in shallower environments (Table 6), due to higher pressure of predators there. It is also correlated with temperature.

The pressure of invertebrate predators is also regulated by their interrelationships which can vary from neutral or positive to negative. The absolute numbers of various coexisting predators can of course be various, depending on the situation (Table 7).

TABLE 4 Increased numbers of "shorter" individuals of Tubificidae due to eating of their posterior portion by Pelopiinae. (Approximative figures). Experimental isolators 55 cm^2, Lake Sniardwy, 9 days exposure. Series A - IX/X, B - V. After Wisniewski, 1978.

Series	Animals	Parameters	Control	Addition of Pelopiinae
	Pelopiinae	$ind.\cdot m^{-2}$	750	2,600
A		$ind.\cdot m^{-2}$	3,000	3,000
	Tubificidae	$g\cdot m^{-2}$	1.2	1.2
		$mg\cdot ind.^{-1}$	0.4	0.3
	Pelopiinae	$ind.\cdot m^{-2}$	800	1,500
B		$ind.\cdot m^{-2}$	1,800	1,800
	Tubificidae	$g\cdot m^{-2}$	2.0	1.5
		$mg\cdot ind.^{-1}$	1.1	0.8

TABLE 5 Stimulation of the production of Tubificidae biomass due to eating of the posterior portion of individuals by predators. Exposure time - 70 days, 15°C. After Wiśniewski, 1978.

Weight of the individual before removal of posterior body portion, mg f.w.	Ratio: growth of regenerating ind. to that of intact ind. of the same initial biomass, after removing various portion (in %) of the body		
	25%	40-50%	55-60%
	of the individual biomass		
2.4	1	1	1
4.2	1.8	1.8	1.8
6.3	2.8	3.5	3.5

TABLE 6 Percentage (data for 20 Masurian lakes) of Tubificidae with posterior portion of the body eaten by predators. After Wiśniewski, 1978.

Zone	Depth	% Tubificidae	
		average	range
Littoral	1.5-4.0	63.2	41-80
Sublittoral	5.0-8.0	46.4	32-69
Upper profundal	15	27.3	0-50
Deep profundal	15	9.1	0.37

TABLE 7 Dependence of distribution of predatory Heleidae and Pelopiinae on the distribution of dominant predator - Crangonyx richmondensis. Marion Lake, Site A and B, both at 0.5 m. After Kajak and Kajak, 1975.

	Predators	No. of ind. per sample (20 cm^2)		
	Crangonyx	0	1	2
A	Pelopiinae	0.1	1.0	1.0
	Heleidae	0.75	1.0	0.0
B	Pelopiinae	4.7	1.8	
	Heleidae	1.3	0.3	

Artifically increased numbers of the dominant predator, Grangonyx, in shallows of Marion Lake, resulted in diminished consumption by both this and other species (Tables 8,9). On the other hand a naturally greater density of Grangonyx, obviously adjusted to the trophic situation, resulted in higher food consumption (Table 9).

Although the food rations of invertebrate predators in approximately natural conditions are smaller than often assumed, and although there are mechanisms which limit predator consumption, this consumption can be several times greater than the production of nonpredatory benthos estimated according to commonly accepted methods (Kajak et al. 1979; Kajak in press). The role of invertebrate predators can vary strongly depending on trophic and other conditions (Hall et al., 1972). Often predators regulate the quantitative relations, or even occurrence, of both dominant and scarce species (Macan, 1966).

TABLE 8 Consumption of prey ($mg \cdot ind.^{-1} \cdot day^{-1}$) by subdominant predators - Pelopiinae and Heleidae, at various densities of the dominant predator - Grangonyx richmondensis (C). Experimental cylinders 20 cm^2 in the lake. After Kajak and Kajak, 1975).

Natural density of Grangonyx /average 0.8 ind. (20 cm^2)		Artificially increased numbers of C. - ind./20 cm^2 1	2
Pelopiinae	0.1	0.03	0.02
Heleidae	0.05	0.02	0.02

TABLE 9 Daily consumption of prey (mg) by 1 Grangonyx (C) in various situations. Experimental 20 cm^2 in the lake, 2 days exposure. After Kajak and Kajak,1975.

	With naturally different numbers of C.		Artifically increased numbers of C.
Numbers of C. per 20 cm^2	1 C	2 C	1.6 C
Consumption of prey	4.8	6.1	3.4

REFERENCES

Dusoge, K. (1980. Occurrence and role of predatory Procladius Skuse (Chironomidae, Diptera) larvae in benthus of lake Sniardwy. *Ekol. pol., 28.*

Hall, D. J., W. E. Cooper and E. E. Werner (1970). An experimental approach to the production dynamics and structure of freshwater animal communities. *Limnol. Oceanogr., 15,* 839-928.

Kajak, Z. (1966). Field experiment in studies on benthos density of some Mazurian lakes. *Gewässer u. Abwässer., 41/42,* 150-158.

Kajak, Z. (1968a). Analiza eksperymentalna csynników decydujacych o obfitości bentosu. (Experimental analysis of factors decisive for benthos abundance). *Zesz. Nauk. IE PAN, 1,* 94 pp.

Kajak, Z. (1968b). Benthos of oxbow lakes situated in the area of the Zegrzyński Reservoir before its filling up with water. *Exol. pol. A, 16,* 821-832.

Kajak, Z. (1977). Factors influencing benthos biomass in shallow lake environments. *Ekol. pol., 25,* 421-429.

Kajak, Z. (in press). Bentos. W: Ekologia powierzchniowych wód śródladowych. (In: Ecology of surface inland waters). *PWN Warszawa.*

Kajak, Z., G. Bretschko and F. Schiemer (in press). Regularities of benthos production in inland freshwaters. *IBP Handbook.*

Kajak, Z. and K. Dusoge. (1975a). Macrobenthos of Mikołajskie Lake. *Ekol. pol., 23,* 437-457.

Kajak, Z. and K. Dusoge (1975b). Macrobenthos of Lake Tałtowisko. *Ekol. pol.*, *23*, 295-316.

Kajak, Z. and K. Dusoge (1976). Benthos of Lake Sniardwy as compared to benthos of Mikołajskie Lake and Lake Tałtowisko. *Ekol. pol. 24*, 77-101.

Kajak, Z. and A. Kajak (1975). Some trophic relations in the benthos of shallow parts of Marion Lake. *Ekol. pol.*, *23*, 573-586.

Kajak, Z., J. Rybak. and I. Spodniewska and W. A. Godlewska-Lipowa (1975). Influence of the planktonivorous fish Hypophtalmichthys molitrix (Val.) on the plankton and benthos of the eutrophic lake. *Pol. Arch. Hydrobiol.*, *22*, 301-310.

Kajak, Z. and R. J. Wiśniewski (1966). Próba oceny intensywności wyzerania Tubificidae przez drapiezco. (An attempt at estimating the intensity of consumption of Tubificidae by predators). *Ekol. pol. B*, *12*, 181-184.

Macan, T. T. (1966). The influence of predation on the fauna of a moorland fishpond. *Arch. Hydrobiol.*, *61*, 432-452.

Wasilewska, B. E. (1978). Bottom fauna in ponds with intense fish rearing. *Ekol. pol.*, *26*, 513-536.

Wisniewski, R. J. (1978). Effect of predators on Tubificidae groupings and their production in lakes. *Ekol. pol.*, *26*, 493-512.

Author Index

Subject Index